Contents

"There is a groping for a new level of struggle,
a groping for new bases and new directions . . .
whatever the struggle is moving toward, it is
moving toward a combining of political issues and
economic issue."
—*Charles V. Hamilton, 1973*

CIVIL RIGHTS

A current guide

A CBS NEWS REFERENCE BOOK

CIVIL RIGHTS

SECOND EDITION

A current guide to the people, organizations, and events

by JOAN MARTIN BURKE

R.R. BOWKER COMPANY
New York & London, 1974
A Xerox Education Company

XEROX

Published by R. R. Bowker Co. (A Xerox Education Company)
1180 Avenue of the Americas, New York, N.Y. 10036
Copyright © by Columbia Broadcasting System, Inc.
Printed and bound in the United States of America

Library of Congress Cataloging in Publication Data
Burke, Joan Martin.
Civil rights; a current guide to the people,
organizations, and events.
(A CBS news reference book)
First ed. (1970) by A. J. Adams and J. M. Burke.
Bibliography: p.
1. Civil rights—United States—Handbooks, manuals,
etc. I. Adams, A. John. Civil rights. II. Title.
III. Series.
JC599.U5B85   1974   323.4′025′73   74-4053
ISBN 0-8352-0722-6

Cover photo from Magnum Photos Inc.

Preface

Civil Rights was originally prepared as a current guide and quick reference for the correspondents, producers, and editors of CBS News. The first edition covered the civil rights movement from 1954 to the end of the 1960s. This second edition was planned to reflect the changes that have occurred since, and to refresh memories of some of the principal persons, dates, and events of the struggle as it has developed over the last 20 years and as it is happening now.

The tumult of the 1960s, with its sit-ins, freedom rides, and protest marches; its cries for black power, its violence, jailings, and sensational trials, gave way to a period of activity with a somewhat different look. Except for the occasional stirrings and outbursts of such groups as the Indians, Chicanos, and feminists, it was a seemingly quieter time, and some wondered if the movement were alive at all. It soon became apparent that the movement was far from dead, but had merely shifted its emphasis. The struggle now was being waged on the community level, rather than on a national scale. The primary goals were no longer federal laws to regulate voting rights, enforce equal access to public accommodations, or desegregate schools, but rather to gain access to economic and political power. The thrust of the movement in the seventies, it would appear, has the potential of making a more profound effect on all our lives than the turbulence of the sixties.

Many of the new leaders to emerge in the early seventies tended to seek elective office as a means of effecting change—people like Yvonne Brathwaite Burke and Ronald Dellums of California, and Herman Badillo of New York. To meet the needs of these new political leaders, as well as to help promote minority causes, two organizations were established in 1970—the Congressional Black Caucus and the Joint Center for Political Studies.

The early 1970s also saw the rise of organizations established specifically for the purpose of pursuing economic rights—like Operation PUSH, founded by Jesse Jackson, and the Puerto Rican Revolutionary Workers Organization, a group that evolved from the Young Lords Party. Most of the old, established groups—National Urban League, for example—have been able to swing with the new directions; others, like the Southern Christian Leadership Conference (Martin Luther King's organization), are floundering because they could not. But, whatever their tactics, the goal is the same—a more equitable piece of the pie for all minorities.

The first section of *Civil Rights* is an alphabetical guide to the people and organizations involved in the movement. Most of the persons listed are black; however, also included are Spanish-speaking Americans, American Indians, and whites who engaged in the struggle for minority rights. Biographical and relevant organizational details are supplied; opinions are stated only when they seem necessary for clarification.

The second part of the volume includes appendixes and a suggested bibliography. Appendix I deals with congressional voting records on civil rights legislation passed by both houses from 1957 to 1970; Appendix II lists the state and federal agencies with civil rights responsibilities; Appendix III is a chronology of the movement from 1954 to the present; Appendix IV is a list of leading black office holders, by state, as of April 1973; Appendix V, new to this edition, lists the libraries and private collections where research materials and information about the movement may be found.

Some of the men involved in shaping the civil rights movement of the sixties have died since publication of the first edition, and are therefore not included here—like Whitney Young, Jr., George Wiley, Saul Alinsky, Adam Clayton Powell, Jackie Robinson, Louis Armstrong, and Ralph Bunche. Organizations like ACT Associates, Deacons for Defense and Justice, the Civil Rights Documentation Project, and the Student National Coordinating Committee— organizations that were important in the early mobilization of the movement— no longer exist and have been dropped. However, information on many of these people and organizations may be found in the Chronology section (Appendix III). Groups that have reorganized and re-emerged as new organizations with new objectives are listed under the names currently used.

Those closely involved with the civil rights movement will undoubtedly think of names and events that are not included. There will also be those who feel that a disproportionate amount of attention has been accorded to certain people and organizations. And still others will wonder at the inclusion of some entries. Our criterion has been information that the well-informed newsman or citizen needs to know—not the specialist.

It is hoped that this volume will be of value to political officials, legislators, teachers, students, agencies, and all individuals who are concerned with the civil rights movement and might like to know more about who's who and what's what in one of the most important and dramatic periods of social change in our country's history.

Joan Martin Burke
February 1974

Acknowledgments

Acknowledgments are due particularly to the assistance and advice of Barbara
Werber; Walter Schatz; Patricia Braden, formerly of the Race Relations
Information Center, Nashville, Tennessee; Barbara Brooks, Civil Rights
Commission, Washington, D.C.; Joint Center for Political Studies, Washington,
D.C.; Peter Bailey, *Ebony* magazine; John Henrik Clarke, *Freedomways*
magazine; Fred Shuttlesworth, former aide to the late Dr. Martin Luther King,
Jr.; Ernest Kaiser, Schomburg Collection of Negro Literature and History;
Eleanor Farrar and Pauline Schneider, MARC (Metropolitan Applied Research
Center), Washington, D.C. and Susan Phillips, MARC, New York; May Dowell
and Katherine Hartley of CBS News Special Projects Library; Robert Skedgell,
Director of CBS News Broadcast Research; Meg Clarke and William Wright of
the CBS News Research staff; A. John Adams, Justin J. Burke; Marjorie Evans;
Bruce F. Jensen; Charlotte M. Lennon; Deborah S. Peterson; F.W. Schmitz
and Dyan Wiley; CBS News Archivist, Samuel T. Suratt, and Director of
Resource Development and Production, Joseph P. Bellon, without whom this
volume would not have appeared; and not least, Richard S. Salant, president
of CBS News, whose concern for civil rights, as for the integrity of CBS News,
provided the inspiration for the original research.

Guide to Acronyms

Note: This list constitutes the more familiar acronyms, and includes those used in connection with civil rights organizations.

ACLU	American Civil Liberties Union	GAO	General Accounting Office
ADL	Anti-Defamation League (B'Nai B'Rith)	HARYOU	Harlem Youth Opportunities Unlimited
AFL-CIO	American Federation of Labor and Congress of Industrial Organizations	HAR-YOU-ACT	Harlem Youth-Action
AIM	American Indian Movement	HUD	Department of Housing and Urban Development
AIO	Americans for Indian Opportunity	ICBIF	Inner City Business Improvement Forum
AJC	American Jewish Committee	IFCO	Interreligious Foundation for Community Organization
BEU	Black Economic Union		
BIA	Bureau of Indian Affairs		
BPP	Black Panther Party	JCPS	Joint Center for Political Studies
BUF	Black United Front		
CORE	Congress of Racial Equality	JOBS	Job Opportunity in the Business Sector
CRC	Civil Rights Congress		
CRS	Community Relations Service (Department of Justice)	KOCO	Kenwood-Oakland Community Organization
CURE	Citizens United for Racial Equality	LDF	Legal Defense and Education Fund, Inc. (NAACP)
D & S	Bedford-Stuyvesant Development and Service Corporation	LHRAA	Lutheran Human Relations Association of America
EEOC	Equal Employment Opportunity Commission	MARC	Metropolitan Applied Research Center
FCC	Federal Communications Commission	MESBIC	Minority Enterprise Small Business Investment Company

NAACP	National Association for the Advancement of Colored People	SBA	Small Business Administration
NAPCR	National Association of Puerto Rican Civil Rights	SCEF	Southern Conference Educational Fund
NCAI	National Congress of American Indians	SCLC	Southern Christian Leadership Conference
NEGRO	National Economic Growth and Reconstruction Organization	SEEK	Search for Education, Elevation and Knowledge
NSRP	National States Rights Party	SERS	Southern Education Reporting Service
OAAU	Organization of Afro-American Unity	SNCC	Student National Coordinating Committee (now defunct)
OEO	U.S. Office of Economic Opportunity	SRC	Southern Regional Council
OIC	Opportunities Industrialization Center	UAW	United Auto Workers
OMBE	Office of Minority Business Enterprise (Department of Commerce)	UFWU	United Farm Workers Union
PUSH	People United to Save Humanity	UNESCO	United Nations Educational, Scientific, and Cultural Organization
PRWO	Puerto Rican Revolutionary Workers Organization	USIA	United States Information Agency
RRIC	Race Relations Information Center	VEP	Voters Education Project
		WLCAC	Watts Labor Community Action Committee

Alphabetical Guide
to Individuals
and Organizations

REV. RALPH D. ABERNATHY
President of Southern Christian Leadership Conference (SCLC) since August 1968. One of Martin Luther King's chief lieutenants and closest companions for more than a decade, he assumed leadership of the organization after King was assassinated in April 1968. Led the Poor People's March on Washington in May 1968, and a demonstration at Republican National Convention in Miami, July 1968. Arrested in September of the same year in Atlanta for blocking emergency garbage pickups in support of striking sanitation workers. Was jailed in June 1969 on charges of inciting Charleston, South Carolina hospital workers to riot. Helped organize SCLC-sponsored march from Perry, Georgia to Atlanta in May 1970. In 1971 and 1973 led marches on Wall Street and against the A & P supermarket chain to protest racism, poverty, the Vietnamese War, and unfair employment practices. Was arrested in May 1973 while demonstrating against the Rich Company in Atlanta for alleged discrimination and unfair practices.

In July 1973 he resigned as president of SCLC, accusing the black middle class of not providing enough financial support to carry on the work of the organization. Also stated that Mrs. Coretta King, widow of SCLC founder, was unwilling to share the money from the Martin Luther King Jr. Center for Social Change with SCLC and as a result SCLC was forced to reduce its staff and curtail its work. At the organization's annual convention in August 1973, the Board of Directors rejected Abernathy's resignation and drafted him to stay on as president for at least a year. "If I get a call from the poor people," he said, "I can't turn my back on them."

After military service in World War II, graduated from Alabama State in 1950 and remained there as an instructor. In 1951, joined the NAACP and became pastor of First Baptist Church in Montgomery. In 1955, worked with Martin Luther King to organize the famous 381-day Montgomery bus boycott. Then helped King establish the SCLC, and in 1961 became its secretary/treasurer. During the next four years went to jail 19 times with King. King named him his successor in 1965. Born Linden, Alabama, March 11, 1926. Married the former Juanita O. Jones in 1952, three children.

O. RUDOLPH AGGREY

Ambassador to Senegal and Gambia—appointed by President Nixon April 1972. Has also served the State Department in France (as vice-consul) and in the Congo (as public affairs officer). Born July 24, 1926 in Salisbury, North Carolina. Educated at Hampton Institute (B.S. in 1946) and Syracuse University (M.S. in 1948).

ALASKA FEDERATION OF NATIVES

Federation of the native regional organizations in Alaska formed in 1966 to assert native claims to 90 percent of the state's land (340 million acres). The state's 60,000 Eskimos, Aleuts, and Indians contend they hold title to the land because, they argue, the United States did not buy Alaska from Russia in 1867, but only purchased the right to tax and govern the territory. Until Alaska became a state in 1958, ownership of the natives' land had not become an issue. In the eight years following statehood, the U.S. Bureau of Land Management ceded land to the state without consulting the native population. In 1966 a "land freeze" was imposed to halt the land transfers until the end of 1970 pending a congressional decision. A compromise proposal passed by Congress in 1972 requires the natives to give up title to all land except 40 million acres (10 percent of the state) for the sum of $500 million plus 2 percent royalties on revenues from the surrendered land. The federation is supported by ten native regional business corporations set up under the Alaska Native Land Claims Settlement Act. Annual budget in 1973 was $200,000. Officers: John Sackett, State Senator from District I, chairman; William L. Hensley, State Senator from District K, president; and John Shively, executive vice-president. Headquarters: 1675 C Street, Anchorage, Alaska 99501.

CLIFFORD ALEXANDER, JR.

Made headlines in April 1969 when he resigned as chairman of Equal Employment Opportunity Commission (EEOC) because he questioned the Nixon Administration's commitment to equal treatment for minorities. At that time, he said, "vigorous efforts to enforce laws on employment and discrimination are not among the goals of this administration." His term as a member of the commission ran until July 1972, but he resigned this membership in July 1969 to accept a partnership in Washington law firm of Arnold and Porter. Received an A.B. degree (cum laude) from Harvard University in 1955, and an LL.B. from Yale University Law School in 1958. From 1959–1961 served as program and executive director of Harlem Youth Opportunities, Unlimited (HARYOU). Moved to Washington in 1967 to become chairman of EEOC and also served as special consultant to President Johnson on civil rights. Currently hosts and co-produces a television program called "Cliff Alexander—Black on White," and teaches a course at Howard University Law School. Born September 21, 1933, in New York City. Married to the former Adele Logan, two children. Office: 1229–19th Street, N.W., Washington, D.C. 20036.

MUHAMMAD ALI see page 87

AMERICAN CIVIL LIBERTIES UNION (ACLU)

Founded in 1920, ACLU claims to be "the nation's oldest civil liberties organization," and states as its aim "to champion the rights of man set forth in the Declaration of Independence and Constitution." Activities include test court cases, opposition to legislation considered in violation of the Constitution, and public protests. Its record includes numerous landmark cases, among them the Scopes anti-evolution trial, the right of the children of Jehovah's Witnesses not to salute the flag on grounds of their religious conscience, and a battle against official efforts to ban the importation of the James Joyce classic, *Ulysses*. Has been heavily involved in efforts to obtain full rights for blacks, from open housing in Chicago to proper representation on juries in Mississippi. In recent years the organization has broadened its work to include litigation on surveillance by government, rights of prisoners, mental patients, women and homosexuals, freedom of the press, and draft amnesty. In its 1972 annual report, executive director Aryeh Neier is quoted as being less than optimistic about the state of civil liberties in this country because of a lack of interest by the federal government, citing the 1972 Supreme Court decision of Apodaca v. Roegon—a decision that strongly dilutes the requirement of guilt beyond a shadow of a doubt by allowing a hung jury to convict a person. The new law applies to all state cases but not to federal government cases. In 1964, ACLU opened a Southern Regional Office to expand its activities in the southern states, where it has fought for proper black legal representation against harassment of attorneys defending black clients, for black voting rights, and against bans on demonstrations. In the case of Cassius Clay (Muhammad Ali), it raised the issue of racial and religious discrimination in the Selective Service System. It is one of the first organizations to call for the impeachment of President Nixon on six grounds "affecting civil liberties." At a news conference October 5, 1973, ACLU's chairman, Edward J. Ennis, listed the grounds as "specific proved violations of the right of political dissent; usurpation of congressional warmaking powers; establishment of personal secret police which committed crimes; attempted interference in the trial of Daniel Ellsberg; distortion of the system of justice; and perversion of other federal agencies." There are 50 affiliates in 46 states with a membership of 235,000. Annual budget (1971–1972) $5,500,000. Executive director, Areyh Neier; chairman, Edward J. Ennis. Office: 22 East 40th Street, New York, N.Y. 10016. *See also* CHARLES MORGAN.

AMERICAN G.I. FORUM

One of the oldest agencies aiding Mexican-Americans. Formed after World War II (1948) to help *chicano* veterans obtain their G.I. benefits. Later expanded into a family service organization. Currently operates two low-rent housing projects in Texas, built with help from the Department of Housing and Urban Development (HUD). In 1972 established an outreach program to help Vietnam veterans—specifically of Mexican-American descent—funded by the U.S. Department of Labor. Currently operating in 12 states, the organization secures jobs for veterans and provides a referral service for education, housing, and medical needs. The Forum has 475 chapters in 28 states and in the District of Columbia, with an estimated membership of 250,000. National chairman: Tony Gallegos. National headquarters: 201 West Cleveland, Room 9, Beeville, Texas 78102. Director of Washington Information Office: Guadalupe Saldana. Washington Office: 2112 S. Randolph, Arlington, Va. 22204.

AMERICAN INDIANS MOVEMENT (AIM)

Organized in 1968 to mobilize Minneapolis' 9,000-member Indian community (one of the largest concentrations of urban Indians). First major effort was the formation of an "Indian patrol" (August 1968) to protect Indians from "indiscriminate" arrests. Also organized boycotts against discriminatory institutions and was instrumental in establishing an all-Indian advisory board that counsels state and local education authorities. Did not start out as a national organization but units were established in Cleveland, Denver, Seattle, Rapid City (South Dakota), and St. Cloud (Minnesota). By 1971 AIM was considered a leading spokesman for the militant Indian movement. In November 1972, AIM leaders occupied the Bureau of Indian Affairs (BIA) building in Washington, D.C., to protest the Bureau's policies, and had to be forcibly ejected by police. On February 27, 1973, 200 members took over Wounded Knee, a South Dakota hamlet on the Oglala-Sioux Reservation, in an effort to oust Richard Wilson, the elected tribal head of the reservation. AIM contended that Wilson was corrupt and dictatorial. After 70 days, two deaths, numerous injuries, many meetings and bureaucratic bickering, AIM surrendered peacefully after receiving concessions from government negotiators. Some of the tangible results were that AIM was able to negotiate directly with the White House for changes in public policy toward Indians; Nixon reshuffled top bureaucrats at BIA; and the BIA budget for the fiscal year 1974 was increased by $50 million to $583 million. AIM slogan: "The Red Giant is on one knee, but he's getting ready to stand up." Claims to have a membership in the thousands and has received financial support from church groups and private donations. President: Carter Camp. Founder: Clyde Bellecourt. See also CLYDE BELLECOURT.

AMERICANS FOR INDIAN OPPORTUNITY (AIO)

Established February 19, 1970, by LaDonna Harris, a Comanche Indian and wife of the former Senator Fred R. Harris (D-Okla). A technical assistance organization which serves as a unifying force in the native American Indian community as well as a catalyst for change, and stresses the need for new approaches to Indian problems. Concentrates its efforts on education, job development, training, and giving opportunities to the young. Is funded through foundation grants and private donations. Mrs. Harris is AIO's president and executive director. (She was a member of the National Council on Indian Opportunity, a government agency concerned with Indian affairs, but resigned in 1970.) Headquarters: 1816 Jefferson Place, N.W., Washington, D.C. 20036.

EARL ANTHONY

Writer and black militant. First became a civil rights activist in 1965 when he helped organize the first public rent strike in San Francisco. Also helped start Independent Action Movement in the same city to fight for more rights for the black community. In 1967, joined the Black Panther party and later was made its deputy minister of information for Southern California. Was expelled in March 1969 when other high ranking members were purged from Panther ranks. His *Picking Up the Gun: A Report on the Black Panthers* (published by Dial Press, 1970) was written after his expulsion and gives an inside look at the organization and its leaders. In 1971 *The Time for the Furnaces: A Study of Black Student Revolt* was published. Born Roanoke, Virginia, 1941; raised in New York and Los Angeles. Holds a B.A. from University of Southern California, 1963. Currently living in San Francisco.

ASSOCIATION ON AMERICAN INDIAN AFFAIRS

Oldest private organization concerned with Indian affairs. Founded in 1922 by white writer Oliver La Farge, its first president. The association turned activist in 1960 and currently has a membership of 75,000. Has initiated programs dealing with health, education, economic development, housing, legal aid, child welfare, and community development by providing financial and technical assistance to 13 Indian communities across the country. Also runs the American Indian Arts Center (1042 Madison Ave., New York, N.Y.) to promote Eskimo and Indian artists and craftsman, and to provide information and reference library facilities. The annual budget for 1974 is $574,200. In 1969, association lawyers worked closely with the American Civil Liberties Union for commutation of the death sentence for a South Dakota Indian, Tom White Hawk, considered by many as a landmark case. Gives grants and was instrumental in establishing the National Indian Council on Alcohol (president: George Melissy; executive director: Harriet Paul) in Minneapolis. Publishes a bi-monthly newsletter, *Indian Affairs*. President: Professor Alfonso Ortiz, a Tewa Indian and an Associate Professor of Anthropology at Princeton University. Executive director: William Byler. Headquarters: 432 Park Avenue South, New York, N.Y., 10016.

HERMAN BADILLO

Democratic congressman from New York's Twenty-first Congressional District, elected first in 1970 and reelected November 1972 with 87 percent of the vote. The first Puerto Rican in the country to win a congressional seat, he is a member of the House education and labor committees. First became prominent in New York City politics in 1960 as chairman of East Harlem Kennedy-for-President Committee. Appointed commissioner of the newly created Department of Relocation in 1962 at the age of 33, the youngest commissioner in the city's administration. Entered the mayoral primary for the first time in 1969, finishing third in the race. Ran again in the 1973 primary but lost.

Worked his way through New York City schools and City College of New York, graduating magna cum laude in 1951. Received a law degree from Brooklyn Law School, 1954, and became a Certified Public Accountant in 1956. Is a partner of the law firm of Permut and Badillo. Author of *A Bill of No Rights: Attica and the American Prison System* published in June 1972. Born in Caguas, Puerto Rico, August 21, 1929; moved to New York City in 1940. Married twice, currently to the former Irma Liebling, three children. Office: 510 Cannon Office Building, Washington, D.C. 20515.

JOAN BAEZ
White folk-singing heroine of the nonconformists. Active in peace marches, ban-the-bomb campaigns, civil rights, and anti-Vietnam war protest movements. In June 1972, organized an antiwar demonstration of women and children in Washington, D.C., called "Ring Around the Congress." Washington's black community opposed it because they said it was irrelevant and pointed up her lack of knowledge of current trends in the civil rights movement. They also felt that monies spent on policing and providing facilities for a large-scale demonstration were monies taken out of municipal funds which could be better spent by the community on local programs. At the end of 1972 she visited Hanoi, North Vietnam, on a trip sponsored by the Committee of Liaison with Families of Servicemen, and was there during the intensified U.S. Christmas bombing. She "felt fear the whole time," she said. "What was most extraordinary to me, was that the people were all back on their bicycles right after a raid and on their way back to work." (*New York Times*, January 2, 1973.) She founded the Institute for Study of Nonviolence in Carmel Valley, California. Arrested in 1967 for participation in an antidraft protest and served 45 days in jail in Oakland, California. Was sued for refusing to pay income tax because of opposition to war. Wrote *Daybreak* (published by Dial Press 1968), an explanation of her pacifist ideas. Studied at Boston University Fine Arts School of Drama in 1958 and became a big hit the following year at the Newport Folk Festival. Since then she has made extensive concert tours of college campuses and has appeared at Carnegie Hall. Avoids television, Hollywood, and Broadway. On August 8, 1969, her appearance at New York's Madison Square Garden was a 20,000 sellout. Born Staten Island, New York, January 1941. Married to David Harris, 1968 (who in July 1969 began a three-year jail sentence in Arizona for failure to register for the draft), one child, Gabriel Earl, born December 2, 1969. Was separated after Harris completed 20 months of his sentence, and finally divorced in 1973.

JAMES BALDWIN
Novelist, essayist, and playwright. Became one of the most articulate spokesmen for the black revolution with publication of his "Letter from a Region in My Mind," in the *New Yorker*, November 17, 1962, described by critics as the most indelible and frightening description ever written of what it means to be a

black in a white society. The essay was subsequently incorporated into the 1963 best-seller, *The Fire Next Time*, and for a while Baldwin was hailed on radio, television, and in lectures across the nation and abroad as the nation's foremost interpreter of the "Negro problem," which he insisted was not a Negro problem, but a white problem. "The victims of segregation are the white people, because the myth of white supremacy prevents them from facing their own weaknesses." Addressing the World Council of Churches in Uppsala, Sweden, in July 1968, he charged that the Christian churches had betrayed the black man—and their own principles—by their identification with racist institutions. Today, Baldwin is considered somewhat passé by the new breed of black militants, and his latest novel, *Tell Me How Long the Train's Been Gone*, was described as "a disaster" by critics. Between 1968 and 1972 published a collection of essays called *No Name in the Street*. Said to have become disillusioned with the direction the civil rights movement has taken in this country over the years, and, in the last decade, his attitude toward the racial question changed from one of optimism and a spirit of reconciliation between blacks and whites in 1962, to one of anger and despair. In 1972 is quoted as being ambivalent about the whole question of race relations.

In 1971 wrote "An Open Letter to My Sister, Miss Angela Davis," in which he said "we must fight for your life as though it were our own—which it is—and render impassable with our bodies the corridor to the gas chamber. For if they take you in the morning, they will be coming for us that night." (*New York Times*, June 30, 1973). Returned to live in France in 1971 after a stay in Turkey. Visits the U.S. only occasionally—once in 1972 for a fund raising tour for Angela Davis and again in 1973 to write the narration for a Ray Charles jazz concert. Born Ausust 2, 1924, in New York City, he attended Frederick Douglass Junior High School and DeWitt Clinton High School. At 14, he became a Holy Roller preacher in Harlem storefront churches, and after graduating from high school worked as handyman, office boy, factory worker, dishwasher, and waiter, while writing book reviews and essays. In 1948, he won a Rosenwald fellowship and went to live in Paris, where he spent most of the next decade. His first novel, the partly autobiographical *Go Tell It on the Mountain*, was published in 1952. It was followed by *Notes of a Native Son* in 1955, *Giovanni's Room* in 1956. His first play, *The Amen Corner*, was first performed in 1954. His collection of essays, *Nobody Knows My Name*, was named one of the outstanding books of 1961. His novel *Another Country* appeared the same year. And a play, *Blues for Mister Charlie*, a story of racial murder dedicated to victims of racial violence in the South, ran for five months at the ANTA theater on Broadway, April through August 1964, and won the Foreign Press Association's dramatic award for the 1963–1964 season. Coauthored *A Rap on Race* with Margaret Mead in 1971.

IMAMU AMIRI BARAKA (LeRoi Jones)
Poet and playwright who since 1967 Newark riots has led efforts to organize that city's black and Puerto Rican communities as a political force, through the United Black Brothers, Black Community Development, and the Committee for

United Newark. In a city whose population is more than 50 percent black, he once declared: "We are out to bring self-government to this town by 1970 . . . it can be taken without a shot being fired." Baraka once summed up his philosophy: "I'm in favor of black people taking power by the quickest, easiest, most successful means they can employ. Malcolm X said 'the ballot or the bullet.' Newark is a particular situation where the ballot seems most advantageous. I believe we have to survive. I didn't invent slavery. I didn't invent white men. What we're trying to do is deal with him the best way we can." In 1970 was a supporter of Kenneth Gibson for mayor but since Gibson took office, the two have clashed openly on a number of issues. Baraka has called Gibson a "puppet" of the business community, leading some to believe that he may make a bid for the office of mayor himself in the spring of 1974. In 1972 he served as co-chairman with Congressman Charles Diggs (D-Mich) and Mayor Richard Hatcher at the Black National Convention in Gary, Indiana, and stressed the theme of "unity with uniformity" saying "the most essential thing, as far as I was concerned, was the creating of a national black political structure. A structure which would function in all the ways the national black community needed to function to gain, maintain, and use power . . . which is my understanding of what politics is." Became a minister of the "Kawaida" faith in the late 1960s, adopting the Swahili title Imamu (spiritual leader) and the Arabic name Amiri Baraka. Arrested in the July 1967 riots for possession of firearms and sentenced to three years, Baraka and his two codefendants were finally acquitted July 2, 1969, after a retrial. Born October 7, 1934, in Newark. Graduated from Howard University in 1953 with a B.A. in English and later obtained an M.A. at Columbia. His poetry and fiction won him a John Hay Whitney Fellowship in 1961, and he received an Obie Award in 1964 for *The Dutchman*, as the best off-Broadway play of the season. Most recent book *Raise Race Rays Raze: Essays since 1965* published in 1971. Heads Spirit House, a black cultural center in Newark, is chairman of the Committee for a United Newark and member of the Steering Committee of the National Black Assembly. Married twice, currently to Ras Jua Al Aziz, six children.

MARION BARRY, JR.

President of the Washington, D.C., Board of Education. Elected to board November 1971 after being asked to run by a group of local politicians and endorsed by Walter Fauntroy, D.C. congressional representative, and subsequently chosen its president. The *Washingtonian* (January 1972) lists him as one of the top ten men in D.C. politics and says "he's very bright, very ambitious and his election to the school board proves he's respected by middle-class blacks as well as young people." Executive director of operations for Pride, Inc. 1968–1972. One of the founders of Student National Coordinating Committee (SNCC), and its first chairman in 1960. In ensuing years, played a leading role in civil rights projects throughout the South, spending time in 15 Southern jails. In January 1968, helped SNCC organize grassroots opposition to the proposed five-cent bus-fare increase in Washington, D.C. Formed "People's Party" slate of candidates for a pilot police district election, February 1970; won 14 of 28 seats. Has been called the "*enfant terrible*" of the civil rights movement. When he joined Pride, he resigned as director of the Washington office of SNCC. Born in Itta Bina, Mississippi, in 1936. Grew up in Memphis and received a B.S. in chemistry from LeMoyne College (1958) and a master's degree from Fisk University (1960). *See also:* PRIDE, INC.

BEDFORD-STUYVESANT DEVELOPMENT AND SERVICE CORPORATION (D&S)

Private, nonprofit corporation formed in 1967 (sponsored by late Senator Robert Kennedy) to develop programs improving living conditions and creating employment in central Brooklyn (New York) with a population of 450,000 people. Its aim is to make Bedford-Stuyvesant a viable community through flourishing businesses, full employment for its residents, and providing a cultural life. Funded by federal grants, private organizations and individuals, it serves as the financial arm of the Restoration Corporation, the operational end of the organization. The Restoration Corporation is headed by Franklin A. Thomas, a black; D & S was headed by John Doar until December 1973. Staffed with experts in law, education, finance, construction, its purpose is to give technical assistance in the following areas: job placement, providing home mortgages, renovation of housing, building five day-care centers, expansion of local business, and the building of a civic and cultural center. Because the Restoration Corporation, one of the largest community development projects in the country, has gained over the years enough expertise and experience, the need for D & S eventually will be phased out, Thomas says, and a merger of the two staffs is planned for early 1974. The Restoration Corporation has five local neighborhood centers, publishes a newsletter called *Restoration*, and provides information for residents on services in the community. Headquarters: 1368 Fulton Street, Brooklyn, N.Y. 11216. *See also:* JOHN DOAR.

HARRY BELAFONTE

On board of directors of Southern Christian Leadership Conference and Dr. Martin Luther King Foundation. Has been leading participant in civil rights marches. Reportedly provided funds for education of the children of the late Martin Luther King. Grew up in West Indies and New York City where he attended high school. Served in the navy 1943 to 1946. Since the early 1950s has enjoyed considerable international success as a singer and actor. Now president of his own company, Belafonte Enterprises, which produces his records. Always in demand as an entertainer, he nevertheless strictly limits his appearances to allow time for outside activities such as political campaigns of Richard Hatcher, Mayor of Gary, Indiana; Andrew Young in Atlanta, Georgia; Shirley Chisholm in New York; and Kenneth Gibson, Mayor of Newark, New Jersey. Born New York City, March 1, 1927. Married, four children.

CLYDE BELLECOURT

Chippewa Indian. Founder and first chairman of American Indians Movement (AIM). Formerly a staff member of Minneapolis Urban Coalition and spent many of his early years in jail, where, he says, he received his only education and learned that he was "not a dirty savage." Spearheaded and considered brains behind the 70-day takeover and occupation of Wounded Knee, South Dakota, in February 1973. On August 28 of same year was shot and critically wounded on the Rosebud Indian Reservation in South Dakota where leaders of the Indian militant movement were meeting. AIM president, Carter Camp, was arrested for the shooting. Born 1937. See also: AMERICAN INDIANS MOVEMENT.

L. HOWARD BENNETT

Acting deputy assistant secretary of defense for civil rights, 1968–1971. Headed panel looking into racial unrest in the military. According to a New York Times November 28, 1969 account, he recommended to the Pentagon "that all services follow the Marine Corps in permitting such open expressions of black pride as the clenched-fist black power salute and the Afro hair style." Resigned November 30, 1971 from the Defense Department in protest charging that the Pentagon wanted to "slow the rate of thrust" and "change the direction of its programs for ending racial discrimination in the armed services." Currently in private law practice in Washington, D.C. Joined the defense department in 1963; civil rights director from 1965. Previously a municipal judge in Minneapolis. Born Charleston, South Carolina, February 22, 1913. Attended University of Chicago, LL.D. (1950). Married, one child.

LERONE BENNETT, JR.

Writer and fellow of the Institute of the Black World, Atlanta, Georgia. Author of Black Power U.S.A., Before the Mayflower, A History of the Negro in America, 1919–1966, and The Challenge of Blackness, published by Johnson in 1972. Worked as a reporter for the Atlanta Daily World (1949–1953). Now with the Johnson Publishing Company as senior editor of Ebony magazine. Born Clarksdale, Mississippi, October 17, 1928. Attended public schools in Jackson, Mississippi, and Morehouse College, A.B. (1949). Married, four children.

AMALIA V. BETANZOS

Currently is a member of the New York City Housing Authority. Former Youth Services Commissioner for the city of New York, concerned with over a million and a half young people under 21 (from 1972–1973). Also was chief advisor to Mayor Lindsay on matters pertaining to Spanish-speaking people in the city and had worked for the Lindsay administration since 1970 in charge of programs for the poor, mentally retarded, and physically handicapped. Was Commissioner of Relocation and Management Services. Has kept close ties with Spanish-speaking, particularly Puerto Rican communities and has been chief executive officer of the Puerto Rican Community Development Project and a past president of the National Association of Puerto Rican Civil Rights. Born 1929, she grew up in the South Bronx, New York. Attended Walton High School and received a B.A. and M.A. from New York University. Married to poet Odon Betanzos, one son.

BLACK ACADEMY OF ARTS AND LETTERS
Formed early in 1969 by a group of 50 black scholars, artists and authors to provide "recognition and encouragement" to those contributing to the interpretation and projection of the black experience in America. In July 1970, announced that the late W. E. B. DuBois, historian Carter G. Woodson, and the artist Henry O. Tanner had been named to its newly established Hall of Fame. Academy also protested denial of visa to the widow of DuBois, who wanted to visit U.S. from her home in Cairo (eventually granted by the Justice Department in 1970). A $150,000 grant from the Twentieth Century Fund expired in October 1972 and since that time the organization has been supported mostly by the black community. Currently engaged in helping young scholars and artists in work relating to the black experience and is trying to raise funds to buy the Langston Hughes house in Harlem for its national headquarters. To date has 65 fellows in the Academy. Academy president: John O. Killens. Secretary to the board: Mrs. Doris Saunder.

BLACK ECONOMIC UNION (BEU)
Formerly called Negro Industrial and Economic Union. Founded in 1967 by football star Jimmy Brown. Encourages blacks to go into business for themselves by making low interest loans available. Has offices in New York, Washington, Cleveland, Los Angeles, Kansas City, and Oakland. Brown and associates began the organization with their own capital before receiving grants from the Ford Foundation and the Economic Development Administration. To date, claims it has been responsible for 150,000 job placements and has helped start 25 to 30 businesses. Recently the organization has instituted a computer-training program for high school dropouts and returning veterans, a Food First Program which sends food and medical supplies to stricken and depressed areas in the country and a job interest and motivation program. *See also:* JAMES NATHANIEL BROWN.

BLACK MUSLIMS
Veteran Chicago-based black nationalist group (also called Nation of Islam) which does not consider itself part of the civil rights movement or an organization, but rather a religious way of life. Has a secret membership estimated between 10,000 (a police estimate) and 250,000, with mosques in 50 cities. Headed by Elijah Muhammad since 1930. Preaching racial separatism and black supremacy, the movement did not gain popularity until 1950s. By early 1960s, had gained reputation as a fanatic and anti-Christian organization whose rigid discipline and doctrines threatened violent rebellion, despite proclaimed policy of nonviolence. Discipline includes rigid personal health habits, abstention from tobacco and alcohol, and extreme modesty for women. Muslims maintain

their own police force and refuse to vote or perform military service. Today, image is less fierce, with chief emphasis on "black capitalism." Aim is reportedly a Muslim-owned financial empire as cornerstone of self-sufficient "Black Islam Nation." In 1968, Muslims reportedly invested $6 million in business ventures and in March 1969, reported negotiating $20 million in loans. In November 1969, more than 2,000 whites protested Muslim plans to buy farmland near Birmingham, Alabama, reportedly part of Muslim program to buy thousands of acres in the South. Following the purchase, the Muslim-owned land was subjected to months of harassment, including poisoning of the water, which killed 30 head of cattle. Subsequently bought vast farmlands in Georgia and Michigan for produce and livestock to supply their stores, supermarkets, and restaurants. Also own a $1.5 million printing plant. In 1972, Muslims borrowed reputedly $3 million from the North African nation of Libya to buy a church even though Muslim assets have been reported to be $70 million, leading to the speculation that they are experiencing financial difficulties. In 1973, the group applied to the Libyan leader Col. Muammar el-Qaddafi for another loan but was turned down. Louis Farrakhan, national representative of Elijah Muhammad, denied the organization was in financial trouble. However, a New York Times investigation (December 1973) reported that the Muslim financial empire was over extended. It also found that because of a lack of funds, some elements within the sect had turned to crime; that a relaxation in the observance of Muslim practices was causing a conflict between hard-line older members and the more liberal younger group; and that there was concern that when the ailing 75-year-old Elijah Muhammad dies, a violent struggle for power within the organization will ensue. Muslims also run 47 schools and a University of Islam. Their newspaper, Muhammad Speaks, has a reported weekly circulation of 500,000. Among prominent Black Muslims were Malcolm X who left the movement in 1964, declaring himself against racism and segregation, and Muhammad Ali, who was expelled in April 1969. See also: MUHAMMAD ALI, ELIJAH MUHAMMAD.

BLACK P. STONE NATION
Considered to be generally inactive since 1971 when a series of incidents with police jailed most of its leadership. Until that time considered the biggest, best-organized youth gang in the United States and active force in Chicago's Coalition for United Community Action formed in 1968. Began in 1960 as a gang of 30 Blackstone Avenue youths on Chicago's South Side, who as Blackstone Rangers gained notoriety in battles with a rival gang, the East Side Disciples. In April of 1971, 23 members of the street gang, who operated on Chicago's South Side, were indicted on charges of defrauding the Office of Economic Opportunity regarding job-training programs. The gang members were charged on 132 counts of systematically stealing $927,341 in federal grants given them in 1967 and 1968. The grants were discontinued after the 1968 hearings before a Senate investigating committee headed by Senator John L. McClellan of Arkansas.

BLACK PANTHER PARTY (BPP)

Organized in 1966 after the Watts riots, by early 1969 the Black Panther party had a membership estimated at three to five thousand with as many as 40 chapters in major cities such as New York, Chicago, and Detroit, and in Georgia, Tennessee, and other states, as well as California (headquaters are in Oakland). Organized by Huey Newton and Bobby Seale while they were students at Merritt College in Oakland, its original purpose was to provide armed patrols to follow the police and intervene when they felt police were out of line. The Black Panther symbol was adopted, Newton explains, to signify that, like the panther, they would not attack unless attacked. The party's purpose is also said to be to break the "oppressive grip of the white power structure on black communities." Panthers stress pride, discipline, and clean living among followers, discouraging the use of drugs and alcohol.

On May 2, 1967, 30 armed Panthers invaded the chambers of the California state legislature in Sacramento, to protest pending legislation to ban the carrying of loaded weapons in public. On April 6, 1968, Panther member Bobby James Hutton, 17, was killed during a gun battle between blacks and police in West Oakland. Panther education minister Eldridge Cleaver was injured, along with two policemen. On September 8, 1968, Panther founder Huey Newton was convicted of manslaughter in the October 28, 1967 shooting of Oakland patrolman John Frey. Newton was sentenced to 2 to 15 years of imprisonment. The seven-week trial touched off extensive "free Huey" demonstrations.

In November 1968, police and Panthers fought gun battles in Berkeley and San Francisco, and there were incidents between Panthers and police in New York and New Jersey, including the machine-gunning of a Jersey City police station on November 29, and a fire-bomb attack on Newark Panther headquarters on December 1.

In an apparent move to improve the Panthers' image, Bobby Seale stated, in January 1969, that efforts were being made to prevent the use of the organization by "provocateur agents, kooks, and avaricious fools" seeking a base for crime, and announced that a number of criminal suspects had been expelled.

On January 17, 1969, two Panther members were shot to death during a student meeting at UCLA, and a Panther spokesman described the deaths as "political assassinations" by a rival organization. On April 2, 1969, 21 members of the Panthers were indicted in New York on charges of conspiring to blow up several public buildings, including five department stores. Bail was set at $100,000 each. Lawyer William Kunstler described the case as a "turning point" in authorities' offensive against militant blacks. After stormy pretrial hearings in 1970, a trial date was set ending in their acquittal May 1971. On July 14, 1969, FBI Director J. Edgar Hoover reported that "of black groups, the Black Panthers without question represent the greatest threat to internal security of the country." July 21, five policemen were shot in a gunfight at Panther offices in Chicago, in a growing series of police–Panther clashes across the country. These appeared to culminate in the killing of Panther leader Fred Hampton in a predawn apartment raid in Chicago on December 4, 1969, and a raid on the Panthers' Los Angeles headquarters December 8, 1969, in which three Panthers and three policemen were wounded in a four-hour gun battle. The raids, particularly the Chicago incident, touched off a wave of protests, public sympathy, and demands for investigation of police actions. A federal investigation led by Assistant Attorney General Jerris Leonard later sharply criticized police and other authorities' procedures in the case, and in June, 1970, a special grand jury investigation was ordered.

On December 5, 1969, Panthers' lawyer Charles R. Garry claimed that a total of 28 Panther members had been killed by police. A study by the ACLU issued December 9 listed 12 Panthers killed and 12 wounded since October 28, 1967. During the same period, three policemen had been killed and 24 wounded in clashes with Panthers, ACLU reported.

On December 28, the American Civil Liberties Union announced that after a survey in nine metropolitan centers it was their conclusion that law enforcement agencies across the country were "waging a drive against the Black Panther party resulting in serious civil liberties violations." A major Panther trial in 1970 involved national chairman Bobby Seale and 13 other Panthers, on charges concerning the murder of Panther member Alex Rackley, in New Haven, Connecticut, but on May 25, 1971 all charges against Seale were dropped. The following December Newton also won dismissal of all charges against him.

In 1970 the party floundered because a series of successful clampdowns and confrontations with police and federal authorities put party leadership in jail or caused it to go into exile. Also a growing rift in ideology finally caused the party to split into two factions in 1971. The more militant wing (headed by Cleaver from Algeria who resigned from the party in 1972 and is currently believed to be underground somewhere in Europe) was based in New York and changed its name to the East Coast Ministry of Self-Defense. Its secretary, Bernice Jones, in describing the purpose of the East Coast faction said in an interview: "We are not a civil rights group. We are not intergrationists or segregationists. We do not relate to the NAACP or the Urban League ideology nor to a pie in the sky idealism. We are a revolutionary organization whose sole function is to wage revolution in America." (New York Post, September 30, 1972.) The West Coast faction headed by Newton and Seale saw the new direction for the Panthers as one of trying to work within the system by combining their resources with others in the community. But Seale says that the Panthers are still working for the liberation of all oppressed people. They have 20 community programs in Oakland including a free medical clinic, sickle cell anemia program, a breakfast program, and a food co-op. They are also into elective politics. In May of 1973, Seale ran (as a Democrat) for mayor of Oakland but lost in a run-off to incumbent John Reading by some 33,000 votes. But Earl Caldwell of the New York Times (May 22, 1973) said "his [Seale's] vote total was evidence enough that the 'new' Black Panthers Party has arrived." Some observers feel that underlying the Panther move into elective politics is the realization that the concentration of blacks in cities now is so great that, once organized, they can take over local governments. Panther membership—always a subject they don't like discussing—was estimated to be under 1000 in 1970. Current estimates are no more than a few hundred but National Chairman Seale claims 28 active chapters mainly in Oakland, Chicago, and on the East Coast. *See also:* STOKELY CARMICHAEL, ELDRIDGE CLEAVER, KATHLEEN CLEAVER, WILLIAM KUNTSLER, HUEY NEWTON, BOBBY SEALE.

BLACK UNITED FRONT (BUF)

Founded during a January 1968 secret meeting called by Stokely Carmichael with some 100 black leaders representing about 20 organizations participating. BUF is a coalition of all black organizations in Washington, D.C., that are concerned with the struggle for equal opportunity. Its structure is informal. In the winter of 1969, the organization's militant faction wanted to adopt a platform calling for the organization of a vigilante black force to protect the ghetto and oust local police from Negro areas altogether. This action was provoked after the killing of a patrolman in July 1968. Some members of BUF issued a resolution stating that the slaying was justified. Mayor Walter E. Washington denounced the resolution and called it inflammatory and irresponsible. This issue split the organization. Rev. Channing Phillips was one of the active early leaders of the organization. Today is a loosely structured organization with chapters in Kansas City, Boston, Baltimore, Cairo (Illinois) and Washington (D.C.). Each chapter concerns itself with major issues confronting its respective communities. The Washington BUF (the largest chapter in the organization) is headed by Rev. Douglas Moore and concentrates on helping blacks get jobs in the news media on transportation issues—currently has a suit pending against the city to keep fares at 25 cents—and does research on racism. In 1973 opposed the nomination of Henry Kissinger as secretary of state because BUF contends that he is not concerned enough with African issues. National chairman: Rev. Charles Koen of Cairo, Illinois. Washington office: 3622 Georgia Avenue, N.W., Washington, D.C.

JULIAN BOND

Georgia state representative. His name was put in nomination for vice-president at 1968 Democratic National Convention, but later withdrawn. Considered one of the most articulate and attractive moderate black voices, is a professed admirer of both Martin Luther King and Stokely Carmichael. Believes emphasis should be on providing jobs and dividing power more equitably rather than on integration or black nationalism. "As power begins to be divided more equitably, then you are going to see a lessening of what you call the racial problem. . . . I don't think it's going to happen quickly." Has been critical of student radicals, black and white: "All they do is talk, but they never do anything."

In 1965, at age 25, elected to Georgia state legislature for new seat created by Supreme Court decision on reapportionment. He and seven others were the first blacks to be elected in 58 years. But by a vote of 184 to 12, the house refused to permit him to take his seat, citing "disloyalty" in a statement by Bond in which he stated he admired draft-card burners. Bond, at the time an official of Student National Coordinating Committee (SNCC), also endorsed an SNCC statement opposing the Vietnam war. He resigned from SNCC in September 1966, "for personal reasons," and was reelected to the legislature in a special election in November 1966, but again denied his seat. On December 5, 1966, the Supreme Court ruled that the Georgia House of Representatives had violated Bond's constitutional rights by excluding him, and he was sworn in on January 9, 1967. (Bond later explained that his draft-card statement had been widely misquoted, that he had stated that he would not burn his draft card, but he understood why people did burn theirs, and admired their courage in view of the known penalties.) Since 1970 has headed the Southern Election Fund, Inc., an interracial group that assists candidates for lower-level government offices. Board of Trustees includes Representatives Shirley Chisholm of Brooklyn and John Conyers, Jr. of Michigan, Charles Morgan, a lawyer and former head of the southern office of the American Civil Liberties Union, Rev. Channing Phillips, Democratic national committeeman, and Representative Andrew Young of Georgia.

Born in 1940 in Pennsylvania, the son of educator H. M. Bond (currently dean of the University of Atlanta), attended a white Quaker private school near Lincoln University (where his father was then president). Later studied philosophy under Martin Luther King at Morehouse College but left during his senior year to work full time for SNCC as communications director. Also worked as reporter and later managing editor of the *Atlanta Inquirer*. Author of *A Time to Speak, A Time to Act: The Movement in Politics*, published by Simon and Schuster, 1972. Married to the former Alice Clopton, four children.

THOMAS BRADLEY

Mayor of Los Angeles, California, elected July 1973 after defeating incumbent Sam Yorty by a margin of 97,000 votes (he received 56 percent of the votes which included nearly half of the white vote) to become the first black mayor of the third largest city in the United States. Ran for mayor the first time in 1969. In a nonpartisan primary on April 1 he defeated incumbent Sam Yorty by 293,753 to 183,334 votes in a city only 18 percent black. However, Bradley fell short of the majority needed to win. A runoff was held May 27, in which Yorty came back to win by 447,030 (53 percent) to 392,379 (47 percent), after accusing Bradley of running a "racist" campaign. Yorty himself was widely accused by the press of playing on racial fears. Bradley's performance and near victory was, nevertheless, considered highly impressive and his campaign attracted national attention. The son of a sharecropper, he was born December 29, 1917, in Calvert, Texas. Moved to Los Angeles with his parents when he was seven, was educated in local schools, and won a scholarship to the University of California. After graduating in 1940, he spent the next 21 years on the Los Angeles police force retiring in 1961 as a lieutenant—the highest rank ever achieved by a black at the time. In 1963 was elected city councilman, and served for the next 10 years. Holds a law degree from Southwestern Law School. In December 1973 became president of National League of Cities—an organization of 15,000 cities throughout the country. Married to the former Ethel Arnold in 1940, two daughters.

MARLON BRANDO

Leading white actor who withdrew from two motion pictures, in 1968, to devote himself to aiding the Southern Christian Leadership Conference and Martin Luther King Foundation. In April 1968, he demonstrated his sympathy with the Black Panther movement by attending the funeral of 17-year-old Bobby James Hutton, killed by a policeman in Oakland, California. Has said major problem in civil rights is communication: "We must inform the blind, bigoted and uninformed people. If not, there will be a revolution in this country unless we change our thinking. I don't believe it will come from the black community, or from the Indians or Mexican-Americans, but from white college students and other young people." Has been an avid supporter of American Indian causes also since the early 1960s and made headlines in 1973 by refusing to accept an Academy Award for the best actor in the movie *The Godfather*. His statement, read to the Academy by an American Indian, said "the motion picture community has been as responsible as any for degrading the Indian and making a mockery of his character, describing him as a savage, hostile and evil. It's hard enough for children to grow up in this world [but] when Indian children watch television and they watch films, and when they see their race depicted as they are in films, their minds become injured in ways we can never know." (*New York Times*, March 30, 1973.) He has traveled across country studying problems of poor and raising money for minority groups. Born Omaha, Nebraska, April 3, 1924. Attended Shattuck Military Academy, 1939–1941. First Broadway success, *A Streetcar Named Desire*, 1948. Won Academy Award for best actor in *On the Waterfront*, 1954.

ANDREW FULTON BRIMMER

First black man to be appointed a member of the Board of Governors of the Federal Reserve System (1966) and as such, the highest ranking black in government. He has been highly critical of the merits of black capitalism, which has put him at odds with the Nixon administration. In a March 1970 speech at Tuskegee Institute in Alabama, he said that while blacks had made significant economic progress during the 1960s, the gains were so unevenly distributed that there was a "deepening schism in the black community." In a speech at the Allied Social Science Association in Detroit, December 28, 1970, took black-owned banks to task saying they "may be a source of racial pride, and they may also render some marginal—although high cost—financial services" and that under these circumstances served "primarily as ornaments rather than vital instruments of economic development" in the black community. His views were immediately denounced by David Harper, president of the First Independent National Bank of Detroit (who said that he was out of his mind) and by the National Bankers Association which said that Brimmer's position as governor of the Federal Reserve did not of itself equip him to set himself up as a supreme one-man judge of black banks, pointing out that the Association and their banks had had significant impact on black community development. Born in Kentucky in 1926 in a log cabin, son of a Mississippi farmer, and one of five children. Served in the army infantry during World War II and resumed his education afterwards. Graduated from the University of Washington in 1947 with a B.A. in economics and in 1951 received an M.A. Won a Fulbright Fellowship to India the same year. From 1953–1954, served as a research assistant on India at M.I.T. From 1955–1958, served as economist with New York Federal Reserve Bank. Received Ph.D. at Harvard in 1957 in monetary economics employment theory and international trade and economics. Taught at Wharton School of University of Pennsylvania in 1961 and joined the Department of Commerce in 1963, where he became assistant secretary in 1965. Married to the former Doris M. Scott, one daughter.

EDWARD BROOKE

Republican senator from Massachusetts, first black man elected to the Senate since Reconstruction. Served on Boston Finance Commission and was the first black in Massachusetts to become state attorney general (1962). Won his Senate seat in 1966 by a plurality of 438,712 votes. Reelected in 1972 for a term expiring in January 1979 by a plurality of 682,654 votes. Supported Rockefeller for president in 1968 and seconded his nomination at the Republican National Convention in Miami in July 1968. Turned down a possible cabinet appointment for secretary of housing and urban development after a meeting with President-elect Nixon on November 27, 1968.

In 1971 was offered an unspecified cabinet post by President Nixon but again turned it down saying that he was honored but felt that, as the only black senator, he had a responsibility both to the people who elected him and to the blacks across the country who called upon him for help. Although he criticized the president in 1971 for not pushing his black enterprise programs enough and for failing to achieve rapport with the black leadership, throughout his first term, Senator Brooke was not considered a vocal spokesman for the black community; in the last few years, however, seems to be moving closer to actively supporting black interests. In 1971, he arranged a meeting between the Congressional Black Caucus and the president but did not attend; in 1973, he was the guest speaker at the third annual dinner of the Congressional Black Caucus. The *New York Times* (September 27, 1973) commented that a "new relationship is seen by political observers here as part of the new black aim at political unity and as a move by the senator for broader support in the black community in case he tries for higher office." On November 4, 1973 became the first Republican publicly to urge Mr. Nixon to resign from office as a result of the Watergate disclosures. Appearing on ABC-TV's "Issues and Answers," said he "reluctantly" had come to the conclusion that the president should resign "in the interests of this nation." Born in Washington, D.C. on October 26, 1919. Received a B.S. from Howard University in 1941. Inducted into an all-Negro infantry unit in World War II, rose to the rank of captain and won the Bronze

Star for intelligence work. Received LL.B. from Boston University law school in 1948, admitted to the Massachusetts bar the same year. Married to the former Remigia Ferrari-Scacco, at Genoa, Italy, on June 7, 1947, two daughters.

CLAUDE BROWN

Author of 1965 best-seller *Manchild in the Promised Land*, a searing account of his Harlem upbringing. Star witness at Senate crime committee hearings on August 30, 1966, when he provided colorful testimony on drugs, drinking, and delinquency. Testified again, August 5, 1969, before House Select Committee on Crime (created May 1, 1969), at which he urged legalization of drugs. Argued that drugs are necessary for release from ghetto life and that legalization would help curb crime. A street fighter at age six; at 11 he was a member of the Buccaneer "bopping gang" and its elite stealing group known as the Forty Thieves. After several stints in the Wiltwyck school for disturbed and deprived boys and the Warwick reform school, he finished high school and graduated from Howard University in 1965. Afterwards attended Rutgers law school. In summer 1969, taught creative writing course at University of California at Santa Barbara. Lectures widely and is currently writing a book about abandoned teenagers in Harlem. Born February 23, 1937, in New York.

H. RAP BROWN

Black militant who succeeded Stokely Carmichael as chairman of Student National Coordinating Committee (SNCC) in May 1967. Did not seek reelection in 1968, but reelected chairman July 22, 1969. Earned notoriety with his televised statement that "violence is as American as cherry pie" at a Washington, D.C., rally on July 27, 1967. Full statement was: "This country was born of violence. Violence is as American as cherry pie. Black people have always been violent, but our violence has always been directed toward each other. If nonviolence is to be practiced, then it should be practiced in our community and end there." At same rally, declared: "If Washington, D.C., doesn't come around, Washington, D.C., should be burned down." At Senate Judiciary Committee hearings, August 2, 1967, police chief cited an inflammatory speech by Brown as "sole reason" for Cambridge, Maryland, riot, July 28. Indicted by Maryland grand jury, August 14. Arrested New York, August 19, 1967, on federal charge of carrying gun across state lines while under indictment. In statement August 20, claimed that he was being held as a political prisoner. After release on bail, August 22, told crowd of blacks on courthouse steps: "We're at war . . . and you better get yourself some guns." During 1968 Columbia University disorders, Brown and Carmichael met with demonstrators at Hamilton Hall, April 26. On May 22, 1968, Brown was convicted by a federal court in New Orleans for violating the Federal Firearms Act. He was sentenced to five years in prison and fined $2,000, the maximum sentence. After serving time in Port Allen jail, near New Orleans, Brown was released in July 1969, into the custody of his lawyer, on two $15,000 bonds, his movements to be restricted to eastern Louisiana and southern New York (Bronx and Manhattan). He was released when the Court of Appeals vacated the conviction, pending a wiretapping appeal. On May 4, 1970 the long-delayed trial for the 1967 Cambridge, Maryland, incident was set to take place in Ellicott City, Maryland. Even though the Kerner Commission on Civil Disorders had concluded that the overreaction by rednecks to black militancy had more to do with the starting of the fires than Brown's speech, Brown went underground rather than stand trial thereby forfeiting his $10,000 bail. (In January 1971 a Maryland prosecutor admitted fabricating the arson charge against Brown because he is reported to have wanted to ensure involvement of FBI in the case.) In November 1973, riot and arson charges were dropped against Brown in an arrangement resulting from a plea-bargaining session. Brown, whose real name is Hubert Gerold Brown, remained underground until his arrest October 16, 1971, for assault and robbery at the Red Carpet Lounge on Manhattan's West 85th Street. After a prolonged trial at which Imamu Baraka appeared as a character witness and he was defended by William Kunstler, Brown was sentenced from 5 to 15 years and is currently at Attica State Prison in upper New York state.

Born in Baton Rouge, Louisiana, October 4, 1943. Attended Southern University, but left in his senior year to work for SNCC. Author of *Die Nigger Die*, published April 1969 by Dial Press. Married (May 3, 1968) New York City school teacher Lynne Doswell.

JAMES BROWN

Nation's king of soul music, called "Soul Brother Number One." Proclaims his faith in America, but adds: "I can't rest until the black man in America is let out of jail, until his dollar's as good as the next man's." Advises kids to stay in school and reportedly gives 10 percent of his income to youth groups and charities. By appearances on radio and television in Boston and Washington, D.C., he helped cool riots which followed Martin Luther King's assassination. Unlike some other soul singers, he believes that the good life is within reach of the black man, and according to a *Newsweek* article of July 1, 1968, he is the man who speaks for the black man on the street. Said *Newsweek*, "It's symptomatic of America's agonizing dilemma that most white people have never heard of him. But to Negroes he is king, the man who made it." Born in 1932 and raised in Augusta, Georgia, he dropped out of school in the seventh grade. Was arrested at 16 (car theft, breaking and entering) and paroled three years later. Earned a precarious living as shoeshine boy, cotton picker, and prize-fighter before singing spirituals in a Toccoa, Georgia, church. Heads his own company, James Brown Enterprises, that brings in $4 million a year and includes two radio stations, music publishing companies, and extensive real estate. Has made 41 gold records and sold more than 80 million records. Endorsed Richard Nixon for President in 1972 because all that blacks know about is Democrats. "My thing," he said, "is to build up this country. If you think Richard Milhous Nixon is wrong, wait until the man's term is gone, then take him as a man." (*Washington Post*, August 12, 1972.) Married twice, currently to Deidre Yvonne Jenkins (1970), one child.

JAMES NATHANIEL BROWN

Movie actor and businessman who played professional football with the Cleveland Browns. Has been called the greatest offensive back in history. Retired from pro ball in 1966 to devote himself to the improvement of black businesses and to a movie career (first major film, *Dirty Dozen*). In 1967, he helped form the Black Economic Union, which aims at encouraging blacks to go into business for themselves by making low interest loans available. Has been brought to court several times in recent years, on charges usually involving illegal use of hands on both men and women. Says Brown: "I walk tall. I do my thing. They try to break you. They won't break me." Born February 7, 1936, on St. Simon Island in Georgia. Moved to Manhasset, New York, at the age of seven and after graduating from Manhasset High School had a choice of 42 college scholarships as well as professional offers to play football. Chose Syracuse University where he became All-American in football and lacrosse. Graduated in 1957 with B.A. degree. Divorced, three sons. *See also:* BLACK ECONOMIC UNION.

WILLIAM H. BROWN III

Former head of Equal Employment Opportunity Commission—the government's chief anti-job discrimination official. Has been outspoken on the issue of back pay. In 1972, as EEOC representative, wrung an agreement from AT&T in which the company was to pay some $15 million to female and minority employees who, he contended, had been illegally confined to low paying jobs that offered little or no advancement. In December 1973, during negotiations between the government and the United Steel Workers of America to promote blacks in low-paying and menial jobs in steel mills, Brown insisted that industry and union pay $45 million in back pay to the aggrieved black workers. Brown's term as EEOC chairman officially expired in June 1973, and President Nixon recently appointed John H. Powell, Jr. to replace him. A Republican appointed by President Nixon, Brown replaced Clifford Alexander, Jr., a Democrat, in April 1969 after Alexander resigned. Holds a B.S. degree from Temple (1952) and LL.D. from the University of Pennsylvania (1955); joined the law firm of Norris, Schmidt, Green, Harris and Higginbotham in Philadelphia becoming a partner in 1963. Born Jan. 19, 1928 in Philadelphia. Married, one daughter.

LOUIS R. BRUCE

Commissioner of the Bureau of Indian Affairs in the Department of the Interior, appointed by President Nixon from 1969 to 1972. Currently works with the Antioch Law Center in Washington, D.C., and the Coalition of Eastern Indians. Member of the Oglala Sioux tribe of South Dakota. In 1961, organized the first National Indian Council on Housing. Recipient of the American Indian Achievement Award. Received Medal of Freedom from President Eisenhower for "outstanding contributions in promoting the American way of life." Born in 1906.

BUREAU OF INDIAN AFFAIRS (BIA)

Agency within Department of the Interior responsible for the administration and welfare of some 400,000 Indians, including 28,000 Aleuts and Eskimos. As trustee of lands owned by the Indians, it controls over 263 separate reservations, pueblos, and colonies, as well as scattered lands in 26 states from Florida to Alaska. With an annual budget of approximately 500 million dollars it attempts to provide improved housing, schools, job training, and health service programs. Despite its status as the nation's largest employer of Indians, the bureau has been described as "a major hurdle to Indian progress" (*Christian Science Monitor*, January 13, 1970), and is criticized for its power over Indians' private and public lives and its fumbling bureaucracy. However many Indian spokesmen claim that, for better or worse, the bureau is their only defense against extinction as a racial and cultural entity.

The BIA was created in 1834 as part of the Department of War to negotiate with hostile Indian tribes. In 1849 it was transferred to the Department of the Interior. President Nixon, in a speech on July 8, 1970, pronounced a doctrine of self-determination for the American Indian which subsequently touched off a bureaucratic struggle within BIA. Two years before, BIA head Louis Bruce began to institute some modest changes by bringing young Indian activists in to replace the complacent and predominately white bureaucrats. He had been supported in his reorganization by then Secretary of Interior, Walter J. Hickel. But after Hickel's dismissal by President Nixon, his successor, Roger C. B. Morton, looked at things differently and, in July 1971, tried to dilute Bruce's power by appointing John D. Crow as deputy commissioner. An old-line bureaucrat and Cherokee Indian, Crow was empowered to bypass Bruce's authority and tried to have the new activists transferred or to make them resign. Tribal leaders in the country saw these actions as a retreat from the president's earlier endorsement of Indian self-determination (even though the government earlier had restored the Sacred Blue Lake to the Taos Pueblo Indians and had helped pass a bill returning 45,000 acres of land back to the Indians). In September 1971, a group of tribal chiefs, headed by Peter MacDonald, Chairman of the Navajo Tribal Council, went to Washington to demand that the BIA be removed from the Department of the Interior and placed in "receivership" in the White House. Simultaneously, a band of young militants invaded BIA offices and attempted a citizen's arrest of Crow (he was not there). The White House then called several high-level conferences and, by the following November, Bruce was reinstated with full powers; but reorganization of the bureau remained stalemated and Bruce resigned in 1972. In October 1973, Morris Thompson, an Athabascan Indian, was appointed as the new commissioner.

YVONNE BRATHWAITE BURKE

Democratic congresswoman from California's newly created Thirty-seventh Congressional District—a predominately black and Democratic section of Los Angeles. Elected in 1972. A former practicing attorney and six-year veteran of the California General Assembly (1966 to 1972) and the first black female legislator in California history. Serves on the Public Works and Interior and Insular Affairs committees and also a member of the Congressional Black Caucus—one of four women members. Came to national attention at the Democratic National Convention in 1972 in Miami when she was elected vice-chairperson (with Lawrence O'Brien). Considered a moderate liberal, and hard working. The only child of James Watson, a retired janitor, and Lola Moore Watson, a successful real estate broker. Born (1933) and raised on Los Angeles' Eastside, she says that she is the product of a middle-class upbringing. Graduated in three and a half years from the University of California at Los Angeles and received her Juris Doctorate at the University of Southern California in 1956. Married twice: first to Louis Brathwaite, a mathematician, which ended in divorce in 1963; currently to William Burke in 1972, a businessman who was voted one of "100 outstanding young men of America" in 1969. One child, Autumn Roxanne, born November 1973. See also: CONGRESSIONAL BLACK CAUCUS.

EUGENE S. CALLENDER
President of the New York Urban Coalition. Elected August 21, 1969. In 1967 he served as a member of the President's Task Force on Manpower and Urban Unemployment. A resident of New York City, he has been actively involved in programs for social change in local communities. Chaired committee that drafted the proposal for Harlem Youth-Action, the nation's first federal program for youth in the ghettos, and for three years was chairman of its board of directors. Former executive director of the New York Urban League. Founder of the street academies program and of Harlem Prep. Born Cambridge, Massachusetts, in 1926, he graduated from Boston University and Westminster Theological Seminary in Philadelphia. An ordained minister, he lectures frequently at colleges across the nation and hosts a weekly television show "Positively Black" now in its fourth year on WNBC-TV. Divorced, three children.

GODFREY CAMBRIDGE
Comedian and actor, noted for his racial satire. In December 1968, became a charter member of a committee to help pay off the $50,000 promissory note for Eldridge Cleaver when he forfeited bail. He has said, "You're not going to find me on any picket lines. In the first place, I'm not non-violent." Born in Harlem, he was sent to Nova Scotia for elementary schooling "to miss the Harlem schools." Returned to New York for high school and attended Hofstra University for two and a half years. Made his Broadway debut in Nature's Way, and won an Obie award for his performance in The Blacks in 1961. Frequently appears on television. In 1969 made the film Cotton Comes to Harlem, in which he plays a Harlem detective, followed by a sequel called Come Back Charleston and a film on drugs called Dead is Dead for use in institutions and schools. Co-chairman of the Committee for the Employment of Negro Performers, an organization, formed in the 1960s, whose aim is to increase the number of minority performers in entertainment. Divorced.

STOKELY CARMICHAEL

Former chairman of Student National Coordinating Committee (SNCC) and one of the most charismatic of the new breed of militant black leaders. First popularized the phrase "black power" during a voting rights march in June 1966. Carmichael asserted the phrase meant nothing more than "a way to help Negroes develop racial pride and use the ballot for education and economic development." In his book *Black Power: The Politics of Liberation in America*, which he wrote with Professor Charles V. Hamilton, he states "the concept of Black Power rests on a fundamental premise: before a group can enter the open society, it must close ranks. By this we mean that group solidarity is necessary before a group can operate effectively from a bargaining position of strength in a pluralistic society." Carmichael broke with SNCC in May 1967. Officially expelled in August 1968 when the alliance between SNCC and the Black Panther party ended at a meeting of the two groups in New York City. SNCC leaders voted to terminate their relationship with Carmichael, who was then prime minister of the Panthers.

From May to December 1967, he went on a world tour, visiting Britain, Czechoslovakia, Cuba (for which the United States revoked his passport), North Vietnam, Algeria, Egypt, Syria, and Guinea. While in Havana, he was quoted as saying: "We must internationalize our struggle, and if we are going to turn into reality the words of Che [Guevara] to create two, three and more Vietnams, we must recognize that Detroit and New York are also Vietnam."

Carmichael returned to the United States amid a storm of legislative protest. His passport was lifted and indictment proceedings were initiated against him by the justice department for preaching sedition. Carmichael settled in Washington, D.C., in 1968 and helped organize the Black United Front, a Washington, D.C., organization to unite blacks in the nation's capital. He married South African singer Miriam Makeba in April 1968 and in the spring of 1969 they went to live in Conakry, Guinea. Carmichael publicly broke with the Black Panthers in July 1969, saying he could no longer support "the present tactics and methods which the party is using to coerce and force everyone to submit to its authority" and was denounced for his action by fellow Panther-in-exile Eldridge Cleaver. In an interview in Algiers, Carmichael said that he intended ultimately to return to the United States, but first wanted to work for the return to power of Ghana's Kwame Nkrumah.

However, Carmichael returned to the United States on March 18, 1970, and declared that he intended to wage "a relentless struggle against the poison of drugs in the black community." A few days later, on March 25, he was called before a closed session of the Senate Internal Security Subcommittee and questioned about his activities while abroad. Later, in November 1972, on a trip to this country from Africa, said he was trying to seek black unity around the ideology of Pan-Africanism and announced plans for starting an All-African People's Revolutionary party—a party less interested in the "electoral politics" of this country than in the ultimate goal of uniting blacks. However, he did point out that the party will eventually run candidates in local races. In 1973,

Carmichael and his wife were given Ugandan citizenship by President Idi Amin.

Carmichael was born in Trinidad, June 21, 1941. He moved to New York City at age 11, and grew up in a predominantly white neighborhood in the Bronx. Has degree in philosophy from Howard University (1964).

ROBERT (SONNY) CARSON

A Brooklyn (New York) black activist who received nation-wide attention in the late 1960s. As chairman of the Brooklyn chapter of the Congress of Racial Equality (CORE), he participated in the Ocean Hill-Brownsville demonstration school district controversy in 1968–1969. During the 1968 CORE national convention in Columbus, Ohio, he and 16 heads of other CORE chapters walked out of the convention. At issue was whether blacks should lead a reform or a revolutionary movement, as Carson's group advocated, and this caused an ideological split in the organization and Carson to break with national CORE organization charging that CORE was more concerned with paper work than with militancy. He then changed the name of the Brooklyn chapter to Independent Brooklyn CORE, and the national organization disavowed any connection with Carson. In recent years has become interested in the "black capitalism movement." Author of a book called *The Education of Sonny Carson*, published in 1972 by W.W. Norton, about his early life; it is currently being made into a movie for which he served as a technical adviser and will share in 50 percent of the movie's profits. In July 1973 was indicted for murder in connection with a man who allegedly held up a black-owned business in the Bedford-Stuyvesant section of Brooklyn. After pleading not guilty, was released on $50,000 bail. Born 1933, married, one son.

LEONARD H. CARTER

West Coast regional director of the NAACP. A native of Minneapolis, Minnesota. Before joining NAACP staff, was secretary-treasurer of the Dining Car Employees Union Local 516 of the Great Northern Railway Company and later auditor to the National Joint Council of Dining Car Employees. Married, four children. Office: 955 Market St., San Francisco, Calif.

LISLE CARTER

Chancellor, Atlanta University Center, Atlanta, Georgia (January 1974). Former vice-president for social and environmental studies at Cornell University, Ithaca, New York (1968–1974). First black assistant secretary in the Department of Health, Education, and Welfare. Appointed January 1966. Born in New York City on November 18, 1925, he graduated from Dartmouth in 1944 and St. John's University law school in 1950. Before working for the government, he practiced law in New York and was legal counsel to the National Urban League. Married to the former Emily E. Ellis in 1950, five children.

ARTHUR A. CHAPIN

Director of Office of Equal Opportunity in the Department of Labor since 1969 and is responsible for carrying out and coordinating all functions and activities of Title VI of the Civil Rights Act of 1964 for the labor department. Has been with the labor department since 1961, and is an assistant to the secretary of labor. Earlier he served as assistant to the president of the New Jersey Congress of Industrial Organizations Council concerned with civil rights legislation, minimum wage, and unemployment compensation. Also served as a member of the New Jersey Committee on Housing and of a state wage panel for restaurant employees. Since joining the labor department has helped compile an annual directory of Negro college graduates for business and industry. Office: Department of Labor, Room 7415, 14th and Constitution Avenue, N.W., Washington, D.C. 20210.

CESAR CHAVEZ

California grape-pickers' leader who since 1965 has won widespread national support for strike and boycott actions against table-grape growers and lettuce growers. President of the United Farm Workers Organizing Committee (AFL-CIO), which he founded in 1962. Began strike against San Joaquin Valley growers in September 1965. In March and April 1966, led 300-mile protest march to Sacramento to gain support of Gov. Pat Brown. By end of 1966, several San Joaquin Valley growers, including the big Di Giorgio Corporation, agreed to sign contracts with the union. In 1967, when bitterness led to outbreaks of violence, Chavez fasted for 25 days "to recall farm workers to the nonviolent roots of their movement."

Chavez began touring the country early in 1969 to broaden support for "La Causa." In September 1969, Chavez charged before the Senate Subcommittee on Migratory Labor that grape growers were "systematically poisoning" field workers with pesticides.

By the end of 1969, Chavez claimed that California grape sales were down 27 percent. The growers responded with a $75 million suit for damages against the union and a $4 million antiboycott campaign. A major breakthrough came April 1, 1970, when three Coachella Valley table-grape growers (constituting 10 percent of table-grape producers) signed a contract with the union, to be followed soon by others. The five-year strike and boycott ended in 1970 when a majority of the grape growers in California negotiated three-year contracts with United Farm Workers Union (UFWU). That same year, however, the Teamsters signed up vegetable growers throughout the state and Chavez called a strike in the lettuce fields from Salinas to Santa Maria. Some 7,000 farm workers joined the strike which was later broken by injunctions. On December 3, 1970 was jailed for violating an injunction and spent 20 days in jail. Two years later (1972), the California Supreme Court ruled the injunctions against farm workers invalid on the grounds the growers used the Teamsters "as a shield" against UFWU.

In 1972 the Farm Bureau sponsored legislation that would outlaw the boycott and strike at harvest time in 15 different states—and effectively thwarted union organizing efforts. When the Arizona legislature passed this legislation into law, Chavez fasted in Phoenix for 24 days and led a successful fight to defeat a similar law in California. Also in that year, the UFWU won two major contracts from the Florida citrus industry making them the first union victory outside of California and Arizona.

In 1973, when the original UFWU contracts expired with the grape growers, the Teamsters again moved in and signed up most of the growers who had previously had UFWU contracts. Chavez called for another strike and boycott in the vineyards that summer but stopped it after two strikers were killed and others wounded. The same year UFWU was chartered as a full-fledged union by AFL-CIO and the Farm Workers Union held its first convention in Fresno, California, in September electing Chavez its first president.

Born the son of Mexican-American migrant workers, he worked in the fields with his parents, attending school intermittently until the seventh grade. Hired by the late Saul Alinsky in 1952 to work for the Community Service Organization to help raise the living standards of Spanish-speaking people but moved to Delano, California, in 1962 to start his own labor movement. Married, 8 children.

SHIRLEY CHISHOLM

Democratic representative from New York, she is the first Negro woman ever elected to Congress. Elected November 5, 1968, from New York's Twelfth Congressional District (Bedford-Stuyvesant), she defeated former Congress of Racial Equality (CORE) chairman James Farmer. Elected to House Veteran Affairs Committee February 18, 1969, after rejecting original assignment to House Agriculture Committee. At a caucus of House Democrats, January 29, 1969, Mrs. Chisholm defied tradition for new members by requesting reassignment, preferably to a committee involved in urban affairs.

In maiden speech, March 26, 1969, declared she would vote against every defense money bill "until our values and priorities have been turned right-side-up again." Was reelected to Congress in 1970 and again in 1972 by an 87.6 percent plurality of the vote over three opponents. On January 24, 1972, announced her candidacy for the presidency declaring that she hoped "to repudiate the ridiculous notion that the American people will not vote for a qualified candidate simply because he is not white or because she is not male." (New York Times, January 25, 1972.) But her candidacy created a controversy within the black community. While she was supported by some black elected officials, such as Percy Sutton and Ronald Dellums (Congressman from California), others such as Walter Fauntroy (District of Columbia Representative) opposed her saying that she had shattered the unity of the black community by not consulting them before her announcement and that she is too much influenced by the Women's Movement. Some black leaders felt that the Chisholm candidacy also threatened their bargaining power with a major candidate who wanted their support. Neither the Congressional Black Caucus, of which she is a member, nor the Black Political Convention, which held its 1972 convention in Gary, Indiana, endorsed her candidacy.

In November 1973, the General Accounting Office recommended that the Justice Department take legal action against her for her alleged mishandling of a $23,000 surplus left over from her campaign fund. "They're just on a fishing expedition," she said about the investigation. "It's because of who I am in America—unbought and unbossed."

Member of the Congressional Black Caucus formed in 1970 and is chairman of the caucus' Military Affairs Committee. She has been a director of a child care center in the Bedford-Stuyvesant section of Brooklyn. Worked behind the scenes in politics until becoming a New York State assemblywoman in 1964. Considers herself part of the "new politics" of Julian Bond and Congressman John Conyers. Author of two books, *Unbought and Unbossed* (1970) and *The Good Fight* (published in 1973 about her presidential campaign). In 1973 was chosen Woman of the Year by the *Ladies Home Journal* magazine. In great demand as a lecturer and reportedly earned $30,419 in lecture fees in 1972— more than any other member of Congress.

Born November 30, 1924 in Brooklyn, New York, she moved to Barbados with her family but returned to Brooklyn at age 11 to finish grade school. Graduated from Brooklyn College, received a M.A. from Columbia University. Married Conrad Chisholm in 1949, no children. *See also:* CONGRESSIONAL BLACK CAUCUS.

CIVIL RIGHTS COMMISSION

Independent, bipartisan federal agency established by Civil Rights Act of 1957 to investigate allegations that citizens are being deprived of their civil rights. Also studies and collects information concerning civil rights legal developments, appraises the laws and policies of the federal government with respect to civil rights, and submits reports of its activities, findings, and recommendations to the president and Congress. Under the staff direction of John A. Boggs serves as a national clearinghouse for civil rights information. It is solely a fact-finding agency with no enforcement or legislative powers. As of 1972, however, more than 60 percent of its recommendations have been adopted in some form—by legislation, executive order, administrative regulation, or policy directive. Greatest achievements include recommendations leading to the 1965 Voting Rights Act and the 1965 Law Enforcement Assistance Act. Its report to President Nixon and Congress in April 1970 demanded stronger safeguards for the rights of Mexican-Americans. The next year a commission report found that five schools in the Southwest gave inferior education not only to Mexican-Americans but to blacks and Indians as well. It also said that nothing was being done to alleviate problems facing Indians in general. Commission reports in the early 1970s criticized the Nixon administration for not taking a more active role in enforcing civil rights laws and regulations (but at the end of 1971 said the government had somewhat improved in this area), for the administration's minimal busing policy which the commission felt undermined 17 years of desegregation (*New York Times* August 13, 1971), and for antipoverty and model cities programs which discriminated against Puerto Ricans. A board of six commissioners, appointed by the president and confirmed by the Senate, listens to grievances throughout the year. After 1972 presidential election, two commissioners and Commission's chairman, Rev. Theodore Hesburgh, who had been sharply critical of the administration on civil rights, resigned claiming the Nixon people had requested it—a charge Nixon officials denied. The post of chairman was filled by Arthur S. Fleming in December 1973. The Commission has regional offices located in Chicago, Los Angeles, Kansas City (Missouri), Atlanta, Denver, San Antonio (Texas), and New York. Headquarters: U.S. Commission on Civil Rights, 1121 Vermont Avenue, N.W., Washington, D.C. 20425.

KENNETH B. CLARK

Distinguished educator and psychologist. Professor of psychology at City College of New York and first Negro to receive permanent appointment as a professor there (1960). Also the only black member of New York Board of Regents. In 1967 founded the Metropolitan Applied Research Center (MARC), a social research organization to "alleviate desperation in ghettos in northern cities not helped directly by federal court decisions or civil rights legislation." Also director of the New York Foundation.

Testified before Supreme Court on school desegregation issue, 1954. Prominent role as arbiter in New York City school strike, 1968. With his wife Dr. Mamie Phipps Clark, also a psychologist, opened the Northside Center for Child Development, a guidance center for emotionally disturbed children, 1946. At Washington conference of black elected officials, September 1969, Dr. Clark stated: "Elected Negro officials are now the only civil rights leaders who are representatives of the aspirations, desires, and the quest for answers posed by their constituents and elected by their people to speak for them. The time has passed when self-appointed individual leaders . . . can speak for the masses of American Negroes." To this end was instrumental in forming the Joint Center for Political Studies, a supportive organization to serve the needs of blacks holding public office. A foe of separatism in schools, which he contends is bad for blacks as well as whites, he testified before a Senate hearing on school desegregation April 20, 1970. Two years later charged that school decentralization in New York City was failing to improve education because the 31 local school boards were more interested in power than improving the quality of education. Dr. Clark was born July 14, 1914, in the Panama Canal Zone, graduated from Howard University in 1933, and received Ph.D. at Columbia University in 1940. Author of four books, the latest of which is *Dark Ghetto*, "a summation of personal . . . experience as a prisoner within the ghetto," published in 1965. Commenting on the movement in a *New York Times* symposium (August 30, 1973) said "It may be that the civil rights movement has, whether it likes it or not, to move toward a think-tank model of effecting the complicated kinds of social change which we clearly are confronted with. And this is threatening . . . it's easier to retreat into rhetoric and costumes and cliches than to develop the model that is appropriate to the present difficulty." Office: City College, New York, N.Y.

JOHN HENRIK CLARKE
Associate editor of *Freedomways* magazine since 1962. Formerly taught African and Afro-American history at both New York University and the New School for Social Research. In 1968, developed format for WCBS-TV series "Black Heritage" and acted as special consultant for the program. Born in Union Springs, Alabama in 1915, he moved to New York City in 1933. Attended high school in Columbus, Georgia, and in New York City and continued studies at New York University and the New School for Social Research. A founding member of the Harlem Writers Guild and the Black Academy of Arts and Letters. Has written and edited fourteen books—the most recent are *American Negro Short Stories* (1966), *Malcolm X: The Man and His Times* (1969), and *Harlem U.S.A.* (1971). Since 1969 has been a professor of African World History at Hunter College in New York City.

WILLIAM CLAY
Democratic representative from Missouri's First Congressional District, he was elected in 1968 as his state's first black congressman. Has been in politics since 1959, when he was elected alderman in St. Louis. Won reelection in 1963. In that year, as an alderman, served 112 days of a 270-day jail sentence for demonstrating to give blacks white-collar jobs at a St. Louis bank. Shortly thereafter became his ward's committeeman and occupied this powerful political seat until election to the House of Representatives. Had been race relations coordinator for Steamfitters' Union Local 526 but resigned this position when he became a congressman. A member of the Congressional Black Caucus, he is organization's treasurer and sits on the House Education and Labor committees. Born in St. Louis on April 30, 1931, he served in the army during the Korean War. In 1955 joined the NAACP and became head of its Youth Council, then joined Congress of Racial Equality. Holds a B.S. degree in political science from the University of St. Louis. Married, three children. *See also:* CONGRESSIONAL BLACK CAUCUS.

REV. ALBERT J. CLEAGE
Leading spokesman of Detroit militants. Headed the Federation for Self-Determination, formed late in 1967 as a unifying force and clearinghouse for black programs and proposals but is no longer associated with the organization. Nominated at National Council of Churches eighth general assembly (1969) in Detroit for its presidency. Defeated by Mrs. Theodore O. Wedel, first woman to hold the office, receiving 93 votes to Mrs. Wedel's 387. At one time pastor of the Shrine of the Black Madonna, formerly the Central United Church of Christ, which is located in the heart of the 1967 riot area of Detroit. In the early 1970s changed his focus from fighting the establishment to building "counter institu-

tions to liberate black people" and expanded the Shrine into an organization called the Shrines of the Black Madonna of the Black Christian National Inc. Organization has established five cadres in Detroit but has plans to expand to Atlanta (Georgia), New York, Washington (D.C.), Philadelphia, and Chicago. Shrines offer job training and education programs which are self-supporting through cultural centers which sell Afro handicrafts. Also receives income from private contributions. Cleage changed his name to Jaramogi Abeb Agyeman (which means liberator, blessed man, savior of the nation in Swahili). Divorced, two daughters.

ELDRIDGE CLEAVER

Former minister of information of the Black Panthers, living in exile abroad since end of 1968. Formally resigned his position in the Panther Party in January 1972 after a party rift became irreconcilable. Disappeared from public view in late November 1968, after refusing to surrender himself for a parole violation. Had been paroled since 1966, after serving nine years of a 14-year sentence on a 1958 conviction for assault with intent to kill. Parole was rescinded after he was involved in a gun battle between Black Panthers and police in Oakland, April 6, 1968. He was released on bail June 12, but this decision was overturned and further appeals were exhausted November 26.

Cleaver joined the Panthers in February 1967, and in a period of less than two years emerged as a dynamic black leader, journalist (*Ramparts* magazine) and author (*Soul on Ice, Post-Prison Writings and Speeches*). In speeches and articles, he expounded the Panthers' demands for the liberation of black America. In August 1968, he became the presidential nominee of the Peace and Freedom Party, said his campaign was aimed at "laying the base for a revolutionary movement that will unite black . . . and white radicals," and in the November 5 election received 36,385 votes, mostly from California.

In October 1968, Cleaver lectured at the University of California at Berkeley on "the roots of racism," and received a standing ovation from students. The lecture took place after weeks of public debate in which Gov. Ronald Reagan led opposition to Cleaver's appearance, denouncing him as "an advocate of racism and violence." Cleaver's lecture, intended as the first of a series, was described as "moderate" and "scholarly."

Cleaver's whereabouts were unknown from November 1968 until May 1969, when he was discovered by reporters living in a small apartment in Havana. In July 1969, Cleaver and his wife Kathleen arrived in Algiers as guests of the Algerian government, to attend the Pan-African Cultural Festival. The festival was marked by a public clash between Cleaver and Stokely Carmichael when the latter announced his break with the Panthers. Reportedly the issue was cooperation with whites, which Cleaver supported and Carmichael denounced. Cleaver told reporters he was homesick and intended eventually to return to the United States either legally or illegally. However, after the festival, Cleaver remained in Algiers with his wife who gave birth to a son there, July 29, 1969. In August 1970, he led Panther delegation to Hanoi for "Solidarity Day" between North Vietnam and American blacks. Since 1970 headed the International Section of the Black Panther Party in Algiers until he fell into disfavor with local government in late 1972 when black militants hijacked two airliners and flew them—with $1.5 million in ransom—to Algiers. After Cleaver protested about the treatment given to hijackers by Algerian authorities, was placed under house arrest. In December of the same year, eight police broke into his house and tried to shoot him but he escaped and went into hiding.

Nothing was heard from Cleaver until April 1973 when he turned up in Paris where it appeared he had been living for several months. He is said to believe that with the "ping-pong entente" between the United States and China, coupled with the mounting preoccupation of Cuba and Algeria, the prospects of an international revolutionary organization may have diminished for him. Currently reported to be working on a new book and preparing for upcoming legal battles at a secret address in France. One of the court battles is the outcome of an appeal against a decision by Interior Ministry of France in May 1973 denying him political asylum. The second legal battle is with the U.S. Treasury which has blocked Cleaver's book royalties based on the 1917 "Trading with the Enemy" Act. For the purpose of the regulation, the Treasury considers Cleaver a national of China, North Korea and North Vietnam—countries he has visited since leaving the U.S. in 1968. Born 1935. Married to the former Kathleen Neal, two children.

KATHLEEN CLEAVER
Wife of Eldridge Cleaver and active spokesman for his causes. Daughter of foreign service officer Ernest Eugene Neal, with whom she had traveled widely in Asia and Africa. Born 1945. Educated at Oberlin and Barnard College. Worked in the Peace Corps and for Student National Coordinating Committee. Met Eldridge Cleaver at black student conference at Fisk University in March 1967 and married him December 27 the same year. On July 29, 1969, in Algiers, she gave birth to a son, named Antonio Maceo after a nineteenth-century black Cuban revolutionary. After two and a half years in Algeria with her husband, returned to New York in late 1971 to reorganize the shattered remnants of the East Coast faction of the Black Panther Party into what she called a revolutionary people's communication network—which would link revolutionary groups of all political persuasions. Said at the time her husband fully intended to return to this country to join in the urban guerrilla struggle which he would like to pattern after the movements in Latin America, Quebec, and Northern Ireland. With backing from supporters started a newspaper called *Babylon* which, although it looks like the West Coast Panther newspaper, minimizes political rhetoric. Currently lectures around the country.

COALITION FOR UNITED COMMUNITY ACTION, RECRUITMENT AND TRAINING
Chicago group of militant organizations, South Side neighborhood groups, and street gangs formed in early summer of 1969 to force an end to discrimination

in the city's construction industry. After it began harassing tactics in late July, more than 20 construction sites representing contracts exceeding $80 million were shut down. Coalition aimed at 10,000 on-the-job training positions for black youths, and more business for black contractors. An agreement, called the Chicago Plan, was reached between Coalition and union and construction officials on January 13, 1970. This agreement scaled down the Coalition's demands to fewer black trainees, rather than continue the impasse. Three major gangs are involved, the Conservative Vice Lords (gold berets), the Black P. Stone Nation (red berets) who are no longer in the Coalition, and the East Side Disciples (black berets) as well as 100 organizations with combined membership of 50,000. Currently engaged in securing jobs for its members in the construction industry and receives federal money. President and executive director: Carl Latimer. David Reed, one of the original organizers of the Coalition and at one time an aide to the governor of Illinois, is on the board of directors. Office: 1369 East 53rd Street, Chicago, Illinois.

CARDISS COLLINS

Elected to Congress on June 5, 1973, to fill the unexpired term of her husband who was killed in an airplane crash in December 1972. A Democrat from Chicago's predominately black Sixth Congressional District whose constituency numbers 420,000. Had been a committeewoman in Chicago's twenty-fourth Ward Regular Democratic Organization and an auditor in the state government. She is on the House Committee on Government Operations and is a member of the Congressional Black Caucus. A widow, one son. See also: CONGRESSIONAL BLACK CAUCUS.

ELLA MAE COLLINS

Chairman of the Organization of Afro-American Unity (OAAU) since death of her brother, Malcolm X. Born in Butler, Georgia, 50 years ago. A former member of the Black Muslims, she left the movement in 1959 because, she says, she believed it was "fishing for suckers." Still considers herself a Muslim, but is not affiliated with any mosque. Has run a nonsectarian school in Boston called the Sarah A. Little School for Preparatory Arts. Says she hopes to bring about brotherhood and understanding between races through the OAAU. In an interview in May 1969, she urged a greater unity among militants and moderates. Also conducted a series of observances of Malcolm X's birthday but in last few years not publicly. See also: ORGANIZATION OF AFRO-AMERICAN UNITY.

CONGRESS OF RACIAL EQUALITY (CORE)

Founded in 1942 by James Farmer and a group of students at the University of Chicago. CORE pioneered such techniques as the sit-in, which it first used in June 1943 at Jact Spratt's restaurant in Chicago's Loop, and the freedom ride, challenging southern bus segregation. Made headlines in May 1961 when freedom-riders tested integration of bus terminal facilities following a 1960 Supreme Court decision. Freedom-riders were attacked by mobs in Birmingham and Montgomery, Alabama, and were arrested in Jackson, Mississippi. In 1965, CORE began an intensive drive for voter registration and desegregation in Bogalusa, Louisiana, which frequently erupted into violence. In March 1966, Farmer resigned from leadership of CORE and was succeeded by Floyd McKissick. Later that year, as McKissick embraced the new slogan of "black power," Farmer denounced it. CORE continued in a black separatist direction under its next leader, Roy Innis, who succeeded McKissick in 1968.

In July 1968, CORE proposed a Community Self-Determination Act, designed to promote black economic development, which was introduced before the Ninetieth Congress. It was not acted upon but was reintroduced to Congress in 1969. In recent years, CORE program has had two principal aims: the Unitary School program—a plan for desegregation by creating two independent and autonomous school systems—as an alternative to "forced" integration, and in 1970 introduced the plan in a brief before the U.S. Supreme Court; the other, a new U.S. Constitution guaranteeing black communities in the country self-determination by a redistribution of political and economic power proportionately to racial percentage of the population.

At one time, CORE was a broad-based organization with a reputed membership of 180,000, including many whites. But in late 1969 the CORE organization was considered by many to be virtually nonexistent as a national civil rights group. In October 1969 *Ebony* magazine reported that CORE was $300,000 in debt and that its ideological switch to black nationalism had been costly in terms of membership, but by 1972 *Ebony* again reported CORE had 200 chapters and over 200,000 members. Innis said in April 1973 the organization was broadening its scope to include the development of links with African nations—starting with Uganda—by encouraging the investment of black American monies in Africa and opening direct trade between the two groups, by offering all black Americans dual citizenship with African nations, by exchanging technical knowledge, and by influencing the U.S. government to increase financial aid to African nations. Its Harlem headquarters reportedly maintains a permanent staff of 40. Office: 200 West 135th Street, New York, N.Y. *See also:* JAMES FARMER, ROY INNIS, FLOYD McKISSICK.

CONGRESSIONAL BLACK CAUCUS
Formed in 1970 by a coalition of the nine black representatives then in Congress for the purpose of shaping a political strategy which would give blacks some bargaining leverage with both the Republican and Democratic parties. Except for a decade during Reconstruction—from 1867 to 1877 when blacks sat in state legislatures and Congress—the Caucus is the first group of black legislators to join in a national effort to promote black causes. Composed of all black members of Congress (except for Senator Edward Brooke who in the last couple of years has begun associating himself more with Caucus business and was guest speaker at its third annual dinner, September 1973). Its current members are Yvonne B. Burke (D-Cal), vice-chairman; Shirley Chisholm (D-NY); Barbara Jordan (D-Tex); Cardiss Collins (D-Ill); William Clay (D-Mo); Ronald

Dellums (D-Cal); Charles Diggs (D-Mich); Walter Fauntroy (D-DC), secretary; Augustus Hawkins (D-Cal); Ralph Metcalfe (D-Ill); Parren Mitchell (D-Md); Robert Nix (D-Pa); Charles Rangel (D-NY), chairman; Louis Stokes (D-Ohio); and Andrew Young (D-Ga), treasurer. The *New York Times* (March 29, 1971) said of the Caucus, "there is a feeling among many blacks that the Caucus now stands as a new kind of black leadership by committee instead of by well-known individuals such as Dr. King, Mr. Young [Whitney], Stokely Carmichael, the former chairman of the Student Non-violent Committee and Roy Wilkins, executive director of NAACP."

Made national headlines in 1970 shortly after its formation when it tried to gain an interview with President Nixon but was put off because of "scheduling difficulties." The requested meeting finally took place nearly a year later only after Caucus members boycotted the president's State of the Union message, January 1971. On the following March 25, the Caucus presented to the president some 60 recommendations which included such items as enforcement of the civil rights laws; replacement of present welfare system with a guaranteed annual income of $6,500 for a family of four; declaration that drug abuse was a national crisis; and withdrawal of troops from Southeast Asia. Nixon then named a committee of five White House staffers to study the recommendations and report back to him. Supported George McGovern in 1972 presidential campaign. The Caucus has its own full-time staff (executive director is Augustus Adair) and meets informally once a week.

JOHN CONYERS, JR.
Democratic representative from the First Congressional District in Detroit, Michigan. Elected first in 1965 and reelected in 1968 and in 1972 with 88 percent of the vote. He serves on the House Judiciary Committee, the first black to do so. In 1971, at the beginning of the Ninety-second Congress, opposed the then Majority Leader Carl Albert for the post of Speaker of the House because Albert refused to take a position on the Mississippi Challenge. This challenge—led by Conyers—was an effort in the House Democratic Caucus to strip the seniority from the five Mississippi Congressmen on the grounds that they were not Democrats but rather members of a racially exclusionary state party which is not recognized by the Democratic National Committee. The challenge failed 111 against 55. The next year again opposed Majority Leader Albert for the post of Speaker because of the failure of the Democratic leadership to assume vigorous and progressive positions on national issues and on congressional reform. House Democrats failed to respond favorably to the challenge. Author of several articles on black politics "Politics and the Black Revolution," (*Ebony*, August 1969) and "A Black Political Strategy for 1972," published in *What Black Politicians Are Saying* in 1972. A native of Detroit, Conyers was born on May 16, 1929. Entered army as a private in 1950 and was honorably discharged 1954 as second lieutenant. Educated at Detroit public schools; B.A. at Wayne State University (1957) and received his LL.D. at Wilberforce University (1969). He worked for three years as legislative assistant to Congressman John Dingell (1958–1961)

before going into politics himself. Always active in union affairs, was a referee for Michigan's Workmen's Compensation Department. In 1963, President Kennedy appointed him to the National Lawyers Committee for Civil Rights under Law. In 1965 had difficulty in winning the primary from his district but did win it by a mere 45 votes. Went on to trounce his opponent in the election, winning by 138,000 votes. He was a cosponsor of the Medicare program under President Johnson and a supporter of 1965 Voting Rights Act. In 1973 sponsored a bill for the Full Opportunity Act which would provide $30 billion yearly for a ten-year period to aid low income Americans in areas of jobs, housing, and education, and of Martin Luther King Holiday Bill which would make January 15—King's birthday—a national holiday. A bachelor. See also: CONGRESSIONAL BLACK CAUCUS.

BILL COSBY
First black actor to star in a network television series ("I Spy"), he won Emmies in 1967 and 1968. Cosby is also one of the most prominent entertainers commited to the black cause and is noted for assistance to young black performers. In 1968, narrated program in CBS series "Of Black America." Created a children's cartoon "Fat Albert" seen on network television in 1973 because he "couldn't stand the junk his kids were watching." Born in 1938 in Philadelphia, Cosby dropped out of high school to become a Navy medic and eventually earned his diploma in the service. Attended Temple University, and started in show business in 1962. Received an M.A. in education from the University of Massachusetts in 1973 and is currently working on his doctorate in education there. In much demand on the night club circuit. In fall of 1969 began a new Sunday night series, the "Bill Cosby Show." He and his family are life members of NAACP and he is active in Operation PUSH (People United to Save Humanity). Married, four children.

GEORGE CROCKETT
Controversial judge of Detroit Recorder's Court, who has frequently clashed with police over the handling of black defendants. A storm of public protest followed his action in freeing suspects following a shoot-out between police and militants at the New Bethel Baptist Church on March 29, 1969, in which a policeman was killed. When the county prosecutor, William L. Cahalan, ordered one of the men held for further questioning, Crockett charged the prosecutor with contempt of court. On March 31, the police commissioner charged that Crockett had hindered police investigation and there were further protests by Detroit Police Officers Association, City Councilman Nicholas Hood, Jr., and Mayor Jerome P. Cavanagh. On April 3, in a public demonstration in sympathy with police, some 2,000 whites marched in the funeral procession for the dead policeman. At the same time, several hundred blacks marched in support of Judge Crockett. At a news conference, Crockett insisted his actions were correct. "Can any of you imagine the Detroit police invading an all-white church and rounding up everyone in sight to be bused to a wholesale lockup in a ga-

rage? Can any of you imagine a (white) church group ... being held incommunicado for seven hours ... without their constitutional rights to counsel? ... Can anyone explain in any other than racial terms the shooting by police inside a closed and surrounded church?" In an earlier case, when suspending sentence of a repeat offender, whom he felt had been mistreated by police, Crockett said: "I think the only thing we can do to bring a stop to that is to prevent the police at least from getting whatever vicarious pleasure there is out of beating up a person and then seeing the person being sentenced. So it's my position that I can take into consideration, in imposing sentence, what the police did to the man after he was arrested." Judge Crockett graduated from the University of Michigan Law School (1934). Was elected judge in 1966 and was reelected in 1972 for another six-year term. Born 1910.

CRUSADE FOR JUSTICE
(LA CRUSADA PARA LA JUSTICIA)
A self-help, human rights organization concerned with the problems of the *chicano* in urban centers. Located in Denver, it claims the distinction of founding the first all-*chicano* free tuition school in the United States called Tlatelolco. Conducts "liberation classes" (to teach leadership, identity, etc.) and publishes a newspaper, *El Gallo* (The Fighting Cock). It also runs a nursery, a gymnasium, and a job-skill "bank." Provides legal aid and a bail-bond service and sponsors a program to develop young artists through its "revolutionary theater" and art gallery. In April 1969, organized Youth Liberation Conference attended by 100 youth and student groups from across the country. Crusade claims about half of Colorado's 185,000 *chicanos* as followers. Headed by Rudolfo Gonzales. Headquarters: 1561 Downing Street, Denver, Co. *See also:* RUDOLFO GONZALES.

HAROLD CRUSE
Author, lecturer, and professor of history. Wrote *The Crisis of the Negro Intellectual* (1967), which was described at the time as "the theoretical base, the intellectual argument for national and ethnic separation of the Negro in America" (*New York Times*, November 21, 1967). An angry tract, it heaped blame for the condition of blacks on white intellectuals, liberals, left-wingers, labor, and heavily on the Jewish community. He was equally scathing of much of the black community. Rejecting integration, he called for black power base—economic, cultural, and political—and, if necessary, an all-black political party. In the early 1960s mainly involved with organizing Freedom Now party and the political, cultural, and economic rehabilitation of Harlem. In 1965–1966 worked to establish Black Arts Theater and school with Imamu Baraka (formerly known as LeRoi Jones). His second book, *Rebellion or Revolution*, was published in 1968. Currently visiting professor of history and Afro-American studies at the University of Michigan. Cruse contributes to the *New Leader, New York Review of Books, Negro Digest, Presence Africaine* (Paris), and other publications. Born in Petersburg, Virginia, his formal education did not go beyond high school. After military service, 1941–1945, he worked in civil service jobs, as a film editor, and in

1960 visited Cuba to study the Castro revolution. Lectures widely, most recently at Princeton, Harvard, Yale, Columbia, and Howard University.

ANGELA DAVIS

Activist and admitted Communist. Born 1944 in Birmingham, Alabama, one of four children. Moved to New York City and graduated from Elizabeth Irwin High School in 1961 and Brandeis University (magna cum laude) in 1965. Did graduate work abroad at Johann Wolfgang von Goethe University in Frankfurt, Germany, but broke off studies suddenly in 1967 to return to the United States because "my commitment to the struggle being waged by my people was something far more important than a doctoral dissertation," she said. Settled in Los Angeles and joined the Student Non-violent Coordinating Committee. When it collapsed, joined the Che Lumumba Club, a black-oriented Marxist collective inside the Communist party, and eventually joined the Party in July 1968. The same year earned her M.A. from the University of California at San Diego where she studied under Marxist professor Herbert Marcuse. Was then hired as an instructor of philosophy at the University of California at Los Angeles but two years later (June 1970), the California Board of Regents notified her that her contract would not be renewed because of her membership in the Communist Party. Shortly afterwards participated in a demonstration for the Soledad Brothers, three black convicts accused of killing a white guard at Soledad State Prison, and there met Jonathan Jackson, the brother of George, one of the three accused men and with whom she had a long correspondence until his death in 1971. On August 7 of that year, Jonathan was involved in a kidnap attempt and shoot-out at the Marin County Civic Center and she was accused of supplying the gun that killed four people, including a judge, as well as plotting the kidnap—an effort designed to free three convicts from San Quentin Prison. Before being arrested, went underground, but was finally apprehended in New York City on October 15, 1970 by the FBI in a midtown motel and extradicted to California to stand trial. After 16 months in jail waiting for trial, was released on $102,500 bail put up by Rodger McAfee, a partner in a farm cooperative and dairy farm in the San Joaquin Valley. On June 4, 1972, was finally acquitted of all charges of murder, kidnapping, and conspiracy by the Santa Clara superior court in San Jose, California.

Currently lectures and is one of the chairpersons of the National Alliance Against Racist and Political Repression (also called the United Defense Committee). Author of *If They Come in the Morning: Voices of Resistance*, published in 1971 by the Third Press.

OSSIE DAVIS AND RUBY DEE

Successful husband-wife acting team for more than 20 years (they have been called "Mr. and Mrs. Broadway"). In recent years they have been closely associated with the civil rights movement and its leaders. Davis delivered an eloquent eulogy at the funeral of Malcolm X, was prominent in raising money for the legal defense of Imamu Baraka, attended the King funeral in Atlanta, and took part in the Martin Luther King memorial march in Memphis in May 1968. Lectures widely on campuses where, he says, "there is a tremendous hunger among blacks and whites for the truth about black experience in this country. This is why I can increasingly be part of the cultural arm of the revolution." Has been involved in the movement for more than 30 years and was one of the first to interpret the black experience through his plays, films, and acting. He is credited with validating the slogan "black is beautiful" when many blacks were unsure of its meaning. Over the years has emerged as a leader of what some call the "black cultural renaissance" in the film industry. Davis wrote screenplay and directed 1969 United Artists production, *Cotton Comes to Harlem*. Film is described as the first major motion picture to be made about black America which is entertaining without either preaching or demeaning the black community, and set the pace for the spate of black films that have followed. Davis was born December 18, 1917, in Cogdell, Georgia, and was a student at Howard University, 1935–1938. After war service, he made his stage debut (1946) in *Jeb*. Another member of the cast was Ruby Dee, and they were married in 1948. In 1959 they were in *Raisin in the Sun*. In 1961–1962, Davis authored and costarred with Ruby Dee in the Broadway hit *Purlie Victorious*, a racial satire which was basis for Broadway smash musical *Purlie* in 1970. They later starred in the film version *Gone Are the Days*. Davis won an Emmy nomination for his role in *Teacher, Teacher*, and has appeared widely in television series and specials. Recipients of the Frederick Douglass Award (May 1970) for "distinguished leadership toward equal opportunity" and the first living black couple ever to receive it. Ruby Dee was born in Cleveland, Ohio, but raised in Harlem. She graduated from Hunter College in 1942. In 1972 recipients of the Dr. Martin Luther King, Jr., award for excellence in family life and the Meritorious Service Award from the Congressional Black Caucus. Active in Operation PUSH (People United to Save Humanity). They have three children and live in Mount Vernon, New York.

SAMMY DAVIS, JR.

One of the most involved of the nation's top entertainers, Sammy Davis has made numerous personal appeals and appearances on behalf of civil rights causes. He took part in the March on Washington in 1963. In 1965 he was named man of the year by B'nai B'rith "for untiring labors on behalf of human rights and the Jewish people." When Martin Luther King was assassinated, Davis called NBC and asked to speak for a few minutes on the "Tonight Show." He announced that he would attend the funeral in Atlanta and called on "black brothers to cool it—white brothers to come forward now, we need each other desperately." In 1968, he campaigned for Robert Kennedy for the presidency and in 1972 supported Richard Nixon for president. Currently active in Operation PUSH (People United to Save Humanity), the National Urban League, and Southern Christian Leadership Conference. Born December 8, 1925, in New York City. Made his stage debut at four as part of the Will Mastin Trio and stayed with them until he joined the army in 1943. Since the war he has been one of the world's top nightclub entertainers, and has starred in numerous Broadway shows and motion pictures. Converted to Judaism in 1956. His autobiography, *Yes, I Can*, appeared in 1965. Married three times, currently to the former Altavise Gore, three children.

SISTER MARTIN DE PORRES (GREY)

The only black nun in the 500-member order of the Sisters of Mercy and founder and former director of the National Black Sisters' Conference. The first conference, held at Mount Mercy College, was attended by 150 black nuns. They met to discuss how they could make themselves more relevant to the needs of the black community by trying to determine their responsibility to their people, their church, and religious community. Sister Martin said the reason for the conference was that "the Church is predominantly a white institution and it caters to white communities. Since white racism is behind the race problem, then we, as black religious women, have to help white clergy and our white sisters teach their people the truth." Currently director of Design Programs, Inc., an educational consultant agency concerned with urban nonpublic schools. Its purpose is to bring about changes in areas of staff training, curriculum designs, administrative development, and parent-community involvement. Sister Martin is from Sewickley, Pennsylvania, and has been a nun since 1960. Born in 1943, she is the daughter of Edgar W. Grey, a steelworker.

RONALD V. DELLUMS

Democratic representative from Oakland, California's Seventh Congressional District—an ethnic potpourri numbering some 450,000 residents. First elected in 1970 and serves on the District of Columbia and Armed Services committees. Also a member of the Congressional Black Caucus. Before his election to Congress, served as a member of the Berkeley City Council from 1967–1970 and came to national attention when former vice-president Spiro Agnew called him an "out-and-out radical" in a speech in Fort Smith, Arkansas, while Dellums was campaigning for his congressional seat in 1970. This was no surprise to Dellums for he has been called many things in his political career and says that he is quite comfortable with the "radical" label but is careful to point out what his brand of militancy means. "Yes, I'm a militant because I'm a member of a race of people who live in a racist society. I'm black, I'm an ethnic minority, I'm a human being. In all three of these categories, I have been oppressed. And I live with millions of people who are also oppressed. I feel anger about what's happening in this country to people. But I don't let that anger hang up my ability to see what has to be done in order to overcome these problems" (*America*, December 5, 1970). Was endorsed for his House seat by Mrs. Coretta King and Cesar Chavez and counts pro-basketball star Bill Russell and Black Panther leader Huey Newton among his friends. Born November 14, 1935, in Oakland, California. Educated at St. Patricks's elementary school, Westlake Junior High, and McClymonds high school. Graduated from University of California in 1953 and received his masters in psychiatric social work there in 1962. Spent two years in the Marines and was honorably discharged in 1956. Did social work and was a manpower development consultant before being elected Berkeley councilman. Married (1962), three children. See also: CONGRESSIONAL BLACK CAUCUS.

VINE DELORIA, JR.

Author of *Custer Died For Your Sins: An Indian Manifesto*, published in September 1969, and *God Is Red* published in 1973. Currently chairman of the Institute for the Development of Indian Law formed in 1971 by Deloria to research and document historically all crucial issues, treaties, and agreements Indians have with the U.S. government and to determine what is the legal status of these agreements and treaties. Financed by Deloria's book royalties and some foundation money. Has a full-time staff of five. Executive director of the National Congress of American Indians, 1946–1967. A Standing Rock Sioux from a distinguished family of American Indians with scholar, churchman, and warrior-chief ancestors, he has served on the executive council of the Episcopal Church and the Board of Inquiry into Hunger and Malnutrition. Received degrees from Iowa State University and Lutheran School of Theology (M.Th.) and School of Law at the University of Colorado. Is a member of Colorado bar and the American Bar Association. Served in the Marines in the 1950s. Born on the Pine Ridge Indian Reservation in South Dakota, 1933. Married, three children. Office: Institute for the Development of Indian Law, 927 Fifteenth Street, N.E., Washington, D.C.

ADOLPHUS SUMNER DICKERSON

Has been active in civil rights movement for over 20 years and is chairman of a grievance committee on civil rights in Atlanta. Is considered a pivotal person on civil rights issues in Georgia because of his ability to communicate with both sides. Currently pastor of United Methodist Church in Atlanta and involved in voter registration activities. He was born in 1914 in western Georgia and educated at the University of Atlanta and Boston University. Was ordained in 1937.

CHARLES C. DIGGS, JR.

Democratic representative from Michigan's Thirteenth Congressional District and senior black representative from Michigan, was first elected in 1954. Currently member of the House Foreign Affairs Committee and chairman of its subcommittee on Africa. Was appointed by President Nixon U.S. delegate to the United Nations in December 1971 but resigned to protest administration's African policy. Member of the Congressional Black Caucus formed in 1970 and served as its chairman in 1971–1972. Before being elected to Congress served in Michigan Senate from 1951–1954. Born December 2, 1922 in Detroit. He was educated there and enrolled first at the University of Michigan in 1940, then transferred to Fisk University in 1942. Drafted into the air force, he spent two years in service, 1943–1945. After the war, graduated from Wayne State University in mortuary science. Married three times, currently to the former Janet Elaine Hall in 1971, five children. See also: CONGRESSIONAL BLACK CAUCUS.

IVAN DIXON
Organized the Negro Actors for Action, which is now disbanded. Has said, "There should be an integrated curriculum that teaches about Frederick Douglass as well as George Washington . . . To identify only with whites makes Negro kids negate themselves. The time has come when my kids won't have to even think of their heritage." Born April 6, 1931 in Harlem. Attended Lincoln Academy in King's Mountain, North Carolina, and graduated from North Carolina College with degree in political science and history. Returned to New York and joined Department of Welfare as a social case investigator. Studied with American Theater Wing in New York and at Western Reserve University as a graduate student in drama. Broadway debut was *Raisin in the Sun*. In 1966 won best actor award given by the first World Festival of Negro Arts, in Dakar, Africa. In 1967, starred in CBS's "The Final War of Olly Winter." Movie parts include the much acclaimed *Nothing But a Man*. Featured in the CBS series, "Hogan's Heroes." In 1970 directed three episodes for the Bill Cosby TV show and the film *Trouble Man* in 1972. Married, four children.

JOHN DOAR
Assistant attorney general in charge of Department of Justice Civil Rights Division, 1964–1967. President of New York City Board of Education, 1968–1969. Head of the Bedford-Stuyvesant Development and Service Corporation from 1968 until his resignation on December 14, 1973. "I just concluded it was time to leave," he said. Is currently Special Counsel to the House of Representative Judiciary Committee concerned with impeachment investigation. A white man, Doar was born December 3, 1921, in Minneapolis. Received a B.A. from Princeton in 1944 and law degree from University of California at Berkeley in 1949. After practicing law in Wisconsin (1950–1960), he joined the Civil Rights Division of the justice department in July 1960 as deputy to Harold Tyler, who was assistant attorney general in charge of the division under Robert Kennedy. Rode with the Freedom Riders in 1960s, shepherded James Meredith through the first weeks at the University of Mississippi, prosecuted more than 30 Southern voting-rights cases in federal courts, the cases involving the murder of three young civil rights workers Michael Schwerner, Andrew Goodman, and James Chaney in June 1964 in Mississippi, and Mrs. Viola Liuzzo, white civil rights worker from Detroit killed March 1965. In 1965 was the government's chief representative during civil rights march from Selma to Montgomery. Divorced.

RICHARD L. DOCKERY
Southwest regional director of the NAACP (area includes Arkansas, Louisiana, Oklahoma, New Mexico, and Texas). Prior to his appointment in 1966 was president of the San Antonio branch of the NAACP and also employed as a procurement data specialist at Kelly Air Force Base. A native of Camden, Alabama, served in U.S. Navy from 1941–1945 and graduated from Dillard University in 1950. In 1951 he was appointed director of the city recreation department in

Pensacola, Florida, the first black to become a city director in the South. The same year lead a protest delegation which confronted the Mobile, Alabama, school board to protest for adequate schooling for blacks. In 1970 appointed member of the Texas Advisory Commission to the U.S. Civil Rights Commission. Married, three children. Office: 2600 Flora Street, Dallas, Texas.

HARRY EDWARDS

Tried to organize a boycott by black field and track athletes on the U.S. Olympic team at 1968 games in Mexico because of an International Olympics Committee decision to admit South Africa to the games. (The committee later reversed its decision and barred South Africa from the competition after U.S.S.R. and 40 other countries threatened to withdraw.) Edwards called off his boycott when he failed to get support of all 26 black athletes on the team. However, Tommie Smith, a gold medal winner, and John Carlos, a bronze medal winner, used the victory ceremony for a black power demonstration. Both men appeared without shoes and in black socks and raised their black-gloved fists in a "black power" salute during the U.S. national anthem. "The revolt of the black athlete is the newest phase of the black liberation movement in America," Edwards has said. In commenting on the boycott he remarked, "It seems as though the only way we can reach a lot of people is by showing them all is not well in the locker room." Received a B.A. from San Jose State College and an M.A. from Cornell University. Taught at San Jose State (1967), and since 1971 is assistant professor of sociology at the University of California at Berkeley. Author of *The Revolt of the Black Athlete*, published by Free Press in September 1969, *Black Students* (1970), and *Sociology of Sport*, published by Dorsey in 1972. Born November 22, 1942, in St. Louis, Missouri. Married, one child.

RALPH W. ELLISON

Best known for his novel *Invisible Man* published in 1952, which won for him the National Book Award the following year. Attended Tuskegee Institute (1935–1936) and served as cook and baker in the Merchant Marine in World War II. In 1955, American Academy of Arts and Letters awarded Ellison the Prix de Rome which enabled him to write in Italy for the next two years. Has lectured on writing at New York University, Columbia, Rutgers, Princeton, and Bennington College. Has published short stories and essays for various journals and magazines since 1939. Last published work was *Shadow and Act*, a collection of essays, in 1964. Albert Schweitzer professor in the Humanities at New York University since 1970. Born March 1, 1914, in Oklahoma City, Oklahoma. Married to the former Fanny McConnell.

FRED (AHMED) EVANS

Cleveland militant sentenced to death by all-white jury May 12, 1969, for first degree murder of three policemen and a civilian in what was described as nation's first armed attack by group of black nationalists. Was scheduled to die in electric chair, September 22, 1969, but won stay of execution and has been wait-

ing on death row in Ohio State Penitentiary in Columbus ever since. Evans allegedly instigated attack by group of his supporters (the Black Nationalists of
New Libya) on a squad car in Glenville ghetto area of Cleveland on July 23, 1968.
Attack led to gunfights and rioting in which 11 persons died, and an estimated
$1.5 million worth of property was damaged. Violence commission report re-
leased after Evans' trial stated Evans had been unaware of the attack on police
until after it started. Before arrest, Evans directed a summer program to train
black youngsters in African crafts and operated store for African products. An
attempt to free Evans by fellow black nationalist prisoners at Cuyahoga County
jail was reported by UPI, May 9, 1969. Born April 23, 1928 in Greenville, North
Carolina, Evans served two enlistments in the regular army. According to an article in Black Scholar (April/May issue 1971) served with distinction in Korean
War, was critically wounded and honorably discharged in 1952 "with half a
dozen medals for meritorious service."

(JAMES) CHARLES EVERS
Mayor of Fayette, Mississippi—a town of 2,000, 70 percent of whom are black.
Elected first on May 14, 1969. Ran on an all-black slate opposing five white men
in a bid for Fayette's five alderman seats. Defeated 77-year-old incumbent, who
had held the office for the last 20 years, by 131 votes, thus becoming first black
mayor in a southern town with white residents since Reconstruction. Reelected
in 1973 for a second four-year term. Ran for governor in 1972 as an independent
candidate but lost receiving only 22 percent of the vote. Said of the defeat "for
me to be running for governor in the state where my brother was killed and for
none of us to get our heads bashed in—its a helluva lot. We changed the whole
political system in this state. It won't ever be the same again." In 1971 published
his autobiography called Evers in which he revealed that he had once earned
his living as a pimp, bootlegger, and numbers racketeer and disclosed these
facts about his past at a press conference just before announcing his candidacy
for governor. Was Mississippi field director of the NAACP. Joined the national
staff in June 1963 following the rifle slaying of his brother, Medgar W. Evers.
Born September 11, 1921 in Decatur, Mississippi, had been a businessman and
disk jockey in Chicago before joining NAACP staff. In 1964 helped avert a riot
by Jackson State College students after police had ringed the college campus
with shotgun-carrying patrolmen, armored tanks, and dogs. The incident occurred after an automobile struck a coed on a campus street. The subsequent
shotgun wounding of three demonstrators resulted in student anger. Made unsuccessful bid for Congress in March 1968, when he led the field against six
white candidates in preliminary election for Mississippi's Third Congressional
District, but lost the run-off. At the 1968 Democratic convention, along with Dr.
Aaron E. Henry, state chairman of the NAACP, and Hodding Carter III, white
publisher of the Delta Democrat-Times in Greenville, Mississippi, Evers led the
biracial coalition known as the Loyal Democrats in their successful challenge
which barred the seating of the all-white regular Mississippi delegation. Graduated from high school in Newton, Mississippi, in 1947 and Alcorn A&M College.

Served in the army in the Korean War and was discharged as a battalion sergeant major. With his brother's widow, Mrs. Myrlie Evers, established the Medgar Evers Fund, in 1970, to provide community facilities for Fayette. See also: MISSISSIPPI FREEDOM DEMOCRATIC PARTY.

JAMES FARMER

One of the nation's leading civil rights activists for more than two decades, he was born in Marshall, Texas, in 1920, the son of a college professor (who was the nation's first black Ph.D.). Received a B.S. in chemistry from Wiley College at 18, and a divinity degree from Howard University, but was not ordained. In 1942, he founded the Congress of Racial Equality (CORE) in Chicago, pioneered the sit-in to desegregate public facilities and later was one of the original Freedom Riders, for which he was jailed in 1961. Led 2,000-strong Pilgrimage of Prayer, 1959, to protest closing of Virginia's public schools. Also led major civil rights actions in Louisiana. After leading CORE to some of its greatest successes in the 1960s, Farmer left the organization in 1966 in disagreement with increasing emphasis on separatism. Ran as Liberal party candidate for Congress in November 1968, losing to Shirley Chisholm.

Appointed assistant secretary of health, education and welfare in 1969 by President Nixon and came under a lot of criticism from former civil rights colleagues for not being more outspoken about Nixon administration policies. Resigned (December 21, 1970) and waited two years more before criticizing his former boss, the president. In a television interview, of January 21, 1973, revealed he had had serious disagreements with the administration and had had difficulty in remaining as long as he did. Said that Nixon had no direct contact with black community and never consulted with black leaders but relied on a white aide, Leonard Garment, as the expert on black affairs. Also disagreed with some of the president's appointments to the Supreme Court. Says of the movement that "full integration is no longer the goal of most blacks. The operative word today is 'liberation,' that's a push for an open pluralistic society in which blacks have a right place alongside other ethnic groups." Married to the former Lula Peterson, two daughters. See also: CONGRESS OF RACIAL EQUALITY (CORE).

WALTER FAUNTROY

Congressional delegate to the House of Representatives from the District of Columbia—the district's first black representative to the House in almost 100 years—elected April 1971. After winning the Democratic primary over six candidates (including Joseph Yeldell and Rev. Channing Phillips who were considered more prominent and influential in Washington politics), went on to win the general election over eight contenders. As a nonvoting member of the House of Representatives, is able to vote in committee and to introduce legislation and participate in debate.

His major efforts in Congress have been to try to win home rule for the District. Has a seat on the House District of Columbia and Banking and Currency committees. Also a member of the Congressional Black Caucus. Has the largest constituency (over 700,000) of any congressman and is only black elected official—aside from school board members—in the district.

Was active in the civil rights movement in the 1960s. Helped coordinate the 1963 March on Washington and was Washington director of Southern Christian Leadership Conference as well as a friend and aide to the late Martin Luther King, Jr. Also helped coordinate the Selma-to-Montgomery march in 1965 and the Poor People's Campaign in Washington in 1969. In 1972 ran in Democratic presidential primary for the district as a favorite son candidate. Born February 6, 1933, in Washington, D.C. Graduated (cum laude) from Virginia Union University (Richmond, Virginia) in 1955 and the Yale Divinity School in 1958. Has been pastor of the New Bethel Baptist Church in Washington since 1959. Married to the former Dorothy Simms, one son. *See also:* CONGRESSIONAL BLACK CAUCUS.

C. CLYDE FERGUSON, JR.

United States representative to the United Nations—on the Economic and Social Council since October 1973. Deputy assistant secretary of state for African affairs from 1972–1973 and before that U.S. ambassador to Uganda (1970–1972). During Nigerian civil war, he served as State Department's special coordinator for relief to civilian victims. He was Dean of Howard University Law School, 1963–1969. During Kennedy administration, he was general counsel to the U.S. Commission on Civil Rights. He also served as an alternate delegate and expert to the United Nations subcommission on prevention of discrimination against minorities, 1963–1965. Represented the United States at UNESCO conference on human rights, 1965, and helped draft UNESCO statement on race, 1966. Born November 4, 1924, in Wilmington, North Carolina. Graduated from Ohio State University and Harvard Law School. Served with United States Army in Europe and Asia, 1942–1946. Widower, three daughters.

FIGHT BACK

Formerly the Harlem Unemployment Center. A privately funded organization founded in 1964 to bring together black and white workers by supporting them in their struggle for employment, training, and democratic trade unionism. Began to broaden its activities in 1968 into areas of antiwar activities, lobbying for housing and jobs, and drug abuse. The main concern, however, and major accomplishment, is in integration of the building trades through the cooperation of both black and white workers. Has also been successful in job placement in construction work. Organization gives counsel to individual workers with specific union and work-related grievances and represents them before federal, state, and city agencies. In 1972, opened chapters in Springfield (Massachusetts), Norfolk (Virginia), and San Francisco. Currently a joint plaintiff with NAACP against the U.S. Department of Labor for what they claim is job discrimination in the building trades. Active membership is 450. Supported by membership dues ($10.00 per month) plus fund raising activities. Director and founder is James Haughton. Office: 1 East 125th Street, New York, N.Y.

ARTHUR S. FLEMING
Chairman of the Civil Rights Commission, appointed by President Nixon December 1973. Succeeds Rev. Theodore M. Hesburgh who was dismissed the year before (November 1972) from the Commission, after serving for 15 years, to resume his duties as president of Notre Dame University. Formerly president of Ohio Wesleyan University and served in the Eisenhower administration as secretary of health, education and welfare from 1958 to 1961. Born 1905, grew up in Kingston, New York, and presently lives in Alexandria, Virginia. Served in the Nixon administration as chairman of the White House Conference on Aging.

ARTHUR A. FLETCHER
Assistant secretary of labor in Nixon administration until September of 1971. According to the New York Times of February 25, 1973, reportedly was eased out of his post because of disagreements with the then secretary of labor, James D. Hodgson. Recognized as originator of the controversial "Philadelphia Plan" to integrate construction unions. After leaving the administration was named alternate delegate to the United Nations and in 1972 took over directorship of the United Negro College Fund until 1973. Currently runs his own consulting firm, Arthur A. Fletcher Associates, in Washington, D.C., and also acts as a consultant to chairman of the Republican National Committee for minority affairs. Previously ran for lieutenant governor of the state of Washington in 1968 but lost even though he received 49 percent of the vote. Also was special assistant to Governor Daniel Evans of Washington, coordinating relations between local communities and state government. Born December 22, 1924, in Phoenix, Arizona. Married twice, currently to the former Bernyce Ayesha Hassan, a former government statistician (1964), five children from his first marriage.

JAMES FORMAN
Field director for the Black Economic Development Conference until it went out of business in the early 1970s. Had been acting chairman of organization, April through August 1969, when he wrote and presented the "Black Manifesto" calling for reparations from white churches. Made headlines (May 4, 1969) when he disrupted communion services to read manifesto at New York's Riverside Church. In 1972 wrote The Making of Black Revolutionaries: A Personal Account, an informal history of the civil rights movement of the 1960s published by Macmillan. New York Times reviewer Thomas Lask said it was an important book because it told what it was like to be black in America. "This idea is so hard for whites to grasp," he says, "for the problem of a black living in a white society is . . . never absent from the consciousness of the black man and to a degree that the most sympathetic white man can simply not imagine." Cur-

rently lives in Detroit. A former Chicago schoolteacher and veteran civil rights activist, he was one of the early leaders of Student National Coordinating Committee (SNCC) and its executive secretary from 1964–1966. During that period he took a prominent role in voter registration drives and demonstrations in Mississippi and Alabama. In 1966, he lost his SNCC leadership position in the shake-up which saw Stokely Carmichael replace John Lewis as chairman, but he remained a member. At the July 1969 meeting of SNCC he was named director of international affairs. Born in Chicago on October 5, 1929. Graduated Roosevelt University, 1951. After serving in the army, joined Juvenile Research Center in Chicago. Separated, one child.

ARETHA FRANKLIN
Top pop singer of soul music, described in a *Time* magazine cover story, June 1968 as "Lady Soul: Singing it like it is." Born March 25, 1942, in Memphis, Tennessee, one of five children of nationally known revivalist minister Rev. Clarance L. Franklin, pastor of Detroit's New Bethel Baptist Church. (Scene of a shoot-out between police and militants in March 1969, *see* George Crockett entry.) Brought up on gospel music at home, at 14 she was a featured performer in her father's evangelist show that traveled across the country. In 1967, her first recording hit "I Never Loved A Man," sold a million copies. This was quickly followed by four other gold single records. Today, she reportedly commands $25,000 a performance. As a star, she has helped define the new black man's sense of identity, and in 1968 was invited to give a "soul" rendition of the national anthem at the Republican National Convention in Miami Beach. Her Grammy and Golden Mike award winning record "Respect" (a song written by the late Otis Redding) has been called "the new Negro national anthem." Has over 100 single gold records and seven gold albums. In 1967, Southern Christian Leadership Conference awarded her a special citation. Does many benefits to help the movement such as the Angela Davis Defense Fund and to raise money for families of prisoners after Attica. Divorced, four children.

ERNEST J. GAINES
Author, has written *Of Love and Dust* (1967), *Bloodline*, a collection of short stories (1968) and *Long Day in November* (1971), all published by Dial Press. Born on a Louisiana plantation in 1933, he worked as a field hand at the age of nine. Served in the army from 1953–1955 and graduated from San Francisco State College in 1957. In 1958 won the Wallace Stegner Creative Writing Fellowship at Stanford University and the Joseph Henry Jackson Literary prize in 1959. Author of the acclaimed 1974 TV production, The Autobiography of Miss Jane Pittman.

MILTON GALAMISON
Militant civil rights activist, and vocal critic of New York City school policies for the last decade. Has been arrested nine times in an effort to end segregation in

that city's school system. First became involved in the school integration issue in 1956 when he made an unsuccessful attempt to integrate an all-black high school in Brooklyn. In 1964, organized the first city-wide school protest to demand integration. In 1965, organized another boycott to support demands for community control of schools. In May 1968, organized still another boycott during the Ocean Hill-Brownsville school decentralization controversy. Appointed a member of the Board of Education by Mayor Lindsay on July 14, 1968, was elected vice-president of the board, October 16, 1968. His term was to expire July 30, 1971 but on May 1, 1969, the New York state legislature in Albany voted to replace the board with an interim one of five members, one from each borough, to deal with the decentralization issue. Galamison has said of decentralization: "The forces that oppose decentralization are concerned about keeping power away from the black community, not obtaining integration. I for one have not abandoned the long-range goal of integration." Is pastor of the Siloam Presbyterian Church in Brooklyn (since 1949) and holds divinity degrees from Lincoln and Princeton Universities. Currently New York chairman of Opportunities Industrialization Center (OIC), a job-training and placement organization, which is affiliated with Leon Sullivan's OIC in Philadelphia. New York chapter was started in 1967 and has five branches in each of the city's boroughs except Staten Island. Has placed over 5,000 people in jobs since it started and is funded by federal government, the city, and private sources. Taught a course on education and urban studies at Harvard University in 1969 for one year. Born 1923. Married, one son.

CARLOS "CHINO" GARCIA

One of the founders of the Real Great Society (RGS) in 1964—a predominately Puerto-Rican self-help organization for youths in New York's Lower East Side and Spanish Harlem. In the early 1970s, RGS became CHARAS (meaning the group) which concentrates on finding better ways to live through communal living. Inspired by R. Buckminister Fuller, who spoke to the group in 1969, they began studying Fuller's theories and to experiment with building geodesic domes. The story of CHARAS was published in a book by Drake Publishers in 1973 called *CHARAS: The Improbable Dome Builders*. Born on the Lower East Side of Manhattan, in 1942. At 12 joined his first gang and at 17 became the leader of the Assassin Lords, a gang whose membership numbered some 500. In 1967, New York police gave him the option of exile in Puerto Rico, or staying in New York to face charges. He chose Puerto Rico and spent a year there. Returned to New York in 1968 to take his present position. He has no formal education and taught himself to read and write. Organization has 50 members. Address: 303 Cherry Street, New York, N.Y. 10003.

JOHN W. GARDNER

Distinguished white educator and social critic who, as President Johnson's secretary of health, education, and welfare, 1965–1968, substantially reorganized and strengthened that department. Resigned March 1, 1968, to head the newly formed National Urban Coalition. A Republican, he was known as one of the most energetic backers of Johnson's "Great Society," and urged the nation to tackle the problems of the cities with "barn-raising enthusiasm." A president of the Carnegie Corporation in New York (1955–1965), sponsored study that led to the new math, and the famous Conant study of education in the United States. Known as a perfectionist, he coined the phrase "pursuit of excellence." In December 1967 warned: "We are in deep trouble as a people. And history is not going to deal kindly with a rich nation that will not tax itself to cure its miseries." In February 1969, presented follow-up to Kerner report entitled *One Year Later*, which declared that the nation was "a year closer to two societies . . . increasingly separate and scarcely less unequal." In July 1970, announced plans to form a national lobby of citizens to exert pressure for governmental reforms and action on domestic issues. By 1973 his "citizens movement," known as Common Cause, had over a quarter million members and had won many nonpartisan political battles. Serves as chairman. In 1972 and 1973 Common Cause citizen lobby concentrated its efforts on ending the pervasive and corrupting influence of money on the political system especially in the financing of political campaigns and to end the policy of secrecy in Congress and in state legislatures. Born in Los Angeles, October 8, 1912, he graduated from Stanford University and University of California at Berkeley and became a professor of psychology. In World War II he served with the Marines in Italy and Austria. He joined the Carnegie staff in 1946. Author of *Excellence, Self-Renewal, No Easy Victories,* and *Recovery of Confidence.* Married, two daughters. Office: 2030 M Street, N.W. Washington, D.C. 20036.

CHARLES R. GARRY

California lawyer who has defended Black Panther leaders since 1967 and whose absence through illness from the trial of the Chicago Eight was nominally the cause of defendant Bobby Seale's numerous outbursts. Seale claimed that he would accept only Garry as his counsel, but Judge Hoffman refused to postpone the trial until Garry was well enough to take part. In addition to Seale, Garry had defended Huey Newton, and won a dismissal for him on December 15, 1971, as well as Eldridge Cleaver, David Hilliard, and others. Born March 17, 1909, in Bridgewater, Massachusetts, to Armenian immigrant parents named Garabedian. Garry's family later moved to Selma, California, where he grew up on a farm. He has said: "I guess one of the things that makes me so incensed about what's happening to black people is I relate it to my early life and the discrimination I received by just being an ethnic Armenian. I was called a Goddamned Armenian and up until the time I finished grammar school I think I had a fight every single night." Worked his way through school and went to law school at night. Admitted to the bar in 1939. Married to the former Louise Evelyn Edgar, no children.

GILBERTO GERENA-VALENTIN

Militant who has been described as the most influential Puerto Rican in New York City. In July 1969, was dismissed from his $19,000 a year job as an official on the city's Commission on Human Rights because he adopted a "destructive role, inflaming and dividing the community" according to the commission's chief, Simeon Golar. Jailed twice, July 12 and 15, 1969, for refusing to vacate his office after his dismissal. Released July 18 when his case was postponed. Finally won the case in arbitration and the city was forced to reinstate him with back pay for two years. In 1963 founded the National Association of Puerto Rican Civil Rights and is currently president of the Congress of Puerto Rican Hometown Inc., which he also founded in 1958. Born January 25, 1919, in Puerto Rico. Separated from his second wife, two children.

KENNETH ALLEN GIBSON

Mayor of Newark, New Jersey, since July 1, 1970—the first black mayor of a major northeastern city and only the third black man in recent times to be elected mayor of any large American city (after Carl Stokes in Cleveland, Ohio, and Andrew Hatcher in Gary, Indiana). Gibson defeated Hugh J. Addonizio, the white two-term incumbent, in a mayoral runoff June 16, 1970 by an unexpectedly large margin of more than 11,000 votes (54,892 to 43,339) in a record 73 percent voter turnout.

Gibson describes himself as only a nominal Democrat, a moderate, and a liberal. However, he was criticized by opponents in the campaign for accepting support of the city's militant black and Puerto Rican factions, particularly the New Ark (sic) Fund headed by Imanu Amiri Baraka (formerly known as LeRoi Jones). However, since his election has lost ground with Baraka and other Newark blacks who say he has not done enough for the black community, especially the central and northern wards of Newark. In 1973 Baraka accused Gibson of being a "puppet" of the city's business community. "I will work with these men," the mayor said, "or any other citizens for the purpose of positive change but this administration will not be intimidated by those who have a flair for the dramatic." (New York Times, August 19, 1973.) Some local political observers feel the confrontation between Baraka forces and the mayor will have a big influence on his upcoming election in 1974.

In his term of office, has been beset by problems—many left over from the previous administration—and was accused by the State Task Force on Urban Problems of having failed to change anything. However, he won a major victory with his compromise plan that ended an 11-week teacher's strike in 1971.

Born in Enterprise, Alabama, May 15, 1932, Gibson is the son of a seamstress and a butcher who moved to Newark when he was eight. He worked his way through Newark College of Engineering after United States Army service, receiving a civil engineering degree in 1963. He was active in community work, the YMCA and NAACP. By 1966, when he first ran unsuccessfully for mayor, he was chief engineer of the Newark Housing Authority, where he had specialized in urban renewal projects. Married, two daughters.

PAUL PEYTON GIBSON, JR.

Deputy mayor of New York City appointed by the newly-elected Mayor Abraham Beame January 17, 1974—the first black ever to hold the office in that city.

Was the mayor's third choice for the $43,255-a-year job, after the first two choices failed to clear the screening process. Gibson is also a lawyer. Previously a vice-president for American Airlines—joining the organization in 1969 as urban affairs director and becoming a full vice-president in 1971. Gibson has long been a worker for equal rights but prefers to work behind the scenes rather than in the limelight. Although he marched on Washington with other black leaders, he has been characterized as a "moderate—in favor of integration and against confrontation." (*New York Times*, January 17, 1974.) Only other time he was interested in public office was in 1965 when he ran for the city council as an independent and lost. Received a bachelor of social science degree from City College in 1950, and a law degree from New York University Law School in 1952. He was admitted to the New York State bar in 1954. Born August 5, 1927 in New York City. Married to the former Marcia Johnson, an assistant school principal, two sons.

NIKKI GIOVANNI

Has been called the high priestess of black poetry. Born Yolanda Cornelila Giovanni in Knoxville, Tennessee, on June 7, 1943. Her parents were both college graduates—her father a probation officer; her mother a social worker. Graduated from Fisk University in 1967 and took part in John O. Killens writing workshop there; attended Columbia University's Graduate School of Social Work and taught creative writing at Rutgers University. While at Fisk joined the Fisk chapter of the Student National Coordinating Committee (SNCC) forbidden on campus but later reinstated in 1964 when she led group of 200 students to demand that SNCC be given the right to exist on campus along with sororities and fraternities.

A Ford Foundation grant enabled her to produce her first published poetry *Black Feeling, Black Talk* (1968). This was followed by *Black Judgement* (which sold over 10,000 copies), *Gemini* (an autobiographical book of essays published in 1971), and *My House* (1972).

Considers herself a "new woman" whose main interest is ending racism. Says black poets are "revolutionaries or try to be. Sometimes they mouth propaganda, but they are creating a powerful record of their people's anguish and accomplishments." (*Time*, April 6, 1970.) Has a large following on college campuses and in 1971 put out her first record album *Truth Is On It's Way* (Right On Records) which sold over 100,000 copies. In 1972, filled Alice Tully Hall in New York for an evening of poetry and music called "Like a Ripple On a Pond." Is an editorial consultant for *Encore* magazine and founded her own publishing cooperative, TomNik Ltd., in 1970. Unmarried, one son.

SIMEON GOLAR

A lawyer. Ran for City Council president in New York City as the Liberal party candidate—only black running for city-wide office on a major party ticket—in 1973 but lost. Formerly chairman of the New York City Housing Authority, appointed by Mayor Lindsay in January 1970. Resigned May 31, 1973. Had previously served as vice-chairman of the agency 1967–1969. In May 1970, he charged that the federal housing program was being "dismantled" and "destroyed" because of administration policies which were beginning "to spell out a pattern that threatens to reverse the historic, social, and humanitarian goals. . ." Had been a strong advocate of the controversial Forest Hills housing project in Queens, New York, sponsored by the city, which embodied a new housing policy to be a used as a model in other parts of the country. Part of a scatter-site housing program, it was to provide low-income housing for blacks, Puerto Ricans, and the elderly, but was bitterly contested by the white middle-class community, and to date the dispute has not been resolved. Has also been chairman of the New York City Human Rights Commission. A member of the Liberal party, he ran as candidate for attorney general of New York state in 1966. Graduated from the Bernard M. Baruch School of Business and Public Administration of City College in New York (cum laude) by going to night school (1953) and received an LL.B. from New York University Law School (1957). Born October 12, 1928 in Chester, South Carolina. Voted "Man of the Year" in 1972 by the National Association of Negro Business and Professional Women. Divorced, two daughters.

RODOLFO "CORKY" GONZALES
Leader of the *chicano* movement in Denver. In 1965, founded the Crusade for Justice (*La Crusada para la Justicia*), a self-help human rights organization for Mexican-Americans. Born in 1928 in a Denver *barrio*. The son of a Mexican emigrant laborer, at ten he was working in the sugar beet fields beside his father. After graduating from high school at 16, became a boxer. He retired in the mid-1950s as the third-ranking contender for the world's featherweight title in the National Boxing Association. For the last 15 years has been working in the civil rights movement and in 1968 led the Southwest *chicano* delegation with Reies Tijerina in the Poor People's March on Washington. A published poet and playwright, best known works: *A Cross for Maclovic* (a play), and *I Am Joaquin* (an epic poem which has sold more than 50,000 copies and subsequently was made into a film which the Crusade sells to universities and libraries throughout the country; proceeds are used to help finance Tlatelolco, his organization's all-*chicano*, free tuition school). Married, eight children. Office: 1561 Downing Street, Denver, Co. *See also:* CRUSADE FOR JUSTICE.

CHARLES GORDONE
He has been called "the most astonishing new American playwright to come along since Edward Albee." First black playwright to win the Pulitzer Prize, Gordone received the award in 1970 for his play *No Place To Be Somebody*, described by one reviewer as a "searing look into racial hangups, black and white, in terms of misfits who frequent a Greenwich Village bar." A former actor, Gordone entered the theater in New York after graduating from California State College at Los Angeles in 1952. The same year was cast in Moss Hart's *The Climate of Eden* followed by *Mrs. Patterson*. In 1961, he joined the off-Broadway

company producing Jean Genet's *The Blacks*. After a long absence, returned to acting to star in the film *Coon Skin*. Gordone describes himself as "part Indian, part French, part Irish, and part nigger." On black militants he says, "I have respect for their politics. I think it's viable. I mean it's happening ain't it and we have to look at what's happening. But these cats (the black militants) today are discovering they need to join with other elements." Born 1925 in Cleveland, he grew up in Elkhart, Indiana. Enlisted in the Air Corps in 1944. Married several times but currently divorced, nine children.

JESSE GRAY

Assemblyman from New York (elected November 1972) and controversial Harlem leader who organized hundreds of Harlem tenants in a 1963 rent strike. Founder of the Harlem Tenants Council and ACT Associates (1964). Currently working with different groups on improving housing conditions in New York City. In June 1969 won the Democratic nomination for New York City councilman from Harlem's Fifth District, to succeed retiring J. Raymond Jones, but was defeated in the November 4 election by Liberal party candidate Charles Taylor (18,059 to 11,604). In January 1970, announced he would run against Adam Clayton Powell. In 1972 challenged Hulan E. Jack in Democratic primary in the Seventh Assembly District in New York and lost again but later that year became an assemblyman. On March 1, 1973, announced his candidacy for the Democratic mayoral nomination but was finally eliminated from the race. Has been called everything from a "grass-roots kind of guy with a finger in every pie in Harlem" by a Harlem welfare worker, to a "venomous little demagogue with a long record of Communist associations, who made a name of sorts for himself (in 1963) when he instigated a rent strike in Harlem" by *Time* magazine (July 31, 1964). In an interview with *New York Post* June 27, 1969, declared "I'm pro-black, not anti-white." Born May 14, 1923, in Tunica, Louisiana, he attended Xavier College in New Orleans and Southern University in Baton Rouge but never graduated. Married Rosa Lee Brown in 1947 and has been separated since 1965, two children.

JACK GREENBERG

Director-counsel of the NAACP Legal Defense and Educational Fund, Inc. (LDF), and directs the activities of 25 staff and 250 cooperating attorneys for the LDF and the National Office for the Rights of the Indigent (newly organized by Greenberg).

Greenberg, a white, succeeded Supreme Court Associate Justice Thurgood Marshall as director-counsel in October of 1961. He has since become nationally known for winning an impressive string of civil rights legal victories. Has argued successfully before the Supreme Court in matters of school segregation, protest demonstrations, recreation, voting, criminal, and other cases. Also served as executive director of the New York State Bar Association's Special Committee to Study the New York Anti-Trust Laws, for which he wrote *New York Anti-Trust Law in the Federal System* (1957) and *The New York Law of Un-*

fair Competition (1950). Is author of *Race Relations and American Law* and has written for *The New York Times Magazine*. Born 1924. A lieutenant in the navy during World War II. Separated, four children. *See also:* LEGAL DEFENSE AND EDUCATIONAL FUND.

DICK GREGORY

Successful $350,000-a-year nightclub comedian turned independent crusader for civil rights and peace in Vietnam. In 1968, ran as presidential candidate of Freedom and Peace party (splinter group of Peace and Freedom party), receiving 148,622 votes. Took "oath of office" as "president-in-exile" in Washington, March 6, 1969. Much in demand as campus lecturer, in 1968 spoke at 150 colleges in 36 states, reportedly earning $5,000 a week in fees. Author of *From the Back of the Bus* (1964), *Political Primer* (1971), and three other books. Twice went on prolonged fasts to protest Vietnam war, the first in November 1967 for 40 days, and the second in June 1968 for 47 days. In 1971 went on a third fast from solid foods—subsisting on fruit juices—until American prisoners of war had returned home and said that when it ends he "wouldn't give up eating again if they were fighting in my living room." Gave up all nightclub engagements (which he did rarely in later years) the summer of 1973 to devote all his time to lecturing at colleges around the country and currently speaks at some 300 campuses a year.

First ventured into politics in 1967 when polled 22,000 votes as write-in candidate against Chicago's Mayor Richard Daley. Since beginning civil rights career in 1962 has been jailed some 20 times, the latest during 1968 Democratic convention in Chicago, for leading marchers through police barricades. During 1965 Watts riots, was shot in leg while attempting to quiet a rioter. In June 1969, attended World Assembly of Peace in East Berlin, "to emphasize racism as the prime cause of war."

Born in St. Louis, Missouri in 1932. Attended Southern Illinois University where he was an outstanding athlete. Served in the army and worked in the United States Post Office in Chicago, from which he was fired, reportedly for impersonating his colleagues and for flipping letters addressed to Mississippi into the overseas mail slot. Became a nightclub comedian in 1958. In 1961 he auditioned at the Playboy Club in Chicago and was an instant hit. From then on he commanded large salaries. Gregory has said: "This is the only country in the world where a man can grow up in a filthy ghetto, go to the worst schools, be forced to ride in the back of the bus, then get $5,000 a week to tell about it." Married, ten children.

JAMES E. GROPPI

Civil rights activist priest of Italian-American descent who, as assistant pastor of St. Boniface Church in Milwaukee's ghetto area, shocked many of Milwaukee's whites and irritated city and state authorities by his militant leadership of local civil rights causes. He first received national attention in 1967, when he led 100 days of marches and demonstrations for open housing, despite repeated warnings and pleas from Milwaukee officials and statements of nonsupport by his church superiors. For resisting arrest during the marches in February 1968, he was sentenced to six months in jail, but the sentence was stayed and after paying a $500 fine he was placed on probation for two years.

On September 29, 1969, Father Groppi led a take-over of the assembly chambers in Madison, Wisconsin, to protest cuts in state's welfare budget. He was sentenced to six-month jail term on October 17, on grounds that his actions had violated the terms of his probation. However, he was released October 27 by the order of Supreme Court Associate Justice Thurgood Marshall, who declared that Groppi was entitled to freedom on bail until the Supreme Court had ruled on the earlier case.

Father Groppi has been jailed at least a dozen times since beginning his civil rights activities and has said he considers going to jail for the cause "a holy act." Born 1931 in Milwaukee, he was appointed assistant pastor at St. Boniface in 1963, and became an advisor to the NAACP's local youth council. He marched in Mississippi in 1964, and in Selma, Alabama in 1965. In answer to some white critics of his militancy, he once declared: "I am white only in complexion. I will picket with the Negro. I will go South with him. I will go to jail with him. And I will hang with him if it need be."

Father Groppi left St. Boniface June 1, 1970, and was reassigned to St. Michael's, a racially mixed parish in Milwaukee. In October 1973 turned up driving a Yellow Cab in downtown Milwaukee on weekends (also works as a night watchman week nights) to pay his way through his second year at Antioch Law School in Washington, D.C. Tuition, he says, costs him $3,000 a year even though his personal savings have been estimated at $75,000; he is saving, he says, for a storefront church. Said about his cab driving experiences: "Everybody ought to take some time and get where it really is. It clears up a lot of that elitism that many people, especially professional and other middle-class types, have."

KENNETH GUSSCOTT

President of New England Conference of NAACP since 1969. Formerly president of the Boston branch of NAACP (1963–1969). Under Gusscott leadership the NAACP Boston office launched a Positive Program for Boston in 1968. Designed to improve opportunities for blacks, it is supported by private businesses, which in 1968 invested some $174,000. A native of Boston, he is regarded as the originator of that city's civil rights movement. Parents were both part of the Garvey movement in the 1920s and they formed the first all-black credit union in the city. An honor graduate from Kings Point Merchant Marine Naval Academy. Also holds a masters degree in engineering from Bettis Engineering School and a doctorate in humanities from Boston University. Served in the air force during World War II and later joined the Defense Department as a marine engineer. Subsequently was chief nuclear test engineer for Bethlehem Steel. Currently is president of his own management consultant firm in Boston. Born July 29, 1925. Married, one child.

JOSE ANGEL GUTIERREZ

Leader of the Mexican-American Youth Organization (MAYO) in Texas, formed in 1967. Also founder of La Raza Unida party in Crystal City, Texas, in 1970. Claims the party has affiliate branches in 23 states and has worked to elect candidates to public office in 15 counties in Texas as well as in Arizona, California, and Michigan. MAYO, originally established as a self-help organization, is currently the organizing arm for La Raza Unida party. Organizer of the successful Crystal City, Texas, school boycott which made national headlines in January 1970. The boycott set a precedent with direct negotiations between students and the predominantly white Crystal City school board to effect demanded curriculum changes. President of Crystal City Board of Education 1970–1973— the first *chicano* ever elected to that board. Gutierrez, born in 1944, is the son of a doctor, formed MAYO with four others in 1967 while a student at St. Mary's College in San Antonio. Home: 124 West Edwards, Crystal City, Texas.

WILLIAM F. HADDAD

Award-winning reporter for *New York Post* 1957–1961, associate director of Peace Corps, 1961–1963, investigative reporter for the *Herald Tribune* 1963–1964, and a leading official in Office of Economic Opportunity until 1965. From 1966 until July 1973 headed own group, the New York-based U.S. Research and Development Corporation, which conducted minority job-training programs. Is copublisher, with CORE director Roy Innis, of *Manhattan Tribune,* an experimental West Side community paper aimed at greater black-white dialogue. Paper also serves as a training ground for black newsmen. Currently teaches a course in decision-making at Sarah Lawrence College in New York state and is vice-chairman of the New York Board of Trade. Author of *Hidden Force* (1963) and *Black Economic Power* (1970). Aide to Senator Estes Kefauver, 1954–1957. Special assistant to Robert Kennedy in 1960 presidential campaign. In 1964, ran unsuccessfully as reform candidate in New York's Nineteenth Congressional District. Born in Charlotte, North Carolina, July 25, 1928. Received B.A. from Columbia University in 1954. Studied Russian and Chinese at Georgetown University, 1954–1956. Married Kate Roosevelt (1959), three children. Office: 1 Lincoln Plaza, New York, N. Y.

FANNIE LOU HAMER

Charismatic leader and founder of the Mississippi Freedom Democrats at the 1964 Democratic National Convention, "the mammy-style grandmother . . . became the symbol of the downtrodden Southern Negro" (*Washington Post,* July 14, 1968). Given an ovation at the 1968 Convention, when her group successfully unseated the regular Mississippi delegation. First became involved in the civil rights movement August 31, 1962, when whe was barred in her attempt to register to vote in Rulesville (Sunflower County), Mississippi. She then joined Student National Coordinating Committee (1962) and became an activist in the voter registration drive. In 1963, joined James Meredith in his march on the University of Mississippi. And, at the 1964 Democratic National Convention, she was the vice-chairman of the predominantly black Mississippi Freedom Democratic party that sought to unseat the all-white regular delegation. In 1968, worked toward the coalition of her Freedom party with other black and liberal white groups, to be known as the Loyal Democrats of Mississippi. This group successfully challenged the state's all-white delegation at the 1968 Democratic Convention. She and her organization still involved at the grassroots level urging people to participate in the elective process. She travels widely throughout the country speaking and supporting black candidates in their campaigns for public office. Born in 1918, the youngest of 20 children, and the daughter of a sharecropper. She is married to Perry (Pap) Hamer.

CHARLES V. HAMILTON
Professor of government at Columbia University since September 1969 and formerly chairman of the Department of Political Science at Roosevelt University, Chicago. One of the nation's most articulate authorities on black power. Coauthor with Stokely Carmichael of *Black Power: The Politics of Liberation in America*; also wrote *The Black Preacher in America* (1972), the *Black Experience in Black Politics,* and others. Lectures widely on race, ethnicity, and public policy and said about the 1963 March on Washington on its tenth anniversary: "When I look back at the march, I see it clearly as the beginning of the spread of the movement beyond the South. Civil rights mass activism became—if I may use the term—'nationalized' rather than 'localized' . . . I suspect that we are experiencing now what I think is a growing manhood. The critical question is going to be the extent to which society—that is to say, primarily the economic system—can equitably accommodate the entry of mass new groupings. My judgement is it cannot. But that's a judgement that has to be tested. It's clear to me that precisely because we're now moving to challenge questions that go beyond the traditionally understood civil rights agenda, we may well find ourselves looking at what I prefer to call 'deracialized' solutions with racial consequences." Graduate of Roosevelt University, Loyola University School of Law (Chicago), and the University of Chicago. Has taught at Tuskegee Institute, Albany State College (Georgia), Rutgers, and Lincoln Universities. Married, two daughters.

VINCENT HARDING
Historian and educator. Currently director of research at the Institute of the Black World, an organization that grew out of the Martin Luther King Library Documentation Project which he headed from 1968–1970. The Institute of the Black World devotes itself to researching the meaning of all black history in America and serves as a liaison for all black studies programs at colleges and universities across the country. Publishes a monthly newsletter called *Black World View* and position papers on the movement. Funded by foundation grants and individual contributions. Harding received a B.A. from City College in New York (1952), an M.S. in journalism from Columbia (1953), and an M.A. in

history from the University of Chicago (1956). Born July 25, 1931, in New York City and married to the former Rosemarie Freeney (1960), two children.

LaDONNA CRAWFORD HARRIS

Half-Comanche, half-Irish wife of former Senator Fred Harris, Democrat of Oklahoma. In 1969–1970, Mrs. Harris emerged as a leading and attractive spokesman for Indian interests. In February 1970 she founded the Americans for Indian Opportunity and has served as its president and executive director ever since. She is a member of the Urban Coalition national steering committee and is honorary president of the Oklahomans for Indian Opportunity. Born February 15, 1931, and raised by Comanche grandparents in Walters, Oklahoma. Three children. *See also:* AMERICANS FOR INDIAN OPPORTUNITY.

PATRICIA ROBERTS HARRIS

Ambassador to Luxembourg, 1965–1967, and first black woman to head an American embassy. In 1966 and 1967, appointed alternate delegate to the United Nations. In 1968 President Johnson appointed Mrs. Harris to the seven-member Commission on Causes and Prevention of Violence. In February 1969, was central figure in dispute at Howard University. Appointed dean of the law school February 1, she was confronted by a student boycott and resigned February 27, charging that Howard President James Nabrit had placed her in "untenable position" by negotiating with student protesters behind her back. Was member of Howard's law faculty for several years. Long active in civil rights and Democratic politics, she was chairman of the Credentials Committee at the 1972 Democratic National Convention. She has held office in Washington chapters of the NAACP, Urban League, American Civil Liberties Union, and YWCA. Was chairman of the National Women's Committee on Civil Rights, 1963–1964, and is a director of the NAACP Legal Defense Fund. Born May 31, 1924, in Mattoon, Illinois, the daughter of a railroad waiter. She graduated from Howard University in 1945 and George Washington University Law Center (J.D. with honors) in 1960. Admitted to practice before the U.S. Supreme Court and the courts of the District of Columbia. Currently in private practice and is a partner in the law firm of Fried, Frank, Harris, Shriver and Kampelman. Is on the board of directors of the Chase Manhattan Bank, IBM, Georgetown University, and Scott Paper Company. In 1971, with the Scott directorship, became the first black woman director of any major corporation. Married to lawyer William Beasley Harris, an attorney with the Federal Power Commission, no children.

JERU-AHMED HASSAN

Free-wheeling black nationalist and antidrug activist. Born in 1924 in Washington, D.C., as Albert Roy Osborne, changed his name to Hassan when he organized the Washington-based Blackman's Volunteer Army of Liberation in the mid-1960s. A back-to-Africa movement, the organization's purpose was said to be to create a mercenary army of American blacks (called the "Black Star Regiment") to fight for independence in Central and South Africa, and thereby to win a nation for themselves. Hassan's paramilitary organization later established the Blackman's Development Center in Washington, D.C., which in July 1970 received financial backing from city and federal government for its successful antidrug program which treats 2,800 addicts a week. Hassan testified before a special Senate subcommittee on alcoholism and narcotics in April 1970. Declared that heroin reaches Washington through a conspiracy of the Mafia, Cosa Nostra, and "the black syndicate." In June 1971, the Department of Health, Education, and Welfare (HEW), which had awarded the center $197,000 job-training grant, suspended it accusing Hassan of sloppy bookkeeping and audited his books. Six months later, HEW charged that the Center had misspent $39,509 of the grant money on unauthorized items such as wine, auto repairs, and repayment of personal loans. At the same time Hassan came under attack from the Anti-Defamation League (ADL) of B'Nai B'Rith which called him anti-semitic for some of the Center's literature. In 1972, $125,000 in debt, the drug program curtailed, his headquarters moved to Columbus, Ohio (to outflank the ADL). Hassan announced he was going into politics and that he planned to run in the primary for the district's nonvoting delegate seat to Congress. He ran as a Republican but lost. Currently in the real estate business and on November 7, 1973, stepped down as head of the drug center to devote full time to his new business venture.

WILLIAM H. HASTIE
First black to be made a federal judge. Appointed to United States Court of Appeals for the Third Circuit in 1949, chief judge 1969–1971, and currently senior circuit judge. Former chairman of national legal committee of the NAACP and tried and argued numerous cases for the organization in 1930s and 1940s. Previously served as U.S. attorney and governor of the Virgin Islands. Born in Knoxville, Tennessee on November 17, 1904, he received an A.B. degree from Amherst College in 1925 and an honorary M.A. in 1940 also from Amherst. Earned an LL.B. in 1930 and S.J.D. in 1933 from Harvard University; was admitted to the bar the same year. Made a federal judge on the Third Circuit Court of Appeals in Philadelphia in 1949. Married the former Beryl Lockhart, two children. Office: United States Courthouse, Philadelphia, Pa. 19107.

RICHARD GORDON HATCHER
Mayor of Gary, Indiana, elected the first time November 1967. Along with Carl Stokes of Cleveland, one of the first blacks elected mayor of a major American city. Democrat Hatcher's victory was a triumph over the active and bitter opposition of the regular Democratic machine. Election was fraught with notorious examples of harassment and attempted vote-rigging. At Hatcher's request, Attorney General Ramsay Clark ordered 22 FBI men to Gary to get purged names restored to the registration lists. On November 6, just prior to the election, a special three-judge federal court ordered 1,000 false names from the lists and the reinstatement of 5,000 black voters. The court acted after consolidating separate suits brought by Hatcher and the justice department. Hatcher finally de-

feated Joseph B. Radigan by 39,330 votes to 37,941. Has been faced with a series of civic problems and racial unrest: garbage collectors' strike, a school boycott, complaints from whites that he padded black payrolls, an outbreak of violence (sniping and looting) after Martin Luther King's death, and a 65 percent crime increase over 1968. In spite of charges of wastefulness, inefficiency, fostering racism, and being a slum landlord, was reelected to a second four-year term in November 1971 with 58 percent of the vote. Regarding the change from 1967 to 1971 election, he said: "Today blacks are living in other parts of town. I see a lessening of tensions and hostility. I know we've still got a long way to go. People still aren't over many of their reservations on race. In 1967 they were literally at each other's throats. But at least this year I can go into the white areas like Glen Park and Miller and be invited to talk in homes I'd never have gone into four years ago, and that, for Gary, is progress." In March 1972, cochaired with Imamu Amiri Baraka and Representative Charles Diggs of Michigan the first National Black Political Convention. Born 1933, the son of a factory worker, Hatcher worked his way through Indiana University and Valparaiso University law school. After graduation he moved to Gary to practice law. He became a deputy prosecutor and, in 1963, a member of the city council. Member of the U.S. Conference of Mayors, the executive board of NAACP, and the Democratic National Committee. Also Chairman of Indiana State Black Caucus.

JAMES HAUGHTON
Director and founder of Fight Back (formerly called Harlem Unemployment Center). Born in 1929 in Brooklyn, New York. Holds bachelor's degree from City College of New York and Master's in public administration from New York University. Served in the Korean War. Teaches a course on blacks and labor politics at Hunter Collge in New York. Member of the New York Taxi and Limousine Commission. Married to Dr. Eleanor Leacock, an anthropologist. See also: FIGHT BACK.

AUGUSTUS F. HAWKINS
Democratic representative from California's Twenty-first Congressional District, elected in 1963. In 1934, elected to the California legislature and served there for the next 28 years working particularly on juvenile delinquency. He has been a vigorous supporter of legislation in civil rights, labor relations, health, welfare, and housing and more than 300 laws on the statute books in California bear his name or acknowledge his coauthorship. Currently serves on the House Committee on Education and Labor as well as the House Administration Committee. He is a member of the Congressional Black Caucus. In private life, has an insurance and real estate business and automobile appliance business. Born in Shreveport, Louisiana, on August 31, 1917, he moved to California at age 11, went to high school there, and graduated in economics from the University of California. See also: CONGRESSIONAL BLACK CAUCUS.

NATHAN C. HEARD

Author whose first novel, *Howard Street*, published November 1968 (Dial Press), is based on his adolescence in the Newark ghetto. *To Reach A Dream*, his second book, was published in 1972. Taught himself to write during three spells in prison between 1958 and 1968 (the last time for armed robbery). He was finally released December 1968, a month after his book was published. Born 1936 in Newark, New Jersey. From September 1969, has lectured in creative writing at Fresno State College in California.

HERBERT HILL

National labor director of NAACP since 1948 and a veteran of hundreds of legal battles against discriminatory unions. A white man, he was an organizer for the United Steel Workers of America in his teens. Joined the NAACP in 1938, first working with its Harlem branch and in 1945 joined the national staff as a field worker. Born January 24, 1924, in Brooklyn, New York, he attended public schools there, and attended New York University and the New School for Social Research but did not receive a degree. Is coauthor of *Citizen's Guide to Desegregation: A Study of Social and Legal Change in American Society* and *Anger and Beyond*. A frequent lecturer and magazine writer. Married.

JULIUS W. HOBSON

Economist with Department of Health, Education, and Welfare for 20 years until his resignation April 1, 1970. He is known as an uncompromising civil rights activist. As local chairman of ACT Associates filed suit against Washington, D.C., school board that resulted in landmark decision by U.S. District Judge J. Skelly Wright, June 19, 1967 that "de facto" segregation in D.C. schools was unconstitutional. Served as school board member until 1969 when he failed to get reelected. Headed Washington Institute for Quality Education, a research organization concerned with minority problems, until his resignation in 1971. Also taught sociology at the American University in Washington. Has been on FBI monthly surveillance list. In 1971 ran on the People's party ticket as vice-presidential candidate with Dr. Benjamin Spock, the party's presidential candidate to Congress in the primary but came out a weak third pulling only 12 percent of the vote. The same year was selected the individual who had fought hardest for possible change in the district in a poll conducted by the *D.C. Gazette*. In recent months failing health has curtailed his activities. Born 1922 in Birmingham, Alabama, and a graduate of Tuskegee Institute. Married twice, currently to the former Tina Lower, a white woman, two children.

JEROME H. HOLLAND

A director of N.Y. Stock Exchange since 1972 and first black to hold the post. Appointed ambassador to Sweden (1970–1972) by President Nixon. The post, which had been vacant for the previous year, presented difficulties because of a growing rift in U.S.–Swedish relations over the Vietnamese War. Prior to his appointment, Dr. Holland had been president of Hampton Institute in Virginia since 1960. Born January 9, 1916, he holds a B.S. from Cornell University (1939), a Ph.D. from University of Pennsylvania (1950), an LL.D. from University of Cincinnati (1960). Married the former Laura Mitchell in 1948, two children.

BEN HOLMAN

Director of Community Relations Service (CRS), Department of Justice, since 1969. On July 24, 1973, started serving his second four-year term. Joined the Justice Department in 1965 as assistant director for media relations. CRS was created by the Civil Rights Act of 1964 and is the only government agency solely designed to mediate racial disputes—most recently mediated at the Indian take-over at Wounded Knee, South Dakota. Formerly a reporter with the *Chicago Daily News* (1952-1962) and with CBS News (1963-1965) in New York. On WNBC-TV program on integration, November 15, 1969, said: "I've personally found that I've drifted away from the integration goal, and I think I'm mirroring the attitude of a lot of blacks. How can you really have integration when 85 percent of the country doesn't want it?" Born December 18, 1930 in Columbia, South Carolina. Graduated from the University of Kansas (1952) and attended University of Chicago's Graduate School of International Relations (1954-1956).

HAMILTON HOLMES

Desegregated the University of Georgia in Athens on January 10, 1961 along with Charlayne Hunter. Graduated valedictorian and class president from high school, and while waiting for admission to University of Georgia, attended Morehouse College. Was under police protection during his first days at the university but afterwards shunned public attention and stuck close to his books. Graduated in 1963 and entered Emory University School of Medicine in Atlanta graduating in 1967. Completed his first year of residency at Detroit General Hospital in 1969, after which he fulfilled his military service in Germany. Currently completing his residency in orthopedics at Emory.

JAMES A. HOOD

Desegregated the University of Alabama in 1963 along with Vivian Malone. But withdrew two months later, on doctor's orders, "to avoid complete mental and physical breakdown," following state-backed demands for his explusion for alleged remarks at a black rally. Went to live in Detroit, where he worked at Ford Motor Company while studying for B.A. in sociology at Wayne State University. Graduated 1969. Became director of central city programs of Interfaith Action group in Detroit, providing ghetto with educational opportunities and other aid. Entered Michigan State Graduate School of Criminal Justice, College of Social Science and received an M.S. in 1972. Born Gadsden, Alabama, November 10, 1942. Married, one son.

BENJAMIN L. HOOKS

Member of the Federal Communications Commission (FCC), appointed by President Nixon April 12, 1972 to a seven-year term—the first black ever to serve on the seven-member commission. Main concern at FCC is equal employment opportunities in the broadcasting industry. A Baptist minister and an attorney, was born in 1925 in Memphis, Tennessee, and graduated from Le Moyne College and De Paul University with a degree in law. From 1942 to 1946 served in the Army. A member of the Southern Christian Leadership Conference, NAACP, and the Memphis-Shelby County Human Relations Council. Considered to be solidly pro-establishment and to espouse black capitalism. "I believe in green power," he has said. "I'm a Baptist minister and I believe we should have love, faith and all that other stuff, but give me a little of that green stuff that say in God we trust and we'll make it somehow brother."

LENA HORNE
Singer and actress, and the first black woman ever to be signed to a long-term Hollywood contract. Considers herself part of the revolution. Has spoken in Mississippi, marched on Washington, sung for Student National Coordinating Committee. In 1963 with James Baldwin met Robert Kennedy to discuss segregation in North, but identifies more particularly with Southern blacks. "My identity is finally very clear to me. I'm a black woman and I'm not alone." "Am I hopeful?" she repeated when a reporter asked her if the color problem might one day conceivably die out. "Honey, I'm so hopeful that sometimes it hurts." Born June 30, 1917, in Brooklyn, New York and joined the chorus line in the Cotton Club in 1933. Sang with the Charlie Barnett Orchestra 1939 and made her first records with him. Also has done films, records, and TV. Wrote her autobiography *Lena* in 1965. Starred in *Cabin in the Sky; Stormy Weather;* and played *Jamaica* on Broadway. Life member of NAACP. Recently widowed, one child.

CHARLAYNE HUNTER
Desegregated the University of Georgia, January 10, 1961, along with Hamilton Holmes. Graduated in 1963 with a degree in journalism. Married white student Walter Stovall in the spring of 1963, and their daughter Susan was born in November of the same year. After graduation, worked for the *New Yorker* magazine as an editorial assistant while her husband was a reporter for the *Bergen* (New Jersey) *Record*. Later worked for WRC, the NBC affiliate in Washington, D.C. and in July 1969, joined the staff of *The New York Times*. Has not been active in the movement in the last three years. Born 1942. Divorced.

RUBY HURLEY
Southeast regional director for the NAACP which includes states of Alabama, Florida, Georgia, Mississippi, Tennessee, North Carolina, and South Carolina. A native of Washington, D.C., she attended public schools there, Miner Teachers College, and Robert H. Terrell Law School. Before joining the NAACP, worked in the Industrial Bank of Washington and later for the federal government. Joined the national staff of NAACP as national youth secretary responsible for reorganizing youth units and directing the youth program and in 1951 was sent

to Birmingham, Alabama, on a temporary assignment to coordinate NAACP membership campaigns for the branches of Alabama, Florida, Georgia, Mississippi, and Tennessee. Subsequently the southeast region was established and expanded to include North and South Carolina. This seven-state area leads all other NAACP regional groups in membership and consists of 76,000 adult members and 8,400 youth. There are also 542 adult branches and 144 youth councils and college chapters in her region. Office: 970 Hunter Street, Atlanta, Georgia 30314.

INNER CITY BUSINESS IMPROVEMENT FORUM (ICBIF)

An all-black, nonprofit corporation formed in Detroit after the 1967 riots, under the auspices of Representative Charles Diggs, for the funding of black business enterprises to help Detroit's inner city blacks to gain economic independence. It provides financial, managerial, and technical assistance to black businesses, employing either its own staff or the efforts of volunteers and specialists from other agencies and universities. ICBIF is controlled by a volunteer board of 40 from all segments of the black community. By mid-1973 was instrumental in raising $7.8 million in loans to help over 100 minority-owned businesses get started, sponsored first black-owned bank, the First Independence Nation Bank (President David B. Harper), which opened in June 1970, assisted 1,000 in obtaining loans and gave management and technical assistance to more than 1,800 small businessmen. The ICBIF has received funds from the Ford Foundation, the Office of Economic Opportunity, and the Detroit Economic Development Corporation—which was set up in 1968 for the specific purpose of aiding black business. (The Economic Development Corporation is an offspring of New Detroit, a coalition of Detroit business and labor leaders formed by then Governor George Romney and Mayor Jerome Cavanagh after the 1967 riots; current president is Larry Doss.) Chairman of the ICBIF is Howard F. Sims, president of Howard Sims Associates, an architectural firm; president is Walter McMurtry, Jr. (born 1934), an accountant and University of Michigan graduate; executive vice-president is Dyctis J. Moses, Jr. (born 1946), a graduate of Harvard Graduate School of Business Administration and Cheney College. ICBIF address: 1672 14th Street, Detroit, Michigan. See also: CHARLES DIGGS.

ROY INNIS

National director of CORE since 1968, when he succeeded Floyd McKissick. Turned CORE from a broad-based civil rights organization into a black nationalist and separatist group. Defining his ideas of separatism in Ebony magazine, Innis said: "Under segregation, black people live together but their institutions are controlled by whites. Under integration, black people are dispersed and the institutions, goods and services are still controlled by whites. In effect, the two are the same. But under separatism, black people will control their own turf." In the New York mayoralty election in November 1969, Innis refused to endorse any of the candidates and urged Harlem voters to boycott the election. As part of his separatist program, he initiated the Community Self-Determination Bill, introduced in Congress July 1968. Has called for the drafting of a new Constitution, because the original ignored black people. Despite his separatist philosophy, Innis joined with former newsman William Haddad to launch the *Manhattan Tribune* in November 1968, with the stated aim of bridging the gap between "the frustrated, angry black community and the frightened white community" of New York City's Upper West Side. In March 1970, Innis proposed a unitary system plan for school integration which would create one white and one black school district, each autonomous and equal. Mobile, Alabama, has been chosen as first test city for his plan. In December 1973, made headlines when he debated with Nobel prize-winning physicist, William B. Shockley, on NBC's TO-MORROW SHOW on the question: Are Blacks Genetically Inferior to Whites in Intelligence? Born in St. Croix, Virgin Islands, on June 6, 1934. Came to New York with his mother at age two and lived in Harlem. Quit high school at 16 to enlist in the army, fought in the Korean War and stayed in the army for two years. While in the service, he passed the high school equivalency exam. Went to City College of New York where he studied chemistry. He has been married twice, presently to the former Doris Funnye of Georgetown, South Carolina, seven children.

INTERRELIGIOUS FOUNDATION FOR COMMUNITY ORGANIZATION (IFCO)

A multiracial foundation dedicated to the pursuit of "self-determination" in the urban ghettos. Sponsored the now defunct National Black Economic Development Conference in April 1969. Founded in December 1966 by ten major Catholic, Protestant, and Jewish social action agencies—including the Executive Council of the Episcopal Church, the American Jewish Committee, and the Catholic Committee for Urban Ministries. Announced its intention to "help mobilize poor communities throughout the country to play a greater role in solving their problems" by coordinating the programs of the member agencies. Agencies now numbering 23, seek grants from other foundations, train community organizers, and sponsor research programs. From September 1967 to September 1973, received a total of five million dollars in grants. Now funds local communities in more than 40 cities and such international organizations as the African Liberation Support Committee and the Farm Labor Organizing Committee. Controlled by a racially balanced board of directors with 43 members and is based in New York. Rev. Lucius Walker is executive director. Office: 475 Riverside Drive, Room 560, New York, N.Y. 10027.

JAPANESE AMERICAN CITIZENS LEAGUE

A national nonprofit organization, founded in 1930, which campaigns for equal rights for Japanese-American citizens. Has an intensive information and education program and serves as a "watchdog" alert for movements and proposals both in Congress and state legislatures that would affect their welfare. Has approximately 28,000 members in 96 chapters in 32 states and is supported primarily by membership dues. Publishes a weekly news magazine called the *Pacific*

Citizen. Offers legal services for Asian Americans and has programs for youth and senior citizens. National Director is David E. Ushio who became director in January 1973. Born November 12, 1945, is a graduate of Brigham Young University with a degree in political science. Headquarters: 22 Peace Plaza, Suite 203, San Francisco, Calif. 94115. Regional offices in Portland (Oregon), Los Angeles, Fresno (California), Chicago, Washington, D.C., and Salt Lake City (Utah).

JESSE JACKSON
Director of Operation PUSH (People United to Save Humanity), an organization he founded in Chicago December 25, 1971, whose goals are economic development and political action for minorities. Is widely considered the city's leading black spokesman. Formerly head of Southern Christian Leadership Conference (SCLC) in Chicago until 1971 and architect of Operation Breadbasket which has led successful boycott campaigns against Chicago's leading chain stores and other businesses. Announced the formation of Operation PUSH a week after his resignation from Operation Breadbasket, an SCLC-sponsored project, and the entire Chicago chapter followed him. The split followed a series of differences between himself and Ralph Abernathy, president of SCLC. The conflict first became public in 1968 when Jackson wanted a higher post in SCLC hierarchy but was turned down by the board of directors. In 1971 he was asked to move Operation Breadbasket to Atlanta, national headquarters of SCLC, but refused. Later that year, the conflict was intensified over the handling of $500,000 earned by Operation Breadbasket in October through the highly successful Black Expo (an exposition of black business and cultural achievements organized by Jackson first in 1969). Charging that he defied SCLC regulations by creating two nonprofit corporations to operate Black Expo without permission, the SCLC board suspended him for 60 days. But Jackson resigned saying he could not continue under these conditions. After organizing PUSH said there was still room for both organizations; "we have the same goals," he said. "Now we can both work to expand on those goals in the interests of black and poor people everywhere." Jackson was supported in his endeavor to form the new organization by a number of prominent black leaders (Percy Sutton, Manhattan Borough president in New York, Richard Hatcher, mayor of Gary, Indiana, actor Ossie Davis, and others) who felt he should not be lost to the movement. Led alternate delegation from Chicago at the Democratic National Convention in 1972 in Miami and won the challenge against the regular delegation, led by Mayor Daley, to be seated. The challenge was the result of the new delegate selection guidelines adopted at the 1972 Convention which opened up that Convention to more representation from minorities, women, and youth. Ordained a Baptist minister in 1968, he does not have a church but conducts Saturday morning meetings at South Side's Capitol Theater (79th & Halstead St. in Chicago), which have developed a phenomenal regular following of up to 5,000 people. In April 1968, it was Jackson who cradled Martin Luther King's head in his arms on the balcony of the Lorraine

Motel in Memphis. In June 1968, he gained national prominence as manager of Poor People's Campaign Resurrection City in Washington, D.C.

Born in Greenville, South Carolina, in 1941, he received an athletic scholarship to the University of Illinois and later studied at North Carolina Agricultural and Technical College. Jackson led his first protest march in Greensboro in 1963. He later became president of the newly formed North Carolina Intercollegiate Council on Human Rights. It was after this that he joined King ("my father figure, my brother figure and my teacher"). At the second annual convention of Operation PUSH, July 1973, said that the civil rights struggle of the sixties was "outdated" and had to be replaced by "the broader struggle of the seventies. To take advantage of the rights we won—in education, housing, politics—in the sixties, we need economic health in the seventies. It costs money to win elections, it costs money to go to school. In short, it costs money to be free." (Washington Post, July 30, 1973.) See also: OPERATION PUSH.

MAYNARD HOLBROOK JACKSON
Mayor of Atlanta, Georgia—the first black man to govern a major deep south city. Elected October 16, 1973, in a run-off election against incumbent Sam Massell. Won by an overwhelming 59 percent of the vote after missing a clear majority by 300 votes in the October 2 election. Even though Atlanta's black community now numbers 52 percent of the city's population, one out of every five white voters voted for him. Comes from a distinguished black southern family whose grandfather, John Wesley Dobbs, founded the Georgia Voters League and whose father, Dr. Maynard H. Jackson, founded the Friendship Baptist Church in Atlanta. Served as vice-mayor of Atlanta from October 1969 to 1973, and as the first black man ever elected to one of the top two offices of the Georgia capital, gained nearly 60 percent of the votes against white candidate, Alderman Milton G. Farris. In 1968, against the advice of local black leaders, he ran against former Governor Herman Talmadge in the Democratic primary for the U.S. Senate and lost heavily. A lawyer and vice-president of the Atlanta NAACP, Jackson is considered to be a progressive liberal. Says of the civil rights movement today "anyone looking for the civil rights movement in the streets is fooling himself. Politics is the civil rights movement in the seventies. Politics is the last nonviolent hurrah." (New York Times, August 26, 1973.)

Born March 23, 1938 in Dallas, Texas, the third eldest in a family of six children, and has lived in Atlanta since he was seven. Entered Morehouse College at 14, graduating with a degree in political science and history. Received a law degree from North Carolina Central University (Durham) where his mother is chairman of modern foreign languages. Has worked for the National Labor Relations Board and has been in private law practice with the all-black firm of Jackson, Paterson, Parks and Franklin in Atlanta. Married, two daughters.

JOHN H. JOHNSON
Millionaire publisher and founder of the $12 million Chicago-based Johnson Publishing Company, and chairman of Supreme Life Insurance Co., reputedly

the nation's largest black-owned business. Named by President Nixon to Advisory Commission on Minority Enterprise, "to eliminate roadblocks on the path of economic opportunity to every citizen." In 1942, Johnson started the monthly *Negro Digest* with a borrowed $500. In 1945, he launched *Ebony* "to emphasize the brighter side of Negro life and success." With more than one-million circulation, it is the nation's biggest black publication and chief money-maker of the Johnson empire. It was followed by *Tan* (1950) and *Jet* (1951). Says of the black movement today that "it's not built around any particular organization or individual at the moment. There is uncertainty around certain issues, [but] a certain pride in being black, being ourselves." In 1951, Johnson was named one of the ten most outstanding men of the year by the Junior Chamber of Commerce. In 1957, accompanied the then Vice-President Nixon on a good-will trip to nine African countries and in 1959 went with Nixon again to Russia and Poland. Was a special ambassadorial representative for United States at independence ceremonies of the Ivory Coast in 1961 and at Kenya's independence ceremonies in 1963. Received the Russworm, Spingarn, and Horatio Alger awards. In 1966 was a member of the National Advisory Council of President's Committee on Economic Opportunity. Is a vice-president of the National Urban League. Born in Arkansas City, Arkansas, on January 19, 1918. Attended University of Chicago and Northwestern University. Married to the former Eunice Waller, two children.

JOINT CENTER FOR POLITICAL STUDIES (JCPS)
Formed in 1970 to meet the needs of a growing number of blacks elected to public office. As the black community gradually shifted from protest to electoral politics in the late 1960s, psychologist Kenneth B. Clark, president of the Metropolitan Applied Research Center (MARC) saw a need for establishing a center to help black officeholders and called a meeting of leading black Democrats and Republicans in December 1968 to develop plans for such a center. The idea became a reality two years later, when a Ford Foundation grant of $820,000 to Howard University enabled MARC and the university to sponsor the center jointly. Provides technical, educational, and research assistance for blacks in office and publishes the *Roster of Black Elected Officials* (annually)—a tally of blacks currently in office—as well as a monthly newsletter called *Focus*. In its first two years has aided some 500 blacks in office directly and another 2000 indirectly. President is Eddie Williams who took office in 1972. Before that was vice-president for public affairs at the University of Chicago, was a journalist, and worked for the federal government. Born in Memphis, Tennessee, in 1932; graduated from the University of Illinois and did graduate work at Howard and Atlanta Universities. Office: 1426 H Street, N.W., Suite 926, Washington, D.C. 20005.

J. RAYMOND JONES
Veteran New York City Democratic party official, who in 1964 was elected chairman of the New York County Democratic Committee (Tammany Hall), reput-

edly the first black in the country to head a county political organization. Re-signed as Tammany Hall leader in March 1967, after Senator Robert Kennedy denied him his support. In 1969 mayoralty campaign, broke his 48-year record of strict party loyalty by endorsing Mayor Lindsay, declaring Democratic can-didate Mario Procaccino's campaign to be "antiblack." Active in Democratic politics since 1921, Jones became district leader in 1959, city councilman in 1962, and was sometimes known by fellow Democrats as "the Fox." Born in St. Thomas, Virgin Islands, November 19, 1899, he settled in New York City in 1918. Currently retired from politics and living in the Virgin Islands. Married, one daughter.

BARBARA JORDAN
Democratic representative to Congress from the Eighteenth Congressional Dis-trict in Texas—the first black woman since Reconstruction. A lawyer, she en-tered politics in 1960 because she had a law degree, no clients, and was looking for something to do; ended up working for the Harris County Democrats in the Kennedy–Johnson presidential campaign. Elected first to State House in 1964, then to the Senate in 1966 for two terms before going to Congress. Considered a protégé of the late Lyndon Johnson, she keeps a low profile and likes working behind the scenes. Member of the Executive Committee of the National Demo-cratic Policy Council, Congressional Black Caucus, and serves on the House Ju-diciary Committee. Born February 21, 1936. Attended Houston public schools, graduated (magna cum laude) from Texas Southern University with a B.A. de-gree in political science in 1956. Received a law degree from Boston University in 1959. On the board of directors of National Urban League and a member of NAACP and Southern Regional Council. Unmarried.

VERNON E. JORDAN, JR.
Executive director of the National Urban League since January 1972 succeeding the late Whitney Young, Jr. Born August 15, 1935, in Atlanta, Georgia, where he attended elementary and high schools. Graduated from DePauw University in 1957 and Howard University School of Law in 1960. Has been active in civil rights movement ever since. Came to national attention in 1961 when he led Charlayne Hunter into the University of Georgia through a mob of white pro-testors—one of the landmark drives for integration of southern schools. As NAACP field director in Georgia, led a boycott of Augusta stores that refused to hire blacks. Was director of the Voter Education Project for the Southern Re-gional Council in Atlanta and executive director of the United Negro College Fund before coming to the League. During the Johnson administration was ap-pointed to the National Advisory Commission on Selective Service and to the White House Conference called "To Fulfill These Rights." Has held fellowships at Harvard University Institute of Politics, the John F. Kennedy School of Gov-ernment, and the Metropolitan Applied Research Center.

Has continued and expanded the "new thrust" programs begun by Young and sees the role of the League as one of implementing the promises of the

1960s. "We're not talking now about integrating lunch counters," he has said. "We're talking about things that were not even considered civil rights issues in the '60s—things like the delivery of comprehensive medical services, welfare reform, revenue sharing." Married to the former Shirley M. Yarborough, one daughter.

PERCY L. JULIAN

One of the nation's most noted black scientists and a pioneer in the chemistry of hormones and steroids. Director of the Julian Research Institute in Chicago, a nonprofit organization engaged in pure and applied research on drugs, particularly in the areas of sex hormones, oral contraceptives, and provitamin D_3. In 1967 was one of 47 leading black business and professional men who formed a fund-raising organization to finance the activities of the NAACP Legal Defense and Educational Fund. Also a generous contributor to civil rights causes. Born in Montgomery, Alabama, 1898. Attended DePauw University (Indiana) by working his way through as a waiter, graduating Phi Beta Kappa (1920), and taught at Fisk and Howard Universities. Did postgraduate work at Harvard (1923) and the University of Vienna (1931). Married, two children.

JUSTICE DEPARTMENT, CIVIL RIGHTS DIVISION

The Civil Rights Division was established by the Attorney General December 9, 1957, following enactment of the 1957 Civil Rights Act. Initially staffed by ten attorneys and eight support personnel, today it employs some 300, 150 of whom are attorneys. Responsibilities include enforcement of civil rights laws and executive orders prohibiting discrimination; authorizing intervention in cases brought by private litigants involving the denial of equal protection of the laws on account of race; supervision and direction of criminal prosecutions of any person acting under cover of the law and private persons acting in conspiracy to interfere with or to deny the exercise of federal rights. Today jurisdiction of the division extends to all federal laws prohibiting discrimination in areas of education, employment, housing, public accommodation and facilities, voting, and federally assisted programs. Division is headed by an assistant attorney general. Noted previous holders were Burke Marshall (1960–1964) and John Doar (1964–1967). Present head is J. Stanley Pottinger, appointed February 1973. Division has field offices in Montgomery, Alabama; Los Angeles, California; New Orleans, Louisiana; Jackson, Mississippi; and Dallas, Texas. In August 1969, a group of 40 of the division's lawyers publicly protested the Nixon administration's desegregation policies. On October 1, the leader of the dissident lawyers, Gary J. Greenberg, was forced to resign after criticizing Attorney General John Mitchell in open court. On October 14, the justice department filed suit to end alleged racial segregation in the elementary schools of Waterbury, Connecticut, the first such action by the federal government in a northeastern state. In July 1970, the department launched widespread legal action against remaining southern school districts which had not desegregated. In 1973 filed and participated in 209 cases to protect individual's civil rights, such as the first suits against public employers (city fire and police departments and public school systems) for patterns and practices of discrimination against minority employees and applicants. Has established two new offices within the division: Office of Institutions and Facilities concerned with protecting the constitutional rights of persons in public facilities such as prisons, mental hospitals, juvenile homes; and the Office of Indian Rights responsible for enforcing federal civil rights laws for the American Indian population. Office: Civil Rights Division, Department of Justice, Washington, D.C. 20530. *See also:* JOHN DOAR, BURKE MARSHALL.

MAU LANA RON KARENGA
Founder of the Los Angeles-based black nationalist organization "US" (as opposed to THEM) and considered one of the most articulate new breed of black militant leaders. Karenga urges blacks to foster their own distinct Afro-American culture instead of trying to adapt to white values. His adopted Swahili name, Karenga, means "keeper of tradition." Among those he has influenced is Imamu Amiri Baraka (LeRoi Jones), whose Black Community Development program in Newark is patterned on US. Though he uses violent language ("When it's 'burn,' let's see how much you can burn. When it's 'kill,' let's see how much you can kill."), and though he adopts a somewhat fearsome pose (shaven head, Genghis Khan mustache, dark glasses, and armed guards), Karenga is credited with a major role in keeping Los Angeles calm after the King assassination, and his aim has been described by a black lawyer "to exploit the fear of violence without actually using it." Played key role in formation of the Black Congress in 1967, an umbrella organization of black groups in Los Angeles, including moderates and militants, which sponsors supplemental schooling for ghetto children, cooperative food stores, etc. Karenga has also had private meetings with Governor Reagan and Los Angeles police chiefs. Former chief Reddin has praised Karenga's peacekeeping efforts. Motto of Karenga's organization is: "Anywhere we are, US is." But actual membership is small, estimated at less than 100. There has been conflict between US and Black Panthers, and when two members of the Panthers were shot dead at UCLA meeting on black studies January 23, 1969, the Panther group accused US of the assassinations. Three members of US were later convicted of the killings and sentenced to life imprisonment, September 17, 1969. In the late 1960s, he instituted *Kwanza*, a seven-day holiday beginning December 26 because black people had no holiday of their own. The *Kwanza* (which means "first fruits" in Swahili) celebration has its roots in traditional African harvest festivals and while it is not to replace Christmas, it is designed to set aside a special time of the year for blacks to reaffirm themselves to the commitment of liberation of their people. Currently serving a one-to-ten-year sentence in the California State Penitentiary for torturing two women members of US he said were plotting against him in 1971. Karenga was born Ronald Everett in 1943, the youngest of 14 children of a Baptist minister. Received an M.A. in political science at University of California at Los Angeles and was first black elected president of the

student body at California Junior College. Says he switched from moderate to militant after Watts riots in 1965, when he took the Swahili name of Karenga and formed US. Married, three children.

NICHOLAS deB KATZENBACH

With the Department of Justice from 1961–1966, first as assistant attorney general, then attorney general (1965–1966). During his time in the department, he faced Governor George Wallace on the steps of the University of Mississippi with James Meredith in 1962 and helped draft and steer through the Civil Rights Act of 1964, and the Voting Rights Act of 1965. In 1966 he was switched by President Johnson from the justice department to the state department as undersecretary of state, a position he held until January 1969. Currently a vice-president and general counsel and director of IBM. A white man, he was born in 1922 in Philadelphia. Graduated from Phillips Exeter Academy (1939), Princeton University (1945), and Yale University (1947) LL.B. A Rhodes Scholar (1947–1949) at Balliol College, Oxford. Admitted to the New Jersey bar 1950; Connecticut bar 1955, and New York bar 1972. Worked for the firm of Katzenbach, Gildea and Rudner in Trenton and taught law at the University of Chicago and Yale Law School until joining the justice department. Married the former Lydia King Philips Stokes in 1946, four children.

CORETTA SCOTT KING

Widow of Dr. Martin Luther King, Jr. Since his death has emerged as an eloquent speaker and internationally recognized public figure in her own right. In January 1969, announced plans for a Martin Luther King memorial, and two years later the Martin Luther King, Jr. Center for Nonviolent Social Change, a family-sanctioned project, was opened. The center has a collection of documents and tapes as well as some 3,000 books on the civil rights movement dating back to 1954. From the beginning the center has been a bone of contention between Mrs. King, its founder and president, and current Southern Christian Leadership Conference (SCLC) head Ralph Abernathy, who said one of the reasons that SCLC was in such poor financial shape was because Mrs. King was unwilling to share monies she had received for the center with SCLC. In 1973 Mrs. King compared the movement to bringing up a child and feels that it has come full circle and is returning to the philosophy of nonviolence and cooperation that her late husband advocated. In 1969, she traveled to India to receive Nehru Award for international understanding, in behalf of her husband. Received further awards in Italy, where she met with Pope Paul VI. In London, in March 1969, became first woman ever to preach in St. Paul's Cathedral, where she called for "a new ministry of conciliation." In April 1969, led 2,000-strong march through streets of Charleston, South Carolina, in support of striking hospital workers. In February 1969, conferred with Henry Kissinger at White House as representative of antiwar group. Gallup Poll (February 1, 1969) placed her fourth on list of nation's most admired women (after Mrs. Ethel Kennedy, Mrs. Rose Kennedy, and Mrs. Mamie Eisenhower), and she was named Woman of the Year, 1968, by the National Association of Television and Radio Announcers. As principal speaker at Poor People's Solidarity Day in Washington, June 19, 1968, appealed to women of America to unite "and form a solid block of woman power to fight the three great evils of racism, poverty and war."

Born in Heiberger, Alabama, April 27, 1927. In 1945, she became one of the first black students accepted at Antioch College in Ohio, where she majored in education and music. Graduating in 1951, she went on to the New England Conservatory of Music in Boston, where she studied voice. While there, she met King, who was doing graduate work in philosophy at Boston University. They were married June 18, 1953, after which she gave up her plans for a singing career to help her husband. In 1954 they moved to Montgomery, Alabama, where King had been appointed a Baptist pastor—and the following year became nationally known for leading the Montgomery bus boycott. In the ensuing years, she participated in marches, meetings, etc., with her husband, and gave more than 30 "freedom concerts" to raise funds for SCLC. She has written a biography of her husband, *My Life with Martin Luther King, Jr.*, published by Holt, Rinehart & Winston in September, 1969. She lives in Atlanta with her four children: Yolanda Denise ("Yoki"), born 1955; Martin Luther, III, born 1957; Dexter Scott, 1961; Bernice Albertine, 1963.

EARTHA KITT

Renowned "down-to-Eartha" singer, she has been an outspoken critic of war in Vietnam. Made her feelings known to Mrs. Lyndon Johnson (then the First Lady) at a White House luncheon in January 1968, saying that the war was having a demoralizing effect on the nation's youth. "I got 5,000 letters about that," she said, "only seven were critical." Was a seamstress, dancer, and Parisian torcher, before capsizing Broadway (in *New Faces of 1952* with her show-stopping rendition of "Monotonous") and Hollywood in *Anna Lucasta*, 1958. Author of *Thursday's Child* (1956) and *A Tart Is Not a Sweet*. Born January 26, 1928, divorced, one daughter.

WILLIAM M. KUNSTLER

Flamboyant defense counsel in the 1969 Chicago Seven conspiracy trial, whose conduct in court and frequent clashes with Judge Julius Hoffman made him a hero among students and radicals, a controversial figure within the legal profession, and the recipient of a four-year, 13-day jail sentence for contempt of court, believed to be the longest sentence for contempt ever imposed on an American lawyer. Kunstler said that the Chicago trial marked the first time in his life that he had openly disobeyed the court.

Active involvement of Kunstler, a white man, in civil rights dates from 1961, when he witnessed the arrest of five Freedom Riders at a lunch counter in Jackson, Mississippi. Describing the incident in his autobiography, published in 1966, he wrote: "The sight of five frightened young people taught me what I had never known before—that only by personal involvement can one justify his existence." In the years following, Kunstler increasingly ignored his private practice in New York to devote himself to civil rights cases, usually without a fee. His clients included Martin Luther King, Jr., Stokely Carmichael, Adam Clayton Powell, Malcolm X, and H. Rap Brown (in 1971 defended Brown again for holding up a New York nightclub). He appeared for the defense of numerous Black Panthers and also represented pacifists, draft protesters, school desegregation litigants, students and teachers involved in campus disorders and free speech issues. In 1966, Kunstler helped found a New York group, the Law Center for Constitutional Rights, to provide legal and financial help in cases involving personal rights, and now maintains his office at the center. He reportedly helped to raise $200,000 for the defense of the Chicago conspiracy defendants, in which his own services were given free. A black militant reportedly described him as "the blackest white man I ever saw," and in 1969, *Life* magazine termed him "the most sought-after civil rights lawyer in the country." However, U.S. Attorney Thomas Foran, chief prosecutor in the Chicago conspiracy trial, called Kunstler "incredibly unprofessional." Judge Julius Hoffman sentenced Kunstler to four years and 13 days on 24 counts of contempt of court, February 15, 1970. The contempt trial finally came to court October 28, 1973, in Federal District Court in Chicago. An attempt by New York Republican Senator James Buckley to have him disbarred for his "contemptuous attitude toward the court" in the Chicago Seven conspiracy trial was rejected by the Association of the Bar of the City of New York in 1971.

On the violence in the movement Kunstler said in 1972 "I, myself, don't think the public really believes anymore that violence ever was the movement's aim, although they probably used to. We have done that much. All the great acquittals we have had—victory after victory in court and not a single Black Panther convicted, for example—is showing the people that the fear of violence was just hysteria."

Kunstler has written ten books, mostly legal, but one is an account of the Hall-Mills murder case of the 1920s, for which film rights have been sold. Born July 7, 1919, in New York City, the son of a physician, Kunstler graduated from Yale in 1941, and served in the Pacific in World War II, being awarded the Bronze Star. He graduated from Columbia University Law School in 1949, and began a law firm with his younger brother, Michael. In the early 1950s, he began taking cases from the American Civil Liberties Union. He is a member of the bars of New York, District of Columbia, U.S. Supreme Court, U.S. Court of Military Appeals, and the U.S. District Courts for the Southern and Eastern Districts of New York. He married in 1942 the former Lotte Rosenberger, two daughters. Home is in Mamaroneck, New York. Office: 370 Lexington Avenue, New York, N.Y. 10017.

LEADERSHIP CONFERENCE ON CIVIL RIGHTS
Founded in 1949, a coalition of 130 national groups working for enactment and enforcement of effective civil rights and social welfare legislation. In March 1970 launched a successful lobbying campaign against Senate confirmation of Judge G. Harrold Carswell for Supreme Court justice. To affiliate with the con-

ference, a group must be a nonpartisan, national organization with a constituency. Issues a regular newsletter. Officers are chairman, Roy Wilkins; legislative
chairman, Clarence Mitchell; secretary, Arnold Aronson; counsel, Joseph L.
Rauh, Jr.; director of Washington office, Marvin Caplan; executive assistant,
Yvonne Price. Office: 2027 Massachusetts Avenue, N.W., Washington, D.C. *See
also:* CLARENCE MITCHELL, JOSEPH L. RAUH, JR., ROY WILKINS.

LEGAL DEFENSE AND EDUCATIONAL FUND, INC. (LDF)

Established in 1939 as an independent agency of the NAACP. Serves as legal arm
of entire civil rights movement. Completely separate and distinct from the parent organization although NAACP is retained in the official name of the fund.
In 1954, won the historic court ruling Brown v. the Board of Education, making
segregation of blacks in schools unconstitutional. Still mainly concerned with
school desegregation. At its nineteenth anniversary celebration in May 1973,
Director Jack Greenberg noted that the Nixon administration, unlike its four
predecessors, had gone to court in 13 cases to oppose the Fund on desegregation. "As integration has approached becoming a reality," Greenberg said,
"many fears, many anxieties, many genuine problems have been turned against
it." Launched a new program in 1973 to broaden employment goals and opportunities for black women through research, community action, and litigation.
Funded by Ford Foundation grants and public contributions. Has 26 full-time
staff lawyers; director-counsel is Jack Greenberg. Office: 10 Columbus Circle,
New York, N.Y. 10019. *See also:* JACK GREENBERG.

JULIUS LESTER

Author, teacher, and broadcaster. Joined Student National Coordinating Committee in 1966 as director of photo department; later became a field secretary
but resigned before demise of the organization. Since July 1968, has hosted a
weekly radio program on WBAI-FM in New York called "The Great Proletarian
Cultural Revolution." Also teaches a course in black history at the New School
for Social Research. His first book, *Look Out, Whitey! Black Power's Gon' Get
Your Mama!*, published in 1968 (Dial Press), is described as a personal interpretation of black power. Also wrote *To Be a Slave* (1968), *Search for the New
Land: History as Subjective Experience*, published October 1969, and in 1971
published *Two Love Stories.* Is currently working on his autobiography. "I think
people's attitudes have hardened," he said in a recent interview, "both blacks
and whites attitudes have hardened. Sometimes you have to go back before
you go forward. The danger in going back is that you can get stuck there. At the
present moment, I see it as a phase of retrogression, rather than any qualitative,
psychological change." Born in St. Louis, Missouri, in 1939. Graduated from Fisk
University in 1960. Married, two children.

JOHN LEWIS

National chairman of Student National Coordinating Committee (SNCC), 1963-
1966. A Baptist, he was one of the founders of SNCC in 1960, and one of the first

to sit-in and make freedom rides. Jailed a total of 40 times. In 1966, when SNCC became more militant and the radical elements began to take over, he was replaced as chairman by Stokely Carmichael, who made "black power" the rallying cry. Resigned from the organization reportedly because he felt it was departing from its principles of nonviolence. At time of leaving SNCC, he stated that the organization had 50 members and offices in New York, Atlanta, Washington, and San Francisco. After working with the Field Foundation in New York (1966–1967), returned to the South and in 1967 became director of community organization projects for the Southern Regional Council in Atlanta, Georgia. Was named director of Council's Voter Education Project Inc. (VEP), March 1970, a program Lewis envisioned as the logical extension of the movement. In 1973 VEP was considered one of the major groups responsible for registering 3.5 million black voters in the 11 southern states. "What's happening," he said in a *New York Times* interview (November 18, 1973), is "a revolution—not as dramatic as the sixties but registration of more than three and a half million black voters, larger numbers of elected officials [over 1,000] and a new breed of white politician ... within the next eight to 10 years, blacks are going to be elected to some of the highest offices." Was selected by *Ebony* magazine one of the nation's most influential blacks in 1971. Married to the former Lillian Miles, curator of the Negro Collection at the Atlanta University Library. *See also:* SOUTHERN REGIONAL COUNCIL.

C. ERIC LINCOLN

Chairman of the Department of Religious Studies (professor of religion and sociology) at Fisk University in Nashville since 1973. Formerly professor of sociology and religion at the Union Theological Seminary in New York City (1967–1973). Is also adjunct professor of ethics and society at Vanderbilt University's School of Divinity. Born in Athens, Alabama, June 23, 1924. Holds an A.B. from LeMoyne (1947), M.A. from Fisk University (1954), a Ph.D. from Boston University (1960). Lectures frequently across the country as well as abroad. The author of several books including *A Profile of Martin Luther King*, and *The New Blacks and The Black Estate*, both published in 1969, and *Black Muslims in America*, 1961, revised in 1973. He is also a published poet. He is the recipient of some 22 awards and honors from universities and foundations, and is on the board of directors of Boston University, the American Forum of African Study, Martin Luther King Memorial, and the Black Academy of Arts and Letters. Married to the former Lucy Cook, four children.

ROBERT LUCAS

Chairman of the board of the Kenwood-Oakland Community Organization (KOCO), a social service organization whose purpose is "to raise the lifestyle in the area," one of Chicago's worst ghettos. Concentrates on housing, health, education, welfare, and mental health. Has a leadership training program supported in part by the Rockefeller Foundation. Employs 100 people and claims a membership of 1,000. Funded by local businesses, private contributions and foundations. In the late 1960s, Lucas was national chairman of the Black Liberation Alliance, a Chicago-based militant group claiming a national membership of 10,000, with 800 members in the Chicago area, forming part of the Chicago Coalition for United Community Action. Lucas achieved national prominence in September 1966, when as chairman of the Chicago chapter of the Congress of Racial Equality (CORE) he led 250 civil rights marchers through the tense all-white suburb of Cicero. The previous year, 1965, he led several marches protesting de facto school segregation and was one of several CORE members arrested for chaining themselves to the Alabama State exhibit at the Chicago boat show.

Born 1924 in Roncevert, West Virginia, Lucas served with the United States Army in Europe in World War II and then settled in Chicago, where he completed his high school education and joined the post office in 1948. In March 1966, he led a demonstration protesting discrimination in promotions at the post office. He is married, one son.

AUTHERINE LUCY

The first black to try to desegregate the University of Alabama in 1956, seven years before Vivian Malone and James A. Hood accomplished it. Enrolled in Mills College in Tuscaloosa, part of the University of Alabama, in 1953. After a three and a half year court fight—masterminded and argued before the Supreme Court by present Supreme Court Justice Thurgood Marshall, then a lawyer for the NAACP—won her legal right to register. At 26 and already a college graduate, her registration caused a series of violent outbursts in the white community and marked the first time federal and state law agencies clashed over the issue of school segregation. Staying only a few weeks, she withdrew and sued the university for conspiracy for barring her from the school dormitories. Born in 1930, she married Rev. Hugh C. Foster in 1956. Currently lives in Shreveport, Louisiana, where she teaches grammar school. Three children. Has not been active in civil rights since 1956 and says she has no plans in that direction.

PETER MacDONALD

Chairman of the 129,000 member Navajo nation elected to a four-year term November 15, 1970. The Navajo nation, whose sovereignty is guaranteed by a treaty with the United States government, is the largest of the American Indian tribes. The Navajo reservation sprawls over 25,000 miles of parts of New Mexico, Arizona, and Utah. Most of its members live on or near the reservation with about 2,000 others living in California. In running the tribal government, MacDonald watches over $200 million of assets and some $67 million in cash deposits and investments. Before becoming tribal chairman, was director of management methods and procurements for the tribe (1964–1966) and after that headed the office of Navajo Economic Opportunity until he became tribal head. After Bureau of Indian Affairs (BIA) shakeup in 1971, headed a group of tribal chiefs who went to Washington in January 1972 to request that BIA be removed from the Department of the Interior and put into "receivership" in the White House. Born 1929 in Teec Nos Pos, in the northern part of the reservation, he quit the sixth grade to enlist in the Marines in World War II. After being discharged, took an electrician's course under the G.I. Bill, but soon discovered he needed a degree to get ahead. At 20 went back to school and in one year received a high school diploma from an Indian school. Then attended junior college until his money ran out but finished—with the help of a Navajo scholarship—graduating from the University of Oklahoma with an engineering degree in 1957. Worked as a project engineer on a Polaris missile guidance system at Hughes Aircraft in California from 1958 until 1964. Married to an Oklahoma Comanche, two children. See also: BUREAU OF INDIAN AFFAIRS.

VIVIAN MALONE
Desegregated the University of Alabama in 1963. On June 11 of that year, Governor George Wallace of Alabama carried out a 1962 campaign promise to prevent integration of Alabama schools, and confronted Deputy Attorney General Nicholas Katzenbach at the university's Foster Hall to bar her and James Hood from registering. In spite of rioting and personal harassment, she became the first black to graduate from Alabama (1965). Worked for the Civil Rights Division of the justice department after graduation, then joined the Veterans Administration, working in both Atlanta and Washington. Currently Director of Civil Rights and Urban Affairs for the Environmental Protection Agency in Atlanta. Born 1942. Married MacArthur Jones, a teacher (September 3, 1966), one son.

BURKE MARSHALL
Assistant attorney general for Civil Rights Division of the Department of Justice from 1961 to 1964. Presently is deputy dean of the Yale Law School. In 1972 was a member of the New York State Commission for Attica prison hearings. Was Robert Kennedy's leading white authority on matters involving civil rights. Kennedy said of him: "he has the world's best judgment on anything." Born on October 1, 1922, in Plainfield, New Jersey, he graduated from Phillips Exeter Academy in 1940, from Yale University in 1943, and received LL.B. from the same university in 1951. Was admitted to the Washington, D.C., bar in 1951 and practiced law as a member of the firm of Covington and Burling until 1961. Married to the former Violet Person in 1946, three children.

THURGOOD MARSHALL
First black Supreme Court justice in United States history. Was appointed by President Johnson in 1968. A friend says of him, "Thurgood feels that the Constitution is a living document that has to be viewed in terms of today but I don't believe he wants to rewrite it. He's more of a legal conservative than one might assume from his civil rights and civil liberties advocacy." In a speech in Abidjan, Ivory Coast, in the fall of 1973 said of the Constitution: "My country's constitution is, in my judgment, a remarkable work—remarkable in its complexity, in

its grandeur of its design, in its nobility of purpose. Yet sometimes, I think that the whole thrust of the document can be summarized in one, short sentence: people are people." Admitted to the Maryland bar in 1933, he joined the NAACP the same year as special counsel and began a career of fighting for civil rights in the courts. Won 29 of the 32 cases he argued before the Supreme Court, including the landmark 1954 decision on school desegregation. In 1956, helped integrate the University of Alabama. In 1957, was at Central High School in Little Rock, Arkansas. *Newsweek* magazine said of him "in three decades he has probably done more to transform the life of his people than any Negro today." Born in Baltimore July 2, 1908, he received an A.B. degree from Lincoln University (1930), and LL.B. from Howard University (1933). Did postgraduate work in Syracuse at the School of Social Research and at the University of Liberia. Married, two children.

THOMAS W. MATTHEW

Described as "perhaps the nation's number one practitioner of black economic power," Matthew is the founder and president of the black self-help group called NEGRO (National Economic Growth and Reconstruction Organization), which runs a string of self-supporting businesses in New York, Pittsburgh, Watts, and other cities. A successful neurosurgeon who gave up a reputed $100,000-a-year private practice to launch NEGRO, Matthew is a foe of handouts and welfare programs, which he believes perpetuate the dependency of blacks. Equally a foe of federal and state taxes on his projects which, he says, in fact save taxpayers' money by getting people off the relief rolls. Convicted October 2, 1969, for failure to pay 1968 income taxes, claiming he wanted to donate his personal resources to NEGRO. After serving 59 days in jail had his sentence commuted by President Nixon in his first act of executive clemency (January 1970). In February 1970, Matthew announced his support of Judge G. Harrold Carswell for the Supreme Court, and his organization placed a full-page advertisement in *The New York Times* endorsing the nomination. Also endorsed New York conservative senatorial candidate James Buckley. In November 1973 was convicted on 71 counts of illegally diverting Medicaid funds intended for his Interfaith Hospital to two NEGRO companies—one a bus line, the other a factory—which Matthew claimed were used to provide employment for drug addicts and alcoholics following their treatment at Interfaith Hospital. On December 27, 1973 was sentenced to three years in prison for having misapplied more than $200,000 medical funds. Currently appealing the decision. In 1972 campaigned vigorously against scatter-site housing because he favored development of housing in black community. Born one of nine children of a New York City janitor in 1926, Matthew was the first black graduate of Manhattan College and the first black neurosurgeon to graduate from Harvard Medical Center. He is director of the Negro-run Interfaith Hospital in Jamaica, Queens. Married to the former Carol Lewis, five children. *See also*: NEGRO.

CARMAN R. MAYMI

Director of Labor Department's Woman's Bureau appointed by President Nixon in June 1973. Succeeded Elizabeth Duncan Koontz who resigned after the president's reelection and is currently assistant secretary for nutrition coordination for the state of North Carolina in Raleigh. Mrs. Maymi previously had been associate director of the bureau under Mrs. Koontz and before that a consultant to the bureau. Is responsible for formulating standards and policies which will promote the welfare of working women and their employment opportunities. Born March 17, 1938, in Puerto Rico but moved to Chicago when she was 15. Was educated at Chicago public schools and earned an A.B. from the University of DePaul and an M.A. in education from the University of Illinois. Divorced, one daughter. Office: Woman's Bureau, Department of Labor, Washington, D.C. 20210.

RHODY ARNOLD McCOY, JR.

Past controversial administrator of New York City's experimental and troubled Ocean Hill-Brownsville school district, which was established in 1967 as an effort to provide effective education for an underprivileged area and to encourage community involvement. The community governing board's attempt to remove several white teachers led to teacher walkouts, pupil boycotts, physical clashes, and eventually a city-wide teachers' strike which closed all New York City public schools for three months in the fall of 1968. In 1969, the district opposed a decentralization bill passed by New York state to phase out the experimental school districts. In September 1969, he urged that the district's programs, which had been criticized as "questionable" by the United Federation of Teachers, be evaluated by a team of independent educators from outside the city school system. A group of parents in November 1969 called for McCoy's dismissal because of his "dictatorial" methods. In July 1970, the school district became part of newly formed District 23 and McCoy was forced to resign. In 1970 was considered for superintendent of schools in Washington, D.C., but was found unacceptable by the Board of Education which alleged that he did not measure up to the established criteria. Currently, associate professor of the School of Education at the University of Massachusetts at Amherst (since 1971). On July 1, 1973, became director of the Committee for Collegiate Education of Black Students at the university—a body that recruits minority students and provides them with supportive services. Also heads the university Institute for Desegregation Resources. Still considered a controversial figure, and the dean of the School of Education, Dr. Dwight Allen, has said of McCoy that he is "more controversial than most faculty members because of his style ... [which] tends to be one of trying to raise issues and confronting them rather than negotiating or compromising" (*New York Times*, June 18, 1973).
   Born in Washington, D.C., January 16, 1923. Graduated from Howard University in 1947 and received his M.A. from New York University in 1949, after

which he became a teacher in the city's public school system. Became a principal in 1965 and administrator of the Ocean Hill-Brownsville district in 1968. Married, seven children.

FLOYD B. McKISSICK

Joined Congress of Racial Equality (CORE) in the early 1960s and succeeded James Farmer as national director in 1966. Embraced the concept of "black power" the same year. Has said, "as long as the white man has all the power and money, nothing will happen because we have nothing. The only way to achieve meaningful change is to take power." In 1967, took a leave of absence from CORE to work on his cities projects—a program to prepare for the rise of blacks to positions of civic, political, and economic responsibilites in cities where they will soon be the majority. He resigned from CORE in 1968 to devote himself full-time to black economic power. One of his projects is to build a new city in North Carolina called "Soul City." The "new town," which McKissick expects to take 20 years to complete, would be open to all races. In 1969 bought over 1,800 acres in Warren County, North Carolina, for a reputed $500,000. He intends to set up small industries in the city and train people to work in them. In 1972, the Department of Housing and Urban Development announced it would put up a $14 million federal guarantee for Soul City bonds. "The roots of the urban crisis," McKissick insists, "are in the migratory pattern of rural people seeking to leave areas of economic and racial oppression. So in building this new city in a rural area, we help solve this." In 1972 endorsed Richard Nixon for reelection to presidency and encouraged blacks to get into the Republican party to reform it. Author of *Three-Fifths of a Man* (published by Macmillan in August 1969), which focuses on black economic equality through a combination of constitutional rights and black nationalism. McKissick denounced the war in Vietnam, decrying "black men going over to Vietnam and dying for something they don't have a right for here." Born in Asheville, North Carolina, March 9, 1922, he was reared with three sisters. Did undergraduate work at Morehouse and North Carolina Colleges. Graduated from University of North Carolina Law School. Married to the former Evelyn Williams, four children.

ARTHUR McZIER

Assistant administrator of Small Business Administration's Minority Enterprise Program since 1968. Responsible for establishing Operation Business Mainstream, May 1969, to coordinate agency's various programs and services for minority enterprises, particularly in ghetto areas. Before joining the government in 1968, McZier was a marketing analyst for the Ford Motor Co. Born Atlanta, 1935, he attended Loyola University on an athletic scholarship and graduated in business management, 1959. In the same year he was all-star basketball player, captain of Loyola team, and named "most valuable player" and "athlete of the year."

JAMES H. MEREDITH

Desegregated the University of Mississippi in 1962. In June of that year, the United States Court of Appeals ruled that Meredith's application for enrollment to "Ole Miss" had been rejected solely on racial grounds and ordered that he be admitted. When he entered the university, he underwent a grueling ten-day ordeal, during which there were riots, and federal troops accompanied him everywhere. Made the decision to desegregate "Ole Miss" while attending Jackson State College in Mississippi. He then asked help from NAACP and Medgar Evers assisted him. "Nobody handpicked me. I made the decision myself. I paid my own tuition." (He later broke with NAACP in 1963.) Considered a loner, an idealist who goes his own way as he sees it. While living in New York became a Harlem landlord and businessman, who according to *The New York Times*, May 10, 1969, experienced difficulties with his tenants and his enterprises because of a series of bad breaks and mismanagements. Was convicted on August 9, 1969 (and spent two days in jail) for harassing tenants in the 34-family apartment house in the Bronx which he bought in December 1967. Tenants charged that he cut off hot water, did not clean halls, or fix the plumbing and the elevator, or make other repairs. In the 17 months as owner claimed he lost $20,000. In May 1971, after six years of living in the North, moved to Jackson, Mississippi, because "on a person-to-person, day-to-day basis the South is a more livable place for blacks," adding that the racial atmosphere in the South was "significantly better" than it was a decade ago and he wanted to give his wife and children a "better quality of life." Said that his goal in life had changed in recent years and so had the civil rights movement, "I don't think anybody cares much anymore about the black thing—whether you got a black mayor or a black police chief just isn't relevant anymore." Claimed since business controls politics, he was going to work to get control over business. In July 1969, staged a cross-country walk from Chicago to New York, to "build and promote Negro pride and positive goals in the black community." On June 5, 1966 went on his now historic 220-mile march from Memphis to Jackson to encourage voter registration. Was shot in the back June 6, and hospitalized. Returned to march June 24 and attended the windup rally in Jackson, June 26. Meredith was born in Kosciusko, Mississippi, June 25, 1933, one of ten children. Attended high school in Florida and spent six years in the army. Graduated from Columbia Law School. On March 7, 1967, announced his intention to run against Adam Clayton Powell for his congressional seat, but withdrew on March 13, after severe criticism from other black leaders. In February 1972 entered the race as a Republican for Senate seat held by James Eastland (D-Miss) but lost. Author of *Three Years in Mississippi*, published in 1966. Married to the former Mary June Wiggins, three sons.

RALPH H. METCALFE

Democratic representative of 412,000 residents of Chicago's black first district. Elected to Congress in 1970 to fill the seat of the late William L. Dawson and as a result is the city's most prominent office holder. Has been in Democratic politics since the 1930's working his way up to Ward Committeeman (1952-55) and finally to alderman (1955-71) before going to Congress. Until 1972 considered close to Chicago's Mayor Daley but broke openly with him that year over the issue of police brutality. The break stemmed from a 1969 incident in which two Black Panther leaders were killed in a police raid authorized by the then State's Attorney, Edward Hanrahan. Hanrahan was subsequently indicted but quietly re-instated by Daley but after loud protests from black leaders, was eventually dumped. This and other "run-ins" between police and responsible blacks finally caused an outraged black community to form a coalition to protest, and also to set up a "program of survival for our people" choosing Metcalfe as their spokesman. (Other members of the coalition included Rev. Jesse L. Jackson and most of the prominent black leaders.) Is a member of the Congressional Black Caucus and serves on the Interstate and Foreign Commerce Committees as well as the Merchant Marine and Fisheries Committee. A former Olympic track star and member of the U.S. Olympic teams of 1932 and 1936, he is married to the former Madalynne Fay Young (1947), one son. Born on June 29, 1910 in Atlanta, Georgia.

MEXICAN-AMERICAN LEGAL DEFENSE AND EDUCATIONAL FUND
Formed in San Antonio, Texas, in 1968, by a group of Mexican-American lawyers to provide legal representation for poor *chicanos*. Modeled after the NAACP legal fund and financed by a $2.2 million Ford Foundation grant for eight years of operation. By April 1970, the fund claimed to be involved in 155 cases affecting 100,000 *chicanos* from Texas to California. However, disagreement was reported between executive director Pete Tijerina (no relation to Reies Tijerina), a San Antonio lawyer, and the Ford Foundation, which wanted to move the fund's headquarters to New York or Washington to give it a national image. Tijerina argued that most of the nation's five million *chicanos* were in the Southwest, and said he would return to private practice if the fund's headquarters were moved. In 1970 it was decided to move national headquarters to San Francisco and Tijerina resigned. Has regional offices in Denver, Albuquerque, San Antonio, and Los Angeles. Vilma S. Martinez is general counsel elected December 1973 to a three-year term. Headquarters: 145 Ninth Street, San Francisco, Cal. 94103.

MISSISSIPPI FREEDOM DEMOCRATIC PARTY
A predominantly black group that made headlines by challenging the regular Mississippi delegation at the 1964 Democratic National Convention, charging that the all-white slate did not adequately represent blacks. Under a compromise settlement by the Credentials Committee, the Freedom delegates received two seats as special delegates. At the 1968 Democratic convention, the Freedom Democrats formed part of a coalition of black and liberal white groups, known as the Loyal Democrats of Mississippi, which this time successfully barred the state's all-white regular delegation from being seated. The biracial coalition based their argument before the Credentials Committee on the

ground that discrimination by whites on the precinct level prevented blacks from being selected as delegates to the county convention. Since the county convention chose the delegates to the state convention, which in turn named the delegates to the national convention, Mississippi's regular delegation, it was argued, failed to meet national standards that would assure full participation of blacks in the political process. The Loyal Democrats were a coalition of the state branch of the NAACP, the Freedom Democratic party, the state's Young Democrats, the Prince Hall Masons, the Mississippi Teachers Association, and the state AFL-CIO. The chairman was Dr. Aaron E. Henry, state chairman of the NAACP; vice-chairman was Hodding Carter III, white publisher of the *Delta Democrat-Times* in Greenville, Mississippi, and chairman of the state's Young Democrats; Charles Evers was the campaign coordinator. In 1972, the Freedom Democrats supported Charles Evers in his attempt to run for governor—the first black candidate in the 154-year history of Mississippi. Are still involved with grassroots politics, and Fannie Lou Hamer, vice-chairman of the group, says "that's what politics is all about—getting the masses involved." Party chairman: Al Robes.

CLARENCE M. MITCHELL, JR.

Director of the Washington bureau of the NAACP since 1950 and as chief NAACP lobbyist closely involved with all civil rights legislation of recent years. "All Americans are in debt to him," commented *Washington Post* after passage of 1968 open housing bill. Was close to President Johnson. Outspokenly out of sympathy with black nationalists and rioters, whom he has denounced as "hoodlums." Critical of media for publicity given to minority dissidents. As legislative chairman of Leadership Conference on Civil Rights was one of the leaders responsible for the defeat of the nominations of Judges Clement Haynsworth and G. Harrold Carswell to the Supreme Court of the United States in 1971. The year before helped lead the successful fight to extend the Voting Rights Act's ban on literacy tests for an additional five years. Former newspaperman in Baltimore, where he was born March 9, 1911. Received an A.B. degree from Lincoln University in Pennsylvania and did graduate work at Atlanta University and the University of Minnesota. Received LL.D. from the University of Maryland. Married to the former Juanita Jackson, a lawyer, four children. Office: Congressional Building, 422 First Street, S.E., Washington, D.C. 20003.

PARREN J. MITCHELL

Elected to Congress in 1970 representing some 400,000 blacks and whites from Baltimore's Seventh Congressional District. A former sociology professor, headed the Community Action of Baltimore and the Maryland Commission of Interracial Problems and Relations before going to Congress. Serves on the Banking and Currency Committee and the Permanent Select Committee on Small Business. Also a member of the Congressional Black Caucus. Born April 29, 1922, in Baltimore, Maryland.

JOSEPH M. MONTOYA
Senator (D-N. Mex.) since 1965 and only *chicano* currently serving in the U.S. Senate. Elected first to House of Representatives in 1957 and served four terms in the lower house before being appointed to the Senate by Governor Ed Mecham in 1964 following the death of Dennis Chavez. Ran for his first full term in the Senate in 1965 and was reelected in 1970. In 1969 was responsible for the Cabinet Committee on Opportunities for Spanish-Speaking Americans which advises federal departments on the needs of Spanish-Americans, and in 1973 authored the Bilingual Courts Act which provides bilingual proceedings in certain district courts (it's still pending). Made headlines in 1973 as a member of the Senate Select Committee on Campaign Activities, the committee involved in investigating the Watergate inquiry. Born September 24, 1915, in Pena Blanca, New Mexico. Worked his way through school, graduating from Regis College (1934) and Georgetown University Law School (1938). Entered politics in 1936, being elected to New Mexico's House of Representatives while still a law student. Married to the former Della Romero (1940), three children.

CECIL B. MOORE
Controversial Philadelphia civil rights leader and past president of the Philadelphia chapter of the NAACP, 1962-68, during which period the chapter tripled its registration to upwards of 30,000. A lawyer, he has twice run for Congress and lost both times. Born in West Virginia and graduated from Bluefield College there. Holds a law degree from Temple University (1953). He joined the marine corps during World War II and stayed in the service for nine years. Came under investigation by the Bar Association of Pennsylvania for making anti-semitic remarks in 1967 and was subsequently suspended from his job with the NAACP the next year. Currently practicing law privately. Office: Room 503, Dewey Building, 1 North 13th Street, Philadelphia, Pa. 19107.

CHARLES MORGAN, JR.
White lawyer who is currently director of American Civil Liberties Union's (ACLU) Washington national office. As director of ACLU's southern regional office in Atlanta from 1964 to 1972, was involved with civil rights legislation there and ACLU efforts to organize throughout the South. When he began there were two ACLU affiliates and 200 members; currently there are 11 affiliates and more than 22,000 members. As a young lawyer in Birmingham, Alabama, he received national attention in 1963 by publicly denouncing the white community for harboring extremists, following the bombing of a church in which four black children were killed. Has defended Julian Bond, Stokely Carmichael, H. Rap Brown, and Muhammad Ali (Cassius Clay), among others. Author, *A Time to Speak*, 1964, and numerous magazine articles. Born 1930. Graduated from University of Alabama, 1955. Serves on the board of directors of the Southern Christian Leadership Conference. Married to the former Camille Walpole, one son. Office: 410 First Street, S.E., Washington, D.C. 20003.

E. FREDERIC MORROW

First black to serve as executive assistant to the President (1955–1961) and author of *Black Man in the White House*. Presently a vice-president of the Bank of America in New York. Born in Hackensack, New Jersey, in 1910, and educated at public schools there. Graduated from Bowdoin College and Rutgers University Law School. Worked as field secretary for NAACP for five years and then joined the Public Affairs Department of CBS. In 1952, he joined the late General Eisenhower's presidential campaign as adviser and administrative assistant. He became administrative assistant to the secretary of commerce after Eisenhower's election and in 1955 went to the White House. In 1961 he became vice-president of the African-American Institute in New York and in 1964 joined the Bank of America. In 1967, he was made a full vice-president. Author of *Way Down South Up North?* published in 1973. Mr. Morrow is married to the former Catherine Gordon of Chicago. Office: 41 Broad Street, New York, N.Y. 10004.

CONSTANCE BAKER MOTLEY

First black woman to become federal judge (January 25, 1966), when she was named U.S. District Judge for Southern District of New York. An active Democrat, in 1965 was first woman (black or white) to hold office as borough president of Manhattan. State senator, 1964–1965. Assistant counsel, NAACP, and associate counsel for the NAACP Legal Defense Fund, 1947–1965. Born in New Haven, Connecticut, on September 14, 1921, she attended grammar and high schools there. Received a B.A. degree from New York University in 1943 and LL.B. from Columbia University Law School in 1946. Married to Joel Motley, real estate and insurance broker, one son.

MUHAMMAD ALI (Cassius Clay)

Undefeated former heavyweight boxing champion of the world, whose title was lifted by the World Boxing Association in 1967 because he refused to be drafted. Adopted Black Muslim faith and name Muhammad Ali in 1964, but was expelled by Muslims (for one year) in April 1969, following his announcement that he would return to boxing to pay off $300,000 worth of debts. His expulsion from the Black Muslims meant that he could no longer claim draft exemption status as a Black Muslim minister. He first refused to be drafted in 1965 and was convicted for draft evasion and sentenced to five years in jail in 1967. Ali appealed and in 1968 the conviction was upheld by the Fifth Circuit Court of Appeals which rejected his plea for exemption as a Black Muslim conscientious objector. In May 1969, a U.S. District Court judge in Houston set a hearing to determine if the 1967 conviction was based on evidence obtained by illegal government wiretapping. But in July 1969, the judge ruled that the government had not used wiretapping information in his conviction, and Ali was resentenced to the same five years and a $10,000 fine. On June 28, 1971, the U.S. Supreme Court reversed unanimously the draft-evasion conviction in an unsigned 8 to 0 decision. The Court held that the U.S. Justice Department had improperly intervened. The ordeal cost Ali $150,000 in legal fees and in-calculable stress and strain according to his attorney Chauncey Eskridge of Chicago.

Born in Louisville, Kentucky, in 1942, he was educated in public schools there. First fought at the age of 12, and at 18 (1960) had fought 108 amateur bouts, losing only eight. Won an Olympic Gold Medal (1960) in Rome and turned professional. Defeated Sonny Liston (1964) in Miami to become heavy-weight champion of the world, and again beat Liston in Lewiston, Maine (1965). Also successfully defended his title against Floyd Patterson (1965), George Chuvalo (1966), Henry Cooper (1966), Brian London (1966), Karl Mildenberger (1966), Cleveland Williams (1966), Ernie Terrell (1967), Zora Folley (1967). Married twice (presently to Belinda Boyd, August 18, 1967), three daughters.

ELIJAH MUHAMMAD
Leader of the Black Muslim movement since 1930. Born Elijah Poole in Sanderville, Georgia, October 10, 1897. One of 13 children, he is believed to have finished only the fourth or fifth grade in school. Left home at age 16, married Clara Evans and produced six sons and two daughters. Worked as a field hand and railroad laborer before moving to Detroit in 1923, where he worked for Chevrolet until 1929. When the Depression came, went on relief and met the founder of the Nation of Islam, W. D. Fard. In 1930 Muhammad took over leadership of the Black Muslims (Fard mysteriously disappeared in 1934), and changed his name from Poole to Muhammad. Embracing a doctrine which later became known as "black supremacy," he founded his Temple Number 1 in Detroit in 1931. Two years later, Muhammad was arrested by Detroit police for refusing to transfer his child from a Muslim school to a public school, and moved to Chicago. Jailed from 1942–1946 in Chicago by the FBI for draft-dodging during World War II. Once released, again began recruiting followers, and by 1959 he had 50 temples in 22 states. Over the years he has steered clear of publicity but in 1963, nation-wide publicity was unavoidable when Malcolm X, his right-hand man for many years, resigned from the Black Muslims. (Malcolm X was shot to death in 1965 in what many observers believe was a vendetta murder and Muhammad was forced to disavow publicly any involvement, although at least one of the men arrested was said to have been a Black Muslim enforcer.) In 1971 to inform the public more about organization's activities, instituted a series of radio broadcasts "to bring accurate information on the Honorable Elijah Muhammad and his program for survival of the black man in America." Muhammad has homes in both Chicago and Phoenix, Arizona. See also: BLACK MUSLIMS.

NATIONAL ALLIANCE OF BUSINESSMEN
Organization representing nation's business leaders, labor, and government conducts program to provide special training and jobs for hard-core unemployed, needy youth, Vietnam veterans, and ex-offenders. Formed in 1968 at the request of President Johnson and subsequently supported by President

Nixon. Has found jobs for more than 2.5 million people since it started. Program is known as JOBS—Job Opportunities in the Business Sector. National headquarters are in Washington and has over 100 branch offices across the country. Has a staff of 5,000, the majority of whom are business executives on loan and paid for by their companies for a period of three months to two years. Address: 1730 K Street, N.W., Washington, D.C. 20006.

NATIONAL ASSOCIATION FOR THE ADVANCEMENT
OF COLORED PEOPLE (NAACP)

Established in 1909 on the 100th anniversary of the birth of Abraham Lincoln. The organization was the outgrowth of and based on the principles of the Niagara Movement, the first black protest organization, which was founded in 1905 by W. E. B. DuBois. Largely the brainchild of William English Walling, a white Southerner who feared racists would carry "the race war to the North," Mary Ovington, a white newspaper reporter, and Dr. Henry Moskowitz, a New York social worker. Its purpose was to achieve by peaceful and lawful means equal citizenship rights for all Americans by eliminating segregation and discrimination in housing, employment, voting, schools, the courts, transportation and recreation. Since it was founded, the organization's scope has widened and gone into every phase of civil rights activity, its principal task now being the implementation of civil rights acts. Disassociated itself publicly, at its July 1966 national convention, from the "black power" concept of reaching its objectives. In 1969, launched nationwide campaigns for school desegregation, more jobs and training for blacks in the building industry, and abolition of housing discrimination, especially in suburbs.

In an unusual departure at its 1970 convention, NAACP chairman Bishop G. Spottswood denounced the Nixon administration as "anti-Negro." The NAACP continues to uphold its long-held principle of working toward integration. In May 1972 withdrew from the National Black Political Convention because of its separatist and nationalist bias but maintains a working relation with the group. In 1973, the Atlanta chapter challenged the national organization in an agreement it had reached with the Atlanta Board of Education which called for leaving 83 out of 141 of the city's schools virtually all black. National NAACP objected to the agreement because it would undermine the fights for desegregation which had been fought for the last 15 years in the courts and schools and was against the 1971 Supreme Court decision. The Atlanta chapter refused to back down and Lonnie King, the chapter's president, and its board of directors were ousted from the national organization (Newsweek, July 30, 1973).

Today, the NAACP is the oldest and largest civil rights organization, with an overall membership of 425,000 with 1,800 chapters, seven regional offices. Publishes monthly magazine, Crisis. Roy Wilkins is executive director. Headquarters: 1790 Broadway, New York, N.Y. 10019. See also: ROY WILKINS, LEONARD H. CARTER, RICHARD L. DOCKERY, (JAMES) CHARLES EVERS, HERBERT HILL, RUBY HURLEY, CLARENCE M. MITCHELL, JR., JULIUS E. WILLIAMS.

NATIONAL CONFERENCE OF BLACK LAWYERS

Created at a conference of lawyers and students in Chicago, June 1969, to establish "a permanent and on-going body of all black lawyers determined to join the black revolution and committed to taking all steps necessary to assist black people to attain the goals to which they are rightfully entitled by the most fundamental principles of law, morality, and justice." Temporary cochairman of the conference was Floyd B. McKissick. Most of the attending lawyers (some 4,000) were members of the National Bar Association (formed in the 1920s when the American Bar Association did not admit blacks). Organization functions as a bar association—conducts seminars for learning and development of skills—and also takes on cases dealing with civil rights and civil liberties such as the Angela Davis and H. Rap Brown cases. Currently involved with the Black Liberation Army case involving Joanne Chesimard and Clark Squires. Receives financial support from the Metropolitan Applied Research Center (MARC), membership dues, and foundation grants. Membership is 250 lawyers and 800 students. Director, Lennox S. Hinds. Office: 126 West 119th Street, New York, N.Y. 10026.

NATIONAL CONGRESS OF AMERICAN INDIANS (NCAI)

Founded in 1944. With a membership of 350 (including a large Alaskan native constituency) it represents 150 tribes and lobbies for Indian interests in Washington. President, Mel Tonasket, a Collville Indian from the state of Washington; executive director, Charles E. Trimble, a Sioux Indian. Headquarters: 1346 Connecticut Avenue, N.W., Washington, D.C. 20036.

NATIONAL COUNCIL OF NEGRO WOMEN, INC.

A charitable and educational organization with objectives of achieving equality of opportunity and eliminating prejudice and discrimination based on race, creed, color, sex, or national origin; reducing neighborhood tensions and fostering understanding and cooperation among people of different races, creeds, colors and backgrounds; strengthening family life; relieving human suffering among the aged and poverty stricken; combating juvenile delinquency; and educating the public generally to a sense of better citizenship. Has claimed membership of 3,850,000 in 25 national affiliates. Has 106 local offices in 40 states. Issues newsletters, press releases, has a quarterly publication and gives special reports on civil rights problems. National president: Miss Dorothy I. Height, who is also director of the Racial Justice Center of YWCA in the United States. Long active in the civil rights movement, she is currently a member of the USIA's Advisory Council for Minority Groups. Born in Richmond, Virginia, received a master's degree from New York University and from 1958 to 1968 was a member of the New York State Board of Social Welfare. In 1966 served on the Council to the White House Conference "To Fulfill These Rights" under President Lyndon Johnson. Office: 1346 Connecticut Avenue, N.W., Washington, D.C. 20036.

NEGRO (NATIONAL ECONOMIC GROWTH AND RECONSTRUCTION ORGANIZATION)

An economic self-help organization for blacks on welfare rolls, started in 1964 and incorporated in 1966. By 1969 employed more than 800 persons in more than 15 business enterprises in New York, Pittsburgh, and Watts. Financed through the sale of bonds, in denominations as small as 25 cents, NEGRO assets exceeded $3 million. Its businesses include an advertising agency, newspaper, chemical plant, clothing factory, bakery, laundry, bus lines, and a hospital. The hospital is the 160-bed Interfaith Hospital in Jamaica, Queens (New York), operated entirely by blacks and directed by neurosurgeon Dr. Thomas W. Matthew, founder and president of the self-help organization. He opposes increased welfare programs and guaranteed incomes as "guaranteed dependency" and instead urges the government and big business to make loans available to help blacks help themselves. Several thousand persons support NEGRO by the purchase of bonds and the organization's future plans include expansion into the construction industry. It has already carried out repairs and renovation of several buildings in Queens and Harlem. In April 1973 the organization's expansion and other plans came to a halt when Matthew was convicted on 71 counts of mishandling Medicaid funds. NEGRO had received, until this time, $8.2 million from Medicaid, $2.4 million in defense contracts, $227,000 from the Small Business Administration (SBA), $20,000 in grants from the Office of Economic Opportunity, and an estimated $1 million in welfare checks paid to his "patients" (*New York Times*, April 24, 1973). In the process the hospital was over-advanced $1.5 million by Medicaid, the factories defaulted on four SBA loans, and Dr. Matthew ran up a tax bill of some $200,000. The investigation into NEGRO's affairs began in 1972 after a narcotics outpatient had been shot and killed by an Interfaith hospital guard. *See also:* THOMAS W. MATTHEW.

NATIONAL WELFARE RIGHTS ORGANIZATION (NWRO)

One of the most militant civil rights organizations specializing in representing welfare recipients and deliberately shuns ideological issues such as black separatism. Membership originally depicted in 1969 as "an army of 30,000 angry welfare mothers." Mostly black, though open to all races. Founded in 1966, the organization now claims a membership of 125,000 in almost every state in the union and 800 chapters. Founded by former Congress of Racial Equality official George A. Wiley, who stepped down in January 1973 as director to form a new organization he called the Movement for Economic Justice but drowned in August of that year in a boating accident in Chesapeake Bay, Maryland. NWRO has staged demonstrations at city halls and welfare department offices. On May 25, 1969, broke into the convention of the National Conference on Social Welfare in New York, to demand $35,000 from convention registration fees "to help organize welfare recipients." In February 1969, the group's leaders met with Department of Health, Education and Welfare (HEW) Secretary Robert Finch, who described them as "an important constituency of HEW." He promised to investigate their charges that the department's policies were being "flagrantly violated" in many areas. The organization adopted a more militant program at its 1969 convention, to fight for $5,500 guaranteed annual income for family of four and to pressure welfare agencies across the country for supplementary payments for children's clothing. In June 1970, some 500 members stormed city welfare offices in Washington, D.C., demanding money to buy furniture. Damage to the offices was estimated at $5,000. A welfare official commented that the rights group apparently felt the need to do "something dramatic" because it was losing membership. As a result of demonstrations, confrontations, and through lawsuits or negotiations, NWRO accomplished radical changes in welfare recipients' image of themselves as well as in the welfare system according to a *New York Times* article dated August 10, 1973. Since 1971 has been responsible for helping establish welfare recipients' right to privacy, for overturning residency requirements, and for making hearings possible for recipients whose grants were threatened (however some of these changes have been curtailed in some states). Currently branching out to work with poor as well as welfare recipients. Organization's slogan is dignity, justice, and an adequate income for all. Executive director, Johnnie Tillman (currently on a leave of absence); acting executive director, Saith Evans. National headquarters: 1424 Sixteenth St., N W., Washington, D.C. 20036. *See also:* BEULAH SANDERS.

HUEY P. NEWTON
Co-founder and supreme commander of the Black Panther party, and hero of American radicals since his 1968 trial and 2-to-15 years sentence for "voluntary manslaughter" in the death of an Oakland policeman the previous year. The trial was marked by numerous "free Huey" demonstrations, and the phrase subsequently became a favorite slogan of both black and white radicals. A blowup of Newton in an African chair, with zebra skin and black beret, rifle in one hand and spear in the other, became a popular poster. In May 1970, the California Court of Appeals reversed Newton's conviction on the grounds that the trial judge had failed to instruct the jury on the defense position that Newton was unconscious during the shooting. In interviews with reporters following the decision, Newton said he felt embarrassed by the famous poster and it did not represent his view of himself. He said he was opposed to violence, but remained a dedicated revolutionary. Once free, he would aim to broaden the base of the Panther movement among the black population, and it would advocate a "democratic socialistic society, free of racism." Newton said he would also seek the return of exiled Panther leader Eldridge Cleaver, possibly through the United Nations. But Newton added that he would never choose exile for himself, even if he were convicted again on a retrial. On December 15, 1971, after almost two years and standing trial three times for killing an Oakland policeman finally won a dismissal of all charges. The same year visited the People's Republic of China. In 1972 said the role of the Panther party was to "participate in every community institution. We believe in intercommunalism—the relatedness of all people. We want to be part of the whole. That's what gives motion to matter and you can't very well drop out of the system without dropping out of

the universe. So you contradict the system while you are in it until it's transformed into a new system." Author of *Revolutionary Suicide* published in 1973.

Newton was born February 17, 1942 in Louisiana, the son of a minister. He was raised in Oakland, California, where he graduated in social sciences from Merritt College. With fellow student Bobby Seale, he founded the Black Panthers in 1966. *See also:* BLACK PANTHER PARTY.

ROBERT N. C. NIX
Democratic representative to Congress from Philadelphia's Second District representing some 415,000 residents. First elected in 1958. Serves on the Foreign Affairs, Post Office, and Civil Service Committees. Is the oldest member of the Congressional Black Caucus. Born August 9, 1905, in Orangeburg, South Carolina. A lawyer (member of the Philadelphia bar association), member of NAACP, and has been Forty-fourth Ward executive committeeman since 1932. Married to the former Ethel Lanier, one son.

OPERATION BOOTSTRAP
Successful self-help, nonprofit operation begun in Watts after 1965 riots, and by 1969 employed some 70 persons in businesses grossing more than half a million dollars a year. Main elements are a job-training center, printing shop, and Shindana Toys, a division of Operation Bootstrap specializing in the manufacture of Baby Nancy, a ten-pound, 13-inch, black doll. Operation started by Lou Smith and Robert Hall, who refused on principle to accept government or private financing. Instead, adopted policy of asking business and education centers for know-how, training, and money as and when needed. In 1970 Mattel, Inc., the world's largest toymaker, trained Bookstrap personnel in administration and marketing. Organizers emphasize aim of helping Watts residents discover their own potential and among other activities organize group therapy sessions. "The thrust is inward rather than outward," Bootstrap president Lou Smith has said.

Smith was born in Philadelphia in 1929 and worked with Congress of Racial Equality for five years (1964–1968). He says he began Bootstrap "without a red cent." Office: 4161 South Central Avenue, Los Angeles, Cal.

OPERATION BREADBASKET
Operation Breadbasket is the name given to the Southern Christian Leadership Conference (SCLC) program to gain jobs and other rights by effective use of the boycott. Patterned on the successful "selective buying" campaign conducted in Philadelphia in the early 1960s by Baptist minister Dr. Leon Sullivan. The first SCLC Breadbasket campaign was in Atlanta, Georgia, but the biggest and most successful operation had been in Chicago, where it was launched in 1966 by Martin Luther King, Jr., and some 60 ministers. Jesse Jackson was named its director, and was the principal architect of its success in Chicago and elsewhere. In 1968, the Chicago operation conducted 40 boycotts which resulted in the hiring of 8,000 blacks. In 1971 after a series of internal differences

between Jackson and SCLC, Ralph Abernathy, SCLC head, requested that Jackson move his Operation Breadbasket back to Atlanta, as the Chicago program, under Jackson, had virtually become autonomous. (The other SCLC programs are directly accountable to the Atlanta headquarters and are considered part of the area programming in its 82 chapters). Jackson refused and broke with the organization taking the Chicago chapter with him and formed Operation PUSH (People United to Save Humanity).

Concerns itself primarily with equal employment opportunities for all people in deprived communities of the South. Rev. Fred E. Taylor, SCLC Program Area Director, is in charge of all Breadbasket programs. See also: JESSE JACKSON, REV. LEON H. SULLIVAN, RALPH ABERNATHY, SOUTHERN CHRISTIAN LEADERSHIP CONFERENCE.

OPERATION PUSH (PEOPLE UNITED TO SAVE HUMANITY)
A Chicago-based economic rights organization founded by Jesse Jackson on Christmas day 1971. In starting PUSH, Jackson ended a six-year association with Operation Breadbasket and its parent organization, the Southern Christian Leadership Conference (SCLC) headed by Ralph Abernathy. A confrontation between Abernathy and Jackson had been brewing ever since Martin Luther King's death in 1968 and finally erupted in the fall of 1971. Abernathy asked Jackson to move Operation Breadbasket to Atlanta. Jackson refused and was put on suspension from SCLC for 60 days. He finally quit, on December 11, taking the entire Operation Breadbasket organization (a staff of 25 and 30 of its 35 board members plus 1,000 loyal followers) with him. In the two years since, Operation PUSH has had two successful Black Expos (a massive trade fair of black products and enterprises) to its credit. It has chapters in 15 cities, including a regional office in New York City, and boasts of $165 million in contracts from three major national corporations as well as 25,000 dues-paying members. By using the weapon of a massive boycott of products and services, PUSH claims it has been able to force a $65 million agreement with Joseph Schlitz Brewing Company, a $40 million agreement with General Foods, and in July 1973 a $59 million agreement with Avon Products. In addition it announced it was currently negotiating agreements with National Distillers, Miller's Brewing Company, Anheuser Busch, Kellogg's products, Quaker Oats, Carnation Milk, General Mills, Columbia Pictures, and Metro-Goldwyn-Mayer to be concluded at the beginning of 1974. Agreements with companies include promises for jobs for blacks, deposits in black banks, business with black insurance companies, contracts with black contractors, and the use of black advertising agencies and publications.

Getting a piece of the economic pie from big business is necessary now because the civil rights mission has been accomplished, Jackson says "the issue is dead now that we have legal, public accommodations, voting and other rights. Now it's civil economics—the cost factor. What good does it do to have the right to go to school when you can't afford the tuition?" President, Rev.

Jesse Jackson; executive vice-president, Thomas N. Todd, a law professor at Northwestern University. Office: 930 E. 50th Street, Chicago, Ill.

OPPORTUNITIES INDUSTRIALIZATION CENTER (OIC)

Launched by Rev. Leon Sullivan as a job-training program in the black ghetto of North Philadelphia in 1964. Has expanded into one of the nation's biggest and most successful self-help operations, with seven branches in Philadelphia and others in 90 cities across the nation. In the Philadelphia area alone, the centers had trained more than 6,000 people and placed 5,000 in jobs by 1969. By 1973 reported to have trained more than 162,000; some 85,000 completed OIC training and more than 45,000 have been placed in meaningful jobs. A prime contractor with the federal government, OIC received more than $32 million in contracts which are held between the national OIC organization and the various federal departments involved in manpower training. Financial support also comes from the business community and private citizens in local communities where OIC programs exist. The first center was established in an abandoned North Philadelphia police station after a boycott program had revealed that there were not enough skilled blacks to fill all the jobs offered. The centers offer courses in electronics, drafting, cabinet making, restaurant skills, welding, department store sales, dry cleaning, and laundry work. They also give training in job interviews, attitude, grooming, wise shopping, etc. Eskimos and Japanese-Americans are trained at centers in such cities as Seattle; Mexican-Americans in San Jose, California. Main office: 1225 N. Broadway, Philadelphia, Pa. *See also:* REV. LEON H. SULLIVAN.

ORGANIZATION OF AFRO-AMERICAN UNITY (OAAU)

Group founded by Malcolm X in 1963 after his break with Black Muslims. Since Malcolm X's death in 1965, it has been headed by his sister, Mrs. Ella Mae Collins, but today is considered largely inactive. *See also:* ELLA MAE COLLINS.

ROSA PARKS

On December 1, 1955, seamstress Rosa Parks refused to "move to the rear" of the Cleveland Avenue bus in downtown Montgomery, Alabama, was arrested and fined $10. Her action triggered a 381-day bus boycott led by Martin Luther King, Jr., bringing him to national prominence, and marking a turning point in the history of black protest. Has been on the staff of Congressman John Conyers in Detroit since 1969. Is active in the NAACP, Women for Conyers, and African Methodist Episcopal Church.

BASIL A. PATERSON

Vice-chairman of the Democratic National Committee elected July 1972 to a four-year term and the first black to hold the post. As Ambassador Arthur Goldberg's running-mate in the New York Democratic primary, June 1970, he became the first black to win a major party's candidacy for Lieutenant Governor of New York, but was defeated. Until his nomination, he was little known outside

Harlem's 27th district, which he had represented as a state senator since 1966. Born April 27, 1926, in Harlem, where he graduated from DeWitt Clinton High School in 1942. After two years of army service, he was graduated from St. John's (Catholic) University, Brooklyn, in 1948, and its Law School in 1951. Currently practices law in Manhattan and a partner in the firm of Paterson, Michael, Dinkins and Jones. Also president of the Institute for Mediation and Conflict Resolution, an independent and nonprofit organization established in 1969 to provide services and new approaches to effect necessary change for groups involved in community disputes by impartial, third party assistance. Funded by the Ford Foundation. Former president of the New York chapter, NAACP. Married to the former Portia Hairston, two sons.

REV. CHANNING E. PHILLIPS
First black to be nominated for the presidency of the United States at a major party convention. At the 1968 Democratic National Convention in Chicago (he received 67 1/2 votes), Phillips said he ran "to show the Negro vote must not be taken for granted." Was favorite-son candidate of the Washington, D.C., delegation, which he headed. The delegation's 23 votes had been originally pledged to Robert Kennedy. As member of Platform Committee, Phillips opposed administration's position on Vietnam. In 1970 ran as one of three candidates for the District of Columbia's first nonvoting delegate to Congress against Joseph P. Yeldell and Rev. Walter E. Fauntroy but lost. Pastor of Lincoln Memorial Temple in Washington, 1956–1970. Is also president since 1967 of the Housing Development Corporation, a nonprofit housing rehabilitation agency funded in part by Office of Economic Opportunity. Was one of the early leaders of the Washington-based militant Black United Front. Participated in Selma marches, 1965. At 1964 Democratic National Convention was active supporter of Mississippi Freedom Democratic party. Currently working with Project for Corporate Responsibility—a pressure group that tries to place minorities on the boards of major corporations in the country. Group's most notable accomplishment to date is helping to promote the election of Leon Sullivan (head of Opportunities Industrialization Center in Philadelphia) to the board of General Motors. Born 1928, holds B.A. in sociology from Virginia Union University, divinity degree from Colgate Divinity School, and a degree in theology from Drew University. Married, five children.

SAMUEL R. PIERCE
General counsel to the treasury department (1970–1973) appointed by President Nixon, and one of the top black appointees in the Nixon administration. A partner in the prominent New York law firm of Battle, Fowler, Stokes, and Kheel since 1961, he resigned in May 1973 to return to private law practice, and was cited by the Nixon administration for "truly outstanding service" (for contributing significantly to the economic stabilization program and the emergency loan guarantee program). Has been a faculty member, since 1958, of New York University Law School. Also a member of the Advisory Committee of New York

Congress of Racial Equality, a life member of the NAACP, and director of the Lawyers' Committee for Civil Rights Under Law (a committee initiated by the late President John F. Kennedy). Served as a judge to the New York Court of General Sessions (1959–1960) and is a strenuous worker for Republican party causes (once ran for Congressman Adam Clayton Powell's seat on the Republican ticket). Received an A.B. from Cornell University (1947) and LL.B. (1949). Served with Office of Strategic Services during World War II. Born September 8, 1922 and married to physician Barbara Wright (1948), one child.

SIDNEY POITIER
In 1965 became the first black to win an Academy Award for a starring role (*Lilies of the Field*). Says he tries to work in films that make a positive contribution to the image of black people in America. Wrote *For Love of Ivy* for this reason. "I try to do and say nothing that might be a step backward." Born February 20, 1927, in Miami, Florida, but moved to the Bahamas. At 15 returned to the United States, first to Miami, then to New York where he worked as a dishwasher. In 1941 enlisted in the army for four years (served with a medical detachment). Studied with the American Negro Theater, which once rejected him because of his unintelligible West Indian accent. In 1950 made first movie *No Way Out*. Starred on Broadway in *Raisin in the Sun* (1959). Most recent movies: *To Sir with Love*, *In the Heat of the Night*, *For Love of Ivy*, *Guess Who's Coming to Dinner*, and *Uptown Saturday Night*. Divorced, four daughters.

POTOMAC INSTITUTE
Nonprofit, independent organization concerned with the study and development of policies for expanding opportunities for lower income and minority groups. Provides advisory and research services to government and private agencies involved in racial problems, particularly in the areas of central city redevelopment, metropolitan land use, and inequities in public funding. Financed by foundation and government grants, the institute has been in operation since 1961. President, Harold C. Fleming (born 1922) was executive director of the Southern Regional Council before joining the institute in 1961; executive vice-president, Arthur J. Levin. Headquarters: 1501 Eighteenth Street, N.W., Washington, D.C. 20036.

LOU POTTER
Editor responsible for the program composition of National Educational Television's series "Black Journal," the first nationwide series by and for black Americans. In summers of 1971 and 1972 coordinated the Michelle Clark Fellows Program for minorities at Columbia University School of Journalism in New York. Currently writer-producer for an independent film company. Graduated from Howard University in 1959, did postgraduate studies at Wharton School of Finance at the University of Pennsylvania.

J. STANLEY POTTINGER

Nixon-appointed (February 2, 1973) assistant attorney general in charge of the Civil Rights Division, Department of Justice. Educated at elementary and secondary public schools in Dayton, Ohio, and at Harvard University. Received an LL.D. from Harvard Law School in 1965. For three years prior to his appointment in Justice Department, was director of the Office for Civil Rights and assistant to the secretary for civil rights in Department of Health, Education and Welfare. Born 1940. Married to the former Gloria Jean Anderson, three children.

ALVIN F. POUSSAINT

One of the country's leading black psychiatrists and an expert on the psychosis of oppression. Best known for his article, *Black Power, A Failure for Integration Within the Civil Rights Movement*. Currently associate professor of psychiatry and associate dean of student affairs at Harvard Medical School. Active in Operation PUSH (People United to Save Humanity). Taught at Tufts University School of Medicine, 1967–1969. Graduated from Columbia University (1956), M.D. from Cornell University Medical School (1960), and M.S. from University of California at Los Angeles (1964). Born May 15, 1934.

PRIDE, INC.

A labor department-financed organization providing employment for ghetto youths in the District of Columbia. Started in 1967 by Rufus Mayfield, a convicted felon, who obtained a $300,000 labor department grant to employ 900 youths in a slum clean-up and rat-control program. Today has three divisions: Youth Pride, Inc.; Pride Economic Enterprises; and Pride Environmental Services. Youth Pride Inc. is a job-training and skills development program for poverty-level inner-city youths. Since 1967 has prepared 6,200 young people for jobs in everything from bakeries to plumbing. Together with job training, youths are encouraged to complete high school, even to seek higher education and work with local universities such as Catholic and American Universities, to place those who want to go on. Pride Economic Enterprises owns and manages a 55-unit apartment complex in southeast Washington and the Pride Mini-Market (opened in the fall of 1973) to serve community and train youths in marketing and retailing. Pride Environmental Services focuses on black economic development within the inner city while providing employment and opportunities to youths. By 1969, Pride Inc. had received more than six million dollars in grants from the labor department. At the beginning had its share of trouble. The program had been attacked in Congress on the grounds that federal funds should not be handled by persons with criminal records. Early in 1969, the General Accounting Office (GAO) charged 269 cases of mismanagement, payroll padding, and kickbacks, but GAO investigators eventually found only $2,100 unaccounted for, less than one percent of Pride's budget. Nevertheless, in July 1969, the organization came under grand jury investigation, and in February 1970, some 17 former and present members were indicted on charges of irregularities involving the organization's funds. Executive director of Youth

Pride Inc. and president of Pride Economic Enterprises and Pride Environmental Services: Mary Treadwell Barry. Headquarters: 1536 U Street, N.W., Washington, D.C.

PROJECT ENTERPRISE
Nixon administration's major program to encourage and expand minority business enterprises. Launched in the fall of 1969, the program expanded the availability of venture capital and management advice and training, chiefly through a series of local investment companies set up for this purpose. The investment companies, sponsored by major U.S. corporations and private-sector organizations in partnership with the federal government, are known as Minority Enterprise Small Business Investment Companies (MESBIC). By August 21, 1970, 16 such companies were in operation and commitments had been received for over 100. One of the first and most successful of the companies, the Arcata Investment Company of Palo Alto, California, financed some 50 minority businightclubs and a delivery service. But by 1972, because of insufficient funds, Arcata Investments collapsed. Big corporations, which publicly said they supported the program, actually "looked upon MESBIC's like they regarded their wives' favorite charities: other things came first," according to Alan Steelman, executive director of the MESBIC advisory council. In 1971 there were 42 MESBIC's, by 1972 there were 47, and to date (December 1973) there are 65. The companies, licensed by the Small Business Administration, work in conjunction with the Commerce Department's Office of Minority Business Enterprise (OMBE). MESBIC head is David Wollard. See also: ARTHUR McZIER.

PUERTO RICAN CIVIL RIGHTS, NATIONAL
ASSOCIATION OF (NAPCR)
Founded in 1964 by Puerto Rican individuals and some 100 Puerto Rican organizations in the United States. Concerned with civil rights problems of Puerto Ricans in legislative, labor, police, legal, and housing matters, particularly in New York City (which has the highest concentration of Puerto Ricans in the country: 1.2 million). Today NAPCR goals are to provide legal help for all races particularly Puerto Ricans; runs a youth development program and works for closer ties among Spanish-speaking groups throughout the country. Claims to have 14 chapters in six states and Puerto Rico and a membership of 15,000. President: Robert Munoz. Headquarters: 175 East 116th Street, New York, N.Y. 10029.

PUERTO RICAN LEGAL DEFENSE AND EDUCATION FUND, INC.
Established in 1972 to provide legal representation for Puerto Ricans throughout the country and to promote education and give information about the law to the Puerto Rican community. Has fought cases in education, employment, welfare, and voting rights in New York, New Jersey, Pennsylvania, and several other states. Staffed with five full-time lawyers, is supported mainly by contribu-

tions from foundations and corporations. Executive director: Cesar A. Perales, former general counsel for Model Cities Administration of New York. Office: 815 Second Avenue, New York, N.Y. 10017.

PUERTO RICAN REVOLUTIONARY WORKERS ORGANIZATION (PRWO)

A new, semisecret militant organization which grew out of a national group called the Young Lords Party. The Young Lords started in 1960 as a Puerto Rican street gang in Chicago, shifted to a social-service club in 1964, and then in January 1969 became a political organization modeled on the Black Panther party. Its proclaimed aim was to promote independence for all *Latinos* (Latin-Americans) through a brand of socialism based on a 13-point program which covered much of the same ground as the Panther's ten-point program. In the summer of 1969, the Lords joined with the Panthers and the Appalachian Young Patriots, a group of poor-white revolutionaries and former Chicago street gang, to form the Rainbow Coalition. Always secretive about their membership, the *Black Panther* newspaper (February 17, 1970) listed Lord chapters in Puerto Rico, New York, Philadelphia, Newark, and Hayward (California) with national headquarters in Chicago. Today The Young Lords Party, as a national group, is no longer considered active.

The New York chapter, called the New York State Central Committee, joined the national organization in January 1969. But in May 1970 split with the group over organizational differences and took the name Young Lords Party. It made headlines in December 1969 when it seized the First Spanish Methodist Church in East Harlem and held it for 11 days, seeking to force church authorities to provide space for a free breakfast program. In July of 1973, after several years of watching the movement splinter and the Black Panthers become more inclined to work within the system, formed the Puerto Rican Revolutionary Workers Organization for the purpose of bettering the lot of the working class. It discarded the paramilitary structure of the Young Lords and set up a small central governing committee. Members go out and get jobs in factories and hospitals, join unions, and press for unionization of nonunion workers. Pablo (called Yoruba) Guzman, a member of PRWO's central committee, points out that just because there are no more sit-ins and taking over buildings with guns, it doesn't mean that nothing is happening or everything is cool. "When the Lords used to hold marches and some of our critics used to jeer . . . 'whyntcha get a job?' " Yoruba said in a recent interview, "there was an aspect of truth in what they said. We've taken their advice." After a visit to China in 1971, Yoruba said the task of his organization was to create a multinational Communist party to replace the "sold-out" U.S. Communist party. Organization puts out a biweekly newspaper called *Palante* (which means "right arm"), distributes leaflets for leftist political conferences, and oversees work of its branches in Boston, Philadelphia, New Jersey, and Connecticut. Membership believed to be about 35. Headquarters: East 142nd Street and Willis Avenue, South Bronx, N.Y.

A. PHILIP RANDOLPH

Considered the "elder statesman" of the civil rights movement. Has worked for almost 50 years to build an alliance between black Americans and the trade union movement. Opposing any form of strike-breaking by blacks, he advocated instead full integration into the American trade union movement (today there are some three million black trade unionists). In 1925, began a long and backbreaking campaign to organize the Brotherhood of Sleeping Car Porters of the AFL which eventually won certification in 1937. Later became the first black vice-president of AFL-CIO. In 1941 organized and directed the first march on Washington which led President Roosevelt to establish the Commission of Fair Employment Practices. In 1963 was one of the major forces behind the march on Washington that year. Retired from AFL-CIO post in 1966 and is presently a member of its executive council. Currently president of the A. Philip Randolph Institute, founded in 1964 for the purpose of supplementing the social and economic changes which civil rights legislation cannot achieve by itself. Born in Crescent City, Florida, on April 15, 1889, he attended City College of New York and received a law degree from Howard University in 1941. Married to the former Lucille E. Campbell. See also: BAYARD RUSTIN.

CHARLES E. RANGEL

Elected to Congress in 1970, a Democrat, from New York's Nineteenth Congressional district with 87 percent of the vote by successfully beating the late Adam Clayton Powell—who had represented the district for 12 consecutive terms—in the primary. Is chairman of the Congressional Black Caucus. Member of Public Works and Science Committees in Congress as well as Select Committee on Crime. Before becoming a Congressman was New York state assemblyman from central Harlem from 1966–1970. Lawyer, former assistant United States attorney, and a former general counsel to the National Advisory Commission on Selective Service. In April 1969, Representative James H. Scheuer, one of the seven candidates running for the Democratic nomination for mayor of New York, picked Rangel to run on his ticket for city council president. Educated at DeWitt Clinton High School and graduated in 1953. After serving in the army (1948–1952) graduated from New York University (1957) and St. John's University Law School in Brooklyn, New York (1960). Born June 11, 1930, in Harlem, New York, winner of the Purple Heart and Bronze Star in Korean War. Married to the former Alma Carter, one child. See also: CONGRESSIONAL BLACK CAUCUS.

JOSEPH L. RAUH, JR.

One of the most prominent white lawyers identified with civil rights legislation and issues. As general counsel of the Leadership Conference on Civil Rights, he and Clarence Mitchell of the NAACP were the chief lobbyists for the Civil Rights Act of 1964, the Voting Rights Act of 1965, and the Fair Housing Act of 1968. At the 1964 Democratic National Convention in Atlantic City, New Jersey, was counsel for the Mississippi Freedom Democratic party which forced the

unseating of the regular delegation and obtained an offer to seat part of the
Freedom delegation. Also Washington counsel of the United Auto Workers,
the Brotherhood of Sleeping Car Porters, Locomotive Firemen and Enginemen,
and other labor groups. For 20 years was vice-chairman and chairman of the
Democratic Central Committee for the District of Columbia. In 1946, helped
form the liberal Americans for Democratic Action, of which he was chairman
from 1948–1952, and currently vice-chairman. Elected to national board of
NAACP at 1973 convention. Born January 3, 1911, in Cincinatti, Ohio, he graduated from Harvard University in 1932 and Harvard Law School in 1935. Married, two sons. See also: FREEDOM DEMOCRATIC PARTY.

REPUBLIC OF NEW AFRICA
Separatist group that advocates the establishment of an independent black nation in five southern states. Originally based in Detroit, it was involved in De-
troit ghetto gun battle, March 29, 1969, in which Patrolman Michael Czapski
was killed. Shooting followed meeting of the separatist group at the New Bethel
Baptist Church (whose pastor, Rev. C. L. Franklin, is father of Aretha Franklin).
After the shooting all 142 blacks inside the church were arrested but within
hours all but two of them had been released through the intervention of Judge
George Crockett, a black, on the grounds that their rights had been violated.
The judge's action led to storm of public and police protest. He defended himself at news conference April 3. Czapski's funeral, April 2, was attended by 2,000
persons. The Republic of New Africa claims to have declared its "independence" from the United States, and is asking for $400 billion in "slavery dam-
ages" from the U.S. government. It has an armed guard which it calls the "Black
Legion." Formed in March 1968 by two brothers, Milton Henry, a lawyer
known within the organization as Brother Gaidi, and Richard Henry who took
the name Imari Abubakari Obadele. At a meeting held in January 1970, group
was reported split into two factions each headed by a founding brother: Milton
leading original group (which has since disbanded and Milton is practising law
in Detroit) and Richard (Brother Imari) leading the dissident faction. In the
Spring of 1971 Brother Imari and his followers tried to buy 20 acres of land in
Jackson, Mississippi, to establish a capital for their separate black nation. A raid
by Jackson police shortly afterwards ended in a gun fight leaving one policeman dead and another wounded. Eleven members of the group were arrested including its president Brother Imari, who was convicted for conspiracy
and currently an appeal is pending in this conviction. See also: GEORGE
CROCKETT, ROBERT F. WILLIAMS.

GLORIA HAYS RICHARDSON
Formed Cambridge Nonviolent Action Committee in Cambridge, Maryland in
1963, to force acceptance of blacks in white restaurants, bowling alleys, taverns,
and other public accommodations. Also one of the founders of ACT Associates.
Not active in recent years. Born in Baltimore, on May 6, 1922, she grew up in

Cambridge, the daughter of a well-to-do druggist. A graduate of Howard University. Divorced, two children.

CLEVELAND ROBINSON

Succeeded A. Philip Randolph as president of the National Afro-American Labor Council (formerly the Negro American Labor Council) in 1966. The council was formed in 1960 to promote employment equality and apprenticeship opportunity for black trade unionists. Robinson is also president of the Distributive Workers of America, and secretary-treasurer of its District 65. Active in civil rights groups, he assisted in organization of 1963 Washington march. Born 1914 in Jamaica, West Indies. Married, two sons.

ISAIAH ROBINSON

Member of New York City's reorganized Board of Education. Was first appointed in May 1969 by Manhattan Borough President Percy Sutton and served as president for a one-year term 1971–1972. Played a leading role in decentralization of city's public school system. Described as "a cool-headed militant" and a strong supporter of community control, he is president of the Harlem Commonwealth Council for Economic Development and an adviser to New York's IS 201 demonstration school district. A commercial artist, he has been involved in Harlem educational activities since 1955. Served as a second lieutenant and pilot in air force during World War II after graduating from Rosedale High School (Birmingham, Alabama), and attending Tuskegee Institute flying school. Also a graduate of Art Career School in New York. Served as consultant to several groups including Teachers Corps, Urban Coalition, the McGeorge Bundy panel on decentralization, and Fordham University's instructional administrators program. Born February 17, 1924, in Birmingham, Alabama. Married, one child.

CARL ROWAN

First black to sit in on National Security Council and cabinet meetings (1964), when he succeeded Edward R. Murrow as director of the U.S. Information Agency. Appointed by President Johnson, he resigned in July 1965, to return to journalism. Currently a nationally syndicated columnist for the *Chicago Daily News* and roving editor for the *Reader's Digest*. Also has a syndicated radio program which goes to some 40 black stations across the country. In August 1967, he criticized Martin Luther King, Jr.'s opposition to the Vietnam war, declaring that this "created doubt about the Negro's loyalty to his country" and endangered civil rights advances. In August 1964, he declared that civil rights demonstrations "for the most part, serve only to becloud the real issues of the Negro's legitimate grievances" and called for "bold, uncompromising efforts to free the civil rights movement from the taint of street rioters." Rowan himself was the center of a civil rights incident in January 1962, when Washington's exclusive Cosmos Club refused him membership, leading to the resignation of several of its big name members, including John Kenneth Galbraith. After 13 years as an award-winning reporter for the *Minneapolis Tribune*, Rowan entered government service in 1961 when he was appointed deputy assistant secretary of state for public affairs in state department. He was a U.S. delegate to the U.N. in 1962 and ambassador to Finland in 1963. Author of two books on the race problem (*South of Freedom* and *Go South to Sorrow*), one on Southeast Asia (*The Pitiful and the Proud*), and the biography of Jackie Robinson (*Wait Till Next Year*). Born in Ravenscroft, Tennessee, August 11, 1925. During World War II became one of the first 15 blacks to be raised to officer rank in the navy. Received B.A. at Oberlin College, Ohio, in 1947 and M.A. in journalism at University of Minnesota in 1948. Married, with three children, he lives in Washington, D.C.

BAYARD RUSTIN
Executive director of the A. Philip Randolph Institute in New York. Rustin was the organizing genius behind the historic 1963 March on Washington (at its time the largest single protest demonstration in the nation's history) when, on August 28, more than 200,000 persons converged on the capital to dramatize black demands. A pacifist and former Communist, Rustin was considered by many to be a dangerous radical. A civil rights activist since 1947, he helped to develop Congress of Racial Equality and Southern Christian Leadership Conference and also organized the first New York City school boycott in 1964. But recently, Rustin has criticized black revolutionaries, and attacked some of their most popular rallying cries—reparations, separatism, black studies, black capitalism—as "myths" which will only divide and isolate the black community and retard real progress. A firm believer in nonviolence, he has said that blacks who choose violence can expect to end up in one of three ways: "in jail, in exile—or shot—and probably by Negroes." Born in West Chester, Pennsylvania, in 1910, one of 12 children, he was a track star, tennis champion, and class valedictorian in high school. Attended City College of New York (1933–1935), and joined the Young Communist League in 1936 but resigned in 1941 to become a pacifist. Was a conscientious objector during World War II and was jailed for 28 months. After the war he became active in civil rights and from 1941–1954 was race relations director of Fellowship and Reconciliation, a pacifist organization that attempts to substitute nonviolence and reconciliation for violence through education and peaceful action. Has worked since 1964, through the A. Philip Randolph Institute, to solidify relations between blacks and the unions and for better laws and policies to promote economic equality. Conceived and put into operation the Institute's recruitment and training program designed to bring black youths into union apprenticeship programs. Also serves as chairman of the executive committee of the Leadership Conference on Civil Rights in Washington. Wrote *Down the Line*, a collection of essays published in 1971. Office: 26 Park Avenue South, New York, N.Y. 10010.

BUFFY SAINTE-MARIE
Successful Indian folksinger and songwriter ("Now That the Buffalo's Gone"), many of whose songs concern the plight of American Indians. In addition

to frequent benefit performances and financial support, she has been an active spokesman for Indian rights. She supported the Indians in their bid for Alcatraz Island, and in April 1970 lobbied the California Legislature on behalf of the Pyramid Lake Indians. She also formed the Nihewan Foundation to provide scholarships and other aid to Indian students. Born a Plains Cree in Saskatchewan, Canada, February 20, 1941. Married to Dewane Bugbee, lives in Hawaii.

BEULAH SANDERS

National chairwoman and a member of the executive board of National Welfare Rights Organization (NWRO) since 1971. Before that had been NWRO's New York chapter head and leader of New York City's dissident welfare recipients, who told House Ways and Means Committee, October 27, 1969, that the poor would "disrupt this country" if not given a share of the nation's wealth. "The middle class," she declared, "is getting it all." Mrs. Sanders appeared before the committee to urge higher guaranteed annual incomes. As chairman of New York's Citywide Coordinating Committee of Welfare Groups, which represents the city's predominantly black welfare recipients, she has led boycotts and other activities against cuts in relief payments and allowances. Born January 14, 1935, in New Bern, North Carolina, she settled in New York in 1955. See also: NATIONAL WELFARE RIGHTS ORGANIZATION.

STANLEY S. SCOTT

Former Tennessee newspaperman appointed in 1973 as the ranking black aide to President Nixon at White House. Replaced Robert J. Brown who returned to private business in High Point, North Carolina. Before his present appointment, was an aide to Herbert C. Klein, the administration's communications director. Born 1934, was a reporter with the United Press International and with radio station WINS in New York.

BOBBY SEALE

National chairman and titular head of the Black Panther party, which he helped found with Huey Newton in 1966, as well as chairman of the California Black Panthers. On August 19, 1969, Seale was arrested by FBI agents in Berkeley on a warrant issued in New Haven, Connecticut, charging him with kidnap, conspiracy to kidnap, murder, and conspiracy to murder Alex Rackley in a Panther building in New Haven in May 1969. Rackley, 24, who had been a member of the Panthers in New York, was found shot after apparent severe torture (his body showed multiple bruises, cigarette burns, ice-pick wounds, and rope marks around the wrists). Police linked his death with the earlier arrest of 21 Panthers in New York on charges of conspiring to bomb several large department stores, believing he was subjected to a kangaroo court and tortured because of suspected disloyalty to the Panthers. Seale was flown from California to Connecticut March 13, 1970, to stand trial on the charges. At a bail hearing, April 22, prosecution witness George Sams, Jr., who had pleaded guilty to second-degree murder in the case, testified that Seale had ordered Rackley's execution after concluding that he was a police informer. It was more than a year before Seale was brought to trial. Part of the delay was caused in selecting a jury—it took four months of questioning 1,035 persons before one was finally selected on March 11, 1971. On the following May 25, a trial that commanded national attention ended in a hung jury and all charges against Seale were dismissed by New Haven Judge Harold M. Mulvey because the "massive publicity" about the aborted trial made it too difficult to try him again—thus ending 21 months of an odyssey that took Seale through a series of jails, courtrooms, and prisons. One observer called it one of the most controversial episodes in legal history.

On March 20, 1969, Seale and seven others (the "Chicago Eight") became the first group indicted under the new antiriot provision of the 1968 Civil Rights Act (which makes it a crime to cross state lines to incite riots or to teach the use of riot weapons) because of their involvement in the demonstrations during the Democratic National Convention in August 1968. The trial began September 24 and was marked from the beginning by dramatic confrontations between Seale and the 74-year-old judge, Julius J. Hoffman. Seale contended that his Constitutional rights were being violated because his own lawyer, who was recovering from an operation, was unable to be present. Seale frequently disrupted the trial with outbursts in which he called the judge a "racist," a "fascist," and "pig" and accused him of lying. On October 29, Seale was ordered gagged and chained to his chair in the courtroom. On November 5, Judge Hoffman convicted Seale on 16 counts of contempt of court and sentenced him to four years in prison, at the same time severing his case from that of the seven other defendants in the conspiracy trial, declaring an individual mistrial, and setting a new date (April 23, 1970) for Seale's trial on the conspiracy charges. On September 27, 1972, the government asked the U.S. District Court in Chicago to dismiss contempt charges against him. In May 1972 announced he would run for office of mayor of Oakland as a Democrat in 1973. Ended up running in a field with nine other contenders which finished in a runoff between Seale and incumbent John Reading. In a May 19 runoff, Seale lost, 43,710 votes to Reading's 77,476. Born in Dallas on October 22, 1926, one of three children of impoverished parents. Lived in Texas before moving to California and then went into the army. Was dishonorably discharged for losing his temper resulting from a run-in with a colonel at Ellsworth Air Force Base in South Dakota but was able to find work back in California as a sheet metal worker, a stand-up comic, and even did a stint at the Neighborhood Youth Corps in Oakland. Attended Merritt College in Oakland off and on and in 1962 met Huey Newton. Author of *Seize the Time: The Story of the Black Panther Party and Huey P. Newton* (Random House, 1970). Married, one son. See also: BLACK PANTHER PARTY, ELDRIDGE CLEAVER, HUEY P. NEWTON.

SEARCH FOR EDUCATION, ELEVATION AND KNOWLEDGE (SEEK)
Program providing compensatory instruction, counseling, and financial aid for educationally and economically disadvantaged students at City University of New York's senior colleges. Started in 1966, by 1973 the program was aiding

more than 9,800 students at a cost of more than $26 million a year, with funds provided by the city and state of New York. The SEEK program enjoys departmental status on the ten senior college campuses. Current head is university dean, Robert Young. Address: 511 East 80th Street, New York, N.Y.

BETTY SHABAZZ
Widow of Malcolm X. Currently lives in virtual seclusion with her six daughters in Mount Vernon, New York. In interview with *Look* magazine (March 4, 1969) said she believed that U.S. government was behind Malcolm X's murder, because "he learned some things the Government did not want him to know." An orthodox Muslim (former Black Muslim), after her husband's death (February 21, 1965), she made pilgrimage to Mecca, took name Haji Bahiyah Betty Shabazz. In May 1971 was named cochairperson of Advisory Board of *Amsterdam News*, largest black weekly in the United States, by new owners headed by Manhattan Borough President Percy Sutton. Born 1937 in Detroit, attended Tuskegee Institute, and studied nursing in New York, where she joined Black Muslims. Her daughters, who attend private schools, all have Arabic names: Attallah, Qubilah, Ilyasah, Gamilah, Lamumbah, Malikah, and Malaak.

FRED SHUTTLESWORTH
Veteran civil rights leader and former chief lieutenant to Martin Luther King, Jr. Led Birmingham, Alabama, integration movement, and was one of clergymen arrested with King for leading 1963 Birmingham demonstrations. Jailed more than 20 times. A founder of the Southern Christian Leadership Conference, of which he is still a board and executive committee member, he is currently a board member of the Southern Conference Educational Fund, a 17-state interracial civil rights group focusing on integration, with headquarters in Louisville, Kentucky. But present residence is in Cincinnati, where he is pastor of Baptist Church of the Greater New Light, and president emeritus of the Alabama Christian Movement for Human Rights. Also works with Operation PUSH (People United to Save Humanity) and is on the board of the Cincinnati branch of Opportunities Industrialization Center. Says that ill health has curtailed his recent civil rights activities. Born March 18, 1922. Married, four children.

SAMUEL J. SIMMONS
President, National Center for Housing Management since September 1972, responsible for directing nationwide training programs and performance standards for managers of government-subsidized housing. Formerly assistant secretary for equal opportunity in Department of Housing and Urban Development (1969–1972). From 1970–1972 also served as chairman of federal Interagency Committee on Minority Enterprise in the construction industry. Director of Field Service Division, U.S. Commission on Civil Rights, 1964–1968. Born April 13, 1927, in Flint, Michigan. Office: 1133 15th Street, N.W., Washington, D.C. 20005.

MARGARET E. SLOAN

A founder of the National Black Feminist Organization formed in August 1973 by 35 black women for the purpose of demolishing the "myths" about black women's relation to family, to black men, and to racism. (Organization claims chapters in San Francisco, Cleveland, and Chicago as well as New York.) Has been active in civil rights, she says, since she was 12 after witnessing a demonstration at a downtown Chicago 5 and 10 store. Soon after she was organizing her own protests—rent strikes against lead poisoning on Chicago's West Side, marching with Dr. Martin Luther King for open housing in 1966, and coordinating a hunger task force investigating poverty in Illinois. A turning point in her life was meeting New York black activist lawyer Florence Kennedy in 1969 through whom she met Gloria Steinem which led to moving to New York and an editor's job at *Ms Magazine* in 1972. Born in Chattanooga, Tennessee, May 31, 1947, the daughter of an insurance salesman turned janitor. Shortly afterwards, moved with her parents to Chicago, attended Catholic grammar school, Loretto Academy high school, and Chicago City College. Has been a cab driver, a salesgirl, and nurse's aid. Divorced, one child.

SOUTHERN CHRISTIAN LEADERSHIP CONFERENCE (SCLC)

Founded by Dr. Martin Luther King, Jr. after his successful Montgomery bus boycott in 1956, the SCLC rose to preeminence in the civil rights movement in the early sixties. Its stress was on nonviolent protest. Its first major campaign was in 1960, when King called on blacks to begin "mass violation of immoral laws." In April and May 1963, King led the drive to desegregate facilities in Birmingham, Alabama, which became a landmark in the struggle to desegregate the South. In a major confrontation between marchers and the authorities, police dogs and fire-hoses were used against the marchers, and thousands of blacks were arrested—including hundreds of children—as well as Dr. King himself. In his now famous "Letter from a Birmingham Jail," King eloquently enunciated his principles. In August of the same year, he was a leading figure in the massive March on Washington, at which he delivered the most memorable of the day's addresses, "I have a dream . . .". In many southern towns, King and his organization led boycotts, sit-ins, marches, voter registrations, and held lectures and forums. In October 1964, King's efforts were given international recognition when he was awarded the Nobel Peace Prize. He was then 35, the youngest recipient ever.

With the emergence of Stokely Carmichael and militant demands for "black power" in 1966, King's unquestioned leadership of the black cause began to wane. His efforts to widen the influence of his organization in the northern cities were only partly successful. After his asassination in April 1968, the SCLC, under his successor Ralph Abernathy, organized the Poor People's March on Washington which took place in May of that year. But the march did not have the impact intended and it became increasingly evident that without the leadership of King SCLC would not play such a national role in the civil rights movement. From 1970 to 1973, SCLC's fortunes waned even further so that in the summer of that year, five years after King's death, it was reported on the brink of extinction (*Washington Post*, July 24, 1973). Several reasons for this have been given by those close to the organization: One, that there are fewer funds available to the civil rights movement generally in the early 1970s. SCLC's budget went from a reported $4 million in 1968 to $500,000 in 1972 thereby forcing it to make drastic cutbacks in staff and programming. Abernathy also admitted that one of the major reasons for SCLS's financial difficulties was the loss of white support. A second reason offered was that most of the organization's bright young leaders had gone on to something else—Rev. Jesse Jackson to Operation PUSH (People United to Save Humanity), Andrew Young to Congress, and Coretta King (the founder's widow) started the Martin Luther King, Jr. Center for Nonviolent Social Change and Abernathy accused her of draining away funds that might otherwise have gone to SCLC coffers. But SCLC also floundered around looking for programs that would recapture the imagination of the public and these programs were not forthcoming. Much of the blame for this has been assigned to Abernathy's leadership. How the future is resolved for SCLC, some feel, may well indicate what tactics will dominate the struggle in the 1970s. Headquarters: 334 Auburn Avenue, N.W., Atlanta, Ga. *See also:* RALPH D. ABERNATHY, JESSE JACKSON, CORETTA SCOTT KING, HOSEA WILLIAMS, ANDREW J. YOUNG.

SOUTHERN REGIONAL COUNCIL

Atlanta-based civil rights research agency. Since 1962, has conducted foundation-funded voter registration programs in the South which have helped to add an estimated 3.5 million blacks to registration rolls in 11 southern states. This program, known as the Voter Education Project, has included seminars, workshops, and conferences for candidates and officeholders. In October 1969, the council issued a report drawing attention to the rapid proliferation of all-white private schools in the South, which, it claimed, threatened to jeopardize public education throughout the region. In March 1970, published a survey (with Metropolitan Applied Research Center) showing almost 1,500 blacks were currently holding public office. In 1970 established the School Desegregation Project to help students, school administrators, and interested agencies to deal with the problems of school desegregation and in 1973 had trained some 105 youths to work as volunteers in their communities. With the University of Texas Human Resource Center developed the Black Women Employment Project in 1972 to assist them in obtaining better and managerial jobs. To date has placed 68 women in better paying jobs. The council was formed in 1918 by a group of southern whites. In addition to special studies, publishes a quarterly review, *New South* and, in 1974, *Southern Voices*, a new magazine of opinion and politics, art, and other items of interest to the South. Income for 1972 was $666,793. Executive director, George H. Esser, Jr.; president, Dr. Raymond Wheeler of Charlotte, North Carolina; Voter Education Project director, John Lewis. Office: 52 Fairlie Street, Atlanta, Ga.

BISHOP STEPHEN G. SPOTTSWOOD

Chairman of the NAACP since 1961, whose outspoken keynote address at 1970 NAACP convention characterized Nixon administration as "anti-Negro." At the 1972 NAACP convention said that black Americans have not been so confused as they are today about their goals and so ready to "applaud the counsels of division and separatism" since the turn of the century. "These lost brothers and sisters," he continued, "need our strength and firmness as never before; they will stumble and fall if we are not ready—with wisdom and understanding—to lend them a hand while we point the true way ahead with the other." (*New York Daily News*, July 4, 1972.) A bishop of the African Methodist Episcopal Zion Church, retired in May of 1972 after 20 years, and veteran of civil rights campaigns since 1919 when he joined the NAACP. Born July 18, 1897 in Boston, Massachusetts. Graduated from Albright College, 1917, and Gordon College of Theology, 1919. Also studied at Yale Divinity School. Married twice, first to Viola Booker (1919–1953) and then to Mrs. Mattie Brownita Johnson Elliott (December 15, 1969), five children.

CARL B. STOKES

Mayor of Cleveland and first black elected mayor of a major U.S. city (November 7, 1967), when he defeated Seth B. Taft (Republican, grandson of President Taft) in a close vote, 129,318 to 127,674. A moderate, Stokes had been opposed in the primary by the regular Democratic organization. He won reelection in November 1969 by a slightly wider margin (118,713 to 116,544) after a hard-fought campaign. As mayor, Stokes had received wide praise for efforts to maintain calm after the King assassination, but was criticized for his handling of the July 1968 rioting that followed a shootout between police and militants. After conferring with black leaders, Stokes had withdrawn national guardsmen and white policemen from ghetto areas of Hough and Glenville on July 24, and had turned over responsibility for law and order to 125 black policemen and hastily organized citizen patrols. After renewed violence and looting, however, he ordered guard units back in ghetto areas on July 25, a move widely interpreted both as surrender to pressure and admission of failure. Decided not to seek reelection for a third term in 1971. Some of the reasons cited by friends were "the personal abuse he has taken locally, his inability to push his programs through, an antagonistic city council—even fear for his life—and the possibility of higher political office." His adversaries said that "racial polarization in the city, the deadlock between the mayor and the council, the 'disenchantment' with the mayor, as some call it, by the white establishment and newspapers" are good reasons (*New York Times*, April 20, 1971). Stokes said he wanted to "devote more time to stressing . . . the need for the reestablishment of priorities at the human level and the necessity for an honest blunt appraisal of the root ills of our cities." Has been a newsman with WNBC-TV's News 4 in New York since May 1972. Stokes was prominent campaigner for Hubert Humphrey in 1968 presidential race and was active in the 1972 Democratic Convention. Born June 21, 1927 in a Cleveland slum. After army service, graduated from

University of Minnesota (1954) and Cleveland-Marshall Law School (1956) with LL.B. degree. First worked as an assistant city prosecutor and then entered private practice with his brother, Representative Louis Stokes, who was elected to Congress from Ohio in 1968. Elected to state legislature, 1962. Was leader of NAACP and Americans for Democratic Action in Cleveland. Author of *Promises of Power*, a political autobiography, published in 1973. Separated, two children.

LOUIS STOKES

Democratic representative, and first black Congressman from Ohio. Brother of Carl Stokes, former mayor of Cleveland. Represents Cleveland's Twenty-first Congressional District (largely the ghetto areas of Eastside, East Cleveland, Warrensville, and Warrensville Heights). Elected November 1968 to Ninety-first Congress and reelected to Ninety-second and Ninety-third. First black Congressman to serve on the House Appropriations Committee and was chairman of the Congressional Black Caucus in 1972 and 1973. Previously a lawyer with NAACP who gained a reputation for representing militants. "If a brother needed a lawyer, all he'd have to do was ask Louis," friends have said. Created his own image in spite of his brother Carl's achievements. Born in 1925, grew up in the Cleveland ghetto raised by his mother (the boys' father died when they were infants). He worked as a shoeshine boy. Served with United States Army in World War II, paid for his schooling at Western Reserve University and Cleveland-Marshall Law School with the G.I. Bill. Married, four children. Office: 315 Cannon Office Building, Washington, D.C. *See also:* CONGRESSIONAL BLACK CAUCUS.

REV. LEON H. SULLIVAN

Philadelphia civil rights leader whose practical job-training and self-help projects have become million-dollar operations and have spread throughout the country. A Baptist minister in the black ghetto of North Philadelphia, he began opening up job opportunities through a quiet consumers' boycott ("don't buy where you can't work"), then discovered he could not find enough skilled blacks to fill all the jobs. Deciding that "integration without preparation is frustration," in 1964 he set up his own job-training program in an abandoned police station, calling it the Opportunities Industrialization Center (OIC). By 1974, 10 years since it started, the center had trained more than 39,152 people in Philadelphia alone. Federal agencies have financed similar centers in 90 cities. In 1969, 20,000 men and women went through OIC training. "My aim," Sullivan says, "is 100,000 by next year and by 1980 I hope . . . two million." OIC's budget across the country was $23 million in 1969. Sullivan's program stresses "attitude" and includes training in job interviews, grooming, and handling money. "You can't train someone by just putting him behind a machine," he says, "you've got to see that he is properly motivated and has a measure of self-respect." In 1968, when OIC centers became too numerous for Sullivan to handle alone, he set up the National Industrial Advisory Council to help guide and develop the operation with the late General Electric board chairman, Gerald Phillippe, as its first chairman. Established similar programs for the unskilled abroad in such countries as Kenya, Ethiopia, Algeria, and the Dominican Republic. Sullivan also pioneered black capitalism with Zion Investment Associates, based on $10 contributions from members of his Zion Baptist Church. Since 1962 it has financed four major projects: a moderate-income apartment complex; a shopping center (the first in the United States to be owned and operated by blacks); a garment-making company; and Aerospace Enterprises, a subcontracting company started in May 1968 with more than $2.5 million worth of contracts from General Electric, for training hard-core unemployed as aerospace technicians. In 1970 the Zion Investment Associates—renamed the Zion Non-Profit Charitable Trust—was given $150,000 by the Ford Foundation under a federal matching program called MESBIC or the Minority Enterprise Small Business Investment Company—the Nixon administration's major program to encourage minority business enterprises. Meanwhile, his church congregation has grown from 600 to 5,000, the largest in Philadelphia. Cited by U.S. Junior Chamber of Commerce as outstanding young man of Philadelphia (1955). Named by *Life* magazine as one of 100 outstanding young adults in United States (1963). Born October 16, 1922, in Charleston, West Virginia. Ordained a Baptist minister at 17. Won athletic scholarship to West Virginia State College, later studied theology at Union Theological Seminary in New York. After going to Philadelphia in 1950, he set up programs to battle juvenile delinquency, and with other ministers, established effective citywide organization for ending gang wars. Elected to the board of General Motors in 1971, the first black ever elected to the 23-man board, and said "I perfectly well realize that I was chosen because I am a black man, but if I am going to stay on the board, they are going to have to have many more black dealers—and black salesmen." Married, three children. *See also:* OPPORTUNITIES INDUSTRIALIZATION CENTER.

PERCY E. SUTTON

Lawyer and Manhattan borough president since 1965 when he replaced Constance Baker Motley. Has served as president of the New York branch of NAACP (1961) and was elected to the New York State Assembly in 1964. Also presided over the 1966 Democratic State Convention. In April 1971 headed an all-black group that bought the *Amsterdam News*, a 62-year-old black weekly, one of the oldest in the United States with a circulation of more than 82,600 in the New York metropolitan area. Said "The most important factor in the developing of black progress in the next decade is the communications system. Black persons must control elements of the news media in order to liberate themselves."

   In 1973, after receiving a public service award from the New York chapter of the NAACP, announced that he would run for mayor in 1977. Came into civil rights at 13 when he handed out leaflets for the NAACP in San Antonio. Studied political science at Columbia University and received a law degree from Brooklyn Law School. Served in army air corps intelligence during World War II, after which he continued his studies at Prairie View College, Tuskegee Institute, and Hampton Institute. Married twice (to the same woman), Leatrice O'Farrell, first in 1942, and again in 1951, two children. Office: 200 West 135th Street, New York, N.Y. 10030.

MORRIS THOMPSON

Commissioner of Bureau of Indian Affairs (BIA) appointed by President Nixon October 1973. An Athabascan Indian, was born in Tanana, Alaska, September 11, 1939. Before his appointment had been Alaska Area Director for BIA and the first Alaskan native to hold the post. Educated at the University of Alaska and at the RCA Institute of Technology in Los Angeles graduating in 1965. Married, three children. See also: BUREAU OF INDIAN AFFAIRS.

REIES LOPEZ TIJERINA

Mercurial former leader of New Mexico's militant Spanish-American land claimants, the Alianza Federal de los Pueblos Libres (Federal Alliance of Free City-States), founded by him in 1963. Alianza asserts historical claim to about 2,500 square miles of northern New Mexico, and in particular a 30-square-mile area they call the "San Joaquin Free City-State." As director of Alianza, still considers the return of the common land to the Pueblos to be the major issue concerning the organization. In recent years has become involved in the Institute for Research and Study of Justice which he founded in 1971 for the purpose of bringing together ethnic leaders of labor and church groups for better understanding of themselves and their mutual problems. Born 1927, a former evangelist and migrant worker, Tijerina made headlines June 5, 1967, when he led an armed raid on the county courthouse at Tierra Amarilla, in which two policemen were wounded. Tijerina claimed his aim was to make a citizen's arrest of district attorney Alfonso Sanchez for his harassment of Alianza's activities. Arrested June 10 on charges of kidnapping and assault with intent to commit murder, he was acquitted December 14, 1968, after conducting his own defense, in which he claimed that his attempted citizen's arrest was justified. Encouraged, in May and June 1969, he made unsuccessful attempts to make a citizen's arrest of New Mexico Governor David F. Cargo, Chief-Justice-Designate Warren Burger, and scientists at the Los Alamos Laboratory. Tijerina and his followers, mainly descendants of Spanish conquistadors and indigenous Indians, claim their ancestors received vast land grants from the Spanish crown and Mexican government before the 1848 Treaty of Guadalupe-Hidalgo which granted what is now New Mexico to the United States. In 1969, Tijerina resigned briefly as Alianza's director because of a mystic experience directing him to focus his energies on the Middle East crisis. He was succeeded by Ramon Tijerina, one of his four brothers. Alianza's membership is reputed to be some 30,000 families throughout New Mexico and the Southwest. Current president is Eddie Chavez. Alianza's headquarters: 1010 Third Street, Albuquerque, N.M.

TERENCE A. TODMAN

A career foreign service officer; ambassador to Guinea since 1972, appointed by President Nixon. Before that was ambassador to Chad (1969–1972). After United States Army service (1945–1949), he received a B.A. (summa cum laude) from Inter-American University in Puerto Rico in 1951 and an M.A. from Syracuse University. Born in the Virgin Islands, March 13, 1926. Married to the former Doris Weston, two sons, two daughters.

STERLING TUCKER

Executive director of Washington Urban League, the capital's major civil rights organization, since 1956 and built the affiliate membership to 10,000—the largest in the national organization. From July 1968, national director of the Urban League's new five-million dollar "new thrust" program aimed at building black ghetto's economic, social, and political power within their communities. In February 1969, appointed by President Nixon as vice-chairman of District of Columbia city council. In June 1968, replaced Bayard Rustin as national coordinator of Poor People's March, after Rustin resigned over disagreement with Southern Christian Leadership Conference leaders. Author of *Beyond the Burning* (Association Press 1968) and *Black Reflections on White Power*, described as "a clear statement of the very important and growing position between the traditional civil rights movement and the violent revolutionary stance," and in 1971 *For Blacks Only* (both published by Wm. B. Erdmans). Has lectured widely for the State Department in Japan, India, Southeast Asia, and Europe and currently is visiting lecturer at the Foreign Institute and USIA.

Born Akron, Ohio December 21, 1923. Graduated from the University of Akron (B.A., 1946, M.A., 1950 in social psychology). Began civil rights activity as a student, then as official of Urban League in Akron and Canton. Married to the former Alloyce Robinson, two daughters. Office: 1424 16th Street, N W., Washington, D.C.

URBAN COALITION, NATIONAL

On July 31, 1967, after the riots of Newark and Detroit, a group of 22 prominent Americans announced the formation of an urban coalition designed to focus attention on urban problems and to get "positive and progressive action" on them. The group, called together by Pittsburgh Mayor Joseph Barr and New York Mayor John Lindsay, announced (August 7, 1969) that it planned to call a national convention of 1,000 business, labor, religious, educational, civil rights, and city government leaders to seek solutions to pressing urban questions. The "emergency convocation," held in Washington, D.C., August 24, named Andrew Heiskell, chairman of the board of Time, Inc., and A. Philip Randolph, president of the Brotherhood of Sleeping Car Porters, as cochairmen of coalition's steering committee. In February 1968, outgoing Department of Health, Education and Welfare Secretary John Gardner was named head of the organization, with the title of chairman. The coalition listed as its goals: an emergency federal program to provide jobs and training for urban poor; promotion of nongovernmental efforts to train hard-core unemployed; and a long-range program for physical and social reconstruction of the cities. The group called upon "the nation and the Congress to reorder our national priorities, with a commitment of national resources equal to the dimension of the problems we face."

The national coalition merged with Urban America in early 1970. (Formed in 1965, Urban America was the first private national group that had focused on critical urban problems.) In 1970 Sol M. Linowitz, former president of Xerox Corporation and a former ambassador to the Organization of American States under President Johnson, became chairman of the Coalition. He replaced John Gardner who currently heads Common Cause, a citizens lobby organization. While Linowitz was chairman, the organization went through serious internal up-heavals—bickering between staff workers and between members of the different civil rights, labor, and religious groups comprising the Coalition—which nearly tore it apart and added to the drop in interest and support, particularly from businessmen on whose financial support the Coalition depends. Since May 1973, after its first national conference and the various factions had solved their differences, support for the organization has been on the increase. Chairman Linowitz attributed this renewed interest to opposition to the Nixon administration's domestic policies. "It was due to what I call constructive backlash to Watergate. It was exhilarating to find that what was disturbing to the *chicanos* and blacks also disturbed labor and business leaders," he said in a *New York Times* interview October 17, 1973. The Coalition is financed by contributions from individuals, business, and foundations and its budget is $2.5 million. There are also some 34 chapters across the country. Recently the Coaliton has tried to encourage reform in the federal budgetary process and has established programs to help minority contractors and to bring minorities into the health field. Linowitz stepped down as chairman in the fall of 1973. New chairman is Walter Rothchild (former president of Abraham & Straus stores) who works with a steering committee of 106 prominent citizens, legislators, and business people. Headquarters: 2100 M Street, N.W., Washington, D.C.

URBAN LEAGUE, NATIONAL

Founded in 1910 and known as one of the most affluent—and among the most effective—of all civil rights groups. Its 101 affiliates in 34 states and the District of Columbia depend on contributions from individuals, including major federal and foundation grants, as well as support from commerce and industry. Claims a professional staff of 3,000 and is considered one of the most stable civil rights organizations in spite of a reported deficit of over $1 million in 1972. In 1973 reported to have received $22 million in federal grants and this federal bankrolling plus the "optimism about the organization's role that is almost startling by contrast to the NAACP and especially the SCLC" is what sets the League apart from most other civil rights organizations according to columnist William Raspberry (*Washington Post*, July 23, 1973). Emphasis is on furthering economic progress for blacks. It operates training programs, helps find jobs, aids in health, education, housing, veteran affairs, and research in areas such as population, drugs, and transportation. In 1972 alone, placed 5,000 men and women in better jobs, 3,000 apprentices and journeymen in formerly closed industries, and some 8,000 veterans in jobs, housing, and schools. Many new programs were begun in the ghetto areas in 1968 and 1969 under League's "new thrust" program designed to answer needs of residents in those areas. They included minority leadership development, day care centers, police-community relations, and in 1972 expanded to include voter registration.

In 1968, the League officially embraced the concept of "black power." The late Whitney Young, Jr., then executive director, said: "The words have caught the imagination; they come to convey, above all, pride and community solidarity and this is a positive and constructive concept." However, Young ruled out acceptance of black separatism. He said, "We do not intend to do the racists' job for them by accepting segregation, and we plan no one-way trips to Africa." After Young's death in 1971, Vernon E. Jordan was appointed executive director. Said that while the League was never in the forefront of the movement in 1960s, times had changed and that "the 1970s are a period of implementation and there is no better time for the Urban League. . . . You look at the civil rights movement and we have the greatest talent for delivering the promise of the 1960s, in terms of local leadership, in terms of credibility across the board, in terms of resources financial and otherwise, we're in better shape than any other agency." Executive director: Vernon E. Jordan, Jr., president: James A. Linen. Office: 55 East 52nd Street, New York, N.Y. 10022.

WYATT TEE WALKER
Resident minister of the Canaan Baptist Church in Harlem with a membership of over 1,000, and special assistant for urban affairs to New York Governor Rockefeller. Also active in antinarcotic efforts in New York City. Had been executive director of Southern Christian Leadership Conference from 1960–1964, and is credited with laying the groundwork for the assault on racial segregation in Birmingham, Alabama, in 1963. Also served briefly as interim pastor of Adam Clayton Powell's Abyssinian Baptist Church but was dismissed in September 1965, in a dispute over a visit by Martin Luther King, Jr. Plans to run for Manhattan Borough President in 1977. Graduated from Virginia Union University in 1950. Married the former Theresa Edwards in 1950, four children. Office: 132 West 116th Street, New York, N.Y. 10026.

WALTER E. WASHINGTON
First mayor of Washington, D.C., and first black mayor of any major city in the United States. Appointed by President Johnson after the capital's municipal government was reorganized in August 1967, and reappointed by President Nixon for two more terms (1969–1973 and 1973–1977). Early in his administration he was faced with the worst riots in the capital's history (for details, see chronology) following the assassination of Dr. Martin Luther King, Jr., in April 1968. Received wide praise as a "moderating influence" during and after the

riots, during which he made nightly television appeals for calm, mobilized the business community to provide emergency food and housing for victims, and organized vacation programs for thousands of young people. Later credited with easing tensions between police and black community and preventing major confrontations during antiwar and other demonstrations. Instituted a crackdown on slum landlords and stepped up efforts to combat the capital's high crime rate, for which he was held partly to blame by some critics. However, crime rate in the District has dropped since his crackdown. In June 1970, visited the Soviet Union as guest of Moscow city council, as part of three-week State Department-sponsored trip to Europe and Asia. A lawyer, Mayor Washington served 25 years with the capital's public housing authority before being appointed chairman of the New York City Housing Authority in 1966. Born in Dawson, Georgia, in 1915, and graduate of Howard University Law School. Admitted to D.C. bar, 1948. His wife, Dr. Bennetta B. Washington, is director of the Women's Job Corps and a trustee of American Field Service, one daughter.

TED WATKINS
Chairman and project administrator of the Watts Labor Community Action Committee (WLCAC). Formed organization in 1965 before the Watts riots. Began working when he was seven. Moved to California at 15 and worked with the Ford Motor Company as a fender specialist for nearly 20 years. Became a United Auto Worker official and with union's support was able to work full time on WLCAC project. Born 1923 in Meridian, Mississippi. See also: WATTS LABOR COMMUNITY ACTION COMMITTEE.

BARBARA WATSON
Administrator of Bureau of Security and Consular Affairs, State Department, since 1968; the first woman and also the first black to hold position at this level in State Department. Joined the department in 1966 after serving as attorney with New York City government, latterly as head of the city's liaison with United Nations. In 1948 founded the first all-black modeling agency which she headed until 1958, and then became coordinator and foreign student adviser at Hampton Institute in Hampton, Virginia. Born New York City, November 5, 1918, daughter of the late Judge James S. Watson and Mrs. Violet Lopez Watson. Graduated Barnard College (1943) and New York University Law School (1962), where she was named "most outstanding law student." Unmarried.

WATTS LABOR COMMUNITY ACTION
COMMITTEE (WLCAC)
A Watts, Los Angeles, self-help organization started in 1965 and reported to have been a major factor in keeping the ghetto cool during aftermath of Dr. Martin Luther King's assassination in 1968, and also after defeat of Councilman Thomas Bradley in mayoralty race in 1969. Headed by former United Auto Workers (UAW) official Ted Watkins, and with UAW support, the organization's primary purpose was to beautify and transform the Watts area and started out

with a staff of five. Today employs over 300 and operates two service stations, two restaurants, a farm, seven supermarkets, a landscaping company, a construction company, and a subsidiary corporation which has been assisting the relocation of Watts residents whose homes were condemned to make room for a new superhighway. Funding comes from participating labor unions, such as UAW, the federal government, and the Ford and Rockefeller foundations. Total membership reportedly around 3,000. Chairman, Ted Watkins; vice-chairman, Ellis Bell. Headquarters: 11401 S. Central Avenue, Los Angeles, Cal. 90059. *See also:* TED WATKINS.

ROBERT C. WEAVER

First black cabinet member. Named by President Johnson, January 13, 1966, as cabinet-level secretary of the newly created Department of Housing and Urban Development (HUD) and sworn in five days later. Resigned November 1968, to become president of the projected Bernard M. Baruch College of the City University of New York (CUNY) which was built in an urban renewal area of Brooklyn to replace CUNY's existing Baruch School of Business Administration. Weaver said he wanted to make the new school "a prototype of the urban university as an idea-generation and action-implementation center for meeting the paramount domestic challenge of our time." In 1971 resigned to become professor of urban affairs at Hunter College, CUNY. Headed the Housing and Home Finance Agency (HHFA), 1961–1966. Born Washington, D.C., December 29, 1907. Interrupted his high school education to become an electrician, but went on to graduate as an economist at Harvard, where he received his Ph.D. in 1934. Adviser on Negro affairs, Department of the Interior, 1933–1937. Taught at Columbia and New York Universities, 1947–1949. New York state rent administrator, 1955–1959. Former chairman, NAACP. Author: *The Urban Complex,* 1964; *Dilemmas of Urban America,* 1965; *The Negro Ghetto,* 1948; and *Negro Labor: A National Problem,* 1946. His wife, Ella, is assistant professor of speech at Brooklyn College, one son. Office: Department of Urban Affairs, Hunter College, 790 Madison Avenue, New York, N Y. 10021.

ROGER WILKINS

In May 1974 became member of editorial board of *The New York Times.* Had been member of the editorial board of the *Washington Post* since 1972. Before that was director of studies in social development at the Ford Foundation in New York City. Nephew of Roy Wilkins, NAACP executive director. From 1966–1968 was director of Community Relations Service in the Department of Justice and prior to that practiced law in New York City and did welfare work in Cleveland, Ohio. Made headlines March 15, 1970, when he declined a White House invitation "out of conscience" because, he said, he felt that Nixon's policies were crushing Negro hopes.

ROY WILKINS

Executive director of the NAACP, which he has headed since 1955, and civil rights activist for 40 years. Wilkins was one of the chief symbols of moderation in the turbulent civil rights scene of the 1960s. In firmly rejecting violence and the concepts of black power and black nationalism, and in voicing support for the use of troops to suppress racial riots, he has been a frequent target of criticism among the new generation of black militants. More recently, he has also voiced strong opposition to student demands for all-black departments on college campuses, describing this as a return to "segregation and Jim Crow." But his position as veteran leader of the nation's most influential civil rights group has remained secure, according to *The New York Times*, because of "his mastery of the geography and mechanics of power in Washington." His ability to get action where others fail has earned him a reputation as "master strategist" and "statesman" in the cause of civil rights. At NAACP's annual meeting held in New York in January 1973, said that the American blacks are under a state of siege which has been launched by the "executive branch of the federal government," pointing out that the government has not fought for jobs for black workers, and to the appointment of Peter J. Brennan as secretary of labor, which Wilkins called "a very real obstacle to the employment of blacks in the construction industry." Author (with Ramsey Clark) of *Search and Destroy: A Report by the Commission of Inquiry into the Black Panthers and the Police*, published in 1973. Born in St. Louis on August 30, 1901, he graduated from the University of Minnesota in 1923. Became a newspaperman with the *Kansas City Call*, a black weekly, until joining the NAACP in 1931 as an assistant to Walter White. Married to the former Aminda Badeau of St. Louis.

HOSEA WILLIAMS

National program director of Southern Christian Leadership Conference (SCLC) and veteran of many of Dr. Martin Luther King's civil rights campaigns. Leader of May 1970 "march against repression," from Perry (Georgia) to Atlanta. March was seen as opening an active new phase in SCLC strategy. During the march, Williams called for "black power," a phrase attacked by the late Dr. King. But Williams explained that black power today meant self-respect, not violence. In June 1970, Williams qualified as Republican primary candidate for secretary of state of Georgia. His wife, Juanita, qualified for 1970 Democratic primary for controller general. In 1968, ran unsuccessfully for Georgia House of Representatives as a Democrat. Ran for city council president in Atlanta in 1973 but lost. In fall of 1971 spent four weeks in China as part of a world tour representing SCLC president Ralph Abernathy. Said that his visit there enabled him "to look back and see vividly the many mistakes we made in the civil rights movement in America. We have moved from the streets into the economic realm, then into the political realm and then into the educational realm—we are not grounded in an ideology the way the Chinese leaders were." In 1973, Williams said on the tenth anniversary of Martin Luther King's "I Have A Dream" speech in Washington: "Integration has failed. It didn't work. One of the main reasons integration has failed is that the black man does not respect himself. No man can respect you if you don't respect yourself. We've got to back up and get our thing together. The second reason that integration failed is that white men cannot shed 400 years of racism just like that."

Born January 5, 1926, in Attapulgus, Georgia, Williams was a chemist with the U. S. Department of Agriculture before joining the civil rights movement, in which he soon became known for his skill in "grass roots" organization. Jailed more than 40 times during rights campaigns in the South.

JULIUS E. WILLIAMS
Director, Armed Services and Veterans Affairs of NAACP since 1969. A long time NAACP worker, has served in various capacities in the organization—Youth Council president, branch secretary, branch executive committee member and vice-president of the Illinois State Conference. A native of Birmingham, Alabama, he was graduated from the Maywood, Illinois public schools. Has a B.A. in business administration from the University of Chicago and M.B.A. degree from the School of Commerce of Northwestern University. A veteran of World War II and Korean conflict, retired with the rank of lieutenant colonel.

ROBERT F. WILLIAMS
Black revolutionary and one time branch president of the NAACP in North Carolina who returned to the United States September 12, 1969, after eight years' self-imposed exile in Cuba, North Vietnam, Communist China, and Tanzania. While abroad, published newsletter for American blacks urging revolution and advising on urban guerrilla-warfare techniques. Also called on blacks to refuse to serve in Vietnam—and if they went, to kill white soldiers. Upon return, wearing Mao uniform, was taken into custody by FBI at Detroit airport. Later released. Told newsmen September 15 that United States today represented "the best chance ever for social changes and racial justice," and he was committed to developing a "selfless society."

In March 1970, he testified in secret before Senate Internal Security Subcommittee, answering questions on his travels abroad and meetings with Mao Tse-Tung, Fidel Castro, and Ho Chi Minh. Some reports linked his activities with U.S. Intelligence but lawyer denied it. Elected president of the Republic of New Africa at group's national convention in Washington, D.C., August 23, 1969, but was ousted from the office after internal party split, December, 1969. Currently at the Center for Chinese Studies at the University of Michigan.

Born 1925, Williams fled United States in August 1961, to avoid trial for allegedly kidnapping Mr. and Mrs. Bruce Stegall of Marshville, North Carolina, during a racial disturbance—a case he says is still open in spite of the fact that the couple in question have asked that the charges be dropped. Lectures widely and said at an Afro-American Society meeting in September 1973 that "students should be in the vanguard of the black liberation movement," and told them to go to their books "and let them be your weapons of vengeance." Now describes himself as a self-determinationist. Married, two sons. See also: REPUBLIC OF NEW AFRICA.

WOODLAWN ORGANIZATION
Formed in early 1961 as a community action group in the black Woodlawn area of Chicago's South Side. The organization has acted as arbiter between street

gangs, led neighborhood improvement projects, and organized job-training and voter registration drives. Coordinated controversial Office of Economic Opportunity-funded job-training program for members of the Rangers and Disciples gangs, which was criticized at the Senate Government Operations Committee hearings in Washington, June 1968. Originally led by Rev. Arthur Brazier who was praised by Senator Charles H. Percy for his "courage, guts and determination." Brazier told the story of his organization in *Black Self-Determination: The Story of the Woodlawn Organization*, published by Wm. B. Eerdmans, September 1969. Serves currently as an advisor. Also is a vice-president for the Center for Community Change in Chicago. *Black Power: White Control* by John Fisk (published December 1973 by the Princeton University Press) also tells the Woodlawn story. Executive director: Leon D. Finney.

FRANK YERBY
Most commercially successful black writer. Has more than 20 novels to his credit—including the 1949 bestseller *Foxes of Harrow; Pride's Castle* (1948); *An Odor of Sanctity* (1965); *Goat Song* (1967); *The Dahomean* (1971)—which have grossed him over $10 million. Has lived abroad since 1952, for the past 13 years in Spain. Born in Augusta, Georgia, September 5, 1916. Graduated from Paine College (1937), receiving M.A. from Fisk University (1938). Married twice, four children.

ANDREW J. YOUNG
Elected to the House of Representatives from Georgia's Fifth Congressional District November 7, 1973 after an unsuccessful attempt in 1970, making him the first black Congressman elected from Georgia since Jefferson Long served in 1870 and 1871. Is also only black elected to Congress from a primarily white district in North or South. He serves on the House Banking and Currency Committee with subcommittee duties in mass transit, consumer affairs, international trade and finance. Is also a member of the Congressional Black Caucus. In a *Washington Post* interview of July 24, 1973 said "the problems we face today are not racial. We are in a class struggle. We are talking about attitudes, redistribution of wealth, oil depletion allowances and the war." He joined the Southern Christian Leadership Conference (SCLC) in 1961 and was its executive director 1964-1967, when he became executive vice-president, the number-two man in the SCLC hierarchy and considered by some to have been the "brains" of the organization. Like Ralph Abernathy, had been a friend of Martin Luther King since the 1955 bus boycott in Montgomery, Alabama. His forte is said to be community organization. Born March 12, 1932, in New Orleans, Louisiana, the son of Dr. A. J. Young, Sr. After studying at Dillard and Howard Universities (1951), graduated from Hartford (Connecticut) Theological Seminary in 1955, was ordained a minister of the United Church of Christ and became a pastor in Marion, Alabama. Married to the former Jean Childs, four children. *See also:* CONGRESSIONAL BLACK CAUCUS.

Appendix I
Congressional Voting Records on Civil Rights Acts from 1957 to 1970

1957 Civil Rights Act

(Provides enforcement for the right to vote by empowering federal government, through the attorney general, to seek court injunctions against obstruction or deprivation of voting rights.)

SENATE

Vote Total: 72 for; 18 against

N Record Vote Against (nay).
X Announced Against, Paired Against.
? Absent, General Pair, "Present."

Y Record Vote For (yea).
• Announced For, Paired For.
— Not a Member when vote was taken.

ALABAMA			GEORGIA			MAINE		
Hill	(D)	N	Russell	(D)	N	Payne	(R)	•
Sparkman	(D)	N	Talmadge	(D)	N	Smith	(R)	Y
ARIZONA			**IDAHO**			**MARYLAND**		
Hayden	(D)	Y	Church	(D)	Y	Beall	(R)	Y
Goldwater	(R)	Y	Dworshak	(R)	Y	Butler	(R)	Y
ARKANSAS			**ILLINOIS**			**MASSACHUSETTS**		
Fulbright	(D)	N	Douglas	(D)	Y	Kennedy	(D)	Y
McClellan	(D)	N	Dirksen	(R)	Y	Saltonstall	(R)	Y
CALIFORNIA			**INDIANA**			**MICHIGAN**		
Knowland	(R)	Y	Capehart	(R)	Y	McNamara	(D)	Y
Kuchel	(R)	Y	Jenner	(R)	Y	Potter	(R)	Y
COLORADO			**IOWA**			**MINNESOTA**		
Carroll	(D)	Y	Hickenlooper	(R)	Y	Humphrey	(D)	Y
Allott	(R)	Y	Martin	(R)	Y	Thye	(R)	Y
CONNECTICUT			**KANSAS**			**MISSISSIPPI**		
Bush	(R)	Y	Carlson	(R)	Y	Eastland	(D)	N
Purtell	(R)	Y	Schoeppel	(R)	Y	Stennis	(D)	N.
DELAWARE			**KENTUCKY**			**MISSOURI**		
Frear	(D)	•	Cooper	(R)	Y	Hennings	(D)	Y
Williams	(R)	Y	Morton	(R)	Y	Symington	(D)	Y
FLORIDA			**LOUISIANA**			**MONTANA**		
Holland	(D)	N	Ellender	(D)	N	Mansfield	(D)	Y
Smathers	(D)	Y	Long	(D)	N	Murray	(D)	Y

Note: Excepted and reprinted from the *Congressional Quarterly.*

NEBRASKA			OHIO			TEXAS		
Curtis	(R)	Y	Lausche	(D)	Y	Yarborough	(D)	Y
Hruska	(R)	Y	Bricker	(R)	Y	Johnson	(D)	Y
NEVADA			**OKLAHOMA**			**UTAH**		
Bible	(D)	Y	Kerr	(D)	Y	Bennett	(R)	Y
Malone	(R)	•	Monroney	(D)	Y	Watkins	(R)	Y
NEW HAMPSHIRE			**OREGON**			**VERMONT**		
Bridges	(R)	•	Morse	(D)	N	Aiken	(R)	Y
Cotton	(R)	Y	Neuberger	(D)	Y	Flanders	(R)	Y
NEW JERSEY			**PENNSYLVANIA**			**VIRGINIA**		
Case	(R)	Y	Clark	(D)	Y	Byrd	(D)	N
Smith	(R)	Y	Martin	(R)	Y	Robertson	(D)	N
NEW MEXICO			**RHODE ISLAND**			**WASHINGTON**		
Anderson	(D)	Y	Green	(D)	Y	Jackson	(D)	Y
Chavez	(D)	Y	Pastore	(D)	Y	Magnuson	(D)	Y
NEW YORK			**SOUTH CAROLINA**			**WEST VIRGINIA**		
Ives	(R)	Y	Johnston	(D)	N	Neely	(D)	•
Javits	(R)	Y	Thurmond	(D)	N	Revercomb	(R)	Y
NORTH CAROLINA			**SOUTH DAKOTA**			**WISCONSIN**		
Ervin	(D)	N	Case	(R)	Y	Vacancy		
Scott	(D)	N	Mundt	(R)	Y	Wiley	(R)	Y
NORTH DAKOTA			**TENNESSEE**			**WYOMING**		
Langer	(R)	Y	Gore	(D)	Y	O'Mahoney	(D)	Y
Young	(R)	Y	Kefauver	(D)	Y	Barrett	(R)	Y

HOUSE OF REPRESENTATIVES   Vote Total: 286 for, 126 against

N Record Vote Against (nay).   Y Record Vote For (yea).
X Announced Against, Paired Against.   • Announced For, Paired For.
? Absent, General Pair, "Present."   — Not a Member when vote was taken.

ALABAMA								
Andrews	(D)	N	Sheppard	(D)	Y	Chenoweth	(R)	Y
Boykin	(D)	N	Sisk	(D)	Y	Hill	(R)	Y
Elliott	(D)	N	Allen	(R)	Y	**CONNECTICUT**		
Grant	(D)	N	Baldwin	(R)	Y	Cretella	(R)	Y
Huddleston	(D)	N	Gubser	(R)	Y	May	(R)	Y
Jones	(D)	N	Mailliard	(R)	Y	Morano	(R)	Y
Rains	(D)	N	Scudder	(R)	Y	Patterson	(R)	Y
Roberts	(D)	N	Teague	(R)	Y	Sadlak	(R)	Y
Selden	(D)	N	Utt	(R)	X	Seely-Brown	(R)	Y
ARIZONA			Wilson	(R)	Y	**DELAWARE**		
Udall	(D)	Y	Younger	(R)	Y	Haskell	(R)	Y
Rhodes	(R)	Y	**Los Angeles County**			**FLORIDA**		
ARKANSAS			Doyle	(D)	Y	Bennett	(D)	N
Gathings	(D)	N	Holifield	(D)	Y	Fascell	(D)	N
Harris	(D)	N	King	(D)	Y	Haley	(D)	N
Hays	(D)	N	Roosevelt	(D)	Y	Herlong	(D)	N
Mills	(D)	N	Hiestand	(R)	Y	Matthews	(D)	N
Norrell	(D)	N	Hillings	(R)	•	Rogers	(D)	N
Trimble	(D)	N	Holt	(R)	Y	Sikes	(D)	N
CALIFORNIA			Hosmer	(R)	Y	Cramer	(R)	N
Engle	(D)	Y	Jackson	(R)	Y	**GEORGIA**		
Hagen	(D)	Y	Lipscomb	(R)	Y	Blitch	(D)	N
McFall	(D)	Y	McDonough	(R)	Y	Brown	(D)	N
Miller	(D)	Y	Smith	(R)	Y	Davis	(D)	N
Moss	(D)	Y	**COLORADO**			Flynt	(D)	N
Saund	(D)	Y	Aspinall	(D)	Y	Forrester	(D)	N
Shelley	(D)	Y	Rogers	(D)	Y	Landrum	(D)	N
						Lanham	(D)	N

Pilcher	(D)	N	Scrivner	(R)	Y	**Detroit-Wayne County**		
Preston	(D)	N	Smith	(R)	N	Diggs	(D)	Y
Vinson	(D)	N	**KENTUCKY**			Dingell	(D)	Y
IDAHO			Chelf	(D)	N	Griffiths	(D)	Y
Pfost	(D)	Y	Gregory	(D)	N	Lesinski	(D)	Y
Budge	(R)	N	Natcher	(D)	N	Machrowicz	(D)	•
ILLINOIS			Perkins	(D)	Y	Rabaut	(D)	Y
Gray	(D)	Y	Spence	(D)	N	**MINNESOTA**		
Mack	(D)	Y	Watts	(D)	N	Blatnik	(D)	Y
Price	(D)	Y	Robsion	(R)	Y	Knutson	(D)	Y
Allen	(R)	Y	Siler	(R)	Y	Marshall	(D)	Y
Arends	(R)	Y	**LOUISIANA**			McCarthy	(D)	Y
Chiperfield	(R)	Y	Boggs	(D)	N	Wier	(D)	Y
Keeney	(R)	N	Brooks	(D)	N	Andersen	(R)	Y
Mason	(R)	N	Hebert	(D)	N	Andresen	(R)	Y
Michel	(R)	Y	Long	(D)	N	Judd	(R)	Y
Simpson	(R)	?	Morrison	(D)	N	O'Hara	(R)	N
Springer	(R)	Y	Passman	(D)	N	**MISSISSIPPI**		
Vursell	(R)	Y	Thompson	(D)	N	Abernethy	(D)	N
Chicago-Cook County			Willis	(D)	N	Colmer	(D)	N
Vacancy			**MAINE**			Smith	(D)	N
Boyle	(D)	Y	Coffin	(D)	Y	Whitten	(D)	N
Dawson	(D)	Y	Hale	(R)	Y	Williams	(D)	N
Gordon	(D)	Y	McIntire	(R)	Y	Winstead	(D)	N
Kluczynski	(D)	Y	**MARYLAND**			**MISSOURI**		
O'Brien	(D)	Y	Fallon	(D)	Y	Bolling	(D)	Y
O'Hara	(D)	Y	Friedel	(D)	Y	Brown	(D)	Y
Yates	(D)	Y	Garmatz	(D)	Y	Cannon	(D)	Y
Byrne	(R)	Y	Lankford	(D)	Y	Carnahan	(D)	Y
Church	(R)	Y	Devereux	(R)	Y	Christopher	(D)	Y
Collier	(R)	Y	Hyde	(R)	Y	Hull	(D)	N
McVey	(R)	Y	Miller	(R)	Y	Jones	(D)	N
Sheehan	(R)	Y	**MASSACHUSETTS**			Karsten	(D)	Y
INDIANA			Boland	(D)	Y	Moulder	(D)	Y
Denton	(D)	Y	Donohue	(D)	Y	Sullivan	(D)	Y
Madden	(D)	Y	Lane	(D)	Y	Curtis	(R)	Y
Adair	(R)	Y	Macdonald	(D)	Y	**MONTANA**		
Beamer	(R)	•	McCormack	(D)	Y	Anderson	(D)	Y
Bray	(R)	Y	O'Neill	(D)	Y	Metcalf	(D)	Y
Brownson	(R)	Y	Philbin	(D)	Y	**NEBRASKA**		
Halleck	(R)	Y	Bates	(R)	Y	Cunningham	(R)	Y
Harden	(R)	Y	Curtis	(R)	Y	Harrison	(R)	Y
Harvey	(R)	Y	Heselton	(R)	Y	Miller	(R)	Y
Nimtz	(R)	Y	Martin	(R)	Y	Weaver	(R)	Y
Wilson	(R)	Y	Nicholson	(R)	Y	**NEVADA**		
IOWA			Rogers	(R)	Y	Baring	(D)	Y
Coad	(D)	Y	Wigglesworth	(R)	Y	**NEW HAMPSHIRE**		
Cunningham	(R)	Y	**MICHIGAN**			Bass	(R)	Y
Gross	(R)	N	Bennett	(R)	N	Merrow	(R)	Y
Hoeven	(R)	Y	Bentley	(R)	•	**NEW JERSEY**		
Jensen	(R)	X	Broomfield	(R)	Y	Addonizio	(D)	Y
LeCompte	(R)	Y	Cederberg	(R)	Y	Rodino	(D)	Y
Schwengel	(R)	Y	Chamberlain	(R)	Y	Sieminski	(D)	Y
Talle	(R)	Y	Ford	(R)	Y	Thompson	(D)	Y
KANSAS			Griffin	(R)	•	Auchincloss	(R)	Y
Breeding	(D)	Y	Hoffman	(R)	N	Canfield	(R)	Y
Avery	(R)	Y	Johansen	(R)	N	Dellay	(R)	Y
George	(R)	Y	Knox	(R)	Y	Dwyer	(R)	Y
Rees	(R)	Y	McIntosh	(R)	•	Frelinghuysen	(R)	Y
			Meader	(R)	Y	Vacancy		

Name	Party	Vote
Kean	(R)	•
Osmers	(R)	Y
Widnall	(R)	Y
Wolverton	(R)	Y
NEW MEXICO		
Dempsey	(D)	Y
Montoya	(D)	Y
NEW YORK		
O'Brien	(D)	Y
Becker	(R)	Y
Cole	(R)	Y
Derounian	(R)	Y
Dooley	(R)	Y
Gwinn	(R)	Y
Kearney	(R)	Y
Keating	(R)	Y
Kilburn	(R)	N
Miller	(R)	Y
Ostertag	(R)	Y
Pillion	(R)	Y
Radwan	(R)	Y
Reed	(R)	Y
Riehlman	(R)	Y
St. George	(R)	Y
Taber	(R)	N
Taylor	(R)	Y
Wainwright	(R)	Y
Wharton	(R)	Y
Williams	(R)	?
New York City		
Anfuso	(D)	Y
Buckley	(D)	Y
Celler	(D)	Y
Delaney	(D)	Y
Dollinger	(D)	Y
Farbstein	(D)	Y
Healey	(D)	Y
Holtzman	(D)	?
Kelly	(D)	Y
Keogh	(D)	Y
Multer	(D)	Y
Powell	(D)	Y
Rooney	(D)	Y
Santangelo	(D)	Y
Teller	(D)	Y
Zelenko	(D)	Y
Bosch	(R)	Y
Coudert	(R)	Y
Dorn	(R)	Y
Fino	(R)	Y
Latham	(R)	Y
Ray	(R)	N
NORTH CAROLINA		
Alexander	(D)	N
Barden	(D)	N
Bonner	(D)	N
Cooley	(D)	N
Durham	(D)	N
Fountain	(D)	N
Kitchin	(D)	N
Lennon	(D)	N
Scott	(D)	N
Shuford	(D)	N
Whitener	(D)	N
Jonas	(R)	N
NORTH DAKOTA		
Burdick	(R)	Y
Krueger	(R)	Y
OHIO		
Ashley	(D)	Y
Feighan	(D)	Y
Hays	(D)	Y
Kirwan	(D)	Y
Polk	(D)	Y
Vanik	(D)	Y
Ayres	(R)	Y
Baumhart	(R)	Y
Betts	(R)	Y
Bolton	(R)	Y
Bow	(R)	Y
Brown	(R)	Y
Clevenger	(R)	N
Dennison	(R)	Y
Henderson	(R)	Y
Hess	(R)	Y
Jenkins	(R)	Y
McCulloch	(R)	Y
McGregor	(R)	Y
Minshall	(R)	Y
Schenck	(R)	Y
Scherer	(R)	?
Vorys	(R)	Y
OKLAHOMA		
Albert	(D)	N
Edmondson	(D)	Y
Jarman	(D)	N
Morris	(D)	Y
Steed	(D)	X
Belcher	(R)	Y
OREGON		
Green	(D)	Y
Porter	(D)	Y
Ullman	(D)	Y
Norblad	(R)	Y
PENNSYLVANIA		
Clark	(D)	Y
Eberharter	(D)	Y
Flood	(D)	Y
Holland	(D)	Y
Kelley	(D)	Y
Morgan	(D)	Y
Rhodes	(D)	Y
Walter	(D)	Y
Bush	(R)	?
Carrigg	(R)	Y
Corbett	(R)	Y
Curtin	(R)	Y
Dague	(R)	Y
Fenton	(R)	Y
Fulton	(R)	Y
Gavin	(R)	Y
James	(R)	Y
Kearns	(R)	Y
McConnell	(R)	Y
Mumma	(R)	?
Saylor	(R)	Y
Simpson	(R)	Y
Stauffer	(R)	Y
Van Zandt	(R)	Y
Philadelphia		
Barrett	(D)	Y
Byrne	(D)	Y
Chudoff	(D)	Y
Granahan	(D)	Y
Green	(D)	Y
Scott	(R)	Y
RHODE ISLAND		
Fogarty	(D)	Y
Forand	(D)	Y
SOUTH CAROLINA		
Ashmore	(D)	N
Dorn	(D)	N
Hemphill	(D)	N
McMillan	(D)	N
Riley	(D)	N
Rivers	(D)	N
SOUTH DAKOTA		
McGovern	(D)	•
Berry	(R)	Y
TENNESSEE		
Bass	(D)	N
Cooper	(D)	N
Davis	(D)	N
Evins	(D)	N
Frazier	(D)	N
Loser	(D)	N
Murray	(D)	X
Baker	(R)	X
Reece	(R)	Y
TEXAS		
Beckworth	(D)	N
Brooks	(D)	N
Burleson	(D)	N
Dies	(D)	N
Dowdy	(D)	N
Fisher	(D)	N
Ikard	(D)	N
Kilday	(D)	N
Kilgore	(D)	N
Mahon	(D)	N
Patman	(D)	N
Poage	(D)	N
Rayburn	(D)	—
Rogers	(D)	N
Rutherford	(D)	N
Teague	(D)	N
Thomas	(D)	N
Thompson	(D)	N
Thornberry	(D)	N
Wright	(D)	N

Young	(D)	N	Tuck	(D)	N	Staggers	(D)	Y
Alger	(R)	N	Broyhill	(R)	N	Moore	(R)	Y
UTAH			Poff	(R)	N	Neal	(R)	Y
Dawson	(R)	Y	**WASHINGTON**			**WISCONSIN**		
Dixon	(R)	Y	Magnuson	(D)	Y	Johnson	(D)	Y
VERMONT			Holmes	(R)	Y	Reuss	(D)	Y
AL Prouty	(R)	Y	Horan	(R)	Y	Zablocki	(D)	Y
VIRGINIA			Mack	(R)	Y	Byrnes	(R)	Y
Abbitt	(D)	N	Pelly	(R)	Y	Laird	(R)	Y
Gary	(D)	N	Tollefson	(R)	Y	O'Konski	(R)	Y
Hardy	(D)	N	Westland	(R)	Y	Smith	(R)	N
Harrison	(D)	N	**WEST VIRGINIA**			Tewes	(R)	Y
Jennings	(D)	N	Bailey	(D)	•	Van Pelt	(R)	Y
Robeson	(D)	N	Byrd	(D)	Y	Withrow	(R)	Y
Smith	(D)	N	Kee	(D)	Y	**WYOMING**		
						Thomson	(R)	Y

1960 Civil Rights Act

(Contains penalties for obstructing school desegregation orders, requires preservation of voting records, provides for court referees, strengthens 1957 Civil Rights Act.)

SENATE   Vote Total: 71 for; 18 against

Y Record Vote For (yea).
• Paired For.
† Announced For.
N Record Vote Against (nay).

X Paired Against.
— Announced Against.
? Absent, General Pair, "Present," Did not announce.

ALABAMA			**GEORGIA**			**MAINE**		
Hill	(D)	N	Russell	(D)	N	Muskie	(D)	Y
Sparkman	(D)	N	Talmadge	(D)	N	Smith	(R)	Y
ALASKA			**HAWAII**			**MARYLAND**		
Bartlett	(D)	Y	Long	(R)	Y	Beall	(R)	Y
Gruening	(D)	Y	Fong	(D)	Y	Butler	(R)	Y
ARIZONA			**IDAHO**			**MASSACHUSETTS**		
Hayden	(D)	Y	Church	(D)	Y	Kennedy	(D)	Y
Goldwater	(R)	†	Dworshak	(R)	†	Saltonstall	(R)	Y
ARKANSAS			**ILLINOIS**			**MICHIGAN**		
Fulbright	(D)	N	Douglas	(D)	Y	Hart	(D)	Y
McClellan	(D)	N	Dirksen	(R)	Y	McNamara	(D)	Y
CALIFORNIA			**INDIANA**			**MINNESOTA**		
Engle	(D)	Y	Hartke	(D)	Y	Humphrey	(D)	†
Kuchel	(R)	Y	Capehart	(R)	Y	McCarthy	(D)	Y
COLORADO			**IOWA**			**MISSISSIPPI**		
Carroll	(D)	Y	Hickenlooper	(R)	Y	Eastland	(D)	N
Allott	(R)	†	Martin	(R)	Y	Stennis	(D)	N
CONNECTICUT			**KANSAS**			**MISSOURI**		
Dodd	(D)	†	Carlson	(R)	†	Hennings	D	Y
Bush	(R)	Y	Schoeppel	(R)	†	Symington	(D)	Y
DELAWARE			**KENTUCKY**			**MONTANA**		
Frear	(D)	Y	Cooper	(R)	Y	Mansfield	(D)	†
Williams	(R)	Y	Morton	(R)	Y	Murray	(D)	Y
FLORIDA			**LOUISIANA**			**NEBRASKA**		
Holland	(D)	N	Ellender	(D)	N	Curtis	(R)	Y
Smathers	(D)	N	Long	(D)	N	Hruska	(R)	Y

NEVADA			OKLAHOMA			UTAH		
Bible	(D)	Y	Kerr	(D)	†	Moss	(D)	Y
Cannon	(D)	Y	Monroney	(D)	Y	Bennett	(R)	Y
NEW HAMPSHIRE			**OREGON**			**VERMONT**		
Bridges	(R)	Y	Morse	(D)	Y	Aiken	(R)	†
Cotton	(R)	Y	Lusk	(D)	Y	Prouty	(R)	Y
NEW JERSEY			**PENNSYLVANIA**			**VIRGINIA**		
Williams	(D)	Y	Clark	(D)	Y	Byrd	(D)	N
Case	(R)	Y	Scott	(R)	Y	Robertson	(D)	N
NEW MEXICO			**RHODE ISLAND**					
Anderson	(D)	Y	Green	(D)	Y	**WASHINGTON**		
Chavez	(D)	Y	Pastore	(D)	Y	Jackson	(D)	Y
NEW YORK			**SOUTH CAROLINA**			Magnuson	(D)	Y
Javits	(R)	Y	Johnston	(D)	N	**WEST VIRGINIA**		
Keating	(R)	Y	Thurmond	(D)	N	Byrd	(D)	Y
NORTH CAROLINA			**SOUTH DAKOTA**			Randolph	(D)	Y
Ervin	(D)	N	Case	(R)	Y			
Jordan	(D)	N	Mundt	(R)	Y	**WISCONSIN**		
NORTH DAKOTA			**TENNESSEE**			Proxmire	(D)	Y
Brunsdale	(R)	Y	Gore	(D)	Y	Wiley	(R)	Y
Young	(R)	Y	Kefauver	(D)	Y	**WYOMING**		
Ohio			**TEXAS**			McGee	(D)	Y
Lausche	(D)	Y	Johnson	(D)	Y	O'Mahoney	(D)	†
Young	(D)	Y	Yarborough	(D)	Y			

HOUSE OF REPRESENTATIVES   Vote Total: 311 for; 109 against

Y Record Vote For (yea).
• Paired For.
† Announced For.
N Record Vote Against (nay).

X Paired Against.
— Announced Against.
? Absent, General Pair, "Present,"
Did not announce.

ALABAMA			McFall	(D)	Y	McDonough	(R)	Y
Andrews	(D)	N	Miller (C.W.)	(D)	Y	Smith	(R)	Y
Boykin	(D)	N	Miller (G.P.)	(D)	Y	**COLORADO**		
Elliott	(D)	N	Moss	(D)	Y	Aspinall	(D)	Y
Grant	(D)	N	Saund	(D)	Y	Johnson	(D)	Y
Huddleston	(D)	N	Shelley	(D)	Y	Rogers	(D)	Y
Jones	(D)	N	Sheppard	(D)	Y	Chenoweth	(R)	Y
Rains	(D)	N	Sisk	(D)	Y	**CONNECTICUT**		
Roberts	(D)	N	Baldwin	(R)	Y	Bowles	(D)	Y
Selden	(D)	N	Gubser	(R)	Y	Daddario	(D)	Y
ALASKA			Mailliard	(R)	Y	Giaimo	(D)	Y
Rivers	(D)	Y	Teague	(R)	Y	Irwin	(D)	Y
ARIZONA			Utt	(R)	N	Kowalski	(D)	Y
Udall	(D)	Y	Wilson	(R)	Y	Monagan	(D)	Y
Rhodes	(R)	Y	Younger	(R)	Y	**DELAWARE**		
ARKANSAS			**Los Angeles County**			McDowell	(D)	Y
Alford	(D)	N	Doyle	(D)	Y	**FLORIDA**		
Gathings	(D)	N	Holifield	(D)	Y	Bennett	(D)	N
Harris	(D)	N	Kasem	(D)	Y	Fascell	(D)	Y
Mills	(D)	N	King	(D)	Y	Haley	(D)	N
Norrell	(D)	N	Roosevelt	(D)	Y	Herlong	(D)	N
Trimble	(D)	N	Hiestand	(R)	Y	Matthews	(D)	N
CALIFORNIA			Holt	(R)	Y	Rogers	(D)	N
Cohelan	(D)	Y	Hosmer	(R)	Y	Sikes	(D)	N
Hagen	(D)	Y	Jackson	(R)	X	Cramer	(R)	N
Johnson	(D)	Y	Lipscomb	(R)	Y			

GEORGIA				Hoeven	(R)	Y		Broomfield	(R)	Y
Blitch	(D)	X		Jensen	(R)	N		Cederberg	(R)	Y
Brown	(D)	N		Kyl	(R)	Y		Chamberlain	(R)	Y
Davis	(D)	N		Schwengel	(R)	Y		Ford	(R)	Y
Flynt	(D)	N		**KANSAS**				Griffin	(R)	Y
Forrester	(D)	N		Breeding	(D)	Y		Hoffman	(R)	N
Landrum	(D)	N		George	(D)	Y		Johansen	(R)	N
Mitchell	(D)	N		Hargis	(D)	Y		Knox	(R)	Y
Pilcher	(D)	N		Avery	(R)	Y		Meader	(R)	N
Preston	(D)	N		Rees	(R)	Y		**Detroit-Wayne County**		
Vinson	(D)	N		Smith	(R)	N		Diggs	(D)	Y
HAWAII				**KENTUCKY**				Dingell	(D)	Y
Inouye	(D)	Y		Burke	(D)	Y		Griffiths	(D)	•
IDAHO				Chelf	(D)	Y		Lesinski	(D)	Y
Pfost	(D)	Y		Natcher	(D)	Y		Machrowicz	(D)	Y
Budge	(R)	N		Perkins	(D)	Y		Rabaut	(D)	Y
ILLINOIS				Spence	(D)	N		**MINNESOTA**		
Gray	(D)	Y		Stubblefield	(D)	Y		Blatnik	(D)	Y
Mack	(D)	Y		Watts	(D)	Y		Karth	(D)	Y
Price	(D)	Y		Siler	(R)	Y		Marshall	(D)	Y
Shipley	(D)	Y		**LOUISIANA**				Wier	(D)	Y
Allen	(R)	Y		Boggs	(D)	N		Andersen	(R)	Y
Arends	(R)	•		Brooks	(D)	N		Quie	(R)	Y
Chiperfield	(R)	•		Hebert	(D)	N		Judd	(R)	Y
Hoffman	(R)	Y		McSween	(D)	N		Langen	(R)	Y
Mason	(R)	N		Morrison	(D)	N		Nelsen	(R)	Y
Michel	(R)	Y		Passman	(D)	N		**MISSISSIPPI**		
Simpson	(R)	Y		Thompson	(D)	N		Abernethy	(D)	N
Springer	(R)	Y		Willis	(D)	N		Colmer	(D)	N
Chicago-Cook County				**MAINE**				Smith	(D)	N
Vacancy				Coffin	(D)	Y		Whitten	(D)	N
Dawson	(D)	Y		Oliver	(D)	Y		Williams	(D)	N
Kluczynski	(D)	Y		McIntire	(R)	Y		Winstead	(D)	N
Libonati	(D)	Y		**MARYLAND**				**MISSOURI**		
Murphy	(D)	Y		Brewster	(D)	Y		Bolling	(D)	Y
O'Brien	(D)	Y		Fallon	(D)	Y		Brown	(D)	Y
O'Hara	(D)	Y		Foley	(D)	Y		Cannon	(D)	Y
Pucinski	(D)	Y		Friedel	(D)	Y		Carnahan	(D)	Y
Rostenkowski	(D)	Y		Garmatz	(D)	Y		Randall	(D)	Y
Yates	(D)	Y		Johnson	(D)	Y		Hull	(D)	Y
Church	(R)	Y		Lankford	(D)	Y		Jones	(D)	N
Collier	(R)	Y		**MASSACHUSETTS**				Karsten	(D)	Y
Derwinski	(R)	Y		Boland	(D)	Y		Moulder	(D)	Y
INDIANA				Burke	(D)	Y		Sullivan	(D)	Y
Barr	(D)	Y		Donohue	(D)	Y		Curtis	(R)	Y
Brademas	(D)	Y		Lane	(D)	Y		**MONTANA**		
Denton	(D)	Y		Macdonald	(D)	Y		Anderson	(D)	?
Harmon	(D)	N		McCormack	(D)	Y		Metcalf	(D)	Y
Hogan	(D)	Y		O'Neill	(D)	Y		**NEBRASKA**		
Madden	(D)	Y		Philbin	(D)	Y		Brock	(D)	Y
Roush	(D)	Y		Bates	(R)	Y		McGinley	(D)	Y
Wampler	(D)	Y		Conte	(R)	Y		Cunningham	(R)	Y
Adair	(R)	Y		Curtis	(R)	Y		Weaver	(R)	Y
Bray	(R)	Y		Keith	(R)	Y		**NEVADA**		
Halleck	(R)	Y		Martin	(R)	Y		Baring	(D)	Y
IOWA				Rogers	(R)	Y		**NEW HAMPSHIRE**		
Coad	(D)	Y		**MICHIGAN**				Bass	(R)	Y
Smith	(D)	Y		O'Hara	(D)	Y		Merrow	(R)	Y
Wolf	(D)	Y		Bennett	(R)	N				
Gross	(R)	Y		Bentley	(R)	Y				

NEW JERSEY

Name	Party	Vote
Addonizio	(D)	Y
Daniels	(D)	Y
Gallagher	(D)	Y
Rodino	(D)	Y
Thompson	(D)	Y
Auchincloss	(R)	Y
Cahill	(R)	Y
Canfield	(R)	Y
Dwyer	(R)	Y
Frelinghuysen	(R)	Y
Glenn	(R)	Y
Osmers	(R)	Y
Wallhauser	(R)	Y
Widnall	(R)	Y

NEW MEXICO

Name	Party	Vote
Montoya	(D)	Y
Morris	(D)	Y

NEW YORK

Name	Party	Vote
Dulski	(D)	Y
O'Brien	(D)	Y
Stratton	(D)	Y
Barry	(R)	Y
Becker	(R)	Y
Derounian	(R)	Y
Dooley	(R)	Y
Kilburn	(R)	X
Miller	(R)	Y
Ostertag	(R)	Y
Pillion	(R)	Y
Pirnie	(R)	Y
Goodell	(R)	Y
Riehlman	(R)	Y
St. George	(R)	Y
Taber	(R)	N
Taylor	(R)	Y
Wainwright	(R)	Y
Weis	(R)	Y
Wharton	(R)	Y

New York City

Name	Party	Vote
Anfuso	(D)	Y
Buckley	(D)	Y
Celler	(D)	Y
Delaney	(D)	Y
Gilbert	(D)	Y
Farbstein	(D)	Y
Healey	(D)	Y
Holtzman	(D)	Y
Kelly	(D)	Y
Keogh	(D)	Y
Multer	(D)	Y
Powell	(D)	?
Rooney	(D)	Y
Santangelo	(D)	Y
Teller	(D)	Y
Zelenko	(D)	Y
Bosch	(R)	Y
Dorn	(R)	Y
Fino	(R)	Y
Halpern	(R)	Y
Lindsay	(R)	Y
Ray	(R)	Y

NORTH CAROLINA

Name	Party	Vote
Alexander	(D)	N
Barden	(D)	X
Bonner	(D)	N
Cooley	(D)	N
Durham	(D)	N
Fountain	(D)	N
Vacancy	(D)	
Kitchin	(D)	N
Lennon	(D)	N
Scott	(D)	N
Whitener	(D)	N
Jonas	(R)	N

NORTH DAKOTA

Name	Party	Vote
Burdick	(D)	Y
Short	(R)	Y

OHIO

Name	Party	Vote
Ashley	(D)	Y
Cook	(D)	Y
Feighan	(D)	Y
Hays	(D)	Y
Kirwan	(D)	Y
Levering	(D)	Y
Moeller	(D)	Y
Vacancy	(D)	X
Vanik	(D)	Y
Ayres	(R)	Y
Baumbart	(R)	Y
Betts	(R)	Y
Bolton	(R)	Y
Bow	(R)	Y
Brown	(R)	Y
Devine	(R)	Y
Henderson	(R)	Y
Hess	(R)	Y
Latta	(R)	Y
McCulloch	(R)	Y
Minshall	(R)	†
Schenck	(R)	Y
Scherer	(R)	Y

OKLAHOMA

Name	Party	Vote
Albert	(D)	Y
Edmondson	(D)	Y
Jarman	(D)	Y
Morris	(D)	Y
Steed	(D)	Y
Belcher	(R)	Y

OREGON

Name	Party	Vote
Green	(D)	Y
Porter	(D)	Y
Ullman	(D)	Y
Norblad	(R)	Y

PENNSYLVANIA

Name	Party	Vote
Clark	(D)	Y
Dent	(D)	Y
Flood	(D)	Y
Holland	(D)	Y
Moorhead	(D)	Y
Morgan	(D)	Y
Prokop	(D)	Y
Quigley	(D)	Y
Rhodes	(D)	Y
Walter	(D)	Y
Corbett	(R)	Y
Curtin	(R)	Y
Dague	(R)	Y
Fenton	(R)	Y
Fulton	(R)	Y
Gavin	(R)	Y
Kearns	(R)	Y
Lafore	(R)	Y
Milliken	(R)	Y
Mumma	(R)	Y
Saylor	(R)	Y
Vacancy		
Van Zandt	(R)	Y

Philadelphia

Name	Party	Vote
Barrett	(D)	Y
Byrne	(D)	Y
Granahan	(D)	Y
Green	(D)	Y
Nix •	(D)	Y
Toll	(D)	Y

RHODE ISLAND

Name	Party	Vote
Fogarty	(D)	Y
Forand	(D)	Y

SOUTH CAROLINA

Name	Party	Vote
Ashmore	(D)	N
Dorn	(D)	N
Hamphill	(D)	N
McMillan	(D)	N
Riley	(D)	N
Rivers	(D)	N

SOUTH DAKOTA

Name	Party	Vote
McGovern	(D)	Y
Berry	(R)	Y

TENNESSEE

Name	Party	Vote
Bass †	(D)	N
Davis	(D)	N
Everett	(D)	N
Evins	(D)	N
Frazier	(D)	N
Loser	(D)	N
Murray	(D)	N
Baker	(R)	Y
Reece	(R)	Y

TEXAS

Name	Party	Vote
Beckworth	(D)	N
Brooks	(D)	N
Burleson	(D)	N
Casey	(D)	N
Dowdy	(D)	N
Fisher	(D)	N
Ikard	(D)	N
Kilday	(D)	Y
Kilgore	(D)	Y
Mahon	(D)	N
Patman	(D)	N

Poage	(D)	N	Gary	(D)	N	Kee	(D)	Y
Rayburn	(D)		Hardy	(D)	N	Slack	(D)	Y
Rogers	(D)	N	Harrison	(D)	N	Staggers	(D)	Y
Rutherford	(D)	N	Jennings	(D)	N	Moore	(R)	Y
Teague	(D)	N	Smith	(D)	N			
Thomas	(D)	N	Tuck	(D)	N	**WISCONSIN**		
Thompson	(D)	N	Broyhill	(R)	N	Flynn	(D)	Y
Thornberry	(D)	Y	Poff	(R)	N	Johnson	(D)	Y
Wright	(D)	Y	**WASHINGTON**			Kastenmeier	(D)	Y
Young	(D)	N	Magnuson	(D)	Y	Reuss	(D)	Y
Alger	(R)	N	Horan	(R)	Y	Zablocki	(D)	Y
UTAH			Mack	(R)	Y	Byrnes	(R)	Y
King	(D)	Y	May	(R)	Y	Laird	(R)	Y
Dixon	(R)	Y	Pelly	(R)	Y	O'Konski	(R)	Y
VERMONT			Tollefson	(R)	Y	Van Pelt	(R)	Y
Meyer	(D)	Y	Westland	(R)	Y	Withrow	(R)	Y
VIRGINIA			**WEST VIRGINIA**					
Abbitt	(D)	N	Bailey	(D)	Y	**WYOMING**		
Downing	(D)	N	Hechler	(D)	Y	Thomson	(R)	Y

1964 Civil Rights Act

(Voting rights, equal access to public accommodations, desegregation of public facilities and schools, equal employment, and nondiscrimination in federally assisted programs.)

SENATE   Vote Total: 73 for; 27 against

Y Record Vote For (yea).
• Paired For.
† Announced For.
N Record Vote Against (nay).

X Paired Against.
— Announced Against.
? Absent, General Pair, "Present,"
   Did not announce.

ALABAMA			**FLORIDA**			**KENTUCKY**		
Hill	(D)	N	Holland	(D)	N	Cooper	(R)	Y
Sparkman	(D)	N	Smathers	(D)	N	Morton	(R)	Y
ALASKA			**GEORGIA**			**LOUISIANA**		
Bartlett	(D)	Y	Russell	(D)	N	Ellender	(D)	N
Gruening	(D)	Y	Talmadge	(D)	N	Long	(D)	N
ARIZONA			**HAWAII**			**MAINE**		
Hayden	(D)	Y	Inouye	(D)	Y	Muskie	(D)	Y
Goldwater	(R)	N	Fong	(R)	Y	Smith	(R)	Y
ARKANSAS			**IDAHO**			**MARYLAND**		
Fulbright	(D)	N	Church	(D)	Y	Brewster	(D)	Y
McClellan	(D)	N	Jordan	(R)	Y	Beall	(R)	Y
CALIFORNIA			**ILLINOIS**			**MASSACHUSETTS**		
Engle	(D)	Y	Douglas	(D)	Y	Kennedy	(D)	Y
Kuchel	(R)	Y	Dirksen	(R)	Y	Saltonstall	(R)	Y
COLORADO			**INDIANA**			**MICHIGAN**		
Allott	(R)	Y	Bayh	(D)	Y	Hart	(D)	Y
Dominick	(R)	Y	Hartke	(D)	Y	McNamara	(D)	Y
CONNECTICUT			**IOWA**			**MINNESOTA**		
Dodd	(D)	Y	Hickenlooper	(R)	N	Humphrey	(D)	Y
Ribicoff	(D)	Y	Miller	(R)	Y	McCarthy	(D)	Y
DELAWARE			**KANSAS**			**MISSISSIPPI**		
Boggs	(R)	Y	Carlson	(R)	Y	Eastland	(D)	N
Williams	(R)	Y	Pearson	(R)	Y	Stennis	(D)	N

MISSOURI			NORTH DAKOTA			TEXAS		
Long	(D)	Y	Burdick	(D)	Y	Yarborough	(D)	Y
Symington	(D)	Y	Young	(R)	Y	Tower	(R)	N
MONTANA			**OHIO**			**UTAH**		
Mansfield	(D)	Y	Lausche	(D)	Y	Moss	(D)	Y
Metcalf	(D)	Y	Young	(D)	Y	Bennett	(R)	Y
NEBRASKA			**OKLAHOMA**					
Curtis	(R)	Y	Edmondson	(D)	Y	**VERMONT**		
Hruska	(R)	Y	Monroney	(D)	Y	Aiken	(R)	Y
NEVADA			**OREGON**			Prouty	(R)	Y
Bible	(D)	Y	Morse	(D)	Y	**VIRGINIA**		
Cannon	(D)	Y	Neuberger	(D)	Y	Byrd	(D)	N
NEW HAMPSHIRE			**PENNSYLVANIA**			Robertson	(D)	N
McIntyre	(D)	Y	Clark	(D)	Y			
Cotton	(R)	N	Scott.	(R)	Y	**WASHINGTON**		
NEW JERSEY			**RHODE ISLAND**			Jackson	(D)	Y
Williams	(D)	Y	Pastore	(D)	Y	Magnuson	(D)	Y
Case	(R)	Y	Pell	(D)	Y	**WEST VIRGINIA**		
NEW MEXICO			**SOUTH CAROLINA**			Byrd	(D)	N
Anderson	(D)	Y	Johnston	(D)	N	Randolph	(D)	Y
Mechem	(R)	N	Thurmond	(D)	N	**WISCONSIN**		
NEW YORK			**SOUTH DAKOTA**			Nelson	(D)	Y
Javits	(R)	Y	McGovern	(D)	Y	Proxmire	(D)	Y
Keating	(R)	Y	Mundt	(R)	Y	**WYOMING**		
NORTH CAROLINA			**TENNESSEE**			McGee	(D)	Y
Ervin	(D)	N	Gore	(D)	N	Simpson	(R)	N
Jordan	(D)	N	Walters	(D)	N			

HOUSE OF REPRESENTATIVES   Vote Total: 290 for; 130 against

Y Record Vote For (yea).	X Paired Against.
• Paired For.	— Announced Against.
† Announced For.	? Absent, General Pair, "Present,"
N Record Vote Against (nay).	Did not announce.

ALABAMA			CALIFORNIA				Teague	(R)	Y
Andrews	(D)	N	Cohelan	(D)	Y		Utt	(R)	N
Elliott	(D)	N	Edwards	(D)	Y		Wilson	(R)	Y
Grant	(D)	N	Hagen	(D)	Y		Younger	(R)	Y
Huddleston	(D)	N	Hanna	(D)	Y		**Los Angeles Co.**		
Jones	(D)	N	Johnson	(D)	Y		Brown	(D)	Y
Rains	(D)	N	Leggett	(D)	Y		Burkhalter	(D)	Y
Roberts	(D)	N	McFall	(D)	Y		Cameron	(D)	Y
Selden	(D)	N	Miller	(D)	Y		Corman	(D)	Y
ALASKA			Moss	(D)	Y		Hawkins	(D)	Y
Rivers	(D)	Y	Vacancy				Holifield	(D)	Y
ARIZONA			Sheppard	(D)	Y		King	(D)	Y
Senner	(D)	Y	Sisk	(D)	Y		Roosevelt	(D)	Y
Udall	(D)	Y	Van Deerlin	(D)	Y		Roybal	(D)	Y
Rhodes	(R)	N	Baldwin	(R)	Y		Wilson	(D)	Y
ARKANSAS			Clausen	(R)	Y		Bell	(R)	Y
Gathings	(D)	N	Gubser	(R)	Y		Clawson	(R)	N
Harris	(D)	N	Mailliard	(R)	Y		Hosmer	(R)	Y
Mills	(D)	N	Martin	(R)	N		Lipscomb	(R)	N
Trimble	(D)	N	Talcott	(R)	Y		Smith	(R)	N

COLORADO			Kluczynski	(D)	Y	Lankford	(D)	?	
Aspinall	(D)	Y	Libonati	(D)	Y	Long	(D)	Y	
Rogers	(D)	Y	Murphy	(D)	Y	Sickles	(D)	Y	
Brotzman	(R)	Y	O'Brien	(D)	•	Mathias	(R)	Y	
Chenoweth	(R)	Y	O'Hara	(D)	Y	Morton	(R)	Y	
CONNECTICUT			Pucinski	(D)	Y	**MASSACHUSETTS**			
Daddario	(D)	Y	Rostenkowski	(D)	Y	Boland	(D)	Y	
Giaimo	(D)	Y	Collier	(R)	Y	Burke	(D)	Y	
Grabowski	(D)	Y	Derwinski	(R)	Y	Donohue	(D)	Y	
Monagan	(D)	Y	Rumsfeld	(R)	Y	Macdonald	(D)	Y	
St. Onge	(D)	Y	**INDIANA**			McCormack	(D)		
Sibal	(R)	Y	Brademas	(D)	Y	O'Neill	(D)	Y	
DELAWARE			Denton	(D)	Y	Philbin	(D)	Y	
McDowell	(D)	Y	Madden	(D)	Y	Bates	(R)	Y	
FLORIDA			Roush	(D)	Y	Conte	(R)	Y	
Bennett	(D)	N	Adair	(R)	Y	Keith	(R)	Y	
Fascell	(D)	N	Bray	(R)	Y	Martin	(R)	Y	
Fuqua	(D)	N	Bruce	(R)	Y	Morse	(R)	Y	
Gibbons	(D)	N	Halleck	(R)	Y	**MICHIGAN**			
Haley	(D)	N	Harvey	(R)	Y	O'Hara	(D)	Y	
Herlong	(D)	N	Roudebush	(R)	Y	Staebler	(D)	Y	
Matthews	(D)	N	Wilson	(R)	Y	Bennett	(R)	Y	
Pepper	(D)	Y	**IOWA**			Broomfield	(R)	Y	
Rogers	(D)	N	Smith	(D)	Y	Cederberg	(R)	Y	
Sikes	(D)	N	Bromwell	(R)	Y	Chamberlain	(R)	Y	
Cramer	(R)	N	Gross	(R)	N	Ford	(R)	Y	
Gurney	(R)	N	Hoeven	(R)	Y	Griffin	(R)	Y	
GEORGIA			Jensen	(R)	N	Harvey	(R)	Y	
Davis	(D)	N	Kyl	(R)	Y	Hutchinson	(R)	N	
Flynt	(D)	N	Schwengel	(R)	Y	Johansen	(R)	N	
Forrester	(D)	N	**KANSAS**			Knox	(R)	N	
Hagan	(D)	N	Avery	(R)	Y	Meader	(R)	N	
Landrum	(D)	N	Dole	(R)	Y	**Detroit—Wayne Co.**			
Pilcher	(D)	N	Ellsworth	(R)	Y	Diggs	(D)	Y	
Stephens	(D)	N	Shriver	(R)	Y	Dingell	(D)	Y	
Tuten	(D)	N	Skubitz	(R)	Y	Griffiths	(D)	Y	
Vinson	(D)	N	**KENTUCKY**			Lesinski	(D)	N	
Weltner	(D)	N	Chelf	(D)	N	Nedzi	(D)	Y	
HAWAII			Natcher	(D)	N	Ryan	(D)	Y	
Gill	(D)	Y	Perkins	(D)	Y	**MINNESOTA**			
Matsunaga	(D)	Y	Stubblefield	(D)	N	Blatnik	(D)	Y	
IDAHO			Watts	(D)	N	Fraser	(D)	Y	
Harding	(D)	Y	Siler	(R)	X	Karth	(D)	Y	
White	(D)	Y	Snyder	(R)	N	Olson	(D)	Y	
ILLINOIS			**LOUISIANA**			Langen	(R)	Y	
Gray	(D)	Y	Boggs	(D)	N	MacGregor	(R)	Y	
Price	(D)	Y	Hebert	(D)	N	Nelsen	(R)	Y	
Shipley	(D)	?	Long	(D)	N	Quie	(R)	Y	
Anderson	(R)	Y	Morrison	(D)	N	**MISSISSIPPI**			
Arends	(R)	Y	Passman	(D)	N	Abernethy	(D)	N	
Findley	(R)	Y	Thompson	(D)	N	Colmer	(D)	N	
Hoffman	(R)	?	Waggonner	(D)	N	Whitten	(D)	N	
McClory	(R)	Y	Willis	(D)	N	Williams	(D)	N	
McLoskey	(R)	Y	**MAINE**			Winstead	(D)	N	
Michel	(R)	Y	McIntire	(R)	Y	**MISSOURI**			
Reid	(R)	Y	Tupper	(R)	Y	Bolling	(D)	Y	
Springer	(R)	Y	**MARYLAND**			Cannon	(D)	Y	
Chicago—Cook Co.			Fallon	(D)	Y	Hull	(D)	N	
Dawson	(D)	Y	Friedel	(D)	Y	Ichord	(D)	Y	
Finnegan	(D)	Y	Garmatz	(D)	Y	Jones	(D)	N	

Name	Party	Vote
Karsten	(D)	Y
Randall	(D)	Y
Sullivan	(D)	Y
Curtis	(R)	Y
Hall	(R)	N
MONTANA		
Olsen	(D)	Y
Battin	(R)	N
NEBRASKA		
Beermann	(R)	N
Cunningham	(R)	Y
Martin	(R)	Y
NEVADA		
Baring	(D)	N
NEW HAMPSHIRE		
Cleveland	(R)	Y
Wyman	(R)	N
NEW JERSEY		
Daniels	(D)	Y
Gallagher	(D)	Y
Joelson	(D)	Y
Minish	(D)	Y
Patten	(D)	Y
Rodino	(D)	Y
Thompson	(D)	Y
Auchincloss	(R)	Y
Cahill	(R)	Y
Dwyer	(R)	Y
Frelinghuysen	(R)	Y
Glenn	(R)	Y
Osmers	(R)	Y
Wallhauser	(R)	Y
Widnall	(R)	Y
NEW MEXICO		
Montoya	(D)	Y
Morris	(D)	Y
NEW YORK		
Dulski	(D)	Y
O'Brien	(D)	Y
Pike	(D)	Y
Stratton	(D)	Y
Barry	(R)	Y
Becker	(R)	Y
Derounian	(R)	Y
Goodell	(R)	Y
Grover	(R)	Y
Horton	(R)	Y
Kilburn	(R)	N
King	(R)	Y
Miller	(R)	Y
Ostertag	(R)	Y
Pillion	(R)	Y
Pirnie	(R)	Y
Reid	(R)	Y
Riehlman	(R)	Y
Robison	(R)	Y
St. George	(R)	Y
Wharton	(R)	Y
Wydler	(R)	Y

Name	Party	Vote
New York City		
Addabbo	(D)	Y
Buckley	(D)	Y
Carey	(D)	Y
Celler	(D)	Y
Delaney	(D)	Y
Farbstein	(D)	Y
Gilbert	(D)	Y
Healey	(D)	Y
Kelly	(D)	Y
Keogh	(D)	Y
Multer	(D)	Y
Murphy	(D)	Y
Powell	(D)	Y
Rooney	(D)	Y
Rosenthal	(D)	Y
Ryan	(D)	Y
Fino	(R)	Y
Halpern	(R)	Y
Lindsay	(R)	Y
NORTH CAROLINA		
Booner	(D)	N
Coolery	(D)	N
Fountain	(D)	N
Henderson	(D)	N
Kornegay	(D)	N
Lennon	(D)	N
Scott	(D)	N
Taylor	(D)	N
Whitener	(D)	N
Broyhill	(R)	N
Jonas	(R)	N
NORTH DAKOTA		
Andrews	(R)	Y
Short	(R)	N
OHIO		
Ashley	(D)	Y
Feighan	(D)	Y
Hays	(D)	Y
Kirwan	(D)	Y
Secrest	(D)	Y
Vanik	(D)	Y
Abele	(R)	Y
Ashbrook	(R)	N
Ayres	(R)	Y
Betts	(R)	Y
Bolton, F.P.	(R)	Y
Bolton, O.P.	(R)	Y
Bow	(R)	Y
Brown	(R)	Y
Clancy	(R)	Y
Devine	(R)	Y
Harsha	(R)	Y
Latta	(R)	Y
McCulloch	(R)	Y
Minshall	(R)	Y
Mosher	(R)	Y
Rich	(R)	Y
Schenck	(R)	Y
Taft	(R)	Y

Name	Party	Vote
OKLAHOMA		
Albert	(D)	Y
Edmondson	(D)	Y
Jarman	(D)	N
Steed	(D)	Y
Wickersham	(D)	N
Belcher	(R)	N
OREGON		
Duncan	(D)	Y
Green	(D)	Y
Ullman	(D)	Y
Norblad	(R)	Y
PENNSYLVANIA		
Clark	(D)	Y
Dent	(D)	Y
Flood	(D)	Y
Holland	(D)	Y
Moorhead	(D)	Y
Morgan	(D)	Y
Rhodes	(D)	Y
Rooney	(D)	Y
Corbett	(R)	Y
Curtin	(R)	Y
Dague	(R)	Y
Fulton	(R)	Y
Goodling	(R)	Y
Johnson	(R)	Y
Kunkel	(R)	Y
McDade	(R)	Y
Milliken	(R)	Y
Saylor	(R)	Y
Schneebeli	(R)	Y
Schweiker	(R)	Y
Weaver	(R)	Y
Whalley	(R)	Y
Philadelphia City		
Barrett	(D)	Y
Byrne	(D)	Y
Vacancy		
Nix	(D)	Y
Toll	(D)	Y
RHODE ISLAND		
Fogarty	(D)	Y
St. Germain	(D)	Y
SOUTH CAROLINA		
Ashmore	(D)	N
Dorn	(D)	N
Hemphill	(D)	N
McMillan	(D)	N
Rivers	(D)	N
Watson	(D)	N
SOUTH DAKOTA		
Berry	(R)	N
Reifel	(R)	Y
TENNESSEE		
Bass	(D)	Y
Davis	(D)	X
Everett	(D)	N
Evins	(D)	N
Fulton	(D)	Y

Murray	(D)	N	Wright	(D)	N	Pelly	(R)	•
Vacancy			Young	(D)	N	Stinson	(R)	Y
Brock	(R)	N	Alger	(R)	N	Tollefson	(R)	Y
Quillen	(R)	N	Foreman	(R)	N	Westland	(R)	Y
TEXAS			**UTAH**			**WEST VIRGINIA**		
Beckworth	(D)	N	Burton	(R)	Y	Hechler	(D)	Y
Brooks	(D)	Y	Lloyd	(R)	Y	Kee	(D)	†
Burleson	(D)	N	**VERMONT**			Slack	(D)	Y
Casey	(D)	N	AL Stafford	(R)	Y	Staggers	(D)	Y
Dowdy	(D)	N	**VIRGINIA**			Moore	(R)	Y
Fisher	(D)	N	Abbitt	(D)	N	**WISCONSIN**		
Gonzalez	(D)	Y	Downing	(D)	N	Johnson	(D)	Y
Kilgore	(D)	N	Gary	(D)	N	Kastenmeier	(D)	Y
Mahon	(D)	N	Hardy	(D)	N	Reuss	(D)	Y
Patman	(D)	N	Jennings	(D)	N	Zablocki	(D)	Y
Pickle	(D)	Y	Marsh	(D)	N	Byrnes	(R)	Y
Poage	(D)	N	Smith	(D)	N	Laird	(R)	Y
Pool	(D)	N	Tuck	(D)	N	O'Konski	(R)	†
Purcell	(D)	N	Broyhill	(R)	N	Schadeberg	(R)	Y
Roberts	(D)	N	Poff	(R)	N	Thomson	(R)	Y
Rogers	(D)	N	**WASHINGTON**			Van Pelt	(R)	N
Teague	(D)	N	Hansen	(D)	Y	**WYOMING**		
Thomas	(D)	Y	Horan	(R)	†	Harrison	(R)	N
Thompson	(D)	?	May	(R)	Y			

1965 Voting Rights Act

(Authorizes federal examiners to register Negro voters at state level.)

SENATE
Vote Total: 77 for; 19 against

Y	Record Vote For (yea).	X	Paired Against.
•	Paired For.	—	Announced Against.
†	Announced For.	?	Absent, General Pair, "Present,"
N	Record Vote Against (nay).		Did not announce.

ALABAMA			**DELAWARE**			**IOWA**		
Hill	(D)	N	Boggs	(R)	Y	Hickenlooper	(R)	Y
Sparkman	(D)	N	Williams	(R)	Y	Miller	(R)	Y
ALASKA			**FLORIDA**			**KANSAS**		
Bartlett	(D)	Y	Holland	(D)	N	Carlson	(R)	Y
Gruening	(D)	Y	Smathers	(D)	N	Pearson	(R)	Y
ARIZONA			**GEORGIA**			**KENTUCKY**		
Hayden	(D)	Y	Russell	(D)	N	Cooper	(R)	Y
Fannin	(R)	Y	Talmadge	(D)	N	Morton	(R)	Y
ARKANSAS			**HAWAII**			**LOUISIANA**		
Fulbright	(D)	N	Inouye	(D)	Y	Ellender	(D)	N
McClellan	(D)	N	Fong	(R)	Y	Long	(D)	N
CALIFORNIA			**IDAHO**			**MAINE**		
Kuchel	(R)	Y	Church	(D)	†	Muskie	(D)	Y
Murphy	(R)	Y	Jordan	(R)	Y	Smith	(R)	Y
COLORADO			**ILLINOIS**			**MARYLAND**		
Allott	(R)	Y	Douglas	(D)	Y	Brewster	(D)	Y
Dominick	(R)	Y	Dirksen	(R)	Y	Tydings	(D)	Y
CONNECTICUT			**INDIANA**			**MASSACHUSETTS**		
Dodd	(D)	Y	Bayh	(D)	Y	Kennedy	(D)	Y
Ribicoff	(D)	Y	Hartke	(D)	Y	Saltonstall	(R)	Y

MICHIGAN			**NEW YORK**			**TENNESSEE**		
Hart	(D)	Y	Kennedy	(D)	Y	Bass	(D)	Y
McNamara	(D)	Y	Javits	(R)	Y	Gore	(D)	Y
MINNESOTA			**NORTH CAROLINA**			**TEXAS**		
McCarthy	(D)	Y	Ervin	(D)	N	Yarborough	(D)	Y
Mondale	(D)	Y	Jordan	(D)	N	Tower	(R)	N
MISSISSIPPI			**NORTH DAKOTA**			**UTAH**		
Eastland	(D)	N	Burdick	(D)	Y	Moss	(D)	Y
Stennis	(D)	N	Young	(R)	Y	Bennett	(R)	Y
MISSOURI			**OHIO**					
Long	(D)	Y	Lausche	(D)	Y	**VERMONT**		
Symington	(D)	Y	Young	(D)	Y	Aiken	(R)	Y
MONTANA			**OKLAHOMA**			Prouty	(R)	Y
Mansfield	(D)	Y	Harris	(D)	Y	**VIRGINIA**		
Metcalf	(D)	Y	Monroney	(D)	Y	Byrd	(D)	N
NEBRASKA			**OREGON**			Robertson	(D)	N
Curtis	(R)	Y	Morse	(D)	Y	**WASHINGTON**		
Hruska	(R)	Y	Neuberger	(D)	Y	Jackson	(D)	Y
NEVADA			**PENNSYLVANIA**			Magnuson	(D)	Y
Bible	(D)	†	Clark	(D)	Y	**WEST VIRGINIA**		
Cannon	(D)	●	Scott	(R)	Y	Byrd	(D)	X
NEW HAMPSHIRE			**RHODE ISLAND**			Randolph	(D)	Y
McIntyre	(D)	Y	Pastore	(D)	Y	**WISCONSIN**		
Cotton	(R)	Y	Pell	(D)	Y	Nelson	(D)	Y
NEW JERSEY			**SOUTH CAROLINA**			Proxmire	(D)	Y
Williams	(D)	Y	Russell	(D)	N			
Case	(R)	Y	Thurmond	(R)	N	**WYOMING**		
NEW MEXICO			**SOUTH DAKOTA**			McGee	(D)	Y
Anderson	(D)	Y	McGovern	(D)	Y	Simpson	(R)	Y
Montoya	(D)	Y	Mundt	(R)	Y			

HOUSE OF REPRESENTATIVES   Vote Total: 328 for; 74 against

Y Record Vote For (yea).	X Paired Against.
● Paired For.	— Announced Against.
† Announced For.	? Absent, General Pair, "Present,"
N Record Vote Against (nay).	Did not announce.

ALABAMA			**CALIFORNIA**			Teague	(R)	Y
Andrews	(D)	N	Burton	(D)	Y	Utt	(R)	N
Jones	(D)	N	Cohelan	(D)	Y	Wilson	(R)	Y
Seldon	(D)	N	Dyal	(D)	Y	Younger	(R)	Y
Andrews	(R)	N	Edwards	(D)	Y	**Los Angeles Co.**		
Buchanan	(R)	N	Hagen	(D)	Y	Brown	(D)	Y
Dickinson	(R)	N	Hanna	(D)	Y	Cameron	(D)	Y
Edwards	(R)	N	Johnson	(D)	Y	Corman	(D)	Y
Martin	(R)	N	Leggett	(D)	Y	Hawkins	(D)	Y
ALASKA			McFall	(D)	Y	Holifield	(D)	●
Rivers	(D)	●	Miller	(D)	Y	King	(D)	Y
ARIZONA			Moss	(D)	Y	Roosevelt	(D)	Y
Senner	(D)	Y	Sisk	(D)	Y	Roybal	(D)	Y
Udall	(D)	Y	Tunney	(D)	Y	Wilson	(D)	Y
Rhodes	(R)	Y	Van Deerlin	(D)	Y	Bell	(R)	Y
ARKANSAS			Baldwin	(R)	Y	Clawson	(R)	Y
Gathings	(D)	N	Clausen	(R)	Y	Hosmer	(R)	●
Harris	(D)	N	Gubsey	(R)	Y	Lipscomb	(R)	Y
Mills	(D)	N	Mailliard	(R)	Y	Reinecke	(R)	Y
Trimble	(D)	Y	Talcott	(R)	Y	Smith	(R)	N

COLORADO

Name	Party	Vote
Aspinall	(D)	Y
Evans	(D)	Y
McVicker	(D)	Y
Rogers	(D)	Y

CONNECTICUT

Name	Party	Vote
Daddario	(D)	Y
Giaimo	(D)	Y
Grabowski	(D)	Y
Irwin	(D)	Y
Monagan	(D)	Y
St. Onge	(D)	Y

DELAWARE

Name	Party	Vote
McDowell	(D)	Y

FLORIDA

Name	Party	Vote
Bennett	(D)	Y
Fascell	(D)	Y
Fuqua	(D)	N
Gibbons	(D)	Y
Haley	(D)	N
Herlong	(D)	Y
Matthews	(D)	N
Pepper	(D)	Y
Rogers	(D)	Y
Sikes	(D)	N
Cramer	(R)	Y
Gurney	(R)	N

GEORGIA

Name	Party	Vote
Davis	(D)	N
Flynt	(D)	N
Hagan	(D)	N
Landrum	(D)	N
Mackay	(D)	Y
O'Neal	(D)	N
Stephens	(D)	N
Tuten	(D)	N
Weltner	(D)	Y
Callaway	(R)	N

HAWAII

Name	Party	Vote
Matsunaga	(D)	Y
Mink	(D)	Y

IDAHO

Name	Party	Vote
White	(D)	Y
Hansen	(R)	N

ILLINOIS

Name	Party	Vote
Gray	(D)	Y
Price	(D)	Y
Schisler	(D)	Y
Shipley	(D)	Y
Anderson	(R)	Y
Arends	(R)	Y
Erlenborn	(R)	Y
Findley	(R)	Y
McClory	(R)	Y
Michel	(R)	N
Reid	(R)	Y
Springer	(R)	Y

Chicago—Cook Co.

Name	Party	Vote
Annunzio	(D)	Y
Dawson	(D)	Y
Kluczynski	(D)	Y
Murphy	(D)	Y
O'Hara	(D)	Y
Pucinski	(D)	Y
Ronan	(D)	Y
Rostenkowski	(D)	Y
Yates	(D)	Y
Collier	(R)	Y
Derwinski	(R)	Y
Rumsfeld	(R)	Y

INDIANA

Name	Party	Vote
Brademas	(D)	Y
Denton	(D)	Y
Hamilton	(D)	Y
Jacobs	(D)	Y
Madden	(D)	Y
Roush	(D)	Y
Adair	(R)	Y
Bray	(R)	Y
Halleck	(R)	Y
Harvey	(R)	Y
Roudebush	(R)	Y

IOWA

Name	Party	Vote
Bandstra	(D)	Y
Culver	(D)	Y
Greigg	(D)	Y
Hansen	(D)	Y
Schmidhauser	(D)	Y
Smith	(D)	Y
Gross	(R)	N

KANSAS

Name	Party	Vote
Dole	(R)	Y
Ellsworth	(R)	Y
Shriver	(R)	Y
Mize	(R)	Y
Skubitz	(R)	Y

KENTUCKY

Name	Party	Vote
Chelf	(D)	Y
Farnsley	(D)	Y
Natcher	(D)	Y
Perkins	(D)	Y
Stubblefield	(D)	Y
Watts	(D)	?
Carter	(R)	Y

LOUISIANA

Name	Party	Vote
Boggs	(D)	Y
Hebert	(D)	N
Long	(D)	N
Morrison	(D)	Y
Passman	(D)	N
Vacancy		
Waggonner	(D)	N
Willis	(D)	N

MAINE

Name	Party	Vote
Hathaway	(D)	Y
Tupper	(R)	Y

MARYLAND

Name	Party	Vote
Fallon	(D)	Y
Friedel	(D)	Y
Garmatz	(D)	Y
Long	(D)	Y
Machen.	(D)	Y
Sickles	(D)	Y
Mathias	(R)	Y
Morton	(R)	†

MASSACHUSETTS

Name	Party	Vote
Boland	(D)	Y
Burke	(D)	Y
Donohue	(D)	Y
Macdonald	(D)	Y
McCormack	(D)	
O'Neill	(D)	Y
Philbin	(D)	Y
Bates	(R)	Y
Conte	(R)	Y
Keith	(R)	Y
Martin	(R)	•
Morse	(R)	Y

MICHIGAN

Name	Party	Vote
Clevenger	(D)	Y
Farnum	(D)	Y
Mackie	(D)	Y
O'Hara	(D)	Y
Todd	(D)	Y
Vivian	(D)	Y
Broomfield	(R)	Y
Cederberg	(R)	Y
Chamberlain	(R)	Y
Ford	(R)	Y
Griffin	(R)	Y
Harvey	(R)	Y
Hutchinson	(R)	Y

Detroit—Wayne Co.

Name	Party	Vote
Conyers	(D)	Y
Diggs	(D)	Y
Dingell	(D)	Y
Ford	(D)	Y
Griffiths	(D)	Y
Nedzi	(D)	Y

MINNESOTA

Name	Party	Vote
Blatnik	(D)	Y
Fraser	(D)	Y
Karth	(D)	Y
Olson	(D)	Y
Langen	(R)	Y
MacGregor	(R)	Y
Nelsen	(R)	†
Quie	(R)	Y

MISSISSIPPI

Name	Party	Vote
Abernethy	(D)	N
Colmer	(D)	X
Whitten	(D)	N
Williams	(D)	X
Walker	(R)	X

MISSOURI

Name	Party	Vote
Bolling	(D)	Y
Hull	(D)	Y
Hungate	(D)	Y
Ichord	(D)	Y
Jones	(D)	—

Karsten	(D)	Y	**New York City**			**OKLAHOMA**		
Randall	(D)	Y	Addabbo	(D)	Y	Albert	(D)	Y
Sullivan	(D)	Y	Bingham	(D)	†	Edmondson	(D)	Y
Curtis	(R)	Y	Carey	(D)	?	Jarman	(D)	Y
Hall	(R)	†	Celler	(D)	Y	Johnson	(D)	Y
MONTANA			Delaney	(D)	Y	Steed	(D)	Y
Olsen	(D)	Y	Farbstein	(D)	Y	Belcher	(R)	Y
Battin	(R)	X	Gilbert	(D)	Y	**OREGON**		
NEBRASKA			Kelly	(D)	Y	Duncan	(D)	Y
Callan	(D)	Y	Keogh	(D)	•	Green	(D)	•
Cunningham	(R)	Y	Multer	(D)	Y	Ullman	(D)	Y
Martin	(R)	Y	Murphy	(D)	Y	Wyatt	(R)	Y
NEVADA			Powell	(D)	?	**PENNSYLVANIA**		
Baring	(D)	?	Rooney	(D)	Y	Clark	(D)	Y
NEW HAMPSHIRE			Rosenthal	(D)	Y	Craley	(D)	Y
Huot	(D)	Y	Ryan	(D)	Y	Dent	(D)	Y
Cleveland	(R)	Y	Scheuer	(D)	†	Flood	(D)	Y
NEW JERSEY			Fino	(R)	N	Holland	(D)	Y
Daniels	(D)	Y	Halpern	(R)	Y	Moorhead	(D)	Y
Gallagher	(D)	Y	Lindsay	(R)	?	Morgan	(D)	Y
Helstoski	(D)	Y	**NORTH CAROLINA**			Rhodes	(D)	Y
Howard	(D)	Y	Bonner	(D)	X	Rooney	(D)	Y
Joelson	(D)	Y	Cooley	(D)	N	Vigorito	(D)	Y
Krebs	(D)	Y	Fountain	(D)	N	Corbett	(R)	Y
Minish	(D)	Y	Henderson	(D)	N	Curtin	(R)	Y
McGrath	(D)	Y	Kornegay	(D)	N	Dague	(R)	Y
Patten	(D)	Y	Lennon	(D)	N	Fulton	(R)	Y
Rodino	(D)	Y	Scott	(D)	N	Johnson	(R)	Y
Thompson	(D)	Y	Taylor	(D)	X	Kunkel	(R)	Y
Cahill	(R)	?	Whitener	(D)	N	McDade	(R)	Y
Dwyer	(R)	Y	Broyhill	(R)	N	Saylor	(R)	Y
Frelinghuyser	(R)	Y	Jonas	(R)	N	Schneebeli	(R)	Y
Widnall	(R)	Y	**NORTH DAKOTA**			Schweiker	(R)	Y
NEW MEXICO			Redlin	(D)	Y	Watkins	(R)	Y
Morris	(D)	Y	Andrews	(R)	Y	Whalley	(R)	Y
Walker	(D)	Y	**OHIO**			**Philadelphia City**		
NEW YORK			Ashley	(D)	†	Barrett	(D)	Y
Dow	(D)	Y	Feighan	(D)	Y	Byrne	(D)	Y
Dulski	(D)	Y	Gilligan	(D)	Y	Green	(D)	Y
Hanley	(D)	Y	Hays	(D)	Y	Nix	(D)	Y
McCarthy	(D)	Y	Kirwan	(D)	Y	Toll	(D)	†
O'Brien	(D)	Y	Love	(D)	Y	**RHODE ISLAND**		
Ottinger	(D)	Y	Moeller	(D)	Y	Fogarty	(D)	Y
Pike	(D)	Y	Secrest	(D)	Y	St. Germain	(D)	Y
Resnick	(D)	Y	Sweeney	(D)	Y	**SOUTH CAROLINA**		
Stratton	(D)	Y	Vanik	(D)	Y	Ashmore	(D)	N
Tenzer	(D)	Y	Ashbrook	(R)	Y	Dorn	(D)	N
Wolff	(D)	Y	Ayres	(R)	Y	Gettys	(D)	N
Conable	(R)	Y	Betts	(R)	Y	McMillan	(D)	X
Goodell	(R)	Y	Bolton	(R)	Y	Rivers	(D)	N
Grover	(R)	Y	Bow	(R)	Y	Watson	(R)	N
Horton	(R)	Y	Brown	(R)	Y	**SOUTH DAKOTA**		
King	(R)	Y	Clancy	(R)	Y	Berry	(R)	Y
McEwen	(R)	N	Devine	(R)	Y	Reifel	(R)	Y
Pirnie	(R)	Y	Harsha	(R)	Y	**TENNESSEE**		
Reid	(R)	Y	Latta	(R)	Y	Anderson	(D)	Y
Robison	(R)	Y	McCulloch	(R)	Y	Everett	(D)	N
Smith	(R)	Y	Minshall	(R)	Y	Evins	(D)	Y
Wydler	(R)	Y	Mosher	(R)	Y	Fulton	(D)	Y
			Stanton	(R)	Y	Grider	(D)	Y

Murray	(D)	N	Thompson	(D)	Y	Hicks	(D)	Y		
Brock	(R)	Y	White	(D)	Y	Meeds	(D)	Y		
Duncan	(R)	Y	Wright	(D)	†	May	(R)	Y		
Quillen	(R)	Y	Young	(D)	Y	Pelly	(R)	Y		
TEXAS			**UTAH**			**WEST VIRGINIA**				
Beckworth	(D)	N	King	(D)	Y	Hechler	(D)	Y		
Brooks	(D)	Y	Burton	(R)	Y	Kee	(D)	Y		
Burleson	(D)	N	**VERMONT**			Slack	(D)	Y		
Cabell	(D)	Y	Stafford	(R)	Y	Staggers	(D)	Y		
Casey	(D)	N	**VIRGINIA**			Moore	(R)	Y		
De la Garza	(D)	Y	Abbitt	(D)	N					
Dowdy	(D)	N	Downing	(D)	N	**WISCONSIN**				
Fisher	(D)	N	Hardy	(D)	N	Kastenmeier	(D)	Y		
Gonzalez	(D)	Y	Jennings	(D)	Y	Race	(D)	Y		
Mahon	(D)	Y	Marsh	(D)	N	Reuss	(D)	Y		
Patman	(D)	Y	Satterfield	(D)	N	Stalbaum	(D)	Y		
Pickle	(D)	Y	Smith	(D)	N	Zablocki	(D)	Y		
Poage	(D)	N	Tuck	(D)	N	Byrnes	(R)	Y		
Pool	(D)	N	Broyhill	(R)	N	Laird	(R)	?		
Purcell	(D)	Y	Poff	(R)	N	O'Konski	(R)	Y		
Roberts	(D)	N	**WASHINGTON**			Thomson	(R)	Y		
Rogers	(D)	N	Adams	(D)	Y	Davis	(R)	N		
Teague	(D)	N	Foley	(D)	Y	**WYOMING**				
Thomas	(D)	?	Hansen	(D)	Y	Roncalio	(D)	•		

1966 Civil Rights Bill

(Included provision to ban racial discrimination in sale or rental of housing. Bill laid aside after Senate filibuster.)

SENATE

Vote Total: 52 for; 41 against

(*Note:* This was the final vote to invoke cloture. It failed to obtain two-thirds majority to stop filibuster and therefore ended consideration of bill by Congress. Later, it was reintroduced and became the 1968 Civil Rights Act.)

Y Record Vote For (yea).
• Paired For.
† Announced For.
N Record Vote Against (nay).

X Paired Against.
— Announced Against.
? Absent, General Pair, "Present," Did not announce.

ALABAMA			**COLORADO**			**HAWAII**			
Hill	(D)	N	Allott	(R)	•	Inouye	(D)	Y	
Sparkman	(D)	N	Dominick	(R)	•	Fong	(R)	Y	
ALASKA			**CONNECTICUT**			**IDAHO**			
Bartlett	(D)	Y	Dodd	(D)	Y	Church	(D)	Y	
Gruening	(D)	Y	Ribicoff	(D)	Y	Jordan	(R)	N	
ARIZONA			**DELAWARE**			**ILLINOIS**			
Hayden	(D)	X	Boggs	(R)	Y	Douglas	(D)	Y	
Fannin	(R)	N	Williams	(R)	N	Dirksen	(R)	N	
ARKANSAS			**FLORIDA**			**INDIANA**			
Fulbright	(D)	N	Holland	(D)	N	Bayh	(D)	Y	
McClellan	(D)	N	Smathers	(D)	N	Hartke	(D)	Y	
CALIFORNIA			**GEORGIA**			**IOWA**			
Kuchel	(R)	Y	Russell	(D)	N	Hickenlooper	(R)	N	
Murphy	(R)	N	Talmadge	(D)	N	Miller	(R)	N	

KANSAS			NEVADA			SOUTH CAROLINA		
Carlson	(R)	N	Bible	(D)	N	Russell	(D)	N
Pearson	(R)	N	Cannon	(D)	N	Thurmond	(R)	N
KENTUCKY			**NEW HAMPSHIRE**			**SOUTH DAKOTA**		
Cooper	(R)	X	McIntyre	(D)	Y	McGovern	(D)	Y
Morton	(R)	N	Cotton	(R)	N	Mundt	(R)	N
LOUISIANA			**NEW JERSEY**			**TENNESSEE**		
Ellender	(D)	N	Williams	(D)	Y	Bass	(D)	Y
Long	(D)	N	Case	(R)	Y	Gore	(D)	Y
MAINE			**NEW MEXICO**			**TEXAS**		
Muskie	(D)	Y	Anderson	(D)	†	Yarborough	(D)	Y
Smith	(R)	Y	Montoya	(D)	Y	Tower	(R)	N
MARYLAND			**NEW YORK**			**UTAH**		
Brewster	(D)	Y	Kennedy	(D)	Y	Moss	(D)	Y
Tydings	(D)	Y	Javits	(R)	Y	Bennett	(R)	N
MASSACHUSETTS			**NORTH CAROLINA**			**VERMONT**		
Kennedy	(D)	Y	Ervin	(D)	N	Aiken	(R)	Y
Saltonstall	(R)	Y	Jordan	(D)	N	Prouty	(R)	N
MICHIGAN			**NORTH DAKOTA**			**VIRGINIA**		
Hart	(D)	Y	Burdick	(D)	Y	Byrd, Jr.	(D)	N
Griffin	(R)	Y	Young	(R)	N	Robertson	(D)	N
MINNESOTA			**OHIO**			**WASHINGTON**		
McCarthy	(D)	Y	Lausche	(D)	N	Jackson	(D)	Y
Mondale	(D)	Y	Young	(D)	Y	Magnuson	(D)	•
MISSISSIPPI			**OKLAHOMA**			**WEST VIRGINIA**		
Eastland	(D)	N	Harris	(D)	•	Byrd	(D)	N
Stennis	(D)	N	Monroney	(D)	Y	Randolph	(D)	Y
MISSOURI			**OREGON**			**WISCONSIN**		
Long	(D)	Y	Morse	(D)	Y	Nelson	(D)	Y
Symington	(D)	Y	Neuberger	(D)	Y	Proxmire	(D)	Y
MONTANA			**PENNSYLVANIA**			**WYOMING**		
Mansfield	(D)	Y	Clark	(D)	Y	McGee	(D)	Y
Metcalf	(D)	Y	Scott	(R)	Y	Simpson	(R)	N
NEBRASKA			**RHODE ISLAND**					
Curtis	(R)	N	Pastore	(D)	Y			
Hruska	(R)	N	Pell	(D)	Y			

HOUSE OF REPRESENTATIVES   Vote Total: 259 for; 157 against

Y Record Vote For (yea).	X Paired Against.
• Paired For.	— Announced Against.
† Announced For.	? Absent, General Pair, "Present."
N Record Vote Against (nay).	

ALABAMA			ARKANSAS			McFall	(D)	Y
Andrews	(D)	X	Gathings	(D)	N	Miller	(D)	Y
Jones	(D)	N	Vacancy			Moss	(D)	Y
Selden	(D)	N	Mills	(D)	N	Sisk	(D)	Y
Andrews	(R)	N	Trimble	(D)	N	Tunney	(D)	Y
Buchanan	(R)	N				Van Deerlin	(D)	•
Dickinson	(R)	N	**CALIFORNIA**			Waldie	(D)	Y
Edwards	(R)	N	Burton	(D)	Y	Clausen	(R)	N
Martin	(R)	N	Cohelan	(D)	Y	Gubser	(R)	N
ALASKA			Dyal	(D)	Y	Mailliard	(R)	Y
Rivers	(D)	Y	Edwards	(D)	•	Talcott	(R)	N
ARIZONA			Hagen	(D)	N	Teague	(R)	N
Senner	(D)	Y	Hanna	(D)	X	Utt	(R)	N
Udall	(D)	Y	Johnson	(D)	Y	Wilson	(R)	N
Rhodes	(R)	N	Leggett	(D)	Y	Younger	(R)	N

Los Angeles Co.

Brown	(D)	Y
Cameron	(D)	N
Corman	(D)	Y
Hawkins	(D)	•
Holifield	(D)	Y
King	(D)	Y
Rees	(D)	Y
Roybal	(D)	Y
Wilson	(D)	Y
Bell	(R)	Y
Clawson	(R)	N
Hosmer	(R)	N
Lipscomb	(R)	N
Reinecke	(R)	N
Smith	(R)	N

COLORADO

Aspinall	(D)	N
Evans	(D)	Y
McVicker	(D)	Y
Rogers	(D)	Y

CONNECTICUT

Daddario	(D)	Y
Giaimo	(D)	Y
Grabowski	(D)	Y
Irwin	(D)	Y
Monagan	(D)	Y
St. Onge	(D)	Y

DELAWARE

McDowell	(D)	Y

FLORIDA

Bennett	(D)	N
Fascell	(D)	Y
Fuqua	(D)	N
Gibbons	(D)	Y
Haley	(D)	N
Herlong	(D)	N
Matthews	(D)	N
Pepper	(D)	Y
Rogers	(D)	N
Sikes	(D)	N
Cramer	(R)	N
Gurney	(R)	N

GEORGIA

Davis	(D)	N
Flynt	(D)	N
Hagan	(D)	N
Landrum	(D)	N
Mackay	(D)	N
O'Neal	(D)	N
Stephens	(D)	N
Tuten	(D)	N
Weltner	(D)	Y
Callaway	(R)	N

HAWAII

Matsunaga	(D)	Y
Mink	(D)	Y

IDAHO

White	(D)	Y
Hansen	(R)	N

ILLINOIS

Gray	(D)	Y
Price	(D)	Y
Schisler	(D)	Y
Shipley	(D)	Y
Anderson	(R)	N
Arends	(R)	Y
Erlenborn	(R)	Y
Findley	(R)	Y
McClory	(R)	Y
Michel	(R)	Y
Reid	(R)	N
Springer	(R)	Y

Chicago—Cook Co.

Annunzio	(D)	Y
Dawson	(D)	Y
Kluczynski	(D)	Y
Murphy	(D)	Y
O'Hara	(D)	Y
Pucinski	(D)	Y
Ronan	(D)	Y
Rostenkowski	(D)	Y
Yates	(D)	Y
Collier	(R)	N
Derwinski	(R)	Y
Rumsfeld	(R)	Y

INDIANA

Brademas	(D)	Y
Denton	(D)	Y
Hamilton	(D)	Y
Jacobs	(D)	Y
Madden	(D)	Y
Roush	(D)	Y
Adair	(R)	Y
Bray	(R)	N
Halleck	(R)	Y
Harvey	(R)	N
Roudebush	(R)	N

IOWA

Bandstra	(D)	Y
Culver	(D)	Y
Greigg	(D)	Y
Hansen	(D)	Y
Schmidhauser	(D)	Y
Smith	(D)	Y
Gross	(R)	N

KANSAS

Dole	(R)	N
Ellsworth	(R)	Y
Shriver	(R)	Y
Mize	(R)	N
Skubitz	(R)	N

KENTUCKY

Chelf	(D)	N
Farnsley	(D)	Y
Natcher	(D)	N
Perkins	(D)	Y
Stubblefield	(D)	N
Watts	(D)	N
Carter	(R)	N

LOUISIANA

Boggs	(D)	N
Hebert	(D)	N
Long, S.O.	(D)	N
Morrison	(D)	?
Passman	(D)	N
Edwards	(D)	X
Waggonner	(D)	N
Willis	(D)	X

MAINE

Hathaway	(D)	Y
Tupper	(R)	Y

MARYLAND

Fallon	(D)	N
Friedel	(D)	Y
Garmatz	(D)	N
Long	(D)	Y
Machen	(D)	N
Sickles	(D)	Y
Mathias	(R)	Y
Morton	(R)	N

MASSACHUSETTS

Boland	(D)	Y
Burke	(D)	Y
Donohue	(D)	Y
Macdonald	(D)	Y
McCormack	(D)	
O'Neill	(D)	Y
Philbin	(D)	Y
Bates	(R)	Y
Conte	(R)	Y
Keith	(R)	Y
Martin	(R)	Y
Morse	(R)	Y

MICHIGAN

Clevenger	(D)	Y
Farnum	(D)	Y
Mackie	(D)	Y
O'Hara	(D)	Y
Todd	(D)	Y
Vivian	(D)	Y
Broomfield	(R)	Y
Cederberg	(R)	Y
Chamberlain	(R)	Y
Ford	(R)	Y
Vacancy		
Harvey	(R)	Y
Hutchinson	(R)	Y

Detroit—Wayne Co.

Conyers	(D)	Y
Diggs	(D)	Y
Dingell	(D)	Y
Ford	(D)	Y
Griffiths	(D)	Y
Nedzi	(D)	Y

MINNESOTA

Blatnik	(D)	•
Fraser	(D)	Y
Karth	(D)	Y
Olson	(D)	Y
Langen	(R)	Y

Name	Party	Vote
MacGregor	(R)	Y
Nelsen	(R)	Y
Quie	(R)	Y
MISSISSIPPI		
Abernethy	(D)	N
Colmer	(D)	N
Whitten	(D)	N
Williams	(D)	N
Walker	(R)	N
MISSOURI		
Bolling	(D)	Y
Hull	(D)	N
Hungate	(D)	N
Ichord	(D)	N
Jones	(D)	N
Karsten	(D)	Y
Randall	(D)	N
Sullivan	(D)	Y
Curtis	(R)	Y
Hall	(R)	N
MONTANA		
Olsen	(D)	Y
Battin	(R)	N
NEBRASKA		
Callan	(D)	Y
Cunningham	(R)	Y
Martin	(R)	N
NEVADA		
Baring	(D)	N
NEW HAMPSHIRE		
Huot	(D)	Y
Cleveland	(R)	Y
NEW JERSEY		
Daniels	(D)	Y
Gallagher	(D)	Y
Helstoski	(D)	Y
Howard	(D)	Y
Joelson	(D)	Y
Krebs	(D)	Y
Minish	(D)	Y
McGrath	(D)	Y
Patten	(D)	Y
Rodino	(D)	Y
Thompson	(D)	Y
Cahill	(R)	Y
Dwyer	(R)	Y
Frelinghuysen	(R)	Y
Widnall	(R)	Y
NEW MEXICO		
Morris	(D)	N
Walker	(D)	N
NEW YORK		
Dow	(D)	Y
Dulski	(D)	Y
Hanley	(D)	Y
McCarthy	(D)	Y
O'Brien	(D)	Y
Ottinger	(D)	Y
Pike	(D)	Y
Resnick	(D)	Y
Stratton	(D)	Y
Tenzer	(D)	Y
Wolff	(D)	Y
Conable	(R)	Y
Goodell	(R)	Y
Grover	(R)	Y
Horton	(R)	Y
King	(R)	?
McEwen	(R)	Y
Pirnie	(R)	Y
Reid	(R)	Y
Robison	(R)	Y
Smith	(R)	Y
Wydler	(R)	Y
New York City		
Addabbo	(D)	Y
Bingham	(D)	Y
Carey	(D)	Y
Celler	(D)	Y
Delaney	(D)	Y
Farbstein	(D)	Y
Gilbert	(D)	Y
Kelly	(D)	Y
Keogh	(D)	Y
Multer	(D)	Y
Murphy	(D)	Y
Powell	(D)	•
Rooney	(D)	Y
Rosenthal	(D)	Y
Ryan	(D)	Y
Scheuer	(D)	Y
Fino	(R)	Y
Halpern	(R)	Y
Kupferman	(R)	Y
NORTH CAROLINA		
Jones	(D)	N
Cooley	(D)	N
Fountain	(D)	N
Henderson	(D)	N
Kornegay	(D)	N
Lennon	(D)	N
Scott	(D)	N
Taylor	(D)	N
Whitener	(D)	N
Broyhill	(R)	N
Jonas	(R)	N
NORTH DAKOTA		
Redlin	(D)	Y
Andrews	(R)	Y
OHIO		
Ashley	(D)	Y
Feighan	(D)	Y
Gilligan	(D)	Y
Hays	(D)	Y
Kirwan	(D)	Y
Love	(D)	Y
Moeller	(D)	Y
Secrest	(D)	N
Sweeney	(D)	Y
Vanik	(D)	Y
Ashbrook	(R)	N
Ayres	(R)	Y
Betts	(R)	N
Bolton	(R)	N
Bow	(R)	Y
Brown, Jr.	(R)	Y
Clancy	(R)	N
Devine	(R)	N
Harsha	(R)	N
Latta	(R)	N
McCulloch	(R)	Y
Minshall	(R)	N
Mosher	(R)	Y
Stanton	(R)	Y
OKLAHOMA		
Albert	(D)	Y
Edmondson	(D)	N
Jarman	(D)	N
Johnson	(D)	Y
Steed	(D)	N
Belcher	(R)	N
OREGON		
Duncan	(D)	Y
Green	(D)	Y
Ullman	(D)	•
Wyatt	(R)	N
PENNSYLVANIA		
Clark	(D)	Y
Craley	(D)	Y
Dent	(D)	Y
Flood	(D)	Y
Holland	(D)	Y
Moorhead	(D)	Y
Morgan	(D)	Y
Rhodes	(D)	Y
Rooney	(D)	Y
Vigorito	(D)	Y
Corbett	(R)	Y
Curtin	(R)	N
Dague	(R)	Y
Fulton	(R)	Y
Johnson	(R)	Y
Kunkel	(R)	Y
McDade	(R)	Y
Saylor	(R)	Y
Schneebeli	(R)	Y
Schweiker	(R)	Y
Watkins	(R)	N
Whalley	(R)	Y
Philadelphia City		
Barrett	(D)	Y
Byrne	(D)	Y
Green	(D)	Y
Nix	(D)	Y
Toll	(D)	?
RHODE ISLAND		
Fogarty	(D)	Y
St. Germain	(D)	Y

SOUTH CAROLINA			Gonzalez	(D)	Y	Broyhill	(R)	N
Ashmore	(D)	N	Mahon	(D)	N	Poff	(R)	N
Dorn	(D)	N	Patman	(D)	N	**WASHINGTON**		
Gettys	(D)	N	Pickle	(D)	N	Adams	(D)	Y
McMillan	(D)	N	Poage	(D)	N	Foley	(D)	N
Rivers	(D)	N	Pool	(D)	N	Hansen	(D)	Y
Watson	(R)	N	Purcell	(D)	N	Hicks	(D)	Y
SOUTH DAKOTA			Roberts	(D)	N	Meeds	(D)	Y
Berry	(R)	N	Rogers	(D)	X	May	(R)	N
Reifel	(R)	Y	Teague	(D)	N	Pelly	(R)	N
TENNESSEE			Thomas, L.	(D)	?	**WEST VIRGINIA**		
Anderson	(D)	N	Thompson	(D)	N	Hechler	(D)	Y
Everett	(D)	N	White	(D)	N	Kee, J.	(D)	Y
Evins	(D)	N	Wright	(D)	N	Slack	(D)	Y
Fulton	(D)	Y	Young	(D)	Y	Staggers	(D)	Y
Grider	(D)	Y	**UTAH**			Moore	(R)	N
Murray	(D)	X	King	(D)	Y	**WISCONSIN**		
Brock	(R)	N	Burton	(R)	Y	Kastenmeier	(D)	Y
Duncan	(R)	N	**VERMONT**			Race	(D)	N
Quillen	(R)	N	Stafford	(R)	Y	Reuss	(D)	Y
TEXAS			**VIRGINIA**			Stalbaum	(D)	Y
Beckworth	(D)	N	Abbitt	(D)	N	Zablocki	(D)	Y
Brooks	(D)	Y	Downing	(D)	N	Byrnes	(R)	Y
Burleson	(D)	N	Hardy	(D)	N	Laird	(R)	Y
Cabell	(D)	N	Jennings	(D)	N	O'Konski	(R)	Y
Casey	(D)	N	Marsh	(D)	N	Thomson	(R)	Y
De la Garza	(D)	Y	Satterfield	(D)	N	Davis	(R)	Y
Dowdy	(D)	N	Smith	(D)	N	**WYOMING**		
Fisher	(D)	N	Tuck	(D)	N	Roncalio	(D)	Y

1968 Civil Rights Act

(Prohibits interference with a person exercising specified federally protected rights, discrimination in the sale or rental of housing, travel in interstate commerce with intent to incite or take part in a riot; guarantees constitutional rights of American Indians.)

SENATE

Vote Total: 71 for; 20 against

Y Record Vote For (yea).
• Paired For.
† Announced For.
N Record Vote Against (nay).

X Paired Against.
— Announced Against.
? Absent, General Pair, "Present" or Did not announce.

ALABAMA			CALIFORNIA			FLORIDA		
Hill	(D)	N	Kuchel	(R)	•	Holland	(D)	N
Sparkman	(D)	N	Murphy	(R)	Y	Smathers	(D)	N
ALASKA			**COLORADO**			**GEORGIA**		
Bartlett	(D)	Y	Allott	(R)	Y	Russell	(D)	N
Gruening	(D)	Y	Dominick	(R)	Y	Talmadge	(D)	N
ARIZONA			**CONNECTICUT**			**HAWAII**		
Hayden	(D)	Y	Dodd	(D)	Y	Inouye	(D)	Y
Fannin	(R)	N	Ribicoff	(D)	Y	Fong	(R)	Y
ARKANSAS			**DELAWARE**			**IDAHO**		
Fulbright	(D)	N	Boggs	(R)	Y	Church	(D)	Y
McClellan	(D)	N	Williams	(R)	N	Jordan	(R)	Y

ILLINOIS			MONTANA			RHODE ISLAND		
Dirksen	(R)	Y	Mansfield	(D)	Y	Pastore	(D)	•
Percy	(R)	Y	Metcalf	(D)	†	Pell	(D)	Y
INDIANA			**NEBRASKA**			**SOUTH CAROLINA**		
Bayh	(D)	Y	Curtis	(R)	Y	Hollings	(D)	N
Hartke	(D)	Y	Hruska	(R)	Y	Thurmond	(R)	N
IOWA			**NEVADA**			**SOUTH DAKOTA**		
Hickenlooper	(R)	X	Bible	(D)	Y	McGovern	(D)	Y
Miller	(R)	X	Cannon	(D)	Y	Mundt	(R)	Y
KANSAS			**NEW HAMPSHIRE**			**TENNESSEE**		
Carlson	(R)	Y	McIntyre	(D)	†	Gore	(D)	Y
Pearson	(R)	Y	Cotton	(R)	Y	Baker	(R)	Y
KENTUCKY			**NEW JERSEY**					
Cooper	(R)	Y	Williams	(D)	Y	**TEXAS**		
Morton	(R)	Y	Case	(R)	Y	Yarborough	(D)	Y
LOUISIANA			**NEW MEXICO**			Tower	(R)	X
Ellender	(D)	N	Anderson	(D)	Y	**UTAH**		
Long	(D)	N	Montoya	(D)	Y	Moss	(D)	Y
MAINE			**NEW YORK**			Bennett	(R)	Y
Muskie	(D)	Y	Kennedy	(D)	Y	**VERMONT**		
Smith	(R)	Y	Javits	(R)	Y	Aiken	(R)	Y
MARYLAND			**NORTH CAROLINA**			Prouty	(R)	Y
Brewster	(D)	Y	Ervin	(D)	N	**VIRGINIA**		
Tydings	(D)	Y	Jordan	(D)	N	Byrd, Jr.	(D)	N
MASSACHUSETTS			**NORTH DAKOTA**			Spong	(D)	N
Kennedy	(D)	Y	Burdick	(D)	Y	**WASHINGTON**		
Brooke	(R)	Y	Young	(R)	Y	Jackson	(D)	Y
MICHIGAN			**OHIO**			Magnuson	(D)	Y
Hart	(D)	Y	Lausche	(D)	Y	**WEST VIRGINIA**		
Griffin	(R)	Y	Young	(D)	Y	Byrd	(D)	Y
MINNESOTA			**OKLAHOMA**			Randolph	(D)	Y
McCarthy	(D)	†	Harris	(D)	•	**WISCONSIN**		
Mondale	(D)	Y	Monroney	(D)	Y	Nelson	(D)	Y
MISSISSIPPI			**OREGON**			Proxmire	(D)	Y
Eastland	(D)	N	Morse	(D)	Y	**WYOMING**		
Stennis	(D)	N	Hatfield	(R)	Y	McGee	(D)	Y
MISSOURI			**PENNSYLVANIA**			Hansen	(R)	Y
Long	(D)	Y	Clark	(D)	Y			
Symington	(D)	Y	Scott	(R)	Y			

HOUSE OF REPRESENTATIVES   Vote Total: 250 for; 172 against

Y Record Vote For (yea).
• Paired For.
† Announced For.
N Record Vote Against (nay).

X Paired Against.
— Announced Against.
? Absent, General Pair, "Present" or
      Did not announce.

ALABAMA			ARKANSAS					
						Cohelan	(D)	Y
Andrews	(D)	N	Gathings	(D)	N	Edwards	(D)	Y
Bevill	(D)	N	Mills	(D)	N	Hanna	(D)	Y
Jones	(D)	N	Pryor	(D)	N	Johnson	(D)	Y
Nichols	(D)	N	Hammerschmidt	(R)	N	Leggett	(D)	Y
Selden	(D)	N	**ARIZONA**			McFall	(D)	Y
Buchanan	(R)	N	Udall	(D)	Y	Miller	(D)	Y
Dickinson	(R)	N	Rhodes	(R)	N	Moss	(D)	Y
Edwards	(R)	N	Steiger	(R)	N	Sisk	(D)	Y
ALASKA			**CALIFORNIA**			Tunney	(D)	Y
Pollack	(R)	Y	Burton	(D)	Y	Van Deerlin	(D)	Y

Name	Party	Vote	Name	Party	Vote	Name	Party	Vote
Waldie	(D)	Y	O'Neal	(D)	N	Shriver	(R)	N
Clausen	(R)	N	Stephens	(D)	N	Skubitz	(R)	N
Gubser	(R)	N	Stuckey	(D)	N	Winn	(R)	Y
McCloskey	(R)	Y	Blackburn	(R)	N	**KENTUCKY**		
Mailliard	(R)	Y	Thompson	(R)	N	Natcher	(D)	N
Mathias	(R)	N	**HAWAII**			Perkins	(D)	Y
Pettis	(R)	N	Matsunaga	(D)	Y	Stubblefield	(D)	N
Talcott	(R)	N	Mink	(D)	Y	Watts	(D)	N
Teague	(R)	N	**IDAHO**			Carter	(R)	N
Utt	(R)	N	Hansen	(R)	N	Cowger	(R)	Y
Wilson	(R)	N	McClure	(R)	N	Snyder	(R)	N
Los Angeles Co.			**ILLINOIS**			**LOUISIANA**		
Brown	(D)	Y	Gray	(D)	N	Boggs	(D)	Y
Corman	(D)	Y	Price	(D)	Y	Edwards	(D)	N
Hawkins	(D)	Y	Shipley	(D)	Y	Hebert	(D)	N
Holifield	(D)	Y	Anderson	(R)	Y	Long	(D)	N
King	(D)	•	Arends	(R)	N	Passman	(D)	N
Rees	(D)	Y	Erlenborn	(R)	Y	Rarick	(D)	N
Roybal	(D)	Y	Findley	(R)	Y	Waggonner	(D)	N
Wilson	(D)	Y	McClory	(R)	Y	Willis	(D)	N
Bell	(R)	Y	Michel	(R)	Y	**MAINE**		
Clawson	(R)	N	Railsback	(R)	Y	Hathaway	(D)	Y
Hosmer	(R)	N	Reid	(R)	N	Kyros	(D)	Y
Lipscomb	(R)	N	Springer	(R)	Y	**MARYLAND**		
Reinecke	(R)	N	**Chicago—Cook Co.**			Fallon	(D)	N
Smith	(R)	N	Annunzio	(D)	Y	Friedel	(D)	Y
Wiggins	(R)	N	Dawson	(D)	Y	Garmatz	(D)	N
COLORADO			Kluczynski	(D)	N	Long	(D)	Y
Aspinall	(D)	N	Murphy	(D)	Y	Machen	(D)	N
Evans	(D)	Y	O'Hara	(D)	Y	Gude	(R)	Y
Rogers	(D)	Y	Pucinski	(D)	N	Mathias	(R)	Y
Brotzman	(R)	Y	Ronan	(D)	Y	Morton	(R)	N
CONNECTICUT			Rostenkowski	(D)	Y	**MASSACHUSETTS**		
Daddario	(D)	Y	Yates	(D)	Y	Boland	(D)	Y
Giaimo	(D)	Y	Collier	(R)	N	Burke	(D)	Y
Irwin	(D)	Y	Derwinski	(R)	N	Donohue	(D)	Y
Monagan	(D)	Y	Rumsfeld	(R)	Y	Macdonald	(D)	Y
St. Onge	(D)	Y	**INDIANA**			McCormack	(D)	
Meskill	(R)	Y	Brademas	(D)	Y	O'Neill	(D)	Y
DELAWARE			Hamilton	(D)	Y	Philbin	(D)	Y
Roth	(R)	?	Jacobs	(D)	Y	Bates	(R)	Y
FLORIDA			Madden	(D)	Y	Conte	(R)	Y
Bennett	(D)	N	Roush	(D)	Y	Heckler	(R)	Y
Fascell	(D)	Y	Adair	(R)	N	Keith	(R)	Y
Fuqua	(D)	N	Bray	(R)	N	Morse	(R)	Y
Gibbons	(D)	N	Halleck	(R)	N	**MICHIGAN**		
Haley	(D)	N	Myers	(R)	N	O'Hara	(D)	Y
Herlong	(D)	—	Roudebush	(R)	N	Broomfield	(R)	Y
Pepper	(D)	Y	Zion	(R)	N	Brown	(R)	Y
Rogers	(D)	N	**IOWA**			Cederberg	(R)	Y
Sikes	(D)	N	Culver	(D)	Y	Chamberlain	(R)	Y
Burke	(R)	N	Smith	(D)	Y	Esch	(R)	Y
Cramer	(R)	N	Gross	(R)	N	Ford	(R)	Y
Gurney	(R)	N	Kyl	(R)	N	Harvey	(R)	Y
GEORGIA			Mayne	(R)	Y	Hutchinson	(R)	Y
Brinkley	(D)	N	Scherle	(R)	N	McDonald	(R)	Y
Davis	(D)	N	Schwengel	(R)	Y	Riegle	(R)	Y
Flynt	(D)	N	**KANSAS**			Ruppe	(R)	Y
Hagan	(D)	N	Dole	(R)	Y	Vander Jagt	(R)	Y
Landrum	(D)	N	Mize	(R)	Y			

Detroit—Wayne Co.

Conyers	(D)	Y
Diggs	(D)	Y
Dingell	(D)	Y
Ford	(D)	Y
Griffiths	(D)	Y
Nedzi	(D)	Y

MINNESOTA

Blatnik	(D)	Y
Fraser	(D)	Y
Karth	(D)	Y
Langen	(R)	Y
MacGregor	(R)	Y
Nelsen	(R)	Y
Quie	(R)	Y
Zwach	(R)	Y

MISSISSIPPI

Abernethy	(D)	N
Colmer	(D)	N
Montgomery	(D)	N
Whitten	(D)	N
Griffin	(D)	N

MISSOURI

Bolling	(D)	Y
Hull	(D)	N
Hungate	(D)	?
Ichord	(D)	N
Jones	(D)	—
Karsten	(D)	?
Randall	(D)	N
Sullivan	(D)	Y
Curtis	(R)	N
Hall	(R)	N

MONTANA

Olsen	(D)	Y
Battin	(R)	N

NEBRASKA

Cunningham	(R)	Y
Denney	(R)	Y
Martin	(R)	N

NEVADA

Baring	(D)	N

NEW HAMPSHIRE

Cleveland	(R)	Y
Wyman	(R)	Y

NEW JERSEY

Daniels	(D)	Y
Gallagher	(D)	Y
Helstoski	(D)	Y
Howard	(D)	Y
Joelson	(D)	Y
Minish	(D)	Y
Patten	(D)	Y
Rodino	(D)	Y
Thompson	(D)	Y
Cahill	(R)	Y
Dwyer	(R)	Y
Frelinghuysen	(R)	Y
Hunt	(R)	Y
Sandman	(R)	Y
Widnall	(R)	Y

NEW MEXICO

Morris	(D)	Y
Walker	(D)	N

NEW YORK

Dow	(D)	Y
Dulski	(D)	Y
Hanley	(D)	Y
McCarthy	(D)	Y
Ottinger	(D)	Y
Pike	(D)	Y
Resnick	(D)	†
Stratton	(D)	Y
Tenzer	(D)	Y
Wolff	(D)	Y
Button	(R)	Y
Conable	(R)	Y
Goodell	(R)	Y
Grover	(R)	Y
Horton	(R)	Y
King	(R)	?
McEwen	(R)	Y
Pirnie	(R)	Y
Reid	(R)	Y
Robison	(R)	Y
Smith	(R)	Y
Wydler	(R)	Y

New York City

Addabbo	(D)	Y
Bingham	(D)	Y
Brasco	(D)	Y
Carey	(D)	Y
Celler	(D)	Y
Delaney	(D)	N
Farbstein	(D)	Y
Gilbert	(D)	Y
Kelly	(D)	Y
Podell	(D)	Y
Murphy	(D)	Y
Vacancy		
Rooney	(D)	Y
Rosenthal	(D)	Y
Ryan	(D)	Y
Scheuer	(D)	Y
Fino	(R)	—
Halpern	(R)	Y
Kupferman	(R)	Y

NORTH CAROLINA

Fountain	(D)	N
Galifianakis	(D)	N
Henderson	(D)	N
Jones	(D)	N
Kornegay	(D)	N
Lennon	(D)	N
Taylor	(D)	N
Whitener	(D)	N
Broyhill	(R)	N
Gardner	(R)	N
Jonas	(R)	N

NORTH DAKOTA

Andrews	(R)	Y
Kleppe	(R)	Y

OHIO

Ashley	(D)	Y
Feighan	(D)	Y
Hays	(D)	Y
Kirwan	(D)	Y
Vanik	(D)	Y
Ashbrook	(R)	N
Ayres	(R)	Y
Betts	(R)	Y
Bolton	(R)	N
Bow	(R)	N
Brown	(R)	Y
Clancy	(R)	N
Devine	(R)	N
Harsha	(R)	N
Latta	(R)	N
Lukens	(R)	Y
McCulloch	(R)	Y
Miller	(R)	N
Minshall	(R)	N
Mosher	(R)	Y
Stanton	(R)	Y
Taft	(R)	Y
Whalen	(R)	Y
Wylie	(R)	N

OKLAHOMA

Albert	(D)	Y
Edmondson	(D)	N
Jarman	(D)	N
Steed	(D)	N
Belcher	(R)	N
Smith	(R)	N

OREGON

Green	(D)	Y
Ullman	(D)	Y
Dellenback	(R)	Y
Wyatt	(R)	Y

PENNSYLVANIA

Clark	(D)	Y
Dent	(D)	Y
Flood	(D)	Y
Holland	(D)	Y
Moorhead	(D)	Y
Morgan	(D)	Y
Rhodes	(D)	Y
Rooney	(D)	Y
Vigorito	(D)	Y
Biester	(R)	Y
Corbett	(R)	Y
Eshleman	(R)	Y
Fulton	(R)	Y
Goodling	(R)	N
Johnson	(R)	N
McDade	(R)	Y
Saylor	(R)	N
Schneebeli	(R)	Y
Schweiker	(R)	Y
Watkins	(R)	N
Whalley	(R)	N
Williams	(R)	N

Philadelphia City			Cabell	(D)	N	Tuck	(D)	N
Barrett	(D)	Y	Casey	(D)	N	Broyhill	(R)	N
Byrne	(D)	Y	de la Garza	(D)	Y	Poff	(R)	N
Eilberg	(D)	Y	Dowdy	(D)	N	Scott	(R)	N
Green	(D)	Y	Eckhardt	(D)	Y	Wampler	(R)	N
Nix	(D)	Y	Fisher	(D)	N	**WASHINGTON**		
RHODE ISLAND			Gonzalez	(D)	Y	Adams	(D)	Y
St. Germain	(D)	Y	Kazen	(D)	Y	Foley	(D)	Y
Tiernan	(D)	Y	Mahon	(D)	N	Hansen	(D)	Y
SOUTH CAROLINA			Patman	(D)	N	Hicks	(D)	Y
Ashmore	(D)	X	Pickle	(D)	N	Meeds	(D)	Y
Dorn	(D)	N	Poage	(D)	?	May	(R)	Y
Gettys	(D)	N	Pool	(D)	N	Pelly	(R)	Y
McMillan	(D)	N	Purcell	(D)	N	**WEST VIRGINIA**		
Rivers	(D)	N	Roberts	(D)	N	Hechler	(D)	Y
Watson	(R)	N	Teague	(D)	N	Kee	(D)	Y
SOUTH DAKOTA			White	(D)	N	Slack	(D)	Y
Berry	(R)	Y	Wright	(D)	Y	Staggers	(D)	Y
Reifel	(R)	Y	Young	(D)	Y	Moore	(R)	Y
TENNESSEE			Bush	(R)	Y	**WISCONSIN**		
Anderson	(D)	N	Price	(R)	N	Kastenmeier	(D)	Y
Blanton	(D)	N	**UTAH**			Reuss	(D)	Y
Everett	(D)	N	Burton	(R)	N	Zablocki	(D)	Y
Evins	(D)	N	Lloyd	(R)	Y	Byrnes	(R)	Y
Fulton	(D)	Y	**VERMONT**			Davis	(R)	N
Brock	(R)	N	Stafford	(R)	Y	Laird	(R)	Y
Duncan	(R)	N	**VIRGINIA**			O'Konski	(R)	Y
Kuykendall	(R)	N	Abbitt	(D)	N	Schadeberg	(R)	N
Quillen	(R)	N	Downing	(D)	N	Steiger	(R)	Y
TEXAS			Hardy	(D)	N	Thomson	(R)	Y
Brooks	(D)	Y	Marsh	(D)	N	**WYOMING**		
Burleson	(D)	N	Satterfield	(D)	N	Harrison	(R)	N

1970 Voting Rights Act

(Extends the 1965 Voting Rights Act for five years, sets uniform resident requirements for voting in national elections, lowering voting age to 18, and suspends use of literacy tests for five years.)

SENATE   Vote Total: 64 for; 12 against

Y Record Vote For (yea).	X Paired Against.
• Paired For.	— Announced Against.
† Announced For.	? Absent, General Pair, "Present" or
N Record Vote Against (nay).	Did not announce.

ALABAMA			**CALIFORNIA**			**FLORIDA**		
Allen	(D)	N	Cranston	(D)	†	Holland	(D)	N
Sparkman	(D(	N	Murphy	(R)	Y	Gurney	(R)	†
ALASKA			**COLORADO**			**GEORGIA**		
Gravel	(D)	†	Allott	(R)	Y	Russell	(D)	X
Stevens	(R)	†	Dominick	(R)	Y	Talmadge	(D)	N
ARIZONA			**CONNECTICUT**			**HAWAII**		
Fannin	(R)	Y	Dodd	(D)	•	Inouye	(D)	†
Goldwater	(R)	•	Ribicoff	(D)	Y	Fong	(R)	Y
ARKANSAS			**DELAWARE**			**IDAHO**		
Fulbright	(D)	Y	Boggs	(R)	Y	Church	(D)	†
McClellan	(D)	X	Williams	(R)	Y	Jordan	(R)	Y

ILLINOIS			MONTANA			RHODE ISLAND		
Percy	(R)	Y	Mansfield	(D)	●	Pastore	(D)	●
Smith	(R)	†	Metcalf	(D)	Y	Pell	(D)	Y
INDIANA			**NEBRASKA**			**SOUTH CAROLINA**		
Bayh	(D)	Y	Curtis	(R)	Y	Hollings	(D)	N
Hartke	(D)	Y	Hruska	(R)	X	Thurmond	(R)	N
IOWA			**NEVADA**			**SOUTH DAKOTA**		
Hughes	(D)	Y	Bible	(D)	Y	McGovern	(D)	Y
Miller	(R)	Y	Cannon	(D)	Y	Mundt	(R)	†
KANSAS			**NEW HAMPSHIRE**					
Dole	(R)	Y	McIntyre	(D)	Y	**TENNESSEE**		
Pearson	(R)	Y	Cotton	(R)	Y	Gore	(D)	Y
KENTUCKY			**NEW JERSEY**			Baker	(R)	Y
Cook	(R)	Y	Williams	(D)	Y	**TEXAS**		
Cooper	(R)	Y	Case	(R)	Y	Yarborough	(D)	†
LOUISIANA			**NEW MEXICO**			Tower	(R)	X
Ellender	(D)	N	Anderson	(D)	Y	**UTAH**		
Long	(D)	X	Montoya	(D)	†	Moss	(D)	●
MAINE			**NEW YORK**			Bennett	(R)	●
Muskie	(D)	Y	Goodell	(R)	Y	**VERMONT**		
Smith	(R)	Y	Javits	(R)	Y	Aiken	(R)	Y
MARYLAND			**NORTH CAROLINA**			Prouty	(R)	Y
Tydings	(D)	Y	Ervin	(D)	N	**VIRGINIA**		
Mathias	(R)	Y	Jordan	(D)	X	Byrd, Jr.	(D)	N
MASSACHUSETTS			**NORTH DAKOTA**			Spong	(D)	Y
Kennedy	(D)	Y	Burdick	(D)	Y	**WASHINGTON**		
Brooke	(R)	Y	Young	(R)	Y	Jackson	(D)	Y
MICHIGAN			**OHIO**			Magnuson	(D)	Y
Hart	(D)	Y	Young	(D)	Y	**WEST VIRGINIA**		
Griffin	(R)	Y	Saxbe	(R)	Y	Byrd	(D)	N
MINNESOTA			**OKLAHOMA**			Randolph	(D)	Y
McCarthy	(D)	†	Harris	(D)	Y	**WISCONSIN**		
Mondale	(D)	Y	Bellmon	(R)	†	Nelson	(D)	Y
MISSISSIPPI			**OREGON**			Proxmire	(D)	Y
Eastland	(D)	N	Hatfield	(R)	Y	**WYOMING**		
Stennis	(D)	N	Packwood	(R)	Y	McGee	(D)	Y
MISSOURI			**PENNSYLVANIA**			Hansen	(R)	Y
Eagleton	(D)	Y	Schweiker	(R)	Y			
Symington	(D)	Y	Scott	(R)	Y			

HOUSE OF REPRESENTATIVES   Vote Total: 272 for; 132 against

Y Record Vote For (yea).	X Paired Against.	
● Paired For.	— Announced Against.	
† Announced For.	? Absent, General Pair, "Present" or	
N Record Vote Against (nay).	Did not announce.	

ALABAMA			ARIZONA					
						Cohelan	(D)	Y
Andrews	(D)	N	Udall	(D)	Y	Edwards	(D)	Y
Bevill	(D)	N	Rhodes	(R)	Y	Hanna	(D)	Y
Flowers	(D)	N	Steiger	(R)	N	Johnson	(D)	Y
Jones	(D)	Y	**ARKANSAS**			Leggett	(D)	Y
Nichols	(D)	N	Alexander	(D)	N	McFall	(D)	Y
Buchanan	(R)	N	Mills	(D)	N	Miller	(D)	Y
Dickinson	(R)	N	Pryor	(D)	Y	Moss	(D)	Y
Edwards	(R)	N	Hammerschmidt	(R)	N	Sisk	(D)	Y
ALASKA			**CALIFORNIA**			Tunney	(D)	Y
Pollack	(R)	?	Burton	(D)	Y	Van Deerlin	(D)	Y

Name	Party	Vote	Name	Party	Vote	Name	Party	Vote
Waldie	(D)	Y	O'Neal	(D)	?	Shriver	(R)	N
Clausen	(R)	Y	Stephens	(D)	N	Skubitz	(R)	N
Gubser	(R)	Y	Stuckey	(D)	Y	Winn	(R)	N
McCloskey	(R)	Y	Blackburn	(R)	N	**KENTUCKY**		
Mailliard	(R)	Y	Thompson	(R)	N	Natcher	(D)	Y
Mathias	(R)	Y	**HAWAII**			Perkins	(D)	Y
Pettis	(R)	Y	Matsunaga	(D)	Y	Stubblefield	(D)	Y
Talcott	(R)	N	Mink	(D)	Y	Watts	(D)	Y
Teague	(R)	Y	**IDAHO**			Carter	(R)	Y
Vacancy			Hansen, O.	(R)	Y	Cowger	(R)	•
Wilson	(R)	Y	McClure	(R)	N	Snyder	(R)	Y
Los Angeles Co.			**ILLINOIS**			**LOUISIANA**		
Anderson	(D)	Y	Gray	(D)	Y	Boggs	(D)	Y
Brown	(D)	Y	Price	(D)	Y	Caffery	(D)	N
Corman	(D)	Y	Shipley	(D)	Y	Edwards	(D)	Y
Hawkins	(D)	Y	Anderson	(R)	Y	Hebert	(D)	X
Holifield	(D)	Y	Arends	(R)	Y	Long	(D)	N
Rees	(D)	Y	Erlenborn	(R)	—	Passman	(D)	N
Roybal	(D)	Y	Findley	(R)	Y	Rarick	(D)	N
Wilson	(D)	†	McClory	(R)	Y	Waggonner	(D)	N
Bell	(R)	Y	Michel	(R)	N	**MAINE**		
Clawson	(R)	N	Railsback	(R)	Y	Hathaway	(D)	Y
Goldwater	(R)	N	Reid	(R)	Y	Kyros	(D)	Y
Hosmer	(R)	Y	Springer	(R)	Y	**MARYLAND**		
Vacancy			**Chicago—Cook Co.**			Fallon	(D)	Y
Smith	(R)	N	Annunzio	(D)	Y	Friedel	(D)	Y
Wiggins	(R)	N	Dawson	(D)	?	Garmatz	(D)	Y
COLORADO			Kluczynski	(D)	Y	Long	(D)	Y
Aspinall	(D)	Y	Mikva	(D)	Y	Beall	(R)	Y
Evans	(D)	Y	Murphy	(D)	Y	Gude	(R)	Y
Rogers	(D)	Y	Pucinski	(D)	Y	Hogan	(R)	Y
Brotzman	(R)	Y	Vacancy			Morton	(R)	Y
CONNECTICUT			Rostenkowski	(D)	Y	**MASSACHUSETTS**		
Daddario	(D)	Y	Yates	(D)	Y	Boland	(D)	Y
Giaimo	(D)	Y	Collier	(R)	N	Burke	(D)	Y
Monagan	(D)	Y	Crane	(R)	N	Donohue	(D)	Y
Vacancy			Derwinski	(R)	N	Harrington	(D)	Y
Meskill	(R)	Y	**INDIANA**			Macdonald	(D)	Y
Weicker	(R)	Y	Brademas	(D)	Y	McCormack	(D)	
DELAWARE			Hamilton	(D)	Y	O'Neill	(D)	Y
Roth	(R)	Y	Jacobs	(D)	Y	Philbin	(D)	Y
FLORIDA			Madden	(D)	Y	Conte	(R)	Y
Bennett	(D)	Y	Adair	(R)	Y	Heckler	(R)	Y
Chappell	(D)	N	Bray	(R)	Y	Keith	(R)	Y
Fascell	(D)	Y	Dennis	(R)	N	Morse	(R)	Y
Fuqua	(D)	N	Landgrebe	(R)	N	**MICHIGAN**		
Gibbons	(D)	Y	Myers	(R)	Y	O'Hara	(D)	Y
Haley	(D)	N	Roudebush	(R)	?	Broomfield	(R)	Y
Pepper	(D)	Y	Zion	(R)	Y	Brown	(R)	Y
Rogers	(D)	Y	**IOWA**			Cederberg	(R)	Y
Sikes	(D)	N	Culver	(D)	?	Chamberlain	(R)	Y
Burke	(R)	N	Smith	(D)	Y	Esch	(R)	Y
Cramer	(R)	X	Gross	(R)	N	Ford	(R)	Y
Frey	(R)	N	Kyl	(R)	Y	Harvey	(R)	Y
GEORGIA			Mayne	(R)	N	Hutchinson	(R)	N
Brinkley	(D)	N	Scherle	(R)	N	McDonald	(R)	Y
Davis	(D)	N	Schwengel	(R)	•	Riegle	(R)	Y
Flynt	(D)	N	**KANSAS**			Ruppe	(R)	Y
Hagan	(D)	N	Mize	(R)	N	Vander Jagt	(R)	Y
Landrum	(D)	N	Sebelius	(R)	N			

Detroit—Wayne Co.

Conyers	(D)	?
Diggs	(D)	Y
Dingell	(D)	Y
Ford	(D)	Y
Griffiths	(D)	Y
Nedzi	(D)	•

MINNESOTA

Blatnik	(D)	Y
Fraser	(D)	Y
Karth	(D)	Y
Langen	(R)	Y
MacGregor	(R)	Y
Nelsen	(R)	Y
Quie	(R)	Y
Zwach	(R)	Y

MISSISSIPPI

Abernethy	(D)	N
Colmer	(D)	N
Griffin	(D)	N
Montgomery	(D)	N
Whitten	(D)	N

MISSOURI

Bolling	(D)	Y
Burlison	(D)	Y
Clay	(D)	Y
Hull	(D)	N
Hungate	(D)	Y
Ichord	(D)	N
Randall	(D)	N
Sullivan	(D)	Y
Symington	(D)	Y
Hall	(R)	N

MONTANA

Melcher	(D)	Y
Olsen	(D)	Y

NEBRASKA

Cunningham	(R)	N
Denney	(R)	N
Martin	(R)	N

NEVADA

Baring	(D)	N

NEW HAMPSHIRE

Cleveland	(R)	Y
Wyman	(R)	N

NEW JERSEY

Daniels	(D)	Y
Gallagher	(D)	Y
Helstoski	(D)	Y
Howard	(D)	Y
Minish	(D)	Y
Patten	(D)	Y
Rodino	(D)	Y
Roe	(D)	Y
Thompson	(D)	Y
Vacancy		
Dwyer	(R)	Y
Frelinghuysen	(R)	Y
Hunt	(R)	N
Sandman	(R)	N
Widnall	(R)	Y

NEW MEXICO

Foreman	(R)	N
Lujan	(R)	Y

NEW YORK

Dulski	(D)	Y
Hanley	(D)	Y
Lowenstein	(D)	Y
McCarthy	(D)	Y
Ottinger	(D)	Y
Pike	(D)	Y
Stratton	(D)	Y
Wolff	(D)	Y
Button	(R)	Y
Conable	(R)	N
Fish	(R)	Y
Grover	(R)	N
Hastings	(R)	Y
Horton	(R)	Y
King	(R)	X
McEwen	(R)	Y
McKneally	(R)	Y
Pirnie	(R)	Y
Reid	(R)	Y
Robison	(R)	Y
Smith	(R)	N
Wydler	(R)	Y

NEW YORK CITY

Addabbo	(D)	Y
Biaggi	(D)	Y
Bingham	(D)	Y
Brasco	(D)	Y
Carey	(D)	?
Celler	(D)	Y
Chisholm	(D)	?
Delaney	(D)	Y
Farbstein	(D)	Y
Gilbert	(D)	Y
Koch	(D)	Y
Murphy	(D)	Y
Podell	(D)	Y
Powell	(D)	Y
Rooney	(D)	Y
Rosenthal	(D)	Y
Ryan	(D)	Y
Scheuer	(D)	Y
Halpern	(R)	Y

NORTH CAROLINA

Fountain	(D)	N
Galifianakis	(D)	Y
Henderson	(D)	N
Jones	(D)	N
Lennon	(D)	N
Preyer	(D)	Y
Taylor	(D)	Y
Broyhill	(R)	N
Jonas	(R)	N
Mizell	(R)	N
Ruth	(R)	N

NORTH DAKOTA

Andrews	(R)	Y
Kleppe	(R)	Y

OHIO

Ashley	(D)	Y
Feighan	(D)	Y
Hays	(D)	Y
Kirwan	(D)	?
Stokes	(D)	Y
Vanik	(D)	Y
Ashbrook	(R)	N
Ayres	(R)	Y
Betts	(R)	N
Bow	(R)	Y
Brown	(R)	Y
Clancy	(R)	Y
Devine	(R)	N
Harsha	(R)	N
Latta	(R)	Y
Lukens	(R)	?
McCulloch	(R)	Y
Miller	(R)	Y
Minshall	(R)	Y
Mosher	(R)	Y
Stanton	(R)	Y
Taft	(R)	Y
Whalen	(R)	Y
Wylie	(R)	N

OKLAHOMA

Albert	(D)	Y
Edmundson	(D)	Y
Jarman	(D)	N
Steed	(D)	Y
Belcher	(R)	N
Camp	(R)	N

OREGON

Green	(D)	N
Ullman	(D)	N
Dellenback	(R)	N
Wyatt	(R)	N

PENNSYLVANIA

Clark	(D)	?
Dent	(D)	†
Flood	(D)	Y
Gaydos	(D)	•
Moorhead	(D)	Y
Morgan	(D)	Y
Rooney	(D)	Y
Vigorito	(D)	Y
Yatron	(D)	Y
Biester	(R)	Y
Corbett	(R)	Y
Coughlin	(R)	Y
Eshleman	(R)	N
Fulton	(R)	Y
Goodling	(R)	N
Johnson	(R)	N
McDade	(R)	Y
Saylor	(R)	N
Schneebeli	(R)	Y
Watkins	(R)	N
Whalley	(R)	N
Williams	(R)	N

Philadelphia City			Cabell	(D)	Y	Broyhill	(R)	N
Barrett	(D)	Y	Casey	(D)	N	Poff	(R)	N
Byrne	(D)	Y	de la Garza	(D)	Y	Scott	(R)	N
Eilberg	(D)	Y	Dowdy	(D)	N	Wampler	(R)	N
Green	(D)	Y	Eckhardt	(D)	Y	Whitehurst	(R)	Y
Nix	(D)	Y	Fisher	(D)	N	**WASHINGTON**		
RHODE ISLAND			Gonzalez	(D)	Y	Adams	(D)	Y
St. Germain	(D)	Y	Kazen	(D)	Y	Foley	(D)	Y
Tiernan	(D)	Y	Mahon	(D)	N	Hansen	(D)	Y
SOUTH CAROLINA			Patman	(D)	N	Hicks	(D)	Y
Dorn	(D)	N	Pickle	(D)	Y	Meeds	(D)	Y
Gettys	(D)	—	Poage	(D)	N	May	(R)	Y
McMillan	(D)	X	Purcell	(D)	N	Pelly	(R)	?
Mann	(D)	N	Roberts	(D)	N	**WEST VIRGINIA**		
Rivers	(D)	N	Teague	(D)	Y	Hechler	(D)	Y
Watson	(R)	N	White	(D)	Y	Kee	(D)	Y
SOUTH DAKOTA			Wright	(D)	Y	Mollohan	(D)	Y
Berry	(R)	N	Young	(D)	Y	Slack	(D)	Y
Reifel	(R)	Y	Bush	(R)	?	Staggers	(D)	Y
TENNESSEE			Collins	(R)	N	**WISCONSIN**		
Anderson	(D)	Y	Price	(R)	N	Kastenmeier	(D)	Y
Blanton	(D)	N	**UTAH**			Obey	(D)	Y
Evins	(D)	Y	Burton	(R)	Y	Reuss	(D)	Y
Fulton	(D)	Y	Lloyd	(R)	Y	Zablocki	(D)	Y
Jones	(D)	N	**VERMONT**			Byrnes	(R)	N
Brock	(R)	N	Stafford	(R)	Y	Davis	(R)	N
Duncan	(R)	Y	**VIRGINIA**			O'Konski	(R)	Y
Kuykendall	(R)	Y	Abbitt	(D)	N	Schadeberg	(R)	N
Quillen	(R)	N	Daniel	(D)	N	Steiger	(R)	Y
TEXAS			Downing	(D)	N	Thomson	(R)	N
Brooks	(D)	Y	Marsh	(D)	N	**WYOMING**		
Burleson	(D)	N	Satterfield	(D)	N	Wold	(R)	N

Appendix II
State and Federal Agencies with Civil Rights Responsibilities

"Laws" column indicates whether state has law against discrimination in employment (E), private schools and colleges (S), housing not receiving public funds (H), public accommodations (A). "Population" columns reflect 1970 Census figures.

State and Agency	Executive Officer	Laws	Total Population	Non-White Population
ALASKA				
Alaska State Commission for Human Rights	Robert Willard	EHA	300,382	63,615 (21.2%)
520 MacKay Bldg. 338 Denali St. Anchorage, 99501 (907) 272-9504				
ARIZONA				
Arizona Civil Rights Division, Arizona State Department of Law	J. Ford Smith	EA	1,770,900	165,952 (9.4%)
1502 West Jefferson St. Phoenix, 85007 (602) 271-5263				
CALIFORNIA				
California Fair Employment Practices Commission	Paul A. Meaney	EH	19,953,134	2.192,107 (11%)
455 Golden Gate Ave. San Francisco, 94102 (415) 557-2000				

State and Agency	Executive Officer	Laws	Total Population	Non-White Population
COLORADO				
Colorado Civil Rights Commission	James F. Reynolds	EHA	2,207,259	94,907 (4.3%)
312 State Services Bldg. 1525 Sherman St. Denver, 80203 (303) 892-2621				
CONNECTICUT				
Connecticut Commission on Human Rights and Opportunities	Arthur L. Green	EHA	3,031,709	196,251 (6.5%)
90 Washington St. Hartford, 06106 (203) 566-3350				
DELAWARE				
Department of Labor and Industrial Relations Division Against Discrimination	Harold T. Bochman	E	548,104	81,645 (14.9%)
618 North Union Wilmington, 19801 (302) 658-9251 Ext. 276, 277				
DISTRICT OF COLUMBIA				
District of Columbia Human Relations Commission	James W. Baldwin	EHA	756,510	547,238 (72.3%)
Room 5, District Bldg. 14th and E Sts. N.W. Washington (202) 629-4723				
FLORIDA				
Florida Commission on Human Relations Department of Community Affairs	Lyman T. Fletcher	None	6,789,443	1,070,100 (15.8%)
2711 Apalachee Pkwy. Tallahasse, 32301 (904) 878-1489				
GEORGIA				
Governor's Council on Human Relations	Harold E. Barrett	None	4,589,575	1,198,333 (26.1%)
Room 104 State Capital Atlanta, 30334 (404) 656-1735				

State and Agency	Executive Officer	Laws	Total Population	Non-White Population
HAWAII				
Department of Labor and Industrial Relations 825 Mililani St. Honolulu, 96813 (808) 548-3150	Robert K. Haseqawa	E	768,561	470,401 (61.2%)
IDAHO				
Idaho Commission on Human Rights State House Boise, 83702 (208) 384-3550	Jesse S. Berain	None	712,567	13,765 (1.9%)
ILLINOIS				
Illinois Commission on Human Relations 160 N. LaSalle St. Chicago, 60601 (312) 793-2893	Beatrice Young	SH	11,113,976	1,513,595 (13.6%)
INDIANA				
Indiana Civil Rights Commission 319 State Office Bldg. 100 North Senate Ave. Indianapolis, 46204 (317) 633-4855	C. Lee Crean, Jr.	ESHA	5,193,669	373,345 (7.2%)
IOWA				
Iowa Civil Rights Commission State Capitol Bldg. Des Moines, 50319 (515) 281-5129	Alvin Hayes, Jr.	EHA	2,824,376	41,614 (1.5%)
KANSAS				
Kansas Commission on Civil Rights Room 1155 W State Office Bldg. Topeka, 66612 (913) 296-3206	Frank L. Ross	ESHA	2,246,578	124,510 (5.5%)
KENTUCKY				
Kentucky Commission on Human Rights Mammoth Life Bldg. 600 West Walnut St. Louisville, 40203 (502) 585-3363	Galen Martin	EAS	3,218,706	236,940 (7.4%)

State and Agency	Executive Officer	Laws	Total Population	Non-White Population
LOUISIANA				
Louisiana Commission on Human Relations, Rights, and Responsibilities	Ben Jeffers	None	3,641,306	1,099,808 (30.2%)
State Office Bldg. 150 Riverside Mall Suite 402 Baton Rouge, 70801 (504) 389-6601				
MAINE				
Maine Human Rights Commission	Robert E. Talbot	EHA	992,048	6,772 (0.7%)
State House Augusta, 04330 (207) 289-2326				
MARYLAND				
Maryland Commission on Human Rights	Treadwell O. Phillips	EHA	3,922,399	727,511 (18.5%)
The Mount Vernon Bldg. 701 St. Paul St. Baltimore, 21202 (301) 383-3680				
MASSACHUSETTS				
Massachusetts Commission Against Discrimination	Walter H. Nolan	ESHA	5,689,170	211,546 (3.7%)
120 Tremont St. Boston, 02108 (617) 727-3990				
MICHIGAN				
Michigan Civil Rights Commission	Mrs. Frank W. Wylie	ESHA	8,875,083	1,041,609 (11.7%)
1000 Cadillac Sq. Bldg. Detroit, 48226 (313) 222-1810				
MINNESOTA				
Department of Human Rights	Samuel L. Richardson	ESHA	3,804,971	68,933 (1.8%)
60 State Office Bldg. St. Paul, 55155 (612) 296-2931				

State and Agency	Executive Officer	Laws	Total Population	Non-White Population
MISSOURI				
Missouri Commission on Human Rights P.O. Box 1129 314 East High St. Jefferson City, 65101 (314) 751-3325	Clyde L. Scott	EA	4,676,501	499,006 (10.7%)
MONTANA				
Montana Department of Labor and Industry 1336 Helena Ave. Helena, 59601 (406) 449-3472	Sidney T. Smith	EA	694,409	31,366 (4.5%)
NEBRASKA				
Nebraska Equal Opportunity Commission 233 South 14th Lincoln, 68508 (402) 471-2024	Reid E. Devoe	EHA	1,483,493	50,626 (3.4%)
NEVADA				
Nevada Commission on Equal Rights of Citizens State Office Bldg. Room 100-B 215 East Bonanza Las Vegas, 89101 (702) 385-0104	Jesse D. Scott	ESHA	488,738	40,561 (8.3%)
NEW HAMPSHIRE				
New Hampshire Commission on Human Rights 66 South St. Concord, 03301 (603) 271-2767	Berel Firestone	EHA	737,681	4,575 (0.6%)
NEW JERSEY				
New Jersey Division on Civil Rights 1100 Raymond Blvd. Newark, 07102 (201) 648-2700	James H. Blair	ESHA	7,168,164	818,256 (11.4%)

State and Agency	Executive Officer	Laws	Total Population	Non-White Population
NEW MEXICO				
Human Rights Commission of New Mexico 120 Villagra Bldg. Santa Fe, 87501 (505) 827-2713	Charles R. Rudolph	EHA	1,016,000	100,185 (9.9%)
NEW YORK				
New York State Division of Human Rights 270 Broadway New York, 10007 (212) 488-7610	Jack M. Sable	ESHA	18,236,967	2,402,877 (13.2%)
NORTH CAROLINA				
North Carolina Human Relations Commission P.O. Box 12525 Raleigh, 27605 (919) 829-7996	Fred L. Cooper	None	5,082,059	1,180,292 (23.2%)
OHIO				
Ohio Civil Rights Commission 240 Parsons Ave. Columbus, 43215 (614) 469-2785	Ellis L. Ross	EHA	10,652,017	1,005,020 (9.4%)
OKLAHOMA				
Oklahoma Human Rights Commission P.O. Box 52945 Oklahoma City, 73105 (405) 521-2360	William Y. Rose	E	2,559,229	278,867 (10.9%)
OREGON				
Civil Rights Division 466 State Office Bldg. Portland, 97201 (503) 229-5741	Gayle Gemmell	EHA	2,091,385	59,306 (2.8%)
PENNSYLVANIA				
Pennsylvania Human Relations Commission 100 North Cameron St. 4th Floor Harrisburg, 17001 (717) 787-4410	Homer C. Floyd	ESHA	11,793,909	1,056,177 (9.0%)

State and Agency	Executive Officer	Laws	Total Population	Non-White Population
RHODE ISLAND				
Rhode Island Commission for Human Rights	—	EHA	946,725	31,968 (3.4%)
244 Broad St. Providence, 02903 (401) 277-2661				
SOUTH DAKOTA				
South Dakota Human Relations Commission	Mary Lynn Myers	EAS	665,507	35,174 (5.3%)
State Capitol Bldg. Pierre, 57501 (605) 224-3692				
TENNESSEE				
Tennessee Commission for Human Development	Cornelius Jones	ESHA	3,923,687	629,757 (16.1%)
Cordell Hull Bldg. Nashville, 37219 (615) 741-2424				
TEXAS				
Good Neighbor Commission of Texas	Glenn E. Garrett	EHA	11,196,730	1,479,602 (13.2%)
P.O. Box 12007 Austin, 78711 (512) 475-3581				
UTAH				
Anti-Discrimination Division, Industrial Commission of Utah	John R. Schone	E	1,059,273	27,347 (2.6%)
State Office Bldg., Room 418 Salt Lake City, 84114 (801) 328-5552				
VERMONT				
Vermont State Human Rights Commission	Margaret Lucenti	None	444,330	1,777 (0.4%)
c/o Attorney General's Office Montpelier, 05602 (802) 828-2717				

State and Agency	Executive Officer	Laws	Total Population	Non-White Population
WASHINGTON				
Washington State Human Rights Commission	—	ESHA	3,409,169	158,114 (4.6%)
W.E.A. Bldg. 319 Seventh Ave. East Olympia, 98501 (206) 753-6770				
WEST VIRGINIA				
West Virginia Human Rights Commission	Carl W. Glatt	EHA	1,744,237	70,757 (4.1%)
1591 East Washington St. Charleston, 25305 (304) 348-2616				
WISCONSIN				
Equal Rights Division, Department of Industry	Thomas W. Dale	EH	4,417,731	158,772 (3.6%)
310 Price Place Madison, 53702 (608) 266-3145				
WYOMING				
Department of Labor and Statistics	Paul H. Bachman	E	332,416	9,392 (2.8%)
304 State Capitol Bldg. Cheyenne, 82001 (307) 777-7261				

Federal Agencies with Civil Rights Offices

Department of Health, Education, and Welfare
Office for Civil Rights
North Bldg.
300 Independence Ave. S.W.
Washington, D.C. 20201

Peter E. Holmes, Director

Department of Housing and Urban Development
Equal Opportunity Office
415 Seventh St. S.W.
Washington, D.C. 20410

Dr. Gloria E. A. Toote

Department of Justice
Civil Rights Division
Constitution Avenue and Tenth St. S.W.
Washington, D.C. 20530

J. Stanley Pottinger

Department of Transportation
Departmental Office of Civil Rights
400 Seventh St. S.W.
Washington, D.C. 20590

James Frazier

Department of Transportation
National Highway Traffic Safety Adminis-
tration
Office of Civil Rights
400 Seventh St. S.W.
Washington, D.C. 20590

Robert L. Harper

Department of Transportation
Urban Mass Transportation Administration
Office of Civil Rights and Service Devel-
opment
400 Seventh St. S.W.
Washington, D.C. 20590

Harold B. Williams

Environmental Protection Agency
Office of Civil Rights and Urban Affairs
Waterside Mall West Tower
401 M St. S.W.
Washington, D.C. 20460

Carol M. Thomas, Director

Equal Employment Opportunity Commission
Room 1246
1800 G St. N.W.
Washington, D.C. 20506

John H. Powell, Jr., Chairman

Small Business Administration
Office of Minority Enterprise
1441 L St. N.W.
Washington, D.C. 20416

Arthur McZier

Small Business Administration
Office of Equal Employment Opportunity
and Compliance
1441 L St. N.W.
Washington, D.C. 20416

Connie Mack Higgins

Appendix III
Civil Rights Chronology
from 1954 to 1974

1954

MAY 17

Brown vs. Board of Education decision paved the way for school desegregation as Supreme Court unanimously ruled racial segregation in public schools unconstitutional. Decision affected 17 states with compulsory public school segregation. Did not affect "separate but equal" doctrine when applied in other areas and does not apply to private schools.

1955

DEC. 5

Montgomery Bus Boycott began, after Mrs. Rosa Parks, a seamstress, arrested and fined $10 for refusing to give up seat to white person. Dr. Martin Luther King, Jr., then a Montgomery pastor, took over leadership of 381-day boycott, was arrested and his home was bombed. On Nov. 13, 1956, Supreme Court unanimously upheld a federal court decision that racial segregation on buses violated the Fifteenth Amendment. On Dec. 21, the same year, blacks and whites rode for the first time on previously segregated buses thus ending the boycott. King gained national prominence.

1956

FEB. 3

University of Alabama in Tuscaloosa ordered by Supreme Court to admit first black student, Autherine Lucy. Students demonstrated. Miss Lucy suspended Feb. 7 for "safety." Ordered reinstated by federal district judge, she was "expelled" Feb. 29 for accusations she had made in court. She made no further attempt to reenter. (University remained segregated until 1963.)

1957

MAY 17
Prayer Pilgrimage to Washington. On steps of Lincoln Memorial, Dr. King delivered first major address, calling for black voting rights. "Give us the ballot. . . ."

SEPTEMBER
Little Rock Central High. President Eisenhower federalized Arkansas National Guard, and sent in 1,000 paratroopers to restore order and escort nine black students to previously all-white high school. Troops remained on call for entire school year. When Supreme Court refused to delay integration, Little Rock schools closed for 1958–1959 school year; reopened on desegregated basis.

SEPT. 9
1957 Civil Rights Act signed. First civil rights legislation passed by Congress since Reconstruction. It empowered federal government to seek court injunctions against obstruction or deprivation of voting rights. Act created Civil Rights Commission, and established Civil Rights Division in Department of Justice.

1960

FEB. 1
Sit-in Movement began with sit-in at a Woolworth store lunch counter in Greensboro, North Carolina, and spread rapidly throughout nation. By end of year, many hotels, movie theaters, libraries, supermarkets, and amusement parks had lowered barriers against blacks.

MAY 6
1960 Civil Rights Act signed, strengthening 1957 act by authorizing judges to appoint "referees" to help blacks register and vote. The 1960 act also provided criminal penalties for bombings, bomb threats, and mob action designed to obstruct court orders.

NOVEMBER '
New Orleans. Desegregation of two elementary schools led to white boycott, picketing, and violence.

DECEMBER
U.S. Supreme Court in a 7-to-2 decision held that discrimination in bus-terminal restaurants operated primarily for the service of interstate passengers is a violation of the Interstate Commerce Act.

1961

JAN. 10
Peaceful Georgia Desegregation. First desegregation in public education in Georgia was peaceful, as black students Charlayne Hunter and Hamilton Holmes enrolled at University of Georgia in Athens.

MAY 4
Freedom Rides began from Washington, D.C., with New Orleans as goal. Bus stoned and burned in Anniston, Alabama, May 14. Riders also attacked in Birmingham May 14, and Montgomery May 20, where riots led to martial law. In Jackson, Mississippi, riders were arrested.

1962

SUMMER
Albany, Georgia. Several civil rights groups combined to force desegregation of all public facilities, but failed. Division among leaders. Dr. King arrested for "parading without a permit," released after anonymous donor paid fine.

SEPT. 30–OCT. 1
Meredith Enters "Ole Miss." Two killed, many injured in riots, as 29-year-old air force veteran, James Meredith, enrolled at University of Mississippi, Oxford. Meredith blocked in school doorway by Ross Barnett. President Kennedy federalized National Guard, sent in army troops. Former Maj. Gen. Edwin A. Walker arrested for "inciting rebellion." Note: Meredith was graduated Aug. 18, 1963.

1963

APR. 23
White Postman Slain. White Baltimore postman, William Moore, shot to death on road in northeastern Alabama during walk from Tennessee to Mississippi, carrying sign urging "Equal Rights for All."

APRIL–MAY
Birmingham Mass Demonstrations began Apr. 3. Dr. King and other ministers arrested Apr. 12 by Police Commissioner "Bull" Connor. Fire hoses and police dogs used on marchers, including school children, May 2–7. On May 10, biracial agreement announced to desegregate public accommodations, increase job opportunities, and free those arrested.

MAY 11

Birmingham Blacks Riot after bombs thrown at home of Dr. King's younger brother, Rev. A. D. King, and at King's motel room. In three-hour riot, houses and stores burned, and police vehicles smashed.

JUNE 11

Governor Wallace in Schoolhouse Door. Alabama Governor George Wallace carried out 1962 campaign pledge to "stand in the schoolhouse door" to prevent integration of Alabama's schools. Confronted Deputy Attorney General Nicholas Katzenbach and other officials at door of University of Alabama's Foster Hall, where black students Vivian Malone and James Hood were to register. Katzenbach brought proclamation from President Kennedy. Wallace read long statement on "oppression of state's rights." But at second confrontation later same day, Wallace withdrew and black students registered.

JUNE 12

Medgar Evers Murdered. NAACP State Chairman Medgar Evers shot to death as he entered his home in Jackson, Mississippi. Byron de la Beckwith of Greenwood, Mississippi, charged with the murder, but two trials resulted in mistrials (Feb. 7 and Apr. 17, 1964).

JUNE 14

Cambridge, Maryland. Governor Tawes called in National Guard after weeks of racial demonstrations and riots. Attorney General Robert Kennedy called both sides to his office for intensive negotiations, and July 23 announced agreement reached on desegregation, low-rent housing, and new biracial committee. Oct. 1, Cambridge voters defeated amendment requiring equal accommodations in restaurants and motels.

AUG. 28

March on Washington. Largest, most dramatic, and among most peaceful of all civil rights demonstrations. Marchers numbering 250,000, 60,000 of them white, filled the mall from Lincoln Memorial to Washington Monument, and urged support for pending civil rights legislation. Highlighted by Martin Luther King speech: "I have a dream . . .". Chief organizer of march was Bayard Rustin.

SEPT. 15

Birmingham Children Killed. Four girls (ages 11 to 14) were killed, and many other black children injured when bomb exploded during Bible class at Birmingham's Sixteenth Street Baptist Church. This was twenty-first bombing incident against Birmingham blacks in eight years—all "unsolved." President Kennedy (on Sept. 16) expressed America's "deep sense of outrage and grief."

1964

JUNE 21

Rights Workers Murdered. Three young civil rights workers, Michael Schwerner and Andrew Goodman, both whites from New York City, and James Chaney, a black from Meridian, Mississippi, missing while working on summer voter registration project. Search joined by more than 400 servicemen before bodies found Aug. 4 in shallow grave. Fifty FBI agents had also joined the search. Grave was six miles southwest of Philadelphia, Mississippi. All three had been shot, and Chaney brutally beaten. On Dec. 4, the FBI arrested 21 white men, including sheriff and deputy sheriff of Neshoba County, Mississippi, on federal charges of conspiracy to violate Civil Rights Code. At preliminary hearing, Dec. 10, charges were dismissed by U.S. Commissioner of the Justice Department Esther Carter, who termed government's evidence "hearsay." (At Meridian, Mississippi, Oct. 20, 1967, after a new trial, an all-white federal court jury convicted seven on charges of conspiracy to murder, including chief deputy sheriff of Neshoba County, Cecil Price, and Klan imperial wizard, Sam Bowers. Neshoba Sheriff Lawrence Rainey was found not guilty. Convictions described as first-ever for civil rights slayings in Mississippi. Dec. 30, Bowers given maximum ten-year sentence; Price, six years; others three to ten years.)

JULY 2

1964 Civil Rights Act signed by President Johnson. Most far-reaching civil rights legislation since Reconstruction contained new provisions to help guarantee blacks the right to vote and access to public accommodations such as hotels, motels, restaurants, and places of amusement; authorized the federal government to sue to desegregate public facilities and schools; extended life of Civil Rights Commission and gave it new powers; provided for cut-off of federal funds where programs administered discriminatorily; required most companies and labor unions to grant equal employment opportunity; established Community Relations Service in Department of Justice to help solve rights problems; required Census Bureau to gather voting statistics by race; and authorized justice department to enter into a pending civil rights case. (Senate, for first time in its history, voted to end a filibuster over civil rights.)

JULY 18–23

New York City Riots. Rioting in Harlem followed shooting of 15-year-old black school boy, James Powell, by off-duty police officer, Lt. Thomas Gilligan, whom boy allegedly attacked with knife. After charges of police brutality at Congress of Racial Equality rally July 18, crowd marched on police station, demanding Gilligan's ouster. In subsequent rioting, one black killed, 81 civilians and 35 police injured, widespread damage and looting occurred. July 19, battle between blacks and Puerto Ricans in Brownsville section of Brooklyn. July 20–22, riots in Bedford-Stuyvesant. Acting Mayor Paul Screvane announced July 20 an investigation of Powell's death and charges against police; also promised more black policemen in Harlem.

JULY 24–26

Rochester, New York Riots. Governor Rockefeller mobilized National Guard. Three hundred guardsmen, 200 state troopers sent into city. One white man killed, 300 persons reported injured, including 22 policemen.

JULY 29

Call for Moratorium. Expressing concern over "white backlash," leaders of several civil rights organizations called for "broad curtailment, if not total moratorium" on all mass marches, picketing, and other demonstrations until after Nov. 3 presidential election.

AUGUST

Other Riots: Jersey City, New Jersey, Aug. 2–4, 56 persons injured including 22 police; Paterson, New Jersey, Aug. 11–12; Elizabeth, New Jersey, Aug. 12–13; Dixmoor suburb of Chicago, Aug. 16; Philadelphia, Aug. 28.

SEPT. 14

New York School Bussing. New York City began controversial program to end segregation by "bussing" pupils of ten "paired" schools, five mostly black, five mostly white. While parent groups organized school boycott, Sept. 14–15.

DEC. 10

1964 Nobel Peace Prize awarded to Dr. Martin Luther King, Jr., in Oslo, Norway. King became fourteenth American, third black, and, at 35 years of age, the youngest person to win the Nobel Peace Prize. Other black recipients were: Dr. Ralph Bunche in 1950, and South African Zulu chief, Albert Luthuli, in 1960.

1965

JANUARY–FEBRUARY

Selma, Alabama Voting Drive, led by Dr. King. During height of demonstrations, Feb. 1–4, more than 3,000 arrested, including King. Feb. 4, federal court bans literacy test and other technicalities used against voter applicants. Feb. 9, King met with President Johnson at White House on voting right guarantees.

FEB. 21

Malcolm X Murdered. Shot to death at rally of his followers in Audubon Ballroom, New York City, at age 39. Black Muslim headquarters in New York and San Francisco burned. (Mar. 10, 1966, three blacks—Talmadge Hayer, Norman 3X Butler, and Thomas 15X Johnson—convicted of first degree murder, sentenced to life imprisonment.)

MAR. 11

Rev. James Reeb Dies after he and two other white Unitarian ministers beaten by white men while assisting Selma vote drive, Mar. 9. (Three white men indicted for Reeb's murder, Apr. 13; acquitted by Selma jury, Dec. 10.)

MAR. 13

President Johnson meets with Governor Wallace on Selma situation. Mar. 15, president addresses joint session of Congress, appeals for passage of legislation to guarantee voting rights, condemns "crippling legacy of bigotry and injustice." Mar. 17, submits draft of voting rights bill.

MAR. 21-25

Selma–Montgomery March. After two earlier attempts turned back by state troopers, King and Ralph Bunche led 54-mile march to Alabama state capitol, the 300 marchers (limited by agreement) protected by hundreds of army troops and National Guardsmen. In Montgomery, crowd grew to estimated 25,000. Governor Wallace twice refused to receive delegation, finally did so Mar. 30.

MAR. 25

Mrs. Viola Liuzzo Killed. A white civil rights worker from Detroit, who operated auto shuttle service for the Selma–Montgomery march, shot to death while driving on U.S. Highway 80 near Selma. (See later entries, re Collie Leroy Wilkins.)

MAR. 26

President Johnson Denounces KKK, announces arrest of four Klan members in connection with Mrs. Liuzzo's murder. (See later entries.)

MAR. 30

House Un-American Activities Committee voted to open full investigation of Klan and its "shocking crimes."

MAY 3

Klansman Collie Leroy Wilkins tried for murder of Mrs. Liuzzo. Trial resulted in hung jury. At later trial, Oct. 22, jury acquitted Wilkins. But Dec. 3, Wilkins and two others, Eugene Thomas and William Eaton, were convicted on charges of conspiracy (1870 law) and sentenced to ten years. Apr. 27, U.S. Court of Appeals upheld convictions. (Meantime, Eaton had died.)

MAY 30

First Black Graduates from University of Alabama—Vivian Malone.

JULY 1-22

Marches in Bogalusa, Louisiana, led by James Farmer of Congress of Racial Equality. July 19, justice department filed criminal and civil contempt actions against Bogalusa officials. July 22, Governor McKeithen announced formation of biracial committee.

JULY 13

Thurgood Marshall nominated solicitor general, first black to hold the office.

AUG. 6
1965 Voting Rights Act signed by President Johnson. Provided for registration by federal examiners of black voters turned away by state officials.

AUG. 11–16
Watts Riots. For six days, anarchy raged in black ghetto of Los Angeles, one of the worst riots in the nation's history. Thirty-five dead (28 blacks), nearly 900 injured, more than 3,500 arrests. More than 12,500 National Guardsmen called in. Entire city blocks burned to the ground, buses and ambulances stoned, snipers fired at policemen, firemen, and airplanes. Damage in millions of dollars.

OCTOBER
"Imperial Wizard" Robert Shelton refused to answer any questions at House Un-American Activities Committee hearing, invoking his constitutional rights.

1966

JAN. 3
Floyd McKissick succeeded James Farmer as national director of Congress of Racial Equality.

JAN. 10
Julian Bond, elected to Georgia legislature, denied seat on grounds of disloyalty, for opposing U.S. Vietnam policy.

JAN. 13
Robert Weaver named head of Department of Housing and Urban Development, became first black to serve in presidential cabinet.

JAN. 25
Constance Baker Motley, former NAACP lawyer and Manhattan borough president, became first black woman to be named a federal judge.

MAR. 25
Supreme Court Bars Poll Tax for all elections.

MAY 4
More than 80 Percent of Alabama's registered blacks vote in Democratic primary. Sheriffs James Clark (Selma) and Al Lingo (Birmingham) fail to get renominated.

MAY 16
Stokely Carmichael named new head of Student National Coordinating Committee, replacing John Lewis.

JUNE 6

James Meredith shot soon after beginning his 220-mile "march against fear" from Memphis, Tennessee, to Jackson, Mississippi. March then continued by assortment of civil rights groups, and ended June 26 with rally in Jackson addressed by Martin Luther King, Stokely Carmichael, and Meredith himself. During march, about 4,000 blacks registered.

JUNE 6–26

"Black Power" is first enunciated by Stokely Carmichael during Meredith march. Concept is endorsed by Congress of Racial Equality at its national convention (July 1–4), but condemned by King, Wilkins, and other moderates.

JULY 10

King Launched Chicago Drive to make Chicago an "open city," demanding end to discrimination in housing, schools, and employment, and a civilian review board for police. July 12–15, three nights of rioting sweep Chicago's West Side black district, two blacks killed, scores of police and civilians injured, more than 350 arrests. King met with Mayor Daley, announced four-point agreement to ease tensions in city.

JULY 18–23

Hough Riots in Cleveland. Four killed, 50 injured as shooting, fire-bombing, and looting sweep black area of Hough, on Cleveland's East Side.

AUG. 5

King Stoned in Chicago as he led march through crowds of angry whites in Gage Park section of Chicago's Southwest Side. A near-riot ensued as whites battled police. King left Chicago August 6.

1967

JANUARY–APRIL

Adam Clayton Powell Ousted as chairman of House Education and Labor Committee, Jan. 9, and barred from taking seat in House, Jan. 10, pending "investigation of his qualifications." House committee recommended Feb. 23 that Powell be seated, but with loss of seniority and public censure, by speaker, after finding he "wrongfully and willfully appropriated to his own use" public funds totaling $46,226. Powell assessed to pay House $40,000 at $1,000 a month. On Mar. 1, House voted to exclude Powell from Ninetieth Congress. Powell's suit to reverse House decision was dismissed Apr. 7. Powell reelected in special election Apr. 11, with 86 percent of the vote.

JAN. 12–13

Alabama Federal Aid Crisis. Alabama was warned that federal support for welfare programs and public health service would be cut off because of refusal to comply with 1964 Civil Rights Act.

FEB. 15
1967 Civil Rights Act, with "open housing" provision, proposed by President Johnson in special message to Congress. Bill also aimed at strengthening laws against interference with federal action, preventing discrimination in selection of juries, and almost doubling appropriations for Community Relations Service. (Bill not passed in 1967; still pending at time of Martin Luther King's death, April 4, 1968.)

FEB. 28
Ramsey Clark named attorney general at age 39.

MAR. 22
Alabama Ordered to Desegregate all public schools at start of fall semester. Federal court order marked first time since 1954 Supreme Court desegregation ruling that entire state was placed under single jurisdiction to end discrimination.

MAR. 25
King Attacks Vietnam Policy. Led Chicago march of 5,000 white and black anti-war demonstrators. At Coliseum, King branded war "a blasphemy against all that America stands for," charged that U.S. forces "committing atrocities equal to any perpetrated by the Vietcong," and war "seeks to perpetrate white colonialism." At New York press conference, April 4, King calls on young whites and blacks to boycott the war by declaring themselves to be conscientious objectors. King position assailed by NAACP and others.

APR. 16
King Warns "Ten Cities Will Explode." At impromptu news conference in New York, King warned that at least ten cities "could explode in racial violence this summer." Described the cities as "powder kegs" and said "the intolerable conditions which brought about racial violence last summer still exist." Cities he named: Cleveland, Chicago, Los Angeles, Oakland (California), Washington, Newark, and New York. Other cities not named.

MAY 3
Alabama Statute "Unconstitutional." Alabama statute countering federal guidelines for school desegregation declared "unconstitutional" by federal court in Montgomery.

MAY 10–11
Black Student Riot. One black killed, two wounded in rioting on campus of all-black Jackson State College, Mississippi.

MAY 12
H. Rap Brown succeeded Stokely Carmichael as chairman of Student National Coordinating Committee.

MAY 17
Rent Subsidies Increase voted down by House, 232 to 171.

MAY 29
California Housing Ruling. Supreme Court declared "unconstitutional" the state's voter-approved amendment to constitution which gave property owners "absolute discretion" in resale and rental of housing.

JUNE 2–5
Boston (Roxbury) experienced first large-scale rioting in many years. Over 60 injured, nearly 100 arrested.

JUNE 11–13
Tampa, Florida Riot after police killed black robbery suspect. At NAACP suggestion, youth patrol replaced National Guard in black section, successfully kept order.

JUNE 12
King Conviction Upheld. Supreme Court upheld contempt-of-court convictions of King and seven other black leaders who led 1963 marches in Birmingham, Alabama, in defiance of a temporary restraining order. King and aides entered jail Oct. 30 to serve out four-day sentence.

JUNE 12–15
Cincinnati Riot. Over 60 injured, 404 arrested.

JUNE 16–17
Black Students Riot at Texas State University. One policeman killed, two wounded. One student wounded, 488 students arrested.

JUNE 17
Atlanta Incidents. Stokely Carmichael provoked police, arrested. Black youth patrol formed, poverty workers and Mayor Allen active, rioting averted.

JUNE 19
***De Facto* Segregation Ruling.** Federal judge ordered schools in Washington, D.C., to end *de facto* segregation by fall semester. Ruling viewed as historic extension of Supreme Court ban on intentional school segregation to include segregation resulting from segregated population patterns.

JUNE 23
Kodak and "Fight" Reached Accord in Rochester, New York. Ended bitter six-month struggle between the company and the militant civil rights group ("Freedom, Independence, God, Honor, Today"). Accord provided for cooperation in job training and placement for hard-core unemployed.

JULY 6

More Than 50 Percent of Blacks Registered. Department of Justice reported that more than 50 percent of all eligible black voters were registered in states of Mississippi, Georgia, Alabama, Louisiana, and South Carolina.

JULY 12–17

Newark Riots. Twenty-three die, 725 injured (revised figures), and more than 1,000 persons arrested in six days of rioting, burning, looting, and street battles. Damage in millions of dollars. Rioting triggered by arrest and rumored death of black cab driver John Smith.

JULY 16

Mob Kills Plainfield Policeman. A white policeman shot and beaten to death by mob of black youths in Plainfield, New Jersey, in racial outbreak which began July 14 and continued for four days of looting and vandalism. National Guard called in.

JULY 20

Rat Extermination Bill Defeated in House, 207 to 176. President Johnson termed action "a cruel blow to the poor children of America."

JULY 20–23

Black Power Conference in Newark. Largest and most diverse group of American black leaders ever assembled. Militant and separatist mood dominated. Press barred.

JULY 23–30

Detroit Riots. Forty-three die, 324 injued (revised figures) in nation's worst riot of the century. Five thousand persons lost homes as fires gutted large parts of city's ghetto areas. Nearly 1,500 separate fires reported. Damage in millions of dollars. July 24, Governor Romney requested federal troops, and nearly 5,000 paratroopers flown to nearby Selfridge Air Force Base; moved into city July 25. Total of more than 15,000 troops, National Guardsmen, and police on duty. First time in 24 years that U.S. troops used to quell civil strife.

JULY 25

Cambridge, Maryland Violence, nearly 20 buildings destroyed, mostly in black business section. National Guard called in. Outbreak followed speech by H. Rap Brown in which he called on crowd of young blacks to "burn this town down."

JULY 26

H. Rap Brown Arrested at Washington airport for "inciting to riot."

JULY 26
Moderate Black Leaders Deplore Riots. In a joint statement, four moderate black leaders, Martin Luther King, Jr., A. Philip Randolph, Roy Wilkins, and Whitney Young appeal for end to riots which, they say, "have proved ineffective, disruptive, and highly damaging to the Negro population, to the civil rights cause and to the entire nation. . . . Killing, arson and looting are criminal acts and should be dealt with as such. Equally guilty are those who incite, provoke and call specifically for such action."

JULY 27
President Appoints Riot Commission. Governor Kerner of Illinois named chairman, and Mayor Lindsay of New York vice-chairman of National Advisory Commission on Civil Disorders, "to investigate origins of recent disorders" and make recommendations "to prevent or contain such disorders in the future."

JULY 30
Milwaukee Riots. Four killed.

Other Riots During July. *Michigan:* Lansing, Kalamazoo, Saginaw, Grand Rapids. *California:* San Francisco, San Bernardino, Long Beach, Fresno, Marin City. *New York:* Rochester, Mt. Vernon, Poughkeepsie, Peeksill, Nyack. *Connecticut:* Hartford. *New Jersey:* Englewood, Paterson, Elizabeth, New Brunswick, Jersey City, Palmyra, Passaic. Also: Philadelphia, Pennsylvania; Providence, Rhode Island; Phoenix, Arizona; Portland, Oregon; Wichita, Kansas; South Bend, Indiana; Memphis, Tennessee; and Wilmington, Delaware.

JULY 31
"Urban Coalition," organization of business, civic, labor, religious, and civil rights leaders, headed by John Gardner, called on nation to revise priorities, bring more resources to bear on domestic problems.

AUG. 10
More Blacks in National Guard urged by president's riot commission.

AUG. 14
Antisemitic issue of Student National Coordinating Committee (SNCC) newsletter caused storm, resignations. Harry Golden resigns from SNCC Aug. 24.

AUG. 28
Father Groppi began series of night marches for open housing in Milwaukee. Led more than 100 marches before sentenced to six-months imprisonment Feb. 13, 1968 for resisting arrest. Sentence stayed for two-year probation, $500 fine.

Sept. 7
McNamara Announced that Pentagon would extend campaign to end housing discrimination against black servicemen.

OCT. 2
"Big-Business" Program announced by President Johnson to attract firms to build or expand in ghetto communities.

NOV. 2
Report on Conditions of Blacks said more blacks in middle-income bracket, but living conditions in hard-core city slums unchanged or deteriorating.

NOV. 7
Carl Stokes elected mayor of Cleveland, Ohio; first black elected mayor of a major U.S. city.

DEC. 9
Rural Poverty Report called widespread rural poverty "acute" and "national disgrace."

1968

JAN. 4
Leroi Jones, black poet and playwright, sentenced to two and a half to three years and fined $1,000 for illegal possession of firearms during Newark riots. Jan. 9 granted $25,000 bail, freed. Feb. 7, headed advisory group at ghetto elementary school in Newark.

JAN. 9
Adam Clayton Powell in Watts declared: "History is going to record that the Second Civil War and the beginning of the black revolution was born here." At UCLA Jan. 10 urged white students to join "black revolution."

Black United Front formed at secret meeting in Washington, D.C.

JAN. 17
President Johnson, in State of Union address, called for programs to train and hire hard-core unemployed, rebuild cities, and immediately build 300,000 housing units for low and middle income families. Jan. 24, sent special message to Congress on civil rights.

JAN. 18
Eartha Kitt Outburst at White House meeting of white and black women. Miss Kitt told Mrs. Lyndon Johnson that young blacks rebel and "take pot" because "they're going to be shot and maimed in Vietnam."

FEB. 8
Orangeburg, South Carolina Violence. Three black youths shot to death, 34 persons wounded in outbreak at South Carolina State College, Orangeburg, triggered by protest over segregated bowling alley. Alley was desegregated.

FEB. 10

New Jersey Riot Report charged that National Guardsmen and police used "excessive and unjustified force" against blacks during Newark riots.

FEB. 27

Charles Evers led six white segregationists in special Congressional election, Mississippi's Third District. Defeated in run-off.

FEB. 29

President's National Advisory Commission on Civil Disorders issued report, warning that nation "is moving toward two societies, one black, one white—separate and unequal." Commission called for "massive and sustained commitment to action," recommended sweeping reforms in federal and local law enforcement, welfare, employment, housing, education, and news-reporting. "There can be no higher priority for national action ...".

MAR. 4

Martin Luther King, Jr. praised riot commission for "wisdom to perceive the truth and courage to state it," and described report as "a physician's warning of approaching death (of American society) with a prescription to life. The duty of every American is to administer the remedy without regard for the cost and without delay."

MAR. 28

King led 6,000-strong protest march through downtown Memphis, Tennessee, in support of city's striking sanitation workers, mostly blacks. Disorders broke out, black youths looted stores, one 16-year-old black killed, 50 persons injured.

APR. 4

King Assassinated as he stood talking on balcony of his second-floor room at Lorraine Motel in Memphis. Died in St. Joseph's Hospital from gunshot wound in neck.

APR. 5–8

Violence, Looting, and Arson flared up in Washington, Chicago, Pittsburgh, Baltimore. Rioting in Washington's black section worst in captial's history. Four P.M. curfew imposed. More than 9,000 U.S. Army troops called in to guard White House, Capitol, etc. Forty-eight hour toll reached eight dead, 987 injured, more than 700 fires, hundreds homeless. Over 4,000 arrests (most for breaking curfew).

APR. 7

National Day of Mourning for Dr. Martin Luther King, Jr.

APR. 8
Mrs. Martin Luther King took husband's place in leading massive, silent, and orderly march through streets of Memphis. Marchers estimated between 20,000 and 40,000 including sympathizers from all parts of nation. At City Hall Plaza, Mrs. King said: "We must carry on" and asked: "How many men must die before we can really have a free and true and peaceful society? How long will it take?"

APR. 9
King Funeral in Atlanta

APR. 11
Reported Figures of Rioting aftermath resulting from King's assassination recorded in 125 cities in 28 states. National figures were: 46 dead (mainly blacks); 2,600 injured (half in Washington, D.C. and mainly blacks); 21,270 arrested (mostly for looting); property damage put at $45 million as estimated by insurance companies; 55,000 troops involved (34,000 National Guard, 21,000 federal).

1968 Civil Rights Act prohibiting racial discrimination in the sale or rental of housing passed by Congress. Affects approximately 80 percent of nation's housing.

MAY 11
Poor People's Campaign, headed by Rev. Ralph Abernathy, Martin Luther King's successor and Southern Christian Leadership Conference president, got underway in Washington, D.C. Purpose of month-long campaign was to pressure Congress and administration for legislation to alleviate poverty. Resurrection City USA, a canvas and plywood encampment built near Lincoln Memorial, housed some 3,000 who participated.

JUNE 5
Senator Robert Kennedy Shot in Los Angeles, after winning California Democratic nomination for president, by Sirhan Bishara Sirhan, a 24-year-old Jordanian Arab. Kennedy died the next day.

JUNE 19
Solidarity Day March climax of Poor People's Campaign. More than 50,000 marched the mile-long route from Washington Monument to Lincoln Memorial. Half of the participants were white and included Vice-President Hubert Humphrey.

JUNE 24

Resurrection City Closed by Washington police after demonstration permit expired. Abernathy and 300 demonstrators staged march to Capitol and Abernathy sent to jail. Released July 16, announcing Washington phase of campaign over. Said Congress had "failed to move meaningfully against problems of poverty."

AUG. 6

Poor People's Campaign moved to Miami Beach, Republican National Convention site, to demonstrate to GOP delegates the aims of campaign against poverty.

1969

MAY 4

James Forman, director of Black Economic Development Conference, presented his "Black Manifesto" at New York's Riverside Church. Document set forth demands for $500 million in reparations from white churches and synagogues to be paid to blacks.

JUNE–SEPTEMBER

Integration of Construction Industry. Most vociferous civil rights action of 1969 was aimed at nation's highly paid construction industry whose tightly-knit union organizations continued to resist employment of minorities throughout the 1960s. Cities where important action took place: Chicago, Pittsburgh, Seattle, Buffalo, Detroit, Philadelphia, and New York.

SEPT. 23

The Philadelphia Plan, a pilot program setting guidelines for hiring minorities on all federally assisted construction projects in Philadelphia, ordered into effect by Secretary of Labor George P. Schultz. He announced on Sept. 29 that similar plans were to be extended to New York, Boston, Chicago, Detroit, Los Angeles, Pittsburgh, St. Louis, San Francisco, and Seattle. Plan seen as signal that Nixon administration planned to concentrate its civil rights activity in area of equal job opportunity.

OCT. 30

Supreme Court Hands Down Unanimous Decision ordering that segregation in schools must end "at once." Court replaced its 1954 decision of "all deliberate speed" with the more rigorous standard of immediate compliance. The decision, upheld also by the Fifth Circuit Court of New Orleans, was result of delaying actions in 33 Mississippi school districts.

NOV. 20

Alcatraz Island seized by a group of 89 Indians and held by them.

DEC. 4–8

A Pre-Dawn Raid by Chicago Police on the apartment of Fred Hampton, Illinois Panther leader, results in his death, the death of Panther Mark Clark, and the arrest of seven other Panthers. Four days later, Los Angeles police raid Panther headquarters there killing three Panthers and wounding four in a four-hour gun battle. Both incidents bring cries from concerned citizen groups as well as militants. By the end of the month, eight official inquiries are instituted to determine if there is a national conspiracy against Panthers which is out to destroy their organization, as Panthers claim. Among those investigating other than governmental, are the all-black Ad Hoc Committee of U.S. Congressmen, headed by Rep. Charles Diggs of Michigan, and the Commission of Inquiry into the Black Panthers and Law Enforcement Officials, headed by Arthur J. Goldberg and Roy Wilkins.

1970

FEB. 2

Pretrial Hearings Start in New York City for 13 Black Panthers charged with conspiring to bomb public places in 1969, after spending a year in jail because they were unable to post the $100,000 bail set on them.

MAR. 8

H. Rap Brown Disappears the day before his trial is to begin in Bel Air, Maryland, for a 1967 indictment for inciting a riot in Cambridge, Maryland. He was subsequently placed on the FBI's "ten most wanted" list.

MAR. 18

Stokely Carmichael Returns to United States saying he intends to wage "a relentless struggle against the poison of drugs in the black community."

MAR. 21

Highest Ranking Black in government, Andrew F. Brimmer, board member of the Federal Reserve System, criticizes Nixon administration's approach to black capitalism, saying that although blacks have made significant progress as a group in 1960s, gains were so unevenly distributed there was a "deepening schism in the black community."

MAR. 24

President Nixon Makes a Policy Statement on school desegregation, saying the administration would not abandon or undermine gains made since 1954 Supreme Court ruling of "separate but equal." Maintains that while applying all government resources toward eliminating *de jure* segregation in South's public schools, he could not require elimination of *de facto* segregation in North or South (resulting from residential housing patterns), until the courts provided further guidance.

APR. 11

The Commission on Civil Rights, an independent six-member federal agency, criticizes President Nixon's March 24 statement on school desegregation calling it inadequate, overcautious, and possibly signaling a major retreat on the issue of school integration.

MAY 1–3

A Peaceful May Day Rally is held at Yale University in New Haven in which 12,000 demonstrators, watched over by 2,500 National Guardsmen, massed in support of Black Panthers on trial for the 1969 murder of Alex Rackley. The rally climaxed a week of student protest which caused the closing down of the university and produced the controversial statement by Yale's president, Kingman Brewster, saying "I am skeptical of the ability of black revolutionaries to achieve a fair trial anywhere in the U.S."

MAY 8

Seven Black Panthers Freed of all criminal charges stemming from Chicago shootout (Dec. 1969). According to Illinois State Attorney Edward V. Hanrahan, the methods used to gather evidence might have prevented "our satisfying judicial standards of proof."

MAY 11

Six Black Men Killed in Augusta, Georgia, when rioting flared up during a peaceful demonstration by the black community protesting the death of a 16-year-old boy who was murdered in prison.

MAY 15

A Student at Jackson State College in Jackson, Mississippi, and a high school senior, both blacks, were killed in a barrage of gun fire that riddled a Jackson State College dormitory. The incident reportedly started when bottles and stones were thrown at cars driven by whites. Police claim they fired in response to sniper fire.

MAY 20

A 100-Mile March Through Georgia's Black Belt started from Perry to Atlanta. Organized by Southern Christian Leadership Conference (SCLC) and masterminded by Hosea Williams, SCLC vice-president, the purpose was to protest the "growing repressions of blacks and students in the state and the nation."

MAY 22

H. Rap Brown in Algiers, reports the Washington Star, "according to government sources."

MAY 29
The California Court of Appeals Reverses its 1968 decision which sentenced Huey P. Newton to 2–15 years in prison for a 1967 Oakland shooting. Released Aug. 5 on $50,000 bail.

JUNE 16
Kenneth A. Gibson, an engineer turned politican, decisively defeated incumbent Hugh J. Addonizio by 11,000 votes in a bitterly fought mayoral runoff-election in Newark, New Jersey. Gibson became the first black mayor in any major city on the Eastern Seaboard.

JUNE 29
NAACP Chairman Bishop Spottswood labeled Nixon administration "anti-Negro" in keynote address to NAACP's 61st Annual Convention in Cincinnati.

JUNE 30
White House Responds to "Anti-Negro" Charge in telegram to NAACP Chairman Spottswood, from Nixon aide Leonard Garment, detailing civil rights achievements and calling charge "unfair" and "disheartening."

JULY 5–8
Asbury Park Rioting. More than 165 injured and 100 arrested in four nights of distrubances in New Jersey seaside resort, where black leaders demanded jobs, better housing, youth programs, and removal of certain city officials.

JULY 8
President Nixon Meets Indian Leaders at White House and endorses bill to restore 48,000 acres of New Mexico to the Taos Pueblos, and signs message to Congress urging better health and economic programs for Indians.

JULY 9
School Desegregation Suits brought by Department of Justice against state of Mississippi and school districts in Arkansas, Florida, and South Carolina which had failed to produce acceptable desegregation plans.

Philadelphia Contractors who failed to hire sufficient blacks under the Philadelphia Plan receive show-cause orders in administration's "first overt enforcement action" to ensure compliance with the plan, which set minority hiring standards as condition of federal contracts.

JULY 10
Segregated Private Schools warned by Internal Revenue Commissioner Randolph Thrower that their tax-exempt status would be revoked. Move seen aimed particularly at many new private schools established in South to evade public school desegregation.

JULY 13
Political Analyst Samuel Lubell, in new book, *The Hidden Crisis in American Politics,* says "Polarization of racial feeling has become probably the strongest political force agitating New York City's voters."

Black Academy of Arts and Letters institutes a black "Hall of Fame," naming as first members the late W. E. B. DuBois, historian Carter G. Woodson, and artist Henry O. Tanner.

JULY 15
U.S. Senate Backs Alaskan Natives. In overwhelming vote, 76 to 8, U.S. Senate passed bill granting Alaskan natives ten million acres and one billion dollars cash compensation in settlement of century-old claims. Bill would establish Alaska Native Commission and two native corporations to handle economic and social services.

First Black Mayor of Dayton, Ohio. City commissioner James Howell McGee appointed first black mayor of Dayton, Ohio following resignation of previous mayor. Born in West Virginia, Nov. 8, 1918, McGee graduated from Ohio State law school and became known as a militant civil rights lawyer. Married, two daughters.

JULY 17
Senator Strom Thurmond (R-SC) denounces Nixon administration's school desegregation policies as "breach of faith" which "could cost the president re-election in 1972."

JULY 19
Black Coalition Urged by Whitney M. Young, Jr., executive director, at National Urban League's 60th Annual Convention in New York. Young denies Nixon administration is antiblack, as charged at NAACP convention, and says a coalition of black forces could more effectively negotiate with the government.

JULY 20
National Urban Coalition announces 2.9 million dollar project to help black contractors compete for large construction jobs in big cities.

JULY 29
Majority of Grape Growers in California (65 percent) sign with Cesar Chavez's farm workers union, making it the first successful union in the history of agriculture.

AUGUST
Chicago Blacks Disillusioned. Chicago black coalition is reported breaking up, due in part to disappointment over job program which had provided only 75 instead of promised 4,000 openings according to *Washington Post*. Gang violence resumed. To protect black community from gangs, Rev. Jesse Jackson forms new group called Black Men Moving, headed by Rev. John Barber.

AUG. 8
Robert J. Brown, only black aide in White House, praises Nixon policies against critics such as NAACP Chairman Bishop G. Spottswood saying that the president was "becoming much more sensitive to the problems of blacks."

AUG. 15
Angela Davis, controversial assistant professor of philosophy at U.C.L.A. who was dismissed on June 19 from her $10,000-a-year faculty post by California's Board of Regents for membership in the Communist party (Miss Davis claimed it was because of her race), was sought in the Aug. 7 shootout at Marin County courthouse in which four were killed including a judge. Local authorities claimed they had evidence that guns used in the killing belonged to Miss Davis. Panther leader, Huey Newton, recently released from jail, called the incident "more significant than either Watts or Detroit."

AUG. 18
Panther Minister of Information, Eldridge Cleaver, arrives in Hanoi with Panther delegation for "Solidarity Day" between North Vietnam and American blacks.

SEPT. 3–7
Congress of African People in Atlanta, Georgia. Goals include plans to build black institutions at local, national, and international levels and "to help eliminate oppression of black people everywhere." Chairman of Coordinating Committee is Haywood Henry of Harvard University.

1971

JAN. 21
Congressional Black Caucus, formed in 1970 and made up of Congressional black elected officials, boycotted President Nixon's State of the Union message protesting his refusal to meet with the group for almost a year. A meeting was finally arranged the following Mar. 25 at which the Caucus presented the president its recommendations.

FEB. 9
Satchel Paige, a pitcher who spent 22 years in the Negro Leagues, was elected to baseball's Hall of Fame in Cooperstown, New York—the first Negro League player to receive the honor.

MAR. 11
Whitney M. Young, Jr., 49, executive director of the National Urban League, drowned while swimming at a beach resort in Lagos, Nigeria. Headed League since 1961 and was one of the nation's most prominent civil rights leaders.

MAR. 23
Rev. Walter E. Fauntroy Becomes First Congressional Delegate from the District of Columbia. Although a nonvoting member, he is the first elected representative from the district in 96 years.

APR. 21
Supreme Court in a unanimous decision upheld the constitutionality of bussing as a means to "dismantle the dual school systems" in the South. Does not affect *de facto* segregation in North based on neighborhood patterns.

MAY 25
Murder Charges Against Black Panther Party chairman Bobby Seale and party member Erica Higgins are dropped in New Haven, Connecticut. Tried on a variety of charges stemming from the murder of New York Panther member, Alex Rackley, presiding judge declared a mistrial.

JULY 6
Jazz Trumpeter Louis "Satchmo" Armstrong died in New York at the age of 71. Perhaps the greatest of all jazz musicians, is credited with having moved black folk music of New Orleans into the mainstream of music. Eulogized by presidents, he popularized scat singing (singing without words).

OCT. 15
H. Rap Brown, a fugitive from justice since May 6, 1970, was shot in a holdup attempt of a westside bar in New York City.

DEC. 9
Ralph Johnson Bunche Died at the age of 67 in New York City after a long illness. A Nobel Peace Prize winner in 1950 for mediating the end of the 1946 Arab–Israeli war, served as undersecretary-general of the United Nations.

1972

JAN. 25
Senator Fred Harris (D-Okla) announced that 12 representatives from as many activist groups met in Washington to draft "the people's state of the union." Groups represented were students, blacks, senior citizens, American Indians, critics of the Vietnam war, and welfare recipients. Speaking for the panel, Harris said the "people's state of the union" was an effort to point out to candidates running for national office the problems and shortcomings relating to civil rights, the Vietnam war, welfare, and the environment.

JAN. 30

Dr. Carl L. Marburger, New Jersey state education commissioner, ordered the Newark Board of Education to "desist" from implementing a resolution it had passed the previous Nov. 30 (1971) ordering the red-black-green flag of black liberation flown in every school and classroom in the city where blacks are a majority. Marburger said the flag lacked "universality of acceptance from all our people" and since it was a symbol for only one group, it had "no place in the schools."

FEB. 8

Representative Louis Stokes (D-Ohio) elected chairman of the Congressional Black Caucus replacing Charles Diggs, Jr. (D-Mich).

FEB. 15

Senate Reversed Itself in a vote of 45 to 39 denying the Equal Employment Opportunity Commission enforcement powers of its own but said it should rely on federal courts to stop discrimination practices. On Jan. 26, it had voted to give the Commission the power to order companies to stop discrimination in its employment practices. The reversal was seen as a victory for the Nixon administration and a setback for civil rights groups, labor, and women's rights organizations.

MAR. 10–12

The First National Black Political Convention met in Gary, Indiana, for the "unification of black people." For the first time, 4,200 delegates and 5,000 observers of nationalist, separatist, and integrationist sympathies unified themselves in a frontal attack on all American institutions. The three cochairmen were Richard Hatcher, mayor of Gary, Congressman Charles Diggs of Michigan, and Newark, New Jersey, activist Imamu Amiri Baraka (formerly known as Leroi Jones). The convention allegedly adopted two resolutions which caused controversy: a resolution to "dismantle" Israel and an antibussing resolution—both were later denied by Convention spokesmen who claimed distortion by the news media.

MAR. 16

A Moratorium on New Court-Ordered Bussing was proposed by President Nixon in an address to the nation on equal opportunity and bussing. One hundred and fifty seven school districts in 25 states would have been affected by the president's proposed legislation.

APR. 4

Adam Clayton Powell Died of complications following prostate surgery at the age of 63 in Miami, Florida. Served 12 consecutive terms in Congress before being defeated by Charles Rangel in 1970. Always controversial, he was, in his lifetime, commended by President Johnson for his "brilliant record of accomplishment" in the Congress as well as excluded from the Ninetieth Congress (in 1967) when a special House committee charged he misused public funds. In 1969, the Supreme Court ruled that his Constitutional rights had been violated and he was reinstated but stripped of his seniority and fined $25,000.

JUNE 4
Angela Davis Acquitted by an all-white jury on all charges of murder, kidnapping, and conspiracy by the Santa Clara Superior Court in San Jose, California. Commenting on the fairness of the trial she said: "the only fair trial would have been no trial."

OCT. 24
Jackie Robinson Died in Stamford, Connecticut, at 53. The first black baseball player to break into the major leagues (in 1947). Named to baseball's Hall of Fame in 1962 for his trailblazing as well as ball playing.

Racial Disorders in the Military (1971–1972): On Mar. 15, 1971, Defense Secretary Melvin Laird announced a pioneering program to improve race relations between whites and blacks in the military. Brought about because of mounting racial tension in the services, the program called for mandatory race relations classes as part of each recruit's basic training. Also established a Defense Department Race Relations Institute to train instructors to teach race relations courses. On the following July 24 the Pentagon announced that a dozen high ranking military officers had been reprimanded and transferred for failure to comply with Defense Department guidelines on racial equality. A series of incidents followed. On Mar. 19, 1971, after black soldiers based overseas had experienced months of discrimination in housing, the Army announced the formation of a housing referral office on all bases to handle requests for off-base residences and to act as an intermediary between landlord and Army tenant. On June 24, 1971, black and white servicemen battled for 24 hours at Travis Air Base near Marysville, California. Trouble began when 200 black airmen marched on a stockade holding three blacks after a fight over discriminatory treatment. On July 19, 1971, a racial melee broke out in an Army mess hall in Darmstadt, West Germany; said to be the result of "a pattern of discrimination and a failure of the military to supress white racism." On Oct. 12–13, 1972, more than 100 men aboard the *Kitty Hawk*—a ship of 5,000 navy personnel—were involved in a two-day skirmish over racial issues. On Nov. 4, 1972, 111 blacks and some 12 white crewmen on the carrier *Constellation* protested "discrimination in assignments, ratings, and discharges" with a sit-down strike. On Nov. 10, 1972, in a Washington meeting, Navy Secretary John W. Warner and Chief of Naval Operations, Admiral Elmo Zumwalt, said that officers who failed to act sufficiently against racial discrimination or actively engaged in condoning discriminatory practices would be subject to punitive or administrative action.

1973

JAN. 20
James Farmer who served as assistant secretary of the Department of Health, Education and Welfare during President Nixon's first term in office said in a TV interview that the president was isolated from any contact with blacks citing that Nixon relied on a white aide, Leonard Garment, White House adviser on civil rights, for matters pertaining to blacks.

JAN. 23
Lyndon Baines Johnson, 36th president of the United States, died of a heart attack in Texas. Cited by the NAACP as the first U.S. president so fully committed to the betterment of racial inequities, his administration saw the passage of major civil rights legislation—the civil rights laws of 1964, 1965, and 1968—and as senate majority leader, the passage of the Civil Rights Acts of 1957 and 1960.

MAY 8
The Occupation of Wounded Knee ended after 70 days, two deaths, numerous injuries, meetings, and bureaucratic bickering as well as a last-minute gunfight. One hundred militants surrendered the occupied reservation town to federal officials. The previous February 27, 200 members of the American Indian Movement (AIM) seized the South Dakota hamlet, Wounded Knee, on the Oglala-Sioux reservation, in a struggle to overthrow the elected tribal government headed by Richard Wilson. They contended it was dictatorial and corrupt. After the cease fire, White House respresentatives were to meet with Oglala Sioux elders two weeks hence to discuss the Indian charges of broken treaties and demands for compensation of lands once ceded to Sioux but no longer in their possession. The government also agreed to begin "an intensive investigation" into the operation and finances of the official tribal government and to protect the rights of all persons against possible abuses by tribal officials.

JUNE 12
Saul Alinsky, a "professional radical" by his own admission who had campaigned for the poor of all races for more than a generation, died of a heart attack at the age of 63.

JULY 2
First National Black Network owned and operated by blacks goes on the air. The New York-based operation feeds five minutes of radio news of special interest to minorities in hourly broadcasts to its 47 affiliates. President Eugene Jackson and Vice-President Sid Young started the venture two years ago with their own money and some financing from the Bank of America (California), Chase Manhattan Bank, and Manufacturers Hanover Trust.

AUG. 8

Dr. George Wiley, founder and director of the National Welfare Rights Organization, died at 42 in a boating accident on Chesapeake Bay.

OCT. 20

20 Years After the 1954 landmark case of Brown vs. Topeka, Kansas Board of Education paved the way for school desegregation, a new suit has been filed in Topeka alleging the city is still "systematically" discriminating against black students. Two decades before, ten-year-old Linda Brown (now Mrs. Linda Smith and the mother of two children who attend an integrated school outside Topeka) was turned away from an all-white school because she was black. The new suit contends that some 50 public schools are still predominately black although the city's population of 130,000 is less than 10 percent black. This contention is based on the Supreme Court's 1970 decision regarding Charlotte, North Carolina, in which the court indicated that the racial makeup of each school should reflect the makeup of the overall system.

Appendix IV
Leading Black Elected Officials by State, as of April 1973

ALABAMA

Fred D. Gray, State Representative, District 31, Tuskegee

Thomas Reed, State Representative, District 31, Tuskegee

A. J. Cooper, Mayor, Prichard

John Ford, Mayor, Tuskegee

Clyde Foster, Mayor, Madison

Willie Louis Gibbs, Mayor, Ridgeville

A. M. Hayden, Mayor, Uniontown

Richard L. Lewis, Mayor, Brighton

Freddie C. Rogers, Mayor, Roosevelt City

Rev. Judge L. Stringer, Mayor, Hobson City

Willie R. Whitehead, Councilman, Mayor Pro Tem, Tuskegee

ALASKA

Willard Bowman, State Representative, District 10, Anchorage

Selwyn Carroll, State Representative, District 17, Fairbanks

ARIZONA

Art Hamilton, State Representative, District 22, Phoenix

Leon Thompson, State Representative, District 23, Minority Floor Leader, Phoenix

ARKANSAS

Dr. Jerry Jewell, State Senator, District 3, Little Rock

Richard Leon Mays, State Representative, District 3, Post 1, Little Rock

Dr. William Townsend, State Representative, District 3, Post 2, Little Rock

Henry Wilkins, III, State Representative, District 54, Pine Bluff

Rev. W. E. Battle, Mayor, Sunset

Arthur Bowens, Mayor, Dumas

Dave Brooks, Mayor, England

Emmitt Jerome Conley, Mayor, Cotton Plant

Moses W. Johnson, Mayor, Tillar

Clifford Minis, Mayor, Edmondson

Frank W. Smith, Mayor, Menifee

Willard Whitaker, Mayor, Madison

Charles Bussey, Assistant Mayor, Little Rock

CALIFORNIA

Mrs. Yvonne Brathwaite Burke, United States Representative, 37th Congressional District, Los Angeles

Ronald V. Dellums, United States Representative, 7th Congressional District, Berkeley

Augustus F. Hawkins, United States Representative, 21st Congressional District, Los Angeles

Wilson C. Riles, State Superintendent of Public Instruction, Sacramento

Mervyn M. Dymally, State Senator, District 29, Los Angeles

Willie L. Brown, Jr., State Assemblyman, District 18, San Francisco

Julian C. Dixon, State Assemblyman, District 65, Los Angeles

Bill Greene, State Assemblyman, District 63, Los Angeles

Source: Excerpted and reprinted from the *National Roster of Black Elected Officials.*

Frank Holoman, State Assemblyman, District 65, Los Angeles

John J. Miller, State Assemblyman, District 17, Berkeley

Leon D. Ralph, State Assemblyman, District 55, Los Angeles

Douglas Dollarhide, Mayor, Compton

Clarence Jackson, Jr., Mayor, East Palo Alto

Herbert White, Mayor, Pittsburg

Warren Widener, Mayor, Berkeley

Booker T. Anderson, Vice Mayor, Richmond

Ben Gross, Vice Mayor, Councilman, Milpitas

Ralph Lee White, Vice Mayor, Stockton

COLORADO
George Brown, State Senator, District 3, Denver

Floyd W. Pettie, State Representative, District 17, Colorado Springs

Mrs. Arie Taylor, State Representative, District 7, Denver

Wellington Webb, State Representative, District 8, Denver

CONNECTICUT
Wilber G. Smith, State Senator, District 2, Hartford

Clyde Billington, Jr., State Representative, District 7, Hartford

James H. Brannen, III, State Representative, District 48, Colchester

Abraham Giles, State Representative, District 4, Hartford

Bruce L. Morris, State Representative, District 94, New Haven

Mrs. Margaret E. Morton, State Representative, District 129, Bridgeport

DELAWARE
Herman M. Holloway, Sr., State Senator, District 2, Wilmington

Mrs. Henrietta Johnson, State Representative, District 3, Wilmington

Amos B. McCluney, State Representative, District 2, Wilmington

DISTRICT OF COLUMBIA
Walter E. Fauntroy, Non-Voting Delegate, At-Large

FLORIDA
Ms. Gwendolyn Cherry, State Representative, District 106, Miami

Joe Lang Kershaw, State Representative, District 105, Miami

Mrs. Mary L. Singleton, State Representative, District 16, Jacksonville

Earnest Barkley, Jr., Mayor, Gretna

John S. Jackson, M.D., Mayor, Lakeland

Nathaniel Vereen, Mayor, Eatonville

Jackie Caynon, Commissioner, Mayor Pro Tem, Fort Pierce

Mrs. Vernita Cox, Vice Mayor, South Bay

James Richard Ford, Commissioner, Mayor Pro Tem, Tallahassee

Leroy (Spike) Gibson, Vice Mayor, South Miami

John T. Saunders, Commissioner, Vice Mayor, Hallandale

GEORGIA
Andrew J. Young, U. S. Representative, Atlanta

Leroy R. Johnson, State Senator, District 38, Atlanta

Horace T. Ward, State Senator, District 39, Atlanta

William H. Alexander, State Representative, District 38, Atlanta

Rev. Jessie Blackshear, State Representative, District 106, Savannah

Julian Bond, State Representative, District 32, Atlanta

Benjamin Brown, State Representative, District 34, Atlanta

Mrs. Betty J. Clark, State Representative, District 55, Decatur

J. C. Daugherty, State Representative, District 33, Atlanta

James E. Dean, State Representative, District 54, Atlanta

R. A. Dent, State Representative, District 78, Augusta

Clarence G. Ezzard, Sr., State Representative, District 29, Atlanta

Mrs. Grace T. Hamilton, State Representative, District 31, Atlanta

ILLINOIS
Ralph H. Metcalfe, United States Representative, 1st Congressional District, Chicago

Charles Chew, Jr., State Senator, District 29, Chicago

Kenneth Hall, State Senator, District 7, East St. Louis

Richard H. Newhouse, State Senator, District 24, Chicago

Cecil A. Partee, State Senator, District 26, Chicago

Fred J. Smith, State Senator, District 22, Chicago

Eugene M. Barnes, State Representative, District 29, Chicago

Lewis A. H. Caldwell, State Representative, District 24, Chicago

Richard A. Carter, State Representative, District 20, Chicago

Corneal A. Davis, State Representative, District 22, Springfield

Raymond W. Ewell, State Representative, District 29, Chicago

Robert H. Holloway, State Representative, District 29, Chicago

Emil Jones, Jr., State Representative, District 28, Chicago

Mrs. Peggy Smith Martin, State Representative, District 26, Chicago

James A. McLendon, State Representative, District 22, Chicago

Langdon Patrick, State Representative, District 21, Chicago

Isaac R. Sims, State Representative, District 21, Chicago

James C. Taylor, State Representative, District 26, Chicago

Robert L. Thompson, State Representative, District 13, Chicago

Harold Washington, State Representative, District 26, Chicago

Luvert Listenbee, Mayor, East Chicago Heights

Curtis Miller, Mayor, Alorton

Ernest Smith, Mayor, Centerville

Marion L. Smith, Mayor, Robbins

George Thomas, Mayor, Brooklyn

L. K. Watkins, Mayor, Harvey

James E. Williams, Sr., Mayor, East St. Louis

INDIANA

Rudolph Clay, State Senator, District 3, Gary

William L. Alexander, State Representative, District 45, Indianapolis

Mrs. Julia Carson, State Representative, District 45, Indianapolis

William Crawford, State Representative, District 45, Indianapolis

Ray P. Crowe, State Representative, District 42, Indianapolis

Robert Freeland, State Representative, District 5, Gary

Jewell G. Harris, State Representative, District 5, Gary

Richard G. Hatcher, Mayor, Gary

IOWA

William J. Hargrave, State Representative, District 74, Iowa City

KANSAS

Billy Q. McCray, State Senator, District 29, Wichita

Eugene Anderson, State Representative, District 83, Wichita

Theo Cribbs, State Representative, District 89, Wichita

Norman E. Justice, State Representative, District 34, Kansas City

Clarence C. Love, State Representative, District 35, Kansas City

Benjamin H. Day, Mayor, Leavenworth

Roy Patterson, Mayor, Coffeyville

LOUISIANA

Louis J. Chabonnet, III, State Representative, District 96, New Orleans

George L. Connor, State Representative, District 97, New Orleans

Alphonse Jackson, State Representative, District 2, Shreveport

Johnnie Jackson, State Representative, District 101, New Orleans

Johnnie A. Jones, State Representative, District 67, Baton Rouge

Theodore J. Marchand, State Representative, District 102, New Orleans

Mrs. Dorothy Mae Taylor, State Representative, District 93, New Orleans

Richard Turnley, Jr., State Representative, District 63, Baton Rouge

MAINE

Gerald Talbot, State Representative, At-Large, Portland

MARYLAND

Parren J. Mitchell, United States Representative, 7th Congressional District, Baltimore

Clarence W. Blount, State Senator, District 11, Baltimore

Robert L. Dalton, State Senator, District 8, Baltimore

Clarence Mitchell, III, State Senator, District 10, Baltimore

Mrs. Verda F. Welcome, State Senator, District 10, Baltimore

Dr. Aris T. Allen, State Delegate, District 6-C, Minority Leader, Annapolis

Ms. Hildegardeis Boswell, State Delegate, District 4, Baltimore

Troy Brailey, State Delegate, District 4, Baltimore

Joseph A. Chester, State Delegate, District 2, Baltimore

Frank M. Conaway, State Delegate, District 4, Baltimore

Walter R. Dean, State Delegate, District 5, Baltimore

Isaiah Ike Dixon, Jr., State Delegate, District 4, Baltimore

Calvin A. Douglas, State Delegate, District 4, Baltimore

John Douglas, State Delegate, District 2, Baltimore

Arthur A. King, State Delegate, District 2, Mount Rainier

Mrs. Leona K. Lee, State Delegate, District 4, Baltimore

Lloyal Randolph, State Delegate, District 4, Baltimore

James A. Scott, Jr., State Delegate, District 2, Baltimore

Kenneth Webster, State Delegate, District 5, Baltimore

Henry Arrington, Mayor, Seat Pleasant

Charles C. Davis, Mayor, Fairmont Heights

Decatur Trotter, Jr., Mayor, Glenarden

MASSACHUSETTS

Edward W. Brooke, United States Senator

Royal Bolling, Jr., State Representative, District 10, Boston

Royal Bolling, Sr., State Representative, District 7, Boston

Mrs. Doris Bunte, State Representative, District 7, Boston

Melvin H. King, State Representative, District 4, Boston

William Owens, State Representative, District 10, Boston

MICHIGAN

John Conyers, Jr., United States Representative, 1st Congressional District, Detroit

Charles C. Diggs, Jr., United States Representative, 13th Congressional District, Detroit

Richard A. Austin, Secretary of State, Lansing

Basil W. Brown, State Senator, District 6, Highland Park

Arthur Cartwright, State Senator, District 5, Detroit

Coleman A. Young, State Senator, District 4, Detroit

James Bradley, State Representative, District 15, Detroit

George H. Edwards, State Representative, District 9, Detroit

Ms. Daisy Elliot, State Representative, District 8, Detroit

Ms. Rosetta Ferguson, State Representative, District 20, Detroit

Charles Harrison, Jr., State Representative, District 62, Pontiac

David S. Holmes, Jr., State Representative, District 21, Detroit

Morris Hood, Jr., State Representative, District 6, Detroit

Raymond W. Hood, State Representative, District 7, Detroit

Matthew McNeeley, State Representative, District 16, Detroit

Earl Nelson, State Representative, District 57, Lansing

Mrs. Alma G. Stallworth, State Representative, District 4, Detroit

Jackie Vaughn, III, State Representative, District 18, Detroit

Edward Bivens, Jr., Mayor, Inkster

Robert B. Blackwell, Mayor, Highland Park

Gilbert H. Bradley, Mayor, Kalamazoo

Charles F. Joseph, Mayor, Benton Harbor

Lyman S. Parker, Mayor, Grand Rapids

Edward E. Little, Councilman, Mayor Pro Tem, Flint

Virgil May, Commissioner, Vice Mayor, Benton Harbor

Carl C. Poston, Jr., Councilman, Mayor Pro Tem, Saginaw

Charles M. Tucker, Commissioner, Mayor Pro Tem, Pontiac

MINNESOTA

Dr. B. Robert Lewis, State Senator, District 41, St. Louis Park

Ray O. Pleasant, State Representative, District 39-B, Bloomington

MISSISSIPPI

Robert G. Clark, State Representative, District 19, Lexington

N. B. Brooks, Mayor, Falcon

Charles Evers, Mayor, Fayette

Moses Lewis, Mayor, Winstonville

Earl S. Lucas, Mayor, Mound Bayou

Herman Johnson, Alderman, Vice Mayor, Mound Bayou

MISSOURI

William L. Clay, United States Representative, 1st Congressional District, St. Louis

Raymond Howard, State Senator, District 5, St. Louis

Franklin Payne, State Senator, District 4, St. Louis

Johnnie S. Aikens, State Representative, District 66, St. Louis

J. B. Banks, State Representative, District 80, St. Louis

Mrs. DeVerne L. Calloway, State Representative, District 81, St. Louis

James M. Carrington, State Representative, District 67, St. Louis

Philip Curls, State Representative, District 28, Kansas City

Russell Goward, State Representative, District 65, St. Louis

Harold Holliday, Sr., State Representative, District 26, Kansas City

Mrs. Orchid I. Jordan, State Representative, District 25, Kansas City

Harold J. (Babe) Martin, Sr., State Representative, District 82, St. Louis

Leo McKamey, State Representative, District 36, Kansas

Raymond (Ray) Quarles, State Representative, District 63, St. Louis

Nathaniel J. Rivers, State Representative, District 79, St. Louis

Fred Williams, State Representative, District 78, St. Louis

Travis B. Howard, Mayor, Howardville

Robert Metcalf, Mayor, Kinloch

NEBRASKA

Ernest W. Chambers, State Senator, District 11, Omaha

NEVADA

Joe Neal, State Senator, District 4, North Las Vegas

Rev. Marion Bennett, State Assemblyman, District 6, Las Vegas

Cranford L. Crawford, Jr., State Assemblyman, District 7, North Las Vegas

NEW HAMPSHIRE

Eric Hare, School Board Member, Amherst

NEW JERSEY

Mrs. Wynona M. Lipman, State Senator, District 11, Montclair

Eldridge Hawkins, State Assemblyman, District 11-D, East Orange

William H. Hicks, State Assemblyman, District 14-B, Paterson

Ronald Owens, State Assemblyman, District 11-A, Newark

George C. Richardson, State Assemblyman, District 11, Newark

Dr. William G. Wilkerson, State Assemblyman, District 12-B, Jersey City

S. Howard Woodson, Jr., State Assemblyman, District 6-B, Trenton

Kenneth A. Gibson, Mayor, Newark

William S. Hart, Sr., Mayor, East Orange

Hilliard R. Moore, Sr., Mayor, Lawnside

George J. Phillips, Mayor, Chesilhurst

Rev. Walter S. Taylor, Mayor, Englewood

William Howard, Deputy Mayor, Somerset

Isaac McNatt, Councilman, Deputy Mayor, Teaneck

NEW MEXICO

Lenton Malry, State Representative, District 15, Albuquerque

NEW YORK

Mrs. Shirley A. Chisholm, United States Representative, 12th Congressional District, Brooklyn

Charles B. Rangel, United States Representative, 19th Congressional District, Manhattan

Vander L. Beatty, State Senator, District 18, Brooklyn

Joseph L. Galiber, State Senator, District 32, Bronx

Robert Garcia, State Senator, District 30, Bronx

Sidney A. Van Luther, State Senator, District 28, Manhattan

Guy Brewer, State Assemblyman, District 29, Queens

Mrs. Estelle B. Diggs, State Assemblyman, District 78, Bronx

Arthur O. Eve, State Assemblyman, District 143, Buffalo

Thomas R. Fortune, State Assemblyman, District 55, Brooklyn

Jesse Gray, State Assemblyman, District 70, Manhattan

Edward Griffith, State Assemblyman, District 40, Brooklyn

Woodrow Lewis, State Assemblyman, District 13, Brooklyn

George W. Miller, State Assemblyman, District 72, Manhattan

Mark T. Southall, State Assemblyman, District 74, Manhattan

Calvin Williams, State Assemblyman, District 56, Brooklyn

Samuel D. Wright, State Assemblyman, District 54, Bronx

NORTH CAROLINA

Henry E. Frye, State Representative, District 23, Greensboro

Joy Joseph Johnson, State Representative, District 21, Fairmont

H. M. Michaux, Jr., State Representative, District 16, Durham

James Boone, Mayor, Cofield

Alex Brown, Mayor, Rose Hill

Elward Jennette, Mayor, Bayboro

Howard N. Lee, Mayor, Chapel Hill

W. Ray Matthewson, Mayor, Tarboro

Frederick D. Alexander, Councilman, Mayor Pro Tem, Charlotte

Ozell K. Beatty, Councilman, Mayor Pro Tem, Salisbury

Marion C. George, Jr., Councilman, Mayor Pro Tem, Fayetteville

Rev. W. C. Horton, Commissioner, Mayor Pro Tem, Morehead City

Thebaud Jeffers, Councilman, Mayor Pro Tem, Gastonia

Clarence E. Lightner, Councilman, Mayor Pro Tem, Raleigh

Leander R. Morgan, Councilman, Mayor Pro Tem, New Bern

Carl H. Russell, Councilman, Mayor Pro Tem, Winston-Salem

Reginald D. Smith, Alderman, Mayor Pro Tem, Chapel Hill

John S. Stewart, Councilman, Mayor Pro Tem, Durham

OHIO

Louis Stokes, United States Representative, 21st Congressional District, Cleveland

William F. Bowen, State Senator, District 9, Cincinnati

M. Morris Jackson, State Senator, District 21, Cleveland

Thomas Bell, State Representative, District 10, Cleveland

Phale D. Hale, State Representative, District 31, Columbus

Troy Lee James, State Representative, District 9, Cleveland

Casey Jones, State Representative, District 45, Toledo

William L. Mallory, State Representative, District 23, Cincinnati

C. J. McLin, Jr., State Representative, District 36, Dayton

James W. Rankin, State Representative, District 25, Cincinnati

Ike Thompson, State Representative, District 13, Cleveland

John D. Thompson, State Representative, District 15, Cleveland

Theodore M. Berry, Mayor, Cincinnati

Robert L. Burton, Jr., Mayor, Springfield

Jesse C. Fox, Mayor, New Miami

James T. Henry, Sr., Mayor, Xenia

James Keels, Mayor, Woodlawn

James Lowry, Mayor, Lincoln Heights

James H. McGee, Mayor, Dayton

Samuel S. Perry, Mayor, Cleveland

OKLAHOMA

E. Melvin Porter, State Senator, District 48, Oklahoma City

Ms. Hannah D. Atkins, State Representative, District 97, Oklahoma City

A. Visanio Johnson, State Representative, District 99, Oklahoma City

Bernard J. McIntrye, State Representative, District 73, Tulsa

Leslie R. Austin, Mayor, Chairman of Trustees, Langston

Mrs. Lelia Foley, Mayor, Taft

J. H. Matlock, Mayor, Tullahassee

R. E. McClendon, Mayor, Rentiesville

T. R. McConmick, Mayor, Boley

Lee Oliver, Mayor, Tecumseh

OREGON

William McCoy, State Representative, District 15, Portland

PENNSYLVANIA

Robert N. C. Nix, Sr., United States Representative, 2nd Congressional District, Philadelphia

Herbert Arlene, State Senator, District 3, Philadelphia

Freeman Hankins, State Senator, District 7, Philadelphia

James D. Barber, State Representative, District 190, Philadelphia

Lucien Blackwell, State Representative, District 188, Philadelphia

Charles P. Hammock, State Representative, District 196, Philadelphia

K. Leroy Irvis, State Representative, District 19, Minority Whip, Pittsburgh

Joel J. Johnson, State Representative, District 197, Philadelphia

Joseph Rhodes, Jr., State Representative, District 24, Pittsburgh

David P. Richardson, State Representative, District 201, Philadelphia

Ulysses Shelton, State Representative, District 191, Philadelphia

Earl Vann, State Representative, District 186, Philadelphia

Hardy Williams, State Representative, District 191, Philadelphia

RHODE ISLAND
Peter J. Coelho, State Representative, District 84, East Providence

SOUTH CAROLINA
Herbert U. Fielding, State Representative, Charleston County, Charleston

Ernest A. Finney, Jr., State Representative, Sumter County, Sumter

Rev. Benjamin Gordon, State Representative, Williamsburg County, Kingstree

Robert Woods, Jr., State Representative, Charleston County, Charleston

TENNESSEE
J. O. Patterson, Jr., State Senator, District 29, Councilman, District 7, Memphis

Avon N. Williams, Jr., Senator, District 19, Nashville

Harper Brewer, Jr., State Representative, District 98, Memphis

Ms. Lois DeBerry, State Representative, District 91, Memphis

Harold Ford, State Representative, District 86, Memphis

Alvin King, State Representative, District 92, Memphis

Harold M. Love, State Representative, District 54, Nashville

I. H. Murphy, State Representative, District 87, Memphis

Charles W. Pruitt, State Representative, District 58, Nashville

Fred L. Davis, Vice Mayor, Memphis

Ms. James Deotha Malone, Vice Mayor, Gallatin

TEXAS
Ms. Barbara C. Jordan, United States Representative, 18th Congressional District, Houston

Anthony Hall, State Representative, District 85, Houston

Samuel W. Hudson, III, State Representative, District 33-C, Dallas

Mrs. Eddie Bernice Johnson, State Representative, District 33-0, Dallas

George M. Leland, State Representative, District 88, Houston

Paul Ragsdale, State Representative, District 33-N, Dallas

G. J. Sutton, State Representative, District 57-E, San Antonio

Ms. Sefronia Thompson, State Representative, District 89, Houston

Craig A. Washington, Sr., State Representative, District 86, Houston

David K. Robinson, Mayor, Easton

Dennis D. Rundles, Mayor, Detroit

Eristus Sams, Mayor, Prairie View

John H. Miles, Councilman, Mayor Pro Tem, Hearne

VERMONT
Nicodemus McCollum, Jr., Councilman, Winooski

VIRGINIA
Lawrence D. Wilder, State Senator, District 9, Richmond

William Ferguson Reid, State Representative, District 35, Richmond

Dr. William P. Robinson, Sr., State Representative, District 39, Norfolk

Charles Lee Barbour, Vice Mayor, Charlottesville

Robert G. Davis, Jr., Vice Mayor, Clifton Forge

Joseph A. Jordan, Jr., Councilman, Vice Mayor, Norfolk

Henry L. Marsh, III, Vice Mayor, Richmond

Hugo Armstrong Owens, D.D.S., Vice Mayor, Chesapeake

Moses Riddick, Vice Mayor, Suffolk

Clarence W. Seay, Vice Mayor, Lynchburg

WASHINGTON
George Fleming, State Senator, District 37, Seattle

Ms. Peggie Joan Maxie, State Representative, District 37, Seattle

WEST VIRGINIA

Ernest C. Moore, State Delegate, McDowell County, Thorpe

Allan Connolly, Councilman, Vice Mayor, Bluefield

WISCONSIN

Monroe Swan, State Senator, District 6, Milwaukee

Lloyd A. Barbee, State Assemblyman, District 18, Milwaukee

Walter Ward, Jr., State Assemblyman, District 17, Milwaukee

WYOMING

Ms. Alberta Johnson, Councilman, Cheyenne

Note. Other black officials have since been elected, notably Thomas Bradley, Mayor of Los Angeles, and Maynard Jackson, Mayor of Atlanta. Up-to-date information may be obtained from the Joint Center for Political Studies (see page 69).

BLACK ELECTED OFFICIALS IN THE UNITED STATES
As of April, 1973

	TOTAL	FEDERAL		STATE			COUNTY		MUNICIPAL				LAW ENFORCEMENT				EDUCATION		
		SENATOR	REPRESENTATIVES	STATE EXECUTIVES	SENATORS	REPRESENTATIVES	COMMISSIONERS, SUPERVISORS; COUNCILMEN	OTHER COUNTY OFFICIALS	MAYORS	VICE MAYORS, MAYORS PRO TEM	COUNCILMEN, ALDERMEN; COMMISSIONERS	OTHER LOCAL OFFICIALS	JUDGES, JUSTICES; MAGISTRATES	CHIEFS OF POLICE; CONSTABLES; MARSHALS; SHERIFFS	JUSTICES OF THE PEACE	OTHER LAW ENFORCEMENT OFFICIALS	STATE AND COLLEGE BOARDS	LOCAL SCHOOL BOARDS	OTHER EDUCATION OFFICIALS
Alabama	149					2	9	11	8	1	46			1	55				16	
Alaska	5					2					1								2	
Arizona	4					2								1					1	
Arkansas	141				1	3		1	8	1	47	11			19				50	
California	130		3	1	1	6			4	3	33	5	14				4	56	
Colorado	8				1	3					3		1						
Connecticut	48				1	5					20	6		4				12	
Delaware	12				1	2					8							1	
District of Columbia	8	1																7	
Florida	58					3			3	5	42	1	1					3	
Georgia	104		1		2	14	8	1		3	39	1	1		5	1		27	1
Illinois	137		1		5	14	2		7		49	7	13				1	38	
Indiana	57				1	6	1	1	1		23	6	3	4				11	
Iowa	8					1					2		1					4	
Kansas	22				1	4	1		2		6		1					7	
Kentucky	55				1	2	3		1	1	33		2	4			1	7	
Louisiana	130					8	29		3	1	24		2	13	11			39	
Maine	3					1						1						1	
Maryland	55		1		4	14			3		22		5			2		4	
Massachusetts	20	1				5					5	4						5	
Michigan	179		2	1	3	12	27	4	5	4	33	13	20	2			8	45	
Minnesota	7				1	1					1		1					3	
Mississippi	152					1	8	19	4	1	39	7		22	19	1		31	
Missouri	85		1		2	13	3	2	2		27	5	8	1			2	19	
Nebraska	3				1						1							1	
Nevada	6				1	2	1							1	1				
New Hampshire	1																	1	
New Jersey	134				1	6	3		5	2	38	2		2			1	74	
New Mexico	4					1					.3								
New York	164		2		4	11	6			1	11	3	25					101	
North Carolina	112					3	7		4	9	57		2					30	
Ohio	111		1		2	9	2	1	8		46	5	14	1			2	20	
Oklahoma	67				1	3			6		27	10	1					18	1
Oregon	6					1					1		1					3	
Pennsylvania	65		1		2	10		1			13		19	3				16	
Rhode Island	7					1					2							4	
South Carolina	99					4	14	1	5		39		12					24	
Tennessee	71				2	7	25			2	19		2	1				13	
Texas	101		1			8			3	1	38		1	1			2	46	
Vermont	2										1							1	
Virginia	62				1	2	16	2		7	28				6				
Washington	13				1	1					5	1	3					2	
West Virginia	5					1				1	3								
Wisconsin	9				1	2	2				4								
Wyoming	2										1							1	
TOTALS	**2621**	**1**	**15**	**2**	**42**	**196**	**167**	**44**	**82**	**43**	**840**	**88**	**154**	**115**	**61**	**4**	**21**	**744**	**2**

Prepared by Office of Research, Joint Center for Political Studies
1426 H Street, N.W., Washington, D.C. 20005

Note: Five states have no black elected officials: Idaho, Montana, North Dakota, South Dakota, and Utah.

Appendix V
Civil Rights Resources

ALABAMA

JACKSONVILLE

JACKSONVILLE STATE UNIVERSITY, RA-
MONA WOOD LIBRARY. 36265.
Facts on Film.
   Papers, 1954–1967. Microfilm. Con-
   tains materials on civil rights and
   race relations in the South.

NORMAL

ALABAMA AGRICULTURAL AND ME-
CHANICAL COLLEGE (1875), JOSEPH F.
DRAKE MEMORIAL LIBRARY (1904). P.O.
Box 306, 35762.
Facts on Film.
   Papers, 1954–1967. Microfilm. Con-
   tains materials on civil rights and
   race relations in the South.

TUSKEGEE

TUSKEGEE INSTITUTE (1881), HOLLIS
BURKE FRISSELL LIBRARY. 36088.
Facts on Film.
   Papers, 1954–1967. Microfilm. Contains materials on civil rights and
   race relations in the South.
Southern Conference for Human Welfare, Southern Conference Educational Fund, Inc. (SCEF).
   Papers. Minutes of executive board
   meetings, correspondence, financial
   papers, clippings, booklets, photographs, documents, and mss. Contains material pertaining to civil
rights and liberties in the South, to
the lives and activities of Carl Braden, Anne Braden, and James A.
Dombrowski, and information on
the Southern Regional Council,
Southern Tenant Farmer's Union,
American Peace Mobilization, the
CIO, and the National Citizens' Political Action Committee. Also included are files of background materials of the *Southern Patriot*,
publication of SCEF.

UNIVERSITY

UNIVERSITY OF ALABAMA LIBRARIES
(1831), AMELIA GAYLE GORGAS LIBRARY
(1831). Box S, 35486.
Facts on Film.
   Papers, 1954–1967. Microfilm. Contains materials on civil rights and
   race relations in the South.

ARIZONA

FLAGSTAFF

NORTHERN ARIZONA UNIVERSITY, LI-
BRARY. 86001.
   Social and Political Action Documents
   Collection.
   Serials, pamphlets, and ephemeral
   material issued by various right-

Source: Excerpts reprinted from *Directory of Afro-American Resources*, ed. by Walter
Schatz, Race Relations Information Center (New York: R.R. Bowker, 1970).

wing and left-wing groups. Contains material pertaining to segregation, religious prejudices, and social views on race during the late 1950s and early 1960s.

ARKANSAS

FAYETTEVILLE

UNIVERSITY OF ARKANSAS (1871), UNIVERSITY LIBRARY (1873). 72701.
Facts on Film.
Papers, 1954–1967. Microfilm. Contains materials on civil rights and race relations in the South.
Race relations clipping file.
Newspaper and magazine clippings about Negroes, race relations, and desegregation in Arkansas.

PINE BLUFF

AGRICULTURAL, MECHANICAL AND NORMAL COLLEGE, JOHN BROWN WATSON MEMORIAL LIBRARY (1939). 71604.
Facts on Film.
Papers, 1954–1967. Microfilm. Contains materials on civil rights and race relations in the South.

CALIFORNIA

BERKELEY

MEIKLEJOHN CIVIL LIBERTIES LIBRARY (1965). 1715 Francisco St., 94703.
The library was founded in honor of Dr. Alexander Meiklejohn, a leading American educator and civil liberties figure, to establish a collection of research materials on civil liberties, due process, civil rights, and law of the poor for practicing lawyers, law professors and students, other scholars, and organizations.
Publ.: *Mieklejohn Civil Liberties Library Acquisitions*, monthly; *Bill of Rights Citator 1955–1966* & *Holdings of Mieklejohn Library and ACLU, 1920–1966*.
Files of legal cases, books, periodicals, newspapers, pamphlets, and clippings. Legal cases concern equal protection of the law in elections without racial, political, or urban discrimination; jury selection without discrimination; and equal protection of the law in housing, transportation, recreational facilities, dining places, hospitals, government facilities and employment, settling family problems of multiracial families, and enforcement of federal civil rights acts. The library has holdings of all publications of the U.S. Civil Rights Commission, and of virtually all state and local human and civil rights agencies, as well as publications of many black organizations and cases and periodicals concerning welfare rights law. Also included are extensive holdings of early civil liberties organizations such as International Labor Defense, International Juridical Association, Constitutional Rights Federation of Michigan, Civil Rights Congress, and the National Lawyers Guild.

UNIVERSITY OF CALIFORNIA AT BERKELEY, SURVEY RESEARCH CENTER (1958), INTERNATIONAL DATA LIBRARY AND REFERENCE SERVICE (1963). 2220 Piedmont Ave., 94720.
Materials. Questionnaires, codes, IBM cards, and magnetic tapes. Copies of domestic and foreign survey studies, covering such topics as attitudes toward governmental welfare programs, racial attitudes, left-wing and right-wing groups, Watts riots, de facto segregation, social work interventions in AFDC families, anti-Semitism (Negro over-sample), civil liberties, student rebellion, aid to needy children, fair housing, media habits, and attitudes of Negro families. The Center also maintains a small library of books, periodicals and documents of special relevance to survey research.

LOS ANGELES

SOUTHERN CALIFORNIA LIBRARY FOR SOCIAL STUDIES AND RESEARCH (1963). 1510 W. Seventh St., 90017.
The library, specializing in radical, progressive, and labor history, contains files of the history of "hundreds of labor and political action groups"; a film section; books (6000 v.); pamphlets (10,000); tape recordings (1000); files of the Los Angeles Civil Rights Congress (1947–1953); periodicals; Scottsboro boys case material; Herndon case; Black Pan-

ther material; tape recordings of black-brown dialog; Rev. Martin Luther King, Jr's, last address in California on tape three weeks prior to assassination.

UNIVERSITY OF CALIFORNIA AT LOS ANGELES, LIBRARY (1919), DEPARTMENT OF SPECIAL COLLECTIONS (1946). 120 Powell Library, 90024.
American Civil Liberties Union of Southern California.
Archives, ca. 1935–   Contains correspondence, ephemera, and clippings related to ACLU issues.
Extremist Movements Collections.
ca. 10 vf. Literature circulated by civil rights and other social, cultural, and political organizations, pro and con.
Facts on Film.
Papers, 1954–1967. Microfilm. Contains materials on civil rights and race relations in the South.

SAN ANSELMO

SAN FRANCISCO THEOLOGICAL SEMINARY (1871), LIBRARY (1871). 2 Kensington Rd., 94960.
Martin Luther King, Jr., Memorial Collecton.
Books (ca. 1,000), periodicals, pamphlets, ms and microforms. A collection of source material in Negro history, the growing collection includes antislavery and abolition pamphlets, publications of modern civil rights groups, pro slavery material, and ms sermons (ca. 100) on assassination of Martin Luther King, Jr.

SAN DIEGO

CITIZENS INTERRACIAL COMMITTEE OF SAN DIEGO COUNTY, INC. (1963). 1501 Sixth Ave., 92101.
News clipping file on race relations.
1963– . Clippings pertaining to housing, education, employment, police, and related subjects.

CITIZENS UNITED FOR RACIAL EQUALITY (CURE) (1968). 502 Robinson Bldg., 520 E St., 92101.
CURE works to promote on a community-wide basis the principles of racial equality; to encourage through discussion, news media, in-

dividual and group effort the implementation of recommendations; to establish effective lines of communication among, to provide support for, and to provide coordination for the activities of individuals and groups having similar objectives; and to enlist the aid and support of increasing numbers of citizens toward these ends.
Publ.: *CURE*, monthly newsletter.
Files, 1968– . Records, reports, correspondence, and other papers concerning the aims and activities of the organization.

SAN DIEGO PUBLIC LIBRARY. 820 E St., 92101.
Facts on Film.
Papers, 1954–1967. Microfilm. Contains materials on civil rights and race relations in the South.

SAN FRANCISCO

CALIFORNIA LABOR FEDERATION, AFL-CIO, LIBRARY. 995 Market St., 94103.
Library includes materials on such subjects as labor legislation (including statistics); union movement and activities; social insurance; and civil rights and liberties.

SAN RAFAEL

MARIN COUNTY FREE LIBRARY (1926). Civic Center Administration Bldg., 94903.
Clement Woodnut Miller (1916–1962) Memorial Collection.
Materials. ca. 1100 v., 200 pamphlets, and four magazine titles. Congressman from California (1959–1962), organizing member of Marin Chapter, American Civil Liberties Union. Collection contains materials by and about black people, on civil liberties and civil rights.

STANFORD

STANFORD UNIVERSITY (1891), LIBRARIES (1891). 94305.
Facts on Film.
Papers, 1954–1967. Microfilm. Contains materials on civil rights and race relations in the South.

COLORADO

BOULDER

UNIVERSITY OF COLORADO LIBRARIES (1876), NORLIN LIBRARY. 80302.
Facts on Film.
　Papers, 1954–1967. Microfilm. Contains materials on civil rights and race relations in the South.

CONNECTICUT

MIDDLETOWN

WESLEYAN UNIVERSITY, OLIN MEMORIAL LIBRARY (1831). 06457.
Facts on Film.
　Papers, 1954–1967. Microfilm. Contains materials on civil rights and race relations in the South.

STORRS

UNIVERSITY OF CONNECTICUT, INSTITUTE OF URBAN RESEARCH (1963). 06268.
Urban Research Library Collection.
　Miscellaneous. ca. 25 vf. Books (ca. 3,000 v.), pamphlets, reports, surveys, bulletins, periodicals, and other materials pertaining to racial integration and segregation in housing and education, social aspects of urban renewal and planning programs, discrimination in employment, welfare and poverty programs, urban unrest and violence, black economic development, civil rights, inner city manpower programs, race relations and materials published for or by the Connecticut Commission on Human Rights and Opportunities. Also includes conference and convention materials and reports concerning race relations.

DISTRICT OF COLUMBIA

AMERICAN FEDERATION OF LABOR AND CONGRESS OF INDUSTRIAL ORGANIZATIONS (AFL-CIO), DEPARTMENT OF CIVIL RIGHTS (1916). 815 16th St., N.W., Washington 20006.
　The Department serves as staff arm to Civil Rights Committee of AFL-CIO; assists in implementation of equal opportunities and non-discrimination policies of AFL-CIO; handles complaints involving any form of union discrimination; helps to set up community civil rights programs; maintains liaison with civil rights groups and government civil rights agencies; staffers serve on equal opportunity workshops at labor schools, appear on panels, and speak to civic groups.
　Publ.: Occasional reports, film list, pamphlets, and other informational materials relative to civil rights and equal opportunity.

AMERICAN FEDERATION OF TEACHERS, AFL-CIO. Sixth Floor, 1012 14th St., N.W., Washington 20005.
　The Federation is a national private organization which seeks to improve status of teachers and public education in U.S. Civil rights programs include Freedom Schools in Mississippi and various conferences on Negro history, especially pertaining to textbooks in elementary and secondary schools.
　Publ.: Various pamphlets and articles on problems of racial distortion in textbooks and integration in schools.

HOWARD UNIVERSITY, FOUNDERS LIBRARY (1867). 2401 Sixth St., N.W., Washington 20036.
Facts on Film.
　Papers, 1954–1967. Microfilm. Contains materials on civil rights and race relations in the South.

LEADERSHIP CONFERENCE ON CIVIL RIGHTS (LCCR) (1950). 2027 Massachusetts Ave., N.W., Washington 20036.
　Files. Correspondence, minutes of meetings, financial records, studies, reports, and other materials concerning the aims, programs, and history of the Conference.

NATIONAL COUNCIL OF NEGRO WOMEN, INC. (1935). Suite 832, 1346 Connecticut Ave., N.W., Washington 20036.
　The Council is a charitable and educational organization which works to eliminate prejudice and discrimination, reduce neighborhood tensions, strengthen family life, and combat juvenile delinquency.

Publ.: Newsletters, press releases, quarterly publication, special reports on civil rights problems.

POTOMAC INSTITUTE (1961), LIBRARY (1961). 1501 18th St., N.W., Washington 20036.

The Institute is concerned with developing human resources by expanding opportunities for racial and economically deprived minorities through advisory and research services to government and private agencies involved in the development of minority programs.

Publ.: Reports and studies on civil rights problems and poverty.

Files, 1961– . Includes documentation dealing with the aim, history, and programs of the Institute. Among papers are correspondence, reports, studies, investigations, and other materials related to race relations. Restricted.

U.S. COMMISSION ON CIVIL RIGHTS (1957), DOCUMENTATION CENTER (reorganized in 1969). 1121 Vermont Ave., N.W., Washington 20425.

Publ.: *Civil Rights Directory;* annually; Transcripts of hearings and conferences; *Civil Rights Digest;* Staff reports; State advisory committee reports; Films; Clearinghouse reports in such areas as school desegregation, mobility in the Negro community, and racial isolation in public schools.

The Center serves as a repository for basic current data on civil rights and other closely related topics: human, intergroup, and community relations; federal programs in civil rights; federal social welfare programs; demographic statistical programs; and the disciplines of the social and behavioral sciences, the humanities, and law as they concern the above topics. Materials include books (ca. 5,300 v.), periodicals (274 titles), pamphlets (1500 v.), vf (12), theses and dissertations (200 v.), and correspondence (9 vf).

Facts on Film.

Papers, 1954–1967. Microfilm. Contains materials on civil rights and race relations in the South.

U.S. DEPARTMENT OF AGRICULTURE. 14th St. and Independence Ave., S.W., Washington 20250.

Civil rights files. Records, reports, correspondence, and other materials concerning the civil rights activities of the Department. Includes materials pertaining to contract compliance and Title VI. Restricted.

U.S. DEPARTMENT OF DEFENSE, OFFICE FOR CIVIL RIGHTS. The Pentagon, Washington 20301.

Publ.: Reports and studies concerning integration and equal opportunities in the Armed Forces.

Files. ca. 190 cu. ft. Records, reports, correspondence, and other papers concerning equal opportunity in the Armed Forces, including material on Title VI, contract compliance and federal employment. Restricted.

U.S. DEPARTMENT OF HEALTH, EDUCATION, AND WELFARE; OFFICE FOR CIVIL RIGHTS (1966), INFORMATION DIVISION—RESOURCES AND MATERIALS UNIT. Room 3210, Regional Office, Bldg. #3, Seventh and D Sts., S.W., Washington 20202.

The Office for Civil Rights is responsible for the administration of departmental policies under Title VI of the Civil Rights Acts of 1964, which prohibits discrimination on account of race, color or national origin in any program or activity receiving federal assistance.

Publ.: *OCR Newsletter.*

Office of Civil Rights.

Files, 1966– . Records, correspondence, reports, and other papers concerning the operation and activities of the Office.

Information Division.

Materials. Included are books, periodicals, pamphlets, clippings, films, and materials in the general area of civil rights. Clipping files (1964–) are maintained in a variety of categories and by state on civil rights progress. An area of special strength lies in materials (unpublished) related to the implementation of Titles IV and VI of the Civil Rights Act of 1964. Use of clipping files restricted.

Facts on Film.
Papers, 1954–1967. Microfilm. Contains materials on civil rights and race relations in the South.

U.S. DEPARTMENT OF JUSTICE, CIVIL RIGHTS DIVISION. Tenth and Pennsylvania Ave., S.W., Washington 20530.
The Civil Rights Division enforces civil rights laws and executive orders prohibiting discrimination, authorizes intervention in cases brought by private litigants involving the denial of equal protection of the laws on account of race, among other responsibilities.
Files. Records, reports, correspondence, briefs, and other legal papers concerning investigations and court cases conducted by the Division. Restricted.

U.S. DEPARTMENT OF JUSTICE, COMMUNITY RELATIONS SERVICE (CRS) (1964). Ninth St. and Pennsylvania Ave., S.W., Washington 20530.
Media Library.
Pamphlets, clippings, films, and tape recordings concerning media–community relations and media coverage of racial incidents. Includes press clippings giving examples of different media practices in covering race relations, and programs designed to improve race relations.

U.S. DEPARTMENT OF LABOR. 14th and Constitution Ave., N.W., Washington 20219.
Civil rights files. Records, correspondence, reports, and other papers concerning civil rights activities of the Department, including material on equal employment opportunity programs and Title VI and contract compliance. Restricted.

U.S. DEPARTMENT OF TRANSPORTATION, OFFICE OF CIVIL RIGHTS. 400 Seventh St., S.W., Washington 20590.
Files. Information on the civil rights and equal opportunity activities of the Department of Transportation relating to Department employment practices; services rendered to the public; employment practices of contractors and subcontractors under direct or federally assisted contracts; operation of federally as-

sisted activities; and other programs and efforts involving Department assistance, participation or endorsement.

U.S. GENERAL SERVICES ADMINISTRATION, CIVIL RIGHTS DIVISION. 18th and F Sts., N.W., Washington 20405.
Files. Records, reports, correspondence, and other papers relating to civil rights matters and activities of the Administration, including material on Title VI, contract compliance, and federal employment.

U.S. LIBRARY OF CONGRESS (1800). 10 First St., S.E., Washington 20540.
The Library of Congress is the reference library and major research arm of the U.S. Congress and is a reference and research library for other government agencies, other libraries, and the adult public.
National Association for the Advancement of Colored People.
Records, 1909–1959; ca. 1.5–2 million items. Correspondence, clippings, legal briefs, trial transcripts, speeches, articles, and other printed and unprinted materials, principally 1919–1959, recording the growth and development of the Association, minutes of the meetings of the board of directors and of the executive committee, office diaries, employment records, financial records including special funds for the Sweet Case, data on life memberships, publicity records including the activities of the Speakers' Bureau. Treated are such subjects as discrimination in business and government, segregation in schools, government, and private establishments, lynchings, mob violence, race riots, antilynching measures, suppression of the Negro vote in the South, labor disputes, unions, politics, "Birth of a Nation," Garvey Movement, armed forces, Pan-Africanism, Ku Klux Klan, Spingarn Medal, American Civil Liberties Union, and providing extensive background on Negro life in urban and rural America, especially in the 1930s. Concern with Negro welfare outside the U.S. is also covered, specifically in the files relating to Haiti, the Virgin Islands, and the Pan-African Congress. Includes correspon-

dence and other material relating to the Association's branches, mainly for the period 1910-1939, and reflecting civil rights infringements and violations, local grievances, requests for advice on legal matters and other local matters.

Pictorial Collection.
The Library's archival collection of motion pictures contains some 35,000 titles representing theatrical feature films and newsreels, documentary and educational films, short subjects, and television films (news, documentaries, and entertainment). Among these motion pictures are a number of feature films produced since the 1940s which deal with Negro life in the U.S. or which feature all-Negro casts; a number of television documentaries dating from the late 1950s to the present and dealing with civil rights, urban problems, etc.;and a small number of educational and documentary films from earlier years involving Negroes in the U.S. Films may be viewed in the Motion Picture Section for research purposes. Appointments should be made in advance.

U.S. NATIONAL AERONAUTICS AND SPACE ADMINISTRATION. 400 Maryland Ave., S.W., Washington 20546.
Office for Civil Rights.
Files. Records, correspondence, reports and other papers concerning equal employment opportunity programs, contract compliance, Title VI, and other matters relating to civil rights.

U.S. NATIONAL SCIENCE FOUNDATION, OFFICE FOR EQUAL OPPORTUNITY. 1800 G St., N.W., Washington 20550.
Files. Records, correspondence, reports, and other papers concerning equal employment opportunity and other civil rights matters.

U.S. OFFICE OF ECONOMIC OPPORTUNITY (OEO), OFFICE OF CIVIL RIGHTS. 1200 19th St., N.W., Washington 20506.
Files, 1964– . Records, correspondence, reports, evaluations and other papers relating to the civil rights policies, directives and procedures for OEO. Includes material relating to research and evaluation, community relations, education, and contract compliance.

FLORIDA

CORAL GABLES

UNIVERSITY OF MIAMI (1926), OTTO G. RICHTER LIBRARY (1926). Box 8214, 33124.
Facts on Film.
Papers, 1954-1967. Microfilm. Contains materials on civil rights and race relations in the South.

GAINESVILLE

UNIVERSITY OF FLORIDA (1853), P.K. YONGE LIBRARY. 32601.
Florida History Collection.
Unique materials concerning minority ethnic and racial groups in Florida, including the Negro. Includes books, newspapers, mss, microforms. Restricted.

TALLAHASSEE

FLORIDA AGRICULTURAL AND MECHANICAL UNIVERSITY (1887), SAMUEL H. COLEMAN MEMORIAL LIBRARY (1947). Box 78, 32307.
Negro Collection.
Miscellaneous, 1840– . Books (ca. 8,000 v.); serials (ca. 40 titles); pamphlets; 2 vf; clippings; photographs; microforms; phonorecords; filmstrips. Subjects include: race relations in communication, religion, economics, athletics; international affairs, business; prejudices and apathies; segregation and education; discrimination; sex and racism; civil rights; Black Muslims; interaction of ethnic and racial groups; Negroes in politics; Negro suffrage; sociological studies; patterns of race relations in the South; riots; moral conditions of Negroes; folk beliefs and folklore; slavery; the Negro in medicine, music, art, literature, religion, science, sports, armed forces, law, politics; and Reconstruction.

FLORIDA STATE UNIVERSITY (1857), ROBERT M. STROZIER LIBRARY (1857). 32306.
Facts on Film.
Papers, 1954-1967. Microfilm. Contains materials on civil rights and race relations in the South.

TAMPA

UNIVERSITY OF SOUTH FLORIDA, LI-
BRARY (1960). 4202 Fowler Ave., 33620.
    Facts on Film.
        Papers, 1954–1967. Microfilm. Con-
        tains materials on civil rights and
        race relations in the South.

GEORGIA

ATHENS

UNIVERSITY OF GEORGIA, ILAH DUNLAP
LITTLE MEMORIAL LIBRARY. 30601.
    Facts on Film.
        Papers, 1954–1967. Microfilm. Con-
        tains materials on civil rights and
        race relations in the South.

ATLANTA

ATLANTA UNIVERSITY (1867), TREVOR
ARNETT LIBRARY (1929). 273 Chestnut St.,
S.W., 30314.
    Facts on Film.
        Papers, 1954–1967. Microfilm. Con-
        tains materials on civil rights and
        race relations in the South.
    Southern Regional Council (SRC).
        Papers, 1944– . The Atlanta Univer-
        sity Negro Collection is a depository
        for Southern Regional Council pa-
        pers. The collection now contains
        only the publications of SRC.

MARTIN LUTHER KING, JR. MEMORIAL
CENTER (1968), LIBRARY PROJECT. 671
Beckwith St., S.W., 30314.
        The Library Project of the Center
        collects materials of organizations
        and individuals involved in the Civil
        Rights Movement (1954–), and ar-
        ranges, indexes, and preserves these
        materials so that they may be used
        by scholars to write the history of
        the Movement. Materials available
        on a restricted basis.
    Clippings File.
        Clippings from newspapers and pe-
        riodicals, ca. 1954– . File includes
        the following collections:
    Bond, Mrs. Horace Mann. collector.
        News clippings, ca. 1954–1968. Col-
        lection contains articles on civil
        rights movement in Atlanta; on Ju-
        lian Bond, member of Georgia
        House of Representatives, and son
        of Mrs. H. M. Bond; and on Dr. Hor-
        ace Mann Bond, professor at Atlanta
        University.

    Coca-Cola Company. collector.
        Newspaper clippings, April–May,
        1968. Articles on Rev. Martin Luther
        King, Jr. and American civil rights
        movement written during the ten
        days between King's assassination
        and funeral, from newspapers col-
        lected by Coca-Cola Co. offices and
        plants all over the world.
    Lewis, Lillian M. collector.
        Clippings, ca. 1960–1968. Contains
        articles on John Lewis, chairman
        (1963–1966) of Student Nonviolent
        Coordinating Committee; on
        SNCC; and on the civil rights move-
        ment in the South.
    Martin Luther King, Jr. Memorial Cen-
    ter. collector.
        Clippings, 1968– . Articles on Afro-
        American life and activities clipped
        from 70 newspaper and periodical
        titles.
    Forman, James, 1929– .
        Tape recordings, ca. 1960–1968. Civil
        rights leader. Collection contains in-
        terviews concerning Student Non-
        violent Coordinating Committee;
        and speeches of James Forman, ex-
        ecutive secretary of SNCC, 1963–
        1966.
    Harding, Vincent.
        Papers, ca. 1961– . Civil rights
        leader and teacher. Large collection
        of correspondence, records, pam-
        phlets, broadsides, clippings, and
        other papers. Collection falls into
        four periods: (1) Harding's work in
        Atlanta as a lay minister for Men-
        nonite Church and director of Men-
        nonite House, an organization in-
        volved in education and work with
        the poor, 1961–1963; (2) his work in
        the civil rights movement in Mont-
        gomery, Selma, and Birmingham,
        Ala., and Albany, Ga., 1963–1965, in-
        cluding his participation in training
        program at Antioch College for civil
        rights workers who came South in
        summers of 1963 and 1964; (3) as
        teacher and head of history depart-
        ment at Spelman College, Atlanta
        University, 1965–1969; and (4) as di-
        rector of Martin Luther King, Jr. Me-
        morial Center in Atlanta, 1968– .
    King, C.B.
        Papers, ca. 1961–1964. Attorney in
        Albany, Ga. Collection contains
        court records of cases arising from
        Albany Movement, 1962.

King, Coretta (Scott).
Papers, ca. 1955–1969. Civil rights leader and wife of Rev. Martin Luther King, Jr. Correspondence, clippings, and other papers of Mrs. King. Includes correspondence and condolences on death of her husband.

King, Martin Luther, Jr., 1929–1968.
Papers, ca. 1950–1968. Baptist clergyman, author, and civil rights leader. Correspondence, personal and family papers relating to King's early life, ca. 1950–1955; his work as pastor of Dexter Avenue Baptist Church, Montgomery, Ala., 1955–1960; his work with Montgomery Improvement Association, 1955–1960, and Montgomery bus boycott, 1955–1956, as copastor with his father of Ebenezer Baptist Church, Atlanta, Ga., 1960–1968; winning Nobel Peace Prize, 1964; his work as president of Southern Christian Leadership Conference, 1957–1968, and involvement in civil rights campaigns, including Memphis, Tenn., sanitation workers' strike, 1968, during which he was shot and killed. Collection contains papers, chiefly from 1962–1968, and some papers from before 1955.

Martin Luther King Speaks.
Tape recordings, ca. 1960– . ca. 1,000 tapes. Includes speeches of Martin Luther King, Jr., Ralph Abernathy, Andrew Young, and other officials of Southern Christian Leadership Conference.

Medical Committee for Human Rights.
Papers, ca. 1964–1966. Correspondence and records of group of physicians, including Dr. Thomas Levin, who went to Mississippi in 1964 to work with black people and civil rights movement.

Montgomery Improvement Association.
Papers, 1955– . Records, correspondence, pamphlets, broadsides, clippings, court records, and transcripts of trials. Some on microfilm. Collection contains materials of Martin Luther King, Jr.; Ralph D. Abernathy; Dr. Anderson, president; E.D. Nixon; and attorney, Fred D. Gray. Includes following collection:

Gray, Fred D.
Papers, 1955–1968. Attorney and clergyman. Court records and transcripts of trials. On microfilm. Includes records of his suit to end segregation of buses in Montgomery, Ala., 1955–1956, and other civil rights cases.

Northern Student Movement.
Papers, 1964. Organization of students who came to Mississippi and other Southern states as civil rights workers in summer, 1964. Papers are chiefly organizational materials. Includes papers of William Strickland.

Photograph Collection.
Photographs, 1954– . Depicts the civil rights movement, chiefly in the South, with photographs contributed by staff photographer of Southern Christian Leadership Conference, and by major news services and magazines.

Southern Christian Leadership Conference.
Papers, 1957– . Atlanta-based civil rights organization. Large collection consisting of correspondence, records, clippings, pamphlets, broadsides, photographs, and other papers. Papers reflect SCLC's involvement in civil rights movement, including Alabama sit-in movement, 1960; Freedom Rides, 1961; Albany Movement, 1962; March on Washington, 1963; SCLC's "long hot summer" campaign for civil rights, 1964; demonstrations in Selma, Ala., 1965; SCLC voter registration drives in Virginia, North Carolina, South Carolina, Georgia, Florida, Alabama, and Louisiana, 1965; Chicago civil rights campaign, 1965; SCLC resolution opposing Vietnam war adopted at annual convention in Jackson, Miss., 1965. Other SCLC campaigns mentioned include Chicago fair housing drive, and demonstrations in Cicero, Ill., 1966; Birmingham voting rights marches, 1966; voting rights demonstrations in Grenada, Miss., 1966; march to Jackson, Miss., led by Martin L. King, Jr. after the wounding of James Meredith, 1966; Memphis sanitation workers' strike, 1968; assassination of Rev. Martin Luther King, Jr., president of SCLC, 1968; Poor People's Campaign, 1968; and the Charleston, S.C., hospital workers' strike, 1969. Collection contains papers of leaders of SCLC, including Rev. Martin L. King, Jr., Rev. Ralph D. Abernathy, Rev. Andrew Young,

Rev. Jesse H. Jackson, Rev. James Bevel, Rev. Fred Shuttlesworth, Hosea Williams, and Rev. Wyatt T. Walker.

SOUTHERN CHRISTIAN LEADERSHIP CONFERENCE (SCLC) (1957). 334 Auburn Ave., N.E., 30303. Rev. Ralph Abernathy, Pres.
> Publ.: Reports, newsletters. Files, 1957– . Correspondence, records, papers and taped speeches of Martin Luther King, Jr., and tape-recorded interviews concerning the activities of the organization.

SOUTHERN REGIONAL COUNCIL (SRC) (1944), LIBRARY. 52 Fairlie St., 30303.
> Publ.: New South, quarterly magazine; Field Activities Newsletter; Voter Education Project Newsletter; Special reports; South Today, monthly.
> Civil Rights Collection.
> Miscellaneous, 1944– . Books (ca. 800 v.); pamphlets (280 4 inch bins or ca. 90 ft.); 132 vf of newspaper and magazine clippings and publications of other organizations. The books contain information on Negro history, Southern history, civil rights and civil liberties issues. SRC publications and the background materials in the collection deal with social issues such as Black Power; black youth in Atlanta; prisons in Arkansas, Mississippi, Louisiana, and other states; starvation of blacks in Mississippi; Atlanta housing and residential patterns for the black population; slums and ghettos; race-related violence; the effects of Negro voting; census reports; racial discrimination by the federal courts; history of the Southern Regional Council (1944–); the civil rights issues such as school desegregation (1954–); University of Mississippi riots (1962); "massacre" of black students at Orangeburg, S.C. (1968); desegregation of Albany, Ga. The collection is kept up to date with clippings from 20 newspapers daily, 20 magazines weekly, and papers from community and voter registration organizations, publications of the Center for the Study of Democratic Institutions, the Citizens'

Council, Negro colleges, scholastic journals, law reviews, student organizations, and church groups.
> Facts on Film.
> Papers, 1954–1967. Microfilm. Contains materials on civil rights and race relations in the South.
> Oral History Project.
> Tape-recorded interviews. Interviews with black political candidates in the South by Julian Bond.
> U.S. Commission on Civil Rights.
> News clippings 1958–1972.

SAVANNAH

NATIONAL STATES RIGHTS PARTY (NSRP) (1948). Box 6263, 31405.
> The Party works "to awaken the American people to the Inequality of man."
> Publ.: The Thunderbolt, monthly tabloid newspaper.
> Files. Books, pamphlets, and NSRP publications covering such subjects as white supremacy, eugenics and race, civil rights, riots, race and social revolution.

SAVANNAH STATE COLLEGE (1890), A. H. GORDON LIBRARY. 31404.
> Facts on Film.
> Papers, 1954–1967. Microfilm. Contains materials on civil rights and race relations in the South.

ILLINOIS

CARBONDALE

SOUTHERN ILLINOIS UNIVERSITY (1869), DELYTE W. MORRIS LIBRARY (1874). 62903.
> Facts on Film.
> Papers, 1954–1967. Microfilm. Contains materials on civil rights and race relations in the South.

CHICAGO

CHICAGO HISTORICAL SOCIETY (1856), LIBRARY (1856). North Ave. and Clark St., 60614.
> Congress of Racial Equality (Chicago Chapter).

Papers, 1956–1966. 2 ft. Minutes, memoranda, reports and other records of the Chicago Chapter of CORE, including items from CORE chapters in various parts of the U.S., and from other Chicago civil rights organizations, the Chicago Urban League in particular.

JOHNSON PUBLISHING COMPANY, LIBRARY (1949). 1820 S. Michigan Ave., 60616.

Publ.: *Ebony*, monthly magazine; *Tan*, monthly magazine; *Jet*, weekly magazine; *Black World* (formerly *Negro Digest*), monthly magazine.

Contemporary Negroes.

Extensive vertical file materials by and about the Negro today, with emphasis on his relation to business, religion, science, sports, and politics, and including biographical information about outstanding persons in these fields.

Negro newspapers.

Complete files of the major black newspapers in the United States.

Photograph collection.

ca. 400,000 photographs of people and events in Negro history.

NATIONAL BLACK LIBERATION ALLIANCE (1968). 75 E. 35th St., 60616.

The Alliance promotes, supports, and advances the interests of black people at local, state and national levels; develops economic power to attain an independent black economy; develops leadership and utilizes to best advantage the political power inherent in the black community; and furthers the educational, cultural, and social interests of black people to fight racism and to prevent the genocide and destruction of black people. Formerly Congress of Racial Equality.

Records, 1960– . Reports, correspondence, minutes of meetings, and other papers concerning the establishment of the Alliance and its activities. Contains records of predecessor organization, Chicago Congress of Racial Equality, 1960–1968 (6 boxes), including correspondence, financial reports, minutes of meetings, publications, clippings, and material on various local and national cases.

UNIVERSITY OF ILLINOIS AT CHICAGO CIRCLE, LIBRARY (1946). P.O. Box 8198, 60680.

Chicago Conference on Religon and Race.

Papers, 1967– . .05 ft. Reports, press releases, newsletters, pamphlets, and leaflets. Included are materials pertaining to open housing, religion's role in racial crises, unemployment, and the activities of the National and Chicago Conference on Religion and Race.

Student Nonviolent Coordinating Committee, The Chicago SNCC Freedom Center.

Papers, 1964–1965. 5 ft. Mimeographed material relating to the purpose and activities of the Chicago SNCC Freedom Center, including the war on poverty program; the housing problem; the direct action projects; and the programs of the youth council.

DeKALB

NORTHERN ILLINOIS UNIVERSITY (1899), SWEN FRANKLIN PARSON LIBRARY (1942). 60115.

Publ.: *A Student Guide to Black Studies.*

Facts on Film.

Papers, 1954–1967. Microfilm. Contains materials on civil rights and race relations in the South.

EVANSTON

NORTHWESTERN UNIVERSITY (1851), LIBRARY (1856). 1937 Sheridan Rd., 60201.

Wright, Richard.

Papers. Ms of *Black Power.*

Ephemeral Literature of Modern Radical Movements.

Materials. Contains a limited but growing collection of materials concerning radical black organizations such as the Black Panthers.

MACOMB

WESTERN ILLINOIS UNIVERSITY, MEMORIAL LIBRARY. 61455.

Facts on Film.

Papers, 1954–1967. Microfilm. Contains materials on civil rights and race relations in the South.

URBANA

UNIVERSITY OF ILLINOIS AT URBANA–CHAMPAIGN (1867), LIBRARY (1867). 61803.
Facts on Film.
> Papers, 1954–1967. Microfilm. Contains materials on civil rights and race relations in the South.

INDIANA

FERDINAND

ST. BENEDICT COLLEGE AND CONVENT OF THE IMMACULATE CONCEPTION (1867), ST. BENEDICT COLLEGE LIBRARY (1946). 47532.
Area Race Relations Clipping Collection.
> Newspaper clippings, 1966– . News relating to race relations around Ferdinand, Ind. Restricted.

LAFAYETTE

PURDUE UNIVERSITY LIBRARIES (1874). 47907.
> The development of a basic collection of book and nonbook materials suitable for a Black Cultural Center is in progress. It will include documentary, historical, and selected contemporary works on such subjects as psychological and socioeconomic-political aspects, and artistic contributions of Afro-Americans.

Facts on Film.
> Papers, 1954-1967. Microfilm. Contains materials on civil rights and race relations in the South.

Tape recordings.
> Included are tape recordings (18 tapes) of the Last Citizen Series, produced by radio station WBAA and Louis Schneider, professor of sociology at Purdue, covering such topics as prejudice, color and race, migration and urbanization, the city and the worker, Negro crime, intimidation, protest, and defense; recordings from the the the City Lecture Series, containing historical information and discussions by Budd Schulberg, Albert Mayor, Jonathan Kozol, Paul Goodman, Dick Gregory, and some Black Panthers.

NOTRE DAME

UNIVERSITY OF NOTRE DAME, MEMORIAL LIBRARY (1873). 46556.
Facts on Film.
> Papers, 1954–1967. Microfilm. Contains materials on civil rights and race relations in the South.

VALPARAISO

LUTHERAN HUMAN RELATIONS ASSOCIATION OF AMERICA (LHRAA) (1953), LIBRARY. Valparaiso University, 46383.
> LHRAA works to help the Church assert leadership in the area of intercultural and interracial relations by alerting the Church to its problems and opportunities, by conducting workshops and institutes, and by working with individuals, organizations and other groups.

Race Relations Collection.
> Books (ca. 600), periodical and newspaper titles, pamphlets, theses and dissertations, and clippings (ca. 3 vf) on race relations and the Church's role.

IOWA

IOWA CITY

UNIVERSITY OF IOWA LIBRARIES (1855). 52240.
Facts on Film.
> Papers, 1954–1967. Microfilm. Contains materials on civil rights and race relations in the South.

KANSAS

ABILENE

U.S. GENERAL SERVICES ADMINISTRATION, NATIONAL ARCHIVES & RECORDS SERVICE (1961), DWIGHT D. EISENHOWER LIBRARY (1961). 67410.
> The Library is a repository for all papers, books and memorabilia of General Dwight D. Eisenhower, including material collected by Eisenhower and members of his administration concerning such subjects as equal employment opportunity, civil rights, school desegregation, the Civil Rights Acts of 1957 and 1960, and discrimination in the Armed Forces.

KENTUCKY

LOUISVILLE

SOUTHERN CONFERENCE EDUCA-
TIONAL FUND (SCEF) (1938). 3210 W.
Broadway, 40211.

SCEF works to end poverty and racial injustice in the South by helping
people of all colors to organize; to
inform people of activities to these
ends through a newspaper and publications; to oppose war as an in-
strument of national policy and to
end the draft. SCEF works with community groups and other civil rights
organizations. It gives staff and financial assistance on education, social welfare, voter registration, and
community organizing. Files. Books,
pamphlets, clippings, photographs,
and recent SCEF records and papers.
SCEF papers more than two years
old are sent to the Wisconsin Historical Society; other SCEF papers are
on deposit at Tuskegee Institute,
Tuskegee, Ala., and at the University
of Tennessee, Knoxville, Tenn.

UNIVERSITY OF LOUISVILLE (1798), LI-
BRARY. 2301 S. Third St., 40208.
Facts on Film.
Papers, 1954–1967. Microfilm. Con-
tains materials on civil rights and
race relations in the South.

MOREHEAD

MOREHEAD STATE COLLEGE, JOHNSON
CAMDEN LIBRARY (1922). 40351.
Facts on Film.
Papers, 1954–1967. Microfilm. Con-
tains materials on civil rights and
race relations in the South.

LOUISIANA

BATON ROUGE

LOUISIANA STATE UNIVERSITY AND AG-
RICULTURAL AND MECHANICAL COL-
LEGE (1860), LIBRARY (1860). 70803.
Facts on Film.
Papers, 1954–1967. Microfilm. Con-
tains materials on civil rights and
race relations in the South.

SOUTHERN UNIVERSITY AND AGRICUL-
TURAL AND MECHANICAL COLLEGE
(1880), LIBRARY (1928). South. Br. Post Off.,
70813.
Facts on Film.
Papers, 1954–1967. Microfilm. Contains materials on civil rights and
race relations in the South.

GRAMBLING

GRAMBLING COLLEGE OF LOUISIANA,
A. C. MEMORIAL LIBRARY. P.O. Box 3,
71245.
Facts on Film.
Papers, 1954–1967. Microfilm. Contains materials on civil rights and
race relations in the South.

NATCHITOCHES

NORTHWESTERN STATE COLLEGE OF
LOUISIANA (1884). RUSSELL LIBRARY
(1884). College Ave., 71457.
Facts on Film.
Papers, 1954–1967. Microfilm. Contains materials on civil rights and
race relations in the South.

NEW ORLEANS

DILLARD UNIVERSITY, AMISTAD RE-
SEARCH CENTER (1966). 70122.
The Center maintains an archives
department for the collection of
manuscripts and other source materials, and promotes research
projects in the study of Negro life
and history.
Race Relations Department, American
Missionary Association.
Archives, 1942– . ca. 100,000 items.
Correspondence, notes and studies,
pamphlets, clippings, lectures, and
other papers pertaining to the history of twenty-five (25) annual institutes of race relations and the activities in race relations during the
tenure of Herman Long, John Hope
II, Lewis W. Jones, and others.

DILLARD UNIVERSITY (1930), WILL W. AL-
EXANDER LIBRARY (1930). 2601 Gentilly
Blvd., 70122.
Facts on Film.
Papers, 1954–1967. Microfilm. Con-
tains materials on civil rights and
race relations in the South.

TULANE UNIVERSITY (1884), HOWARD-TILTON MEMORIAL LIBRARY (1940). Freret and Newcomb Place, 70118.
  School integration.
    Papers, 1954–   . Leaflets and broadsides (ca. 20 boxes) representing positions for and against integration of schools in the South.

RUSTON

LOUISIANA POLYTECHNICAL INSTITUTE (1895), PRESCOTT MEMORIAL LIBRARY. 71270.
  Facts on Film.
    Papers, 1954–1967. Microfilm. Contains materials on civil rights and race relations in the South.

MARYLAND

BALTIMORE

THE JOHNS HOPKINS UNIVERSITY (1876), MILTON S. EISENHOWER LIBRARY (1876). 21218.
  Facts on Film.
    Papers, 1954–1967. Microfilm. Contains materials on civil rights and race relations in the South.

THE JOHNS HOPKINS UNIVERSITY, RESEARCH AND DEVELOPMENT CENTER FOR THE STUDY OF SOCIAL ORGANIZATION OF SCHOOLS (1966), THE J.H.U. RESEARCH AND DEVELOPMENT LIBRARY. 3505 N. Charles St., 21218
    The Center studies various organizational and administrative arrangements and scheduling, the racial and socioeconomic integration of schools' informal social structures among students and teachers, organizational patterns throughout school systems, and the relations between levels of education. Continuing research focuses on the problem of school desegregation and its effects on students of varying racial and ethnic backgrounds.
    Publ.: Research reports.
  Race relations collection.
    Papers concerning race relations and school desegregation, including studies about differences of economic, social, and political indicators between Negroes and whites, and studies of the effects of school desegregation on the attitudes and behavior of Negro and white students.

MORGAN STATE COLLEGE (1867), SOPER LIBRARY (1939). Hillen Rd. and Cold Spring Lane, 21212.
  Facts on Film.
    Papers, 1954–1967. Microfilm. Contains materials on civil rights and race relations in the South.

COLLEGE PARK

UNIVERSITY OF MARYLAND, McKELDIN LIBRARY. 20742.
  Facts on Film.
    Papers, 1954–1967. Microfilm. Contains materials on civil rights and race relations in the South.

PRINCESS ANNE

MARYLAND STATE COLLEGE (1886), LIBRARY (1886). 21853.
  Facts on Film.
    Papers, 1954–1967. Microfilm. Contains materials on civil rights and race relations in the South.

MASSACHUSETTS

AMHERST

HAMPSHIRE INTER-LIBRARY CENTER, INC. (HILC) (1951). c/o Univ. of Massachusetts, 01002.
  Facts on Film.
    Papers, 1954–1967. Microfilm. Contains materials on civil rights and race relations in the South.

UNIVERSITY OF MASSACHUSETTS, LIBRARY. 01002.
    Publ.: *Selected Negro Reference Books and Bibliographies,* annotated guide.
  Facts on Film.
    Papers, 1954–1967. Microfilm. Contains materials on civil rights and race relations in the South.

BOSTON

BOSTON PUBLIC LIBRARY (1852). Copley Square, 02117.
  Facts on Film.
    Papers, 1954–1967. Microfilm. Contains materials on civil rights and race relations in the South.

BOSTON UNIVERSITY (1870), MUGAR MEMORIAL LIBRARY. 771 Commonwealth Ave., 02215.
  King, Martin Luther, Jr., 1929–1968.
    Papers, 1956–1961. 30 ft. Baptist clergyman, author, and Negro civil

rights leader. Personal and business correspondence relating to King's work as president of the Southern Christian Leadership Conference in Atlanta, Ga.; correspondence of King with Senator Paul Douglas, Medgar Evers, Bayard Rustin, and others; records of awards and honors in connection with King's work in civil rights; and records of the various civil rights campaigns, including the Montgomery, Ala., bus boycott.

Kunstler, William M.
Papers. Attorney, American Civil Liberties Union; author.

U.S. GENERAL SERVICES ADMINISTRATION, NATIONAL ARCHIVES AND RECORDS SERVICE, JOHN F. KENNEDY LIBRARY, INC. 122 Bowdoin St., 02108.
The Library, a division of the National Archives, will house a complete record of the life, the times, and the administration of the 35th president.

John F. Kennedy Library.
Personal papers of John Fitzgerald Kennedy, 1917–1963, 35th president of the United States; and copies of public records of the Kennedy administration. Original mss (ca. 14,900,000 pages), microfilm copies of mss (ca. 2,500,000 pages), oral history interviews (ca. 600), books and other printed items (ca. 12,000), museum objects (ca. 10,500), photographs (ca. 73,000), motion pictures (ca. 860,000 ft.), and sound recording tapes and discs (ca. 1,000). Included are many documents relating to civil rights.

CAMBRIDGE

CIVIL DISORDER RESEARCH INSTITUTE (1969). P.O. Box 185, Harvard Square Sta., 02138.
The Institute is a private organization which collects, researches, analyzes and verifies data relating to civil disorders in the U.S. The chief program of the Institute is the publication of Civil Disorder Digest, a summary of all available information on disorders precipitated by racial and political conflicts, high school and university issues, sabotage, and labor disputes where violence occurs.
Publ.: Civil Disorder Digest, biweekly newsletter.

HARVARD UNIVERSITY, HARVARD COLLEGE LIBRARY, WIDENER LIBRARY. 02138.
Facts on Film.
Papers, 1954–1967. Microfilm. Contains materials on civil rights and race relations in the South.

WALTHAM

BRANDEIS UNIVERSITY, LEMBERG CENTER FOR THE STUDY OF VIOLENCE (1966). 02154.
The Center conducts research on the causes and consequences of collective violence. Currently research is directed to violence arising from rapid social change and the polarization of attitudes in regard to the admission of minority groups—blacks, Puerto Ricans, students, and women—into the decision-making and opportunity structures of the social system. Attention is also given to the development of an integrated theory of collective violence embracing cultural, political, sociological, psychological and biological factors.
Publ.: Riot Data Review, newsletter; Confrontation, newsletter; Monographs, documentary film series.
Tape recordings.
Recordings of meetings and conferences (ca. 450). Interviews with "decision-makers" in ten cities (Boston, San Francisco, Cleveland, Pittsburgh, Dayton, Akron, Nashville, Birmingham, New Orleans, Atlanta) in which political styles of the city government have been compared with respect to race-related hostility. These consist of black and white government officials, business, civil rights, church, and labor leaders. Use restricted to persons having a bona fide research interest.

MICHIGAN

ANN ARBOR

UNIVERSITY OF MICHIGAN, GENERAL LIBRARY (1838). 48104.
Facts on Film.
Papers, 1954–1967. Microfilm. Contains materials on civil rights and race relations in the South.

UNIVERSITY OF MICHIGAN, INSTITUTE OF PUBLIC POLICY STUDIES (1914). 1516 Rackham Bldg., 48104.
> Research projects of the Institute include studies of urban growth patterns, urban land use, effects of riots on community attitudes, racial discrimination, political behavior in the city, public health programs, and race relations.
> Publ.: Discussion papers, such as *Alienation and Political Behavior*, and *The Meaning of Black Power*.

DEARBORN

DEARBORN PUBLIC LIBRARY (1921), HENRY FORD CENTENNIAL LIBRARY. 16301 Michigan Ave., 48126.
> Negroes in Michigan.
>> Materials, including newspaper clippings (ca. 293), chiefly from local newspapers, regarding race relations in the city of Dearborn; and pamphlets on Negroes in Michigan, the Detroit race riots, and other related topics.

DETROIT

INTER-FAITH CENTERS FOR RACIAL JUSTICE, INC. 10344 Puritan Ave., 48238.
> The Centers comprise a network in the Detroit metropolitan area and seek to organize people to confront racial issues in whatever form they may emerge. Each Center maintains a basic library of written and audiovisual material concerning racial issues. In addition, each Center compiles additional data about the community in which it is located, and conducts on a continuing basis, education for action programs and maintains files of these program materials.

WAYNE STATE UNIVERSITY (1868), LIBRARY. 5210 Second St., 48202.
> Facts on Film.
>> Papers, 1954–1967. Microfilm. Contains materials on civil rights and race relations in the South.

EAST LANSING

MICHIGAN STATE UNIVERSITY (1855), LIBRARY. 48823.
> U.S. Commission on Civil Rights.
>> Reports, 1957–date.

U.S. Congress.
> Hearings and reports of various committees dealing with civil rights.

HIGHLAND PARK

McGREGOR PUBLIC LIBRARY (1919). 12244 Woodward Ave., 48203.
> Included in the general holdings are a large book collection about Negroes; a collection of clippings and pamphlets on Negroes and race relations, particularly concerning southeastern Michigan; a picture file; and recordings of Negroes.

KALAMAZOO

KALAMAZOO LIBRARY SYSTEM, KING MEMORIAL COLLECTION OF BLACK CULTURE (1969). 315 S. Rose St., 49006.
> Martin Luther King, Jr., Memorial Collection.
>> Books, films, records, and other materials on the heritage, culture, and contributions of black people to the world.

WESTERN MICHIGAN UNIVERSITY (1903), DWIGHT B. WALDO LIBRARY (1903). 49001.
> Facts on Film.
>> Papers, 1954–1967. Microfilm. Contains materials on civil rights and race relations in the South.

MISSISSIPPI

HATTIESBURG

UNIVERSITY OF SOUTHERN MISSISSIPPI, LIBRARY. Box 53, Southern Station, 39401.
> Facts on Film.
>> Papers, 1954–1967. Microfilm. Contains materials on civil rights and race relations in the South.

STATE COLLEGE

MISSISSIPPI STATE UNIVERSITY (1878), MITCHELL MEMORIAL LIBRARY. P.O. Drawer 5408, 39762.
> Facts on Film.
>> Papers, 1954–1967. Microfilm. Contains materials on civil rights and race relations in the South.
> Mississippi Integration.
>> Miscellaneous. ca. 6 vf and bound materials. Publications, literature, speeches, broadsides, special edi-

tions, reprints, "hate sheets," clippings, concerning the many phases of integration and the civil rights struggle in Mississippi, including phonotapes (418 titles) of Citizens Council radio program entitled "Citizens Council Forums."

Mississippi State University, State College, Mississippi, 1888–1963.
500 items Correspondence, speeches, notes, articles, clippings, and other papers of persons connected with the University. Most of the papers relate to the University but other subjects include the election of John F. Kennedy and integration on the campus.

MISSOURI

INDEPENDENCE

U.S. GENERAL SERVICES ADMINISTRATION, NATIONAL ARCHIVES AND RECORDS SERVICE, HARRY S. TRUMAN LIBRARY (1957). 24 Highway at Delaware, 64050.
The Library collects and provides reference service for material relating to the career and administration of President Truman and to the office of the president.

Nash, Philleo.
Files, 1946–1952. 11 ft. Special assistant to President Truman for problems of minority groups.

President's Committee on Civil Rights.
Records, 1946–1947. 13 ft. General correspondence and administrative records; correspondence with government departments and agencies, Committee members, individuals, institutions, and private organizations; records relating to meetings, hearings, and staff interviews; statements of witnesses appearing before the Committee; records relating to reports and recommendations of the Committee and its subcommittees; and a reference file.

Truman, Harry S, 1884–1972.
Files 1945–1952. ca. 7 ft. White House papers of President Truman relating to race relations.

ST. LOUIS

ST. LOUIS UNIVERSITY, HUMAN RELATIONS CENTER FOR TRAINING AND RESEARCH (1952), HUMAN RELATIONS LIBRARY (1956). 221 N. Grand St., 63103.
The Center offers a degree program for training teachers, hospital administrators, agency directors, etc., and services the community in human relations projects.

Human Relations Library Collection.
Materials, ca. 16,000 items. Includes books (ca. 2,500), periodicals, newspapers (20), pamphlets (ca. 2,000), vf, theses, mss, correspondence and clippings (ca. 10,500), relating to employment, housing, integration, the culturally disadvantaged, health services, civil rights and liberties, history of state, local and federal human rights commissions.

NEVADA

RENO

UNIVERSITY OF NEVADA (1874), NOBLE H. GETCHELL LIBRARY, SPECIAL COLLECTIONS DEPARTMENT (1963). 89507.
Hulse, James W.
Papers, 1964–1966. ca. 1 ft. Materials from membership on Nevada Commission on Equal Rights of Citizens.

Nevada Commission on Equal Rights of Citizens.
Hearings, 1964. ca. 1 reel. On microfilm.

Scott, Eddie.
Reno civil rights leader. An oral history of Scott's career.

NEW HAMPSHIRE

HANOVER

DARTMOUTH COLLEGE, BAKER LIBRARY. 03755.
Facts on Film.
Papers, 1954–1967. Microfilm. Contains materials on civil rights and race relations in the South.

NEW JERSEY

NEWARK

NEW JERSEY DEPARTMENT OF LAW AND PUBLIC SAFETY, DIVISION ON CIVIL RIGHTS (1945). 1100 Raymond Blvd., 07102.
Division on Civil Rights.
Contains books, pamphlets, mss, correspondence, clippings, films, and tapes in the area of civil rights covering employment, the draft, discrimination, housing, Negro history, and other subjects.

NEWARK PUBLIC LIBRARY. 5 Washington St., 07101.
Facts on Film.
Papers, 1954–1967. Microfilm. Contains materials on civil rights and race relations in the South.
Negro Art.
Contains phonograph records, biographies of Negro musicians and artists, original art works, and a picture file of famous Negroes.
Negro in New Jersey.
Includes books, pamphlets, periodicals, and files on the Negro in New Jersey.
Newark Rebellion of 1967.
Includes clippings, documents, and books on the Newark rebellion.

PRINCETON

PRINCETON UNIVERSITY (1756), HARVEY S. FIRESTONE LIBRARY. 08540.
Facts on Film.
Papers, 1954–1967. Microfilm. Contains materials on civil rights and race relations in the South.

NEW YORK

BROOKLYN

THE CITY UNIVERSITY OF NEW YORK, BROOKLYN COLLEGE (1930), LIBRARY (1930). Bedford Ave. and Ave. H, 11210.
Facts on Film.
Papers, 1954–1967. Microfilm. Contains materials on civil rights and race relations in the South.

BROOKLYN PUBLIC LIBRARY (1892). Grand Army Plaza, 11238.
Facts on Film.
Papers, 1954–1967. Microfilm. Contains materials on civil rights and race relations in the South.

HYDE PARK

U.S. GENERAL SERVICES ADMINISTRATION, NATIONAL ARCHIVES AND RECORDS SERVICE (1934), FRANKLIN D. ROOSEVELT LIBRARY (1939). Albany Post Rd., 12538.
Roosevelt, Franklin Delano, 1882–1945.
Papers, 1935–1945. 3600 cu. ft. Material from Presidential years, 1933–1945, includes items relating to race relations generally, segregation, anti-lynching legislation, and the Negro in the armed services.

ITHACA

CORNELL UNIVERSITY, LIBRARY (1865). 14850.
Facts on Film.
Papers, 1954–1967. Microfilm. Contains materials on civil rights and race relations in the South.
Tape recording of Afro-American Lecture Series.
Tape recording and transcripts, 1968. Proceeding of symposia (speeches and panel discussions) including the following subjects: "Slavery and Racial Prejudice" (October 29, 1968); "Manpower Programs in the Ghetto: Private Business With Pride" (December 6, 1968); "Can White Bureaucracy Bring About Black Progress?" (November 1, 1968); "Racism in a White Society" (September 14, 1968); and "The Modern State Against the Blacks" (December 12, 1968).

NEW YORK

A. PHILIP RANDOLPH INSTITUTE. 260 Park Ave. South, 10010.
The Institute was formed to raise economic issues that underlie the civil rights movement. It prepares educational materials for all civil rights groups.
Randolph, Asa Philip, 1889– .
Papers.

AMERICAN CIVIL LIBERTIES UNION (ACLU) (1920), LIBRARY AND ARCHIVES (1920). 156 Fifth Ave., 10010.
American Civil Liberties Union Archives.
1912– . Books, pamphlets, vf, theses, mss, correspondence, clippings, records, and other materials classified under Equality Before the Law. The collection includes correspondence, records of minutes, and

working papers of the Equality Committee of the ACLU National Board, and of legal cases in which the ACLU has been involved. Among subjects mentioned are race relations, education, employment, housing, public accommodations, voting rights, private organizational discrimination, court proceedings, welfare recipients, and indigents. The Princeton University Library holds the ACLU archives, 1914 to four years prior to any current date.

AMERICAN JEWISH COMMITTEE (AJC) (1906), BLAUSTEIN LIBRARY (1939). 165 E. 56th St., 10022.

AJC is a national human relations agency devoted to intergroup understanding and the protection of civil liberties and human rights.

The Blaustein Library has materials on all aspects of intergroup relations and Jewish community relations, including such topics as prejudice and discrimination, hate movements, civil rights and civil liberties, intergroup education, interreligious affairs and church-state problems, and religious, racial, and ethnic groups in American society. The holdings include books and pamphlets (ca. 40,000), ca. 1,000 periodical and newspaper titles, and 50 vf. Open to qualified persons with permission.

AMERICAN JEWISH CONGRESS (1918), INFORMATION CENTER ON JEWISH-NEGRO RELATIONS (1970). 15 E. 84th St., 10028.

The Center collects, collates, and makes available to interested individuals and organizations all published materials dealing with activities in the area of Jewish-Negro relations.

Files, 1970– . Included are reports, studies, press releases, newspaper and periodical articles, pamphlets, books, and other material pertaining to Jewish-Negro relations and activities, and a file of organizations actively working in this area.

AMERICAN JEWISH CONGRESS (1918), LIBRARY. 15 E. 84th St., 10028.

The Congress, a voluntary membership organization of American Jews, works to foster the unity and creative survival of the Jewish people,

combat anti-Semitism and all forms of racism, combat and extend the democratic way of life, protect the rights and status of Jews everywhere, and advance civil rights and civil liberties to achieve full equality in a free society for all Americans.

The Library includes materials on civil liberties, civil rights, discrimination, and church-state relations.

BROTHERHOOD-IN-ACTION (BIA) (1965), LIBRARY. 560 Seventh Ave., 10018.

Contains ca. 2,500 items, including books, periodical titles, pamphlets, theses and dissertations, correspondence, clippings, and tape recordings on such subjects as race relations and human and intergroup relations. Primarily for use in conference, consultation, and research efforts of the BIA staff. Restricted, in part.

COLUMBIA UNIVERSITY, COLUMBIA UNIVERSITY LIBRARIES, DEPARTMENT OF SPECIAL COLLECTIONS. 10027.

Facts on Film.

Papers, 1954–1967. Microfilm. Contains materials on civil rights and race relations in the South.

COLUMBIA UNIVERSITY, ORAL HISTORY RESEARCH OFFICE (1948). Butler Library, 10027.

The Office was established to collect, by means of tape-recorded interviews, primary source material that would not otherwise exist.

Publ.: Annual Reports; *The Oral History Collection* (1964), descriptive catalog.

Civil Rights in Alabama.

Material about the civil rights movement in Tuscaloosa, Ala., in 1964. Includes interviews with leaders and participants, and transcripts of two mass meetings and interviews with residents expressing widely varying attitudes. 259 pp. of transcript copy.

CONGRESS OF RACIAL EQUALITY (CORE) (1943). 200 W. 135 St., 10030.

Files, 1943– . Records and reports of the operation and activities of CORE.

FREEDOMWAYS ASSOCIATES, INC. (1959). 799 Broadway, 10003.

Publ.: *Freedomways: A Quarterly Review of the Negro Freedom Movement.*

Files, 1959– .

METROPOLITAN APPLIED RESEARCH CENTER (MARC). 60 E. 86th St., 10019.

The Center is concerned with civil rights and urban problems, especially in low-income, minority group neighborhoods. Projects of the Center include an investigation of welfare services for minority group children, and a fellowship program to bring civil rights leaders and social science scholars into closer working relationships on problems and policies involving social change. The Center also acts as a national clearing house for information about black elected officials.

NAACP LEGAL DEFENSE AND EDUCATIONAL FUND (1939). 10 Columbus Circle, 10019.

The Fund is an organization, independent of the NAACP, which operates as the major legal arm of the civil rights movement. It represents groups like the Southern Christian Leadership Conference, the Congress of Racial Equality, and the NAACP, as well as individual citizens.

Facts on Film.
Papers, 1954–1967. Microfilm. Contains materials on civil rights and race relations in the South.

NATIONAL COUNCIL OF THE CHURCHES OF CHRIST IN THE U.S.A., DIVISION OF CHRISTIAN LIFE AND MISSION, COMMISSION ON RELIGION AND RACE (1963). 475 Riverside Dr., 10027.

The Commission seeks to focus the concern, conviction, resources, and action of the member communions on issues of religion and race.

Publ.: Commission reports; Other literature such as a statement on black power, and information on Metropolitan Rural Development for Equal Opportunity.

NEW YORK PUBLIC LIBRARY (1895). Manuscript Division, Fifth Ave. and 42nd St., 10018.

Facts on Film.
Papers, 1954–1967. Microfilm. Contains materials on civil rights and race relations in the South.

THE NEW YORK PUBLIC LIBRARY, 135th STREET BRANCH, SCHOMBURG COLLECTION OF NEGRO LITERATURE AND HISTORY (1925). 103 W. 135th St., 10030.

Publ.: *Dictionary Catalog of the Schomburg Collections of Negro Literature and History* (1962, 1968); *Harlem: A Bibliography; The Negro: A Bibliography.*

The Schomburg Collection is a reference and research library devoted to the life and history of Afro-Americans. The nucleus of this Collection is the private library assembled by Arthur A. Schomburg, a Puerto Rican of African descent, purchased by the Carnegie Corporation of New York and presented to the New York Public Library. The Collection provides books of black authorship, literary and historical works, and magazines, pamphlets, mss, photographs, pictures, prints, newspaper clippings, playbills, programs, broadsides, sheet music, tape and phonograph recordings and films.

Civil Rights Congress (CRC).
Papers, 1946–ca. 1956. ca. 138 boxes. Formed from a merger of the International Labor Defense and the Federation for Constitutional Liberties. Correspondence, press releases, clippings, photographs, tapes, phonodiscs, film, and trial transcripts.

Facts on Film.
Papers, 1954–1967. Microfilm. Contains materials on civil rights and race relations in the South.

Tape Recording Collection.
Ca. 240 tapes. Interviews, speeches, readings, recordings of meetings, and documentary recordings. The Collection contains tapes by Herbert Aptheker, Osceola Archer, Byron Baer, James Baldwin, Jack Barnes, Ross Barnett, David Berkman, Arna Bontemps, George Breitman, Gavin Bushell, Emile Capouya, Robert C. Chapman, Alice Childress, John Henrik Clarke, Albert Cleague, Horace Clayton, W. Montague Cobb, John Conyers, Ossie Davis, Clifton DeBerry, James DeLoach, Thomas Dent, W.E.B. DuBois, Dwight Lowell Dumond, P.D. East, Ralph Ellison, James Farmer, George Grief, John Howard Griffin, Fannie Lou Hamer, John

Hammond, Lorraine Hansberry, Milton Henry, Nat Hentoff, Nora Hicks, Herbert Hill, Langston Hughes, Harold Jackman, LeRoi Jones, Elayne Jones Kaufman, Kenneth Kaunda, Alfred Kazin, John O. Killens, Martin Luther King, Jr., Sidney Kingsley, Franz J.T. Lee, Mr. and Mrs. Lemmon (Brownsville, Tenn.), R.W.B. Lewis, Louis Lomax, Malcolm (Little) X (11 tapes), Mrs. Z.K. Mathews, Gertrude McBrown, James Meredith, Howard Meyer, Charles Morgan, Jr., Frederick O'Neal, Douglas Pugh, Saunders Redding, William Reed, Grant Reynolds, Andrew Robinson, Phillip Rose, Bayard Rustin, John Scott, Evelyn Sell, James Shabazz, Ed Shaw, Charles Sims, Lillian Smith, Mildred Stock, William Styron, Wilbert Tatum, Ernest Thomas, Jackie Vaughn, Robert Vernon, Brenda Wolcott, Wyatt Tee Walker, Solomon Wangboje, Dave Weber, Milton P. Webster, Hilda Weiss, Robert Williams, William Worthy, J. Skelly Wright. The tapes cover such subjects as the Democratic party, Brotherhood of Sleeping Car Porters, Puerto Rican problems in New York, Committee Against Jim Crow in the Army, freedom movement in Mississippi, Marxism, Committee for the Schomburg Collection, Africa, Racism, Militant Labor Forum, Haryou-Act, Freedom Democratic party, Freedom Now party, Deacons for Self Defense, abolitionist movement, White Citizens Council, Robert Gould Shaw, March on Washington (1963), Freedom Schools, Mississippi Freedom Summer (1964), James Chaney, Asilomar Negro Writers Conference, Watts, housing, African theatre, Black Muslim movement, Tent City, On Guard, Fayette County, Tennessee, Radio Free Dixie, Hazel Brannon Smith, Southern Conference Educational Fund, Mississippi Delta blues music, and de facto segregation.

PHELPS-STOKES FUND (1911), EDITORIAL RESEARCH LIBRARY (1964). 22 E. 54th St., 10022.
Files, 1964– . 26 vf. Includes correspondence; ca. 2,000 research monographs, pamphlets, govern-ment publications, and periodical articles; ca. 150 theses and dissertations; books; and a newspaper clipping file. Materials cover all aspects of contemporary Negro American urban and rural life: population and migration, housing, health, education, employment, income, social welfare dependency, crime and juvenile delinquency, civil rights, civil disorder, politics. The principal aim of the library is to keep abreast of trend data which measure the changing economic, social and cultural condition of the Negro in the U.S. Restricted.

PURCHASE

MANHATTANVILLE COLLEGE (1841), BRADY MEMORIAL LIBRARY (1841). 10577.
Martin Luther King, Jr., Collection.
ca. 1200 v. Books and periodicals, concerning the history of the Negro and race relations in general.

ROCHESTER

UNIVERSITY OF ROCHESTER (1850), RUSH RHEES LIBRARY. River Campus Sta., 14627.
Facts on Film.
Papers, 1954–1967. Microfilm. Contains materials on civil rights and race relations in the South.

SYRACUSE

SYRACUSE UNIVERSITY, CARNEGIE LIBRARY. 13210.
Facts on Film.
Papers, 1954–1967. Microfilm. Contains materials on civil rights and race relations in the South.
New York State Council of Churches.
Papers, 1934–1968. 4 ft. Correspondence, agenda, minutes, memoranda and reports, dealing mainly with legislation and social issues including abortion, alcoholism, church and state, civil rights and segregation, drug addiction, family relations, health and hospitals, labor migratory workers, and pornography; and material related to Christian education and church planning. Restricted.

NORTH CAROLINA

CHAPEL HILL

UNIVERSITY OF NORTH CAROLINA LI-
BRARIES, LOUIS ROUND WILSON LI-
BRARY (1795). 27514.
Facts on Film.
  Papers, 1954–1967. Microfilm. Con-
  tains materials on civil rights and
  race relations in the South.

CHARLOTTE

INSTITUTE FOR URBAN STUDIES AND
COMMUNITY SERVICE (1969), J. MURREY
ATKINS LIBRARY. P.O. Box 12665, 28205.
Materials pertaining to Negroes.
  Miscellaneous. Books and journals
  (ca. 370) on Negro life, civil rights,
  Negro history, Negro authors, and
  Negro psychology.

MECKLENBURG ORGANIZATION ON
POLITICAL AFFAIRS, COMMITTEE ON
CIVIL RIGHTS (1948). 1703 Madison Ave.,
28208.
  The Organization works to achieve
  full rights and privileges for American Negroes.
  Files, 1948– . Includes correspondence, minutes of meetings, financial records, and other material
  dealing with the aims, history, and
  programs of the Organization.

DURHAM

NORTH CAROLINA CENTRAL UNIVER-
SITY (1910), JAMES E. SHEPARD MEMO-
RIAL LIBRARY (1951). 27707.
Facts on Film.
  Papers, 1954–1967. Microfilm. Con-
  tains materials on civil rights and
  race relations in the South.

GREENSBORO

NORTH CAROLINA AGRICULTURAL
AND TECHNICAL STATE UNIVERSITY
(1891), F. D. BLUFORD LIBRARY (1894).
27410.
Facts on Film.
  Papers, 1954–1967. Microfilm. Contains materials on civil rights and
  race relations in the South.

GREENVILLE

EAST CAROLINA UNIVERSITY (1907), J. Y.
JOYNER LIBRARY (1954). Box 2547, ECU
Station, 27834.

Contains books (10,000) and pamphlets (5000) relating to race relations.
Facts on Film.
  Papers, 1954–1967. Microfilm, Contains materials on civil rights and
  race relations in the South.

MONTREAT

PRESBYTERIAN CHURCH IN THE UNITED
STATES, HISTORICAL FOUNDATION
(1927). Assembly Dr., 28757.
  Papers relating to Negroes.
  Pamphlets. Subjects include slavery,
  Negro work, and race problems.

OHIO

CINCINNATI

HEBREW UNION COLLEGE, JEWISH INSTI-
TUTE OF RELIGION, AMERICAN JEWISH
ARCHIVES. 3101 Clifton Ave., 45220.
  Desegregation papers.
  1957–1963. 247 items. Letters, articles, and other papers relating to
  the desegregation activities of various rabbis. Includes proceedings
  (1963) of the Steering Committee of
  Metropolitan Houston, Tex., Conference on Religion and Race, and
  correspondence (1962) relating to
  an interfaith meeting in Wichita,
  Kan., to commemorate the 1954 Supreme Court desegregation decision; correspondence, sermons, and
  newspaper clippings (1957–1958)
  from rabbis serving congregations
  in the South; together with an article (1961) by Rabbi Joseph H. Gam-
  biner, describing his efforts in Jackson, Miss., to end segregation.
  Access restricted.

CLEVELAND

CLEVELAND PUBLIC LIBRARY (1869). 325
Superior Ave., 44114.
Facts on Film.
  Papers, 1954–1967. Microfilm. Contains materials on civil rights and
  race relations in the South.
Materials relating to Negroes.
  Miscellaneous. Although not
  housed in a separate collection, the
  library holds in superior strength
  books, periodical titles, clippings,
  films, and microforms by and about
  Negroes.

COLUMBUS

OHIO STATE UNIVERSITY LIBRARIES (1870), WILLIAM OXLEY THOMPSON MEMORIAL LIBRARY (1870). 1858 Neil Ave., 43210.
Facts on Film.
> Papers, 1954–1967. Microfilm. Contains materials on civil rights and race relations in the South.

KENT

KENT STATE UNIVERSITY LIBRARIES (1913). 44240.
Facts on Film.
> Papers, 1954–1967. Microfilm. Contains materials on civil rights and race relations in the South.

Materials pertaining to Negroes.
> Miscellaneous. Monographs (ca. 5000) on history and accomplishments of Negroes, slavery, and the slave trade; Negro newspapers, including all titles (209) listed in Library of Congress bibliography *Negro Newspapers on Microfilm*, plus 17 other titles including three editions of the *Baltimore Afro-American* and a complete file of the *Cleveland Call and Post*.

PENNSYLVANIA

EASTON

LAFAYETTE COLLEGE (1826), DAVID BISHOP SKILLMAN LIBRARY. 18042.
Facts on Film.
> Papers, 1954–1967. Microfilm. Contains materials on civil rights and race relations in the South.

HARRISBURG

PENNSYLVANIA STATE LIBRARY. Box 1601, 17126.
Facts on Film.
> Papers, 1954–1967. Microfilm. Contains materials on civil rights and race relations in the South.

PHILADELPHIA

UNIVERSITY OF PENNSYLVANIA, VAN PELT LIBRARY. 3420 Walnut St., 19104.
Facts on Film.
> Papers, 1954–1967. Microfilm. Contains materials on civil rights and race relations in the South.

NATIONAL BLACK SISTERS' CONFERENCE (NBSC) (1968). 3333 Fifth Ave., 15213.
National Black Sisters' Conference and Black Priests' Conference.
> Records, 1968– . Minutes of meetings; conference and workshop proceedings; speakers bureau and black skills bank materials; Conference publications; reports; tapes from NBSC speakers, symposiums and workshops; and research in such areas as black sisters in the Catholic Church, and analysis of racism and the intercultural orientation of Catholic-affiliated institutions. Restricted.

UNITED STEELWORKERS OF AMERICA, COMMITTEE ON CIVIL RIGHTS. 1500 Commonwealth Bldg., 15222.
> The Committee implements the United Steelworkers of America's policies in the area of civil rights through 24 district directors and civil rights coordinators.
> Files. Documentation dealing with the aims, programs, and history of the Committee. Includes correspondence, minutes of meetings, financial reports, studies, investigations, and other material related to its activities.

UNIVERSITY PARK

PENNSYLVANIA STATE UNIVERSITY, FRED LEWIS PATTEE LIBRARY (1857). 16802.
Facts on Film.
> Papers, 1954–1967. Microfilm. Contains materials on civil rights and race relations in the South.

United Steelworkers of America.
> Records, 1946–1967. 99 ft. Correspondence, petitions, agreements, statements, reports, memos, pamphlets, booklets, reprints, circulars, clippings, and exhibits comprising the union's legislative office files from Washington, D.C., concerning various labor activities. Subjects covered include the AFL-CIO, area redevelopment, budget, civil rights, depressed areas, education, government grants and loans, housing, legislation and labor, manpower utilization and training, and minimum wages.

SOUTH CAROLINA

ROCK HILL

WINTHROP COLLEGE (1886), IDA JANE DACUS LIBRARY. 29730.
Facts on Film.
Papers, 1954–1967. Microfilm. Contains materials on civil rights and race relations in the South.

TENNESSEE

COOKEVILLE

TENNESSEE TECHNOLOGICAL UNIVERSITY (1918), JERE WHITSON MEMORIAL LIBRARY. 38501.
Facts on Film.
Papers, 1954–1967. Microfilm. Contains materials on civil rights and race relations in the South.

JOHNSON CITY

EAST TENNESSEE STATE UNIVERSITY (1911), SHERROD LIBRARY. 37602.
Facts on Film.
Papers, 1954–1967. Microfilm. Contains materials on civil rights and race relations in the South.

KNOXVILLE

UNIVERSITY OF TENNESSEE (1794), JAMES D. HOSKINS LIBRARY, DEPARTMENT OF SPECIAL COLLECTIONS. 37916.
Civil Rights Collection.
ca. 3,000 items. Tapes, correspondence, miscellaneous printed materials, photographs, posters, and other materials relating to the civil rights movement in general.
Facts on Film.
Papers, 1954–1967. Microfilm. Contains materials on civil rights and race relations in the South.

MEMPHIS

MEMPHIS STATE UNIVERSITY (1912), JOHN WILLARD BRISTER LIBRARY. Southern and Patterson, 38111.
Facts on Film.
Papers, 1954–1967. Microfilm. Contains materials on civil rights and race relations in the South.

NASHVILLE

FISK UNIVERSITY (1866), LIBRARY (1866). 37203.
Facts on Film.
Papers, 1954–1967. Microfilm. Contains materials on civil rights and race relations in the South.

RACE RELATIONS INFORMATION CENTER (RRIC) (1969), LIBRARY (1955). 1109 19th Ave. S., 37212.
The Center, a private, nonprofit organization that gathers and distributes information about race relations in the U.S., is the successor to Southern Education Reporting Service, an agency established in 1954 to provide accurate, unbiased information on race-related developments in education in the southern and border states. The Center's Special Reports are intended for use especially by newspapers, magazines, broadcasting stations and educational institutions.
Publ.: *Special Reports*; *Race Relations Reporter*, semi-monthly newsletter.
Facts on Film.
Microfilm. 1954– . ca. 230 reels (through 1967–68 supplement). Commercially available microfilm series which reproduces materials collected by the SERS and RRIC library. Included are news stories, editorial cartoons, magazine articles, SERS and RRIC publications, *Race Relations Law Reporter*, reports, studies and surveys, speeches, pamphlets, newsletters, other miscellaneous printed matter, and a card catalog for the entire collection, on such subjects as race in education, race relations, and compensatory education.
Race Relations Information Center (RRIC).
Files, 1969– . ca. 10 vf. Correspondence, minutes of meetings, financial reports, personnel files. Includes materials relating to the operation of the Center, to its publications, and to research data used to prepare *Directory of Afro-American Resources*. Subjects mentioned include Black Muslims, "soul radio," Title IV of the Civil Rights Act of 1964, Newark (N.J.) politics, racial

protest in the South, United Methodist Church, school desegregation, and Cubans. Restricted.

Race Relations Information Center Library.

Files, ca. 1954– . ca. 81 vf (ca. 300,000 items) and ca. 800 v. Correspondence, mss, newspaper and magazine clippings, magazines, books, pamphlets, reports, surveys, laws, court decisions, speeches, "underground" newspapers, broadsides, microfilms, and card catalog. The library collects materials on all aspects of race relations in the U.S., including such subjects as school and college desegregation, politics, public accommodations, racism, federal, state and local legislation, civil rights, violence, riots, demonstrations, housing, employment, Citizens Council, Ku Klux Klan, SNCC, Black Panthers, Council of Federated Organizations, sit-ins, SCLC, and Southern Regional Council. Also included are complete runs of publications of numerous civil rights organizations; mss and statistical data for the *Statistical Summary of School Segregation-Desegregation in the Southern and Border States* (1957–1967) and for *School Desegregation in the Southern and Border States* (1967–1968); and extensive file of government publications with racial topics. Back files of library materials are periodically sent to Fisk University Library. In part restricted.

Southern Education Reporting Service (SERS).

Files, 1954–1969. ca. 20 vf. Correspondence, minutes of meetings, reports, press releases, mss, photos, galleys, page proofs, financial records, mailing lists, and subscription records. Included are materials relating to SERS publications, *Facts on Film, Southern Schools: Progress and Problems* (1959), *With All Deliberate Speed* (1957), *Ordeal of Desegregation* (1966), *Southern School News* (1954–1965), *Southern Education Report* (1965–1969), and *Statistical Summary* (1957–1967); survey research data concerning "high risk" programs, and college attitudes; distribution records for *Race Relations Law Reporter*. Subjects mentioned include school desegregation, race relations, the "Brown decision," politics, Negro migration, Negro journalists, and compensatory education for the disadvantaged.

VANDERBILT UNIVERSITY, RACE RELATIONS LAW SURVEY (1969). 37203.

The *Survey* consists of summaries of court decisions and occasional summaries of legislation and administrative rulings in which the issue of race and color is a significant factor. Formerly *Race Relations Law Reporter* (1955–1969).

Publ.: *Race Relations Law Survey*, bimonthly.

Race Relations Law Survey.

Records, 1956– . Correspondence, reports, studies, investigations, court decisions, administrative agency rulings, legislation, opinions of attorneys general, other materials concerning race relations and related issues. Also included is a complete set (12 v.) of former publication, *Race Relations Law Reporter*.

TEXAS

AUSTIN

U.S. GENERAL SERVICES ADMINISTRATION, NATIONAL ARCHIVES AND RECORDS SERVICE, LYNDON BAINES JOHNSON LIBRARY (1972). 2313 Red River St., 78705.

The library is a repository for all materials collected by Johnson and members of his administration including prepresidential papers while in the Senate (1949–1960) and as vice-president (1961–1963); presidential papers relating to civil rights (1963–1969); White House central files on such subjects as public opinion mail (1964–1965), reports on pending legislation (1963–1968), reports of aides (1963–1969), and task force reports (1966–1968). Also contains statements of Johnson relating to civil rights (1937–1968); oral history interviews (19 in all, including Roy Wilkins, Whitney Young, Jr., and Robert Weaver); records of White House conference "To Fulfill These Rights" 1965–1966); records of the presidential commissions—National Crime Commission (1965–

1967), National Advisory Commission on Civil Disorders (1967–1968); and National Commission on Causes and Prevention of Violence (1968–1969).

UNIVERSITY OF TEXAS AT AUSTIN (1883), LIBRARY. 78712.
Facts on Film.
    Papers, 1954–1967. Microfilm. Contains materials on civil rights and race relations in the South.

HOUSTON

UNIVERSITY OF HOUSTON (1934), M.D. ANDERSON MEMORIAL LIBRARY (1949). 77004.
Facts on Film.
    Papers, 1954–1967. Microfilm. Contains materials on civil rights and race relations in the South.

PRAIRIE VIEW

PRAIRIE VIEW AGRICULTURAL AND MECHANICAL COLLEGE, W. R. BANKS LIBRARY (1912). 77445.
Facts on Film.
    Papers, 1954–1967. Microfilm. Contains materials on civil rights and race relations in the South.

SAN MARCOS

SOUTHWEST TEXAS STATE COLLEGE, LIBRARY. 78666.
Facts on Film.
    Papers, 1954–1967. Microfilm. Contains materials on civil rights and race relations in the South.

VIRGINIA

PETERSBURG

VIRGINIA STATE COLLEGE (1882), JOHNSTON MEMORIAL LIBRARY. 23803.
Facts on Film.
    Papers, 1954–1967. Microfilm. Contains materials on civil rights and race relations in the South.

RADFORD

RADFORD COLLEGE, JOHN PRESTON McCONNELL LIBRARY (1913). 24141.
Facts on Film.
    Papers, 1954–1967. Microfilm. Contains materials on civil rights and race relations in the South.

WASHINGTON

TACOMA

TACOMA PUBLIC LIBRARY (1886). 1102 Tacoma Ave. S., 98402.
Newspaper Clipping Collection.
    Newspaper clippings, 1909–   . ca. 44 vf. Clippings of Tacoma area newspapers are kept in a subject file and include such subjects as Negroes, civil rights, and segregation in housing and employment.

WISCONSIN

MADISON

STATE HISTORICAL SOCIETY OF WISCONSIN (1846). 816 State St., 53706.
Congress of Racial Equality (CORE).
    Papers, 1941–1967. 104 boxes. Included are files of the director, 1945–1964; assistant director, 1942–1964, executive secretary, 1941–1962; national action council, 1945–1965; and departments and related organizations, 1946–1967. Groups represented include CORE, New York, N.Y., CORE, Berkeley, Calif., and Southern Regional Council, Atlanta, Ga.
Library Division.
    Among the holdings of the Library are a collection of American Negro newspapers; materials (ca. 2,000 books and pamphlets) on the American Negro, slavery, civil rights, and the contemporary black movement in the U.S.

UNIVERSITY OF WISCONSIN, THE MEMORIAL LIBRARY (1850). 728 State St., 53706.
Facts on Film.
    Papers, 1954–1967. Microfilm. Contains materials on civil rights and race relations in the South.

MILWAUKEE

MARQUETTE UNIVERSITY, MEMORIAL LIBRARY. 1415 W. Wisconsin Ave., 53233.
Facts on Film.
    Papers, 1954–1967. Microfilm. Contains materials on civil rights and race relations in the South.

RACINE

RACINE PUBLIC LIBRARY (1896). 75 Seventh St., 53403.
> Publ.: *The American Negro* (1963), a selected bibliography.

Papers relating to Negroes in Racine, Wisconsin.
> Miscellaneous, 1949–1969. Reproductions of material on Negro history, Negro biography, housing, de facto school segregation, racial problems. Publications of Mayor's Commission on Human Rights, Racine Environment Committee, Urban League, NAACP. Clippings on civil rights questions from local papers.

WHITEWATER

WISCONSIN STATE UNIVERSITY-WHITEWATER (1868), HAROLD ANDERSEN LIBRARY (1868). W. Main St., 53190.

Facts on Film.
> Papers, 1954–1967. Microfilm. Contains materials on civil rights and race relations in the South.

VIRGIN ISLANDS

ST. THOMAS

COLLEGE OF THE VIRGIN ISLANDS (1963). LIBRARY (1963). P.O. Box 1826, 00801.
> Newspaper Clipping Collection.
>> Clippings of Virgin Islands area newspapers are kept in subject files and include such subjects as West Indians and American Negroes, civil rights, and segregation in housing and employment.

Suggested Bibliography

Note: The following is a selection of books thought by the editor to be of particular importance in gaining a wider understanding of the struggle for equal rights by minority groups, especially over the last twenty years.

Allport, Gordon W., *The Nature of Prejudice*. Reading, Mass.: Addison-Wesley, 1954.

Altshuler, Alan A., *Community Control*. New York: Pegasus, 1970.

Anthony, Earl, *Picking Up the Gun: A Report on the Black Panthers*. New York: Dial Press, 1970.

Baily, Paul *Concentration Camp: U.S.A.* New York: Tower Publications, 1972.

Baldwin, James, *The Fire Next Time*. New York: Dial Press, 1963.

Banfield, Edward, *The Unheavenly City*. Boston: Little, Brown & Co., 1970.

Barbour, Floyd B., ed., *The Black Power Revolt*. New York: Collier Books, 1969.

Bayley, David H., and Mendelsohn, Harold, *Minorities and the Police*. New York: Free Press, 1969.

Bedford, Denton R., *Civil Rights* (Vols. 1 & 2). New York: Facts on File, 1973.

Bedford, Denton R., *Tsali*. San Francisco, Calif.: The Indian Historian Press, 1972.

Bennett, Lerone, Jr., *Confrontation: Black and White*. Chicago: Johnson Publishing Co., 1965.

Berry, Brewton, *Almost White*. New York: Macmillan Co., 1969.

Berube, Maurice, and Gittell, Marilyn, eds., *Confrontation at Ocean Hill Brownsville: The New York School Strikes of 1968*. New York: Praeger, 1969.

Blaustein, Albert P., and Zangrando, Robert, eds. *Civil Rights and the American Negro*. New York: Washington Square Press, 1968.

Bosmajian, Haig A., and Hamida, *The Rhetoric of the Civil Rights Movement*. New York: Random House, 1969.

Boulware, Marcus H., *The Oratory of Negro Leaders: 1900–1968*. Westport, Conn.: Negro Univ. Press, 1969.

Bracey, John H., Jr., et al., eds., *Black Nationalism in America*. Indianapolis: Bobbs-Merrill Co., 1970.

229

Brazier, Arthur M., *Black Self-Determination: The Story of the Woodlawn Organization.* Grand Rapids, Mich.: William B. Eerdmans Publishing Co., 1969.

Broderick, Francis L., and Meier, August, eds., *Negro Protest Thought in the Twentieth Century.* Indianpolis: Bobbs-Merrill Co., 1966

Brown, H. Rap, *Die Nigger Die.* New York: Dial Press, 1969.

Bullock Paul, ed. *Watts: The Aftermath.* New York: Grove Press, 1970.

Cahn, E. S., ed. *Our Brother's Keeper: The Indian in White America.* Cleveland: World Publishing Co., 1969

Carmichael, Stokely, and Hamilton, Charles V., *Black Power: The Politics of Liberation in America.* New York: Random House, 1967.

Carson, Josephine, *Silent Voices: The Southern Negro Woman Today.* New York: Delacorte Press, 1969.

Carson, Sonny, *The Education of Sonny Carson.* New York: W.W. Norton, 1972.

Chase, William M., and Collier, Peter, eds., *Justice Denied: The Black Man in White America.* New York: Harcourt, Brace & World, 1970.

Clark, John Hendrik, *Malcolm X: The Man and His Time.* New York: Macmillan, 1969.

Clark, Kenneth B., *Dark Ghetto.* New York: Harper & Row, 1965.

Cleaver, Eldridge, *Post-Prison Writings and Speeches.* New York: Random House, 1969.

Cleaver, Eldridge, *Soul on Ice.* New York: McGraw-Hill, 1968.

Connery, Robert H., ed., *Urban Riots: Violence and Social Change.* New York: Random House, 1969.

Cruse, Harold, *Rebellion or Revolution?* New York: Apollo Editions, 1969.

Cruse, Harold, *The Crisis of the Negro Intellectual.* New York: Apollo Editions, 1968

Daniels, Roger, *The Politics of Prejudice.* New York: Atheneum, 1969.

Daniels, Roger, and Kitano, Harry H., *American Racism.* Englewood Cliffs, N.J.: Prentice-Hall, 1970.

Davenport Lawrence, and Petty, Reginald, eds., *Minorities and Career Education.* Ohio: Ecca Publications, 1973.

Davis, Angela, *If They Come in the Morning: Voices of Resistance.* New York: Third Press, 1971.

Deloria, Vine, Jr., *Custer Died for Your Sins: An Indian Manifesto.* New York: Macmillan Co., 1969.

Deloria, Vine, Jr., *God Is Red.* New York: Grosset & Dunlap, 1973.

Drake, St. Clair, and Cayton, Horace R., *Black Metropolis: A Study of Negro Life in a Northern City.* New York: Harcourt, Brace & World, 1970.

Dunne, John G., *Delano: The Story of the California Grape Strike.* New York: Farrar, Straus & Giroux, 1967.

Edwards, Henry, *Sociology of Sport.* Homewood, Ill.: Dorsey Press, 1972.

Edwards, Henry, *The Revolt of the Black Athlete.* New York: Free Press, 1969.

Eichelberger, William L., *Reality in Black and White.* Philadelphia: Westminster, 1969.

Essien-Udom, Essien Udosen, *Black Nationalism: A Search for Identity in America.* Chicago: Univ. of Chicago Press, 1962.

Fager, Charles, *Uncertain Resurrection: The Poor People's Washington Campaign.* Grand Rapids, Mich.: William B. Eerdmans Publishing Co., 1969.

Fager, Charles, *White Reflections on Black Power*. Grand Rapids, Mich.: William B. Eerdmans Publishing Co., 1967.

Fanon, Frantz, *Black Skin, White Masks*. New York: Grove Press, 1967.

Fanon, Frantz, *The Wretched of the Earth*. New York: Grove Press, 1965.

Fisher, Sethard, ed., *Power and the Black Community*. New York: Random House, 1970.

Fisk, John, *Black Power, White Control*. Princeton, N.J.: Princeton University Press, 1973.

Forman, J., *Making of Black Revolutionaries: a Memoir*. New York: Macmillan, 1972.

Franklin, John Hope, *Color and Race*. Boston: Beacon Press, 1969.

Franklin, John Hope, and Starr, Isidore, eds., *The Negro in Twentieth Century America: A Reader on the Struggle for Civil Rights*. New York: Random House, 1967.

Ginzberg, Eli, *The Troublesome Presence*. New York: Free Press, 1964.

Glock, Charles Y., and Siegleman, Ellen, eds., *Prejudice, U.S.A.* New York: Praeger, 1969.

Good, Paul, *The American Serfs*. New York: Ballantine, 1969.

Goro, Herb, *The Block*. New York: Random House, 1970.

Grant, Joan, *Black Protest*. New York: St. Martin's Press, 1970.

Gregory, Dick, *Dick Gregory's Political Primer*. New York: Harper & Row, 1972.

Haddad, William F., and Pugh, G. Douglas, *Black Economic Development*. Englewood Cliffs, N.J.: Prentice-Hall, 1969.

Hale, Frank W., ed., *The Cry for Freedom*. Cranbury, N.J.: A. S. Barnes, 1970.

Hayden, Thomas, *Rebellion in Newark: Official Violence and Ghetto Response*. New York: Random House, 1967.

Henry, Jeanette, *The American Indian Reader: Anthropology*. San Francisco, Calif.: The Indian Historian Press, 1972.

Herndon, James, *The Way It Spozed to Be*. New York: Simon & Schuster, 1968.

Hilton, Bruce, *The Delta Ministry*. New York: Macmillan Co., 1969

Hines, Paul D., *A Guide to Human Rights Education*. Washington, D.C.: Natl. Council for the Social Studies, 1969.

Holloway, Harry, *The Politics of the Southern Negro*. New York: Random House, 1969.

Hornsby, Alton, Jr., *The Black Almanac*. Woodbury, N.Y.: Barron's Educational Series, 1973.

Hosokawa, Bill, *Nisei: The Quiet Americans*. New York: Morrow, 1969.

Howell, Leon, *Freedom City: The Substance of Things Hoped For*. Richmond: John Knox Press, 1969.

Jordan, Winthrop D., ed., *The Negro Versus Equality*. Chicago: Rand McNally Co., 1969.

Keech, William R., *The Impact of Negro Voting*. Chicago: Rand McNally Co., 1970.

Killens, John O., *Black Man's Burden*. New York: Simon & Schuster, 1970.

Killian, Lewis M., *The Impossible Revolution?* New York: Random House, 1968.

King, Coretta Scott, *My Life with Martin Luther King, Jr.* New York: Holt, Rinehart & Winston, 1969.

King, Martin Luther, Jr., *Where Do We Go from Here: Chaos or Community?* New York: Harper & Row, 1967.

Knowles, Louis L., and Prewitt, Kenneth, eds., *Institutional Racism in America.* Englewood Cliffs, N.J.: Prentice-Hall, 1970.

Kohl, Herbert R., *Thirty-Six Children.* New York: New American Library, 1968.

Kozol, Jonathan, *Death at an Early Age.* Boston: Houghton Mifflin Co., 1967.

Kvaraceus, William C., et al., *Negro Self-Concept: Implications for Schools and Citizenship.* New York: McGraw-Hill Book Co., 1965.

Leinwand, Gerard, ed., *Civil Rights and Civil Liberties.* New York: Washington Square Press, 1969.

Leinwand, Gerard, ed., *The Negro in the City.* New York: Washington Square Press, 1969.

Lester, Julius, *Look Out Whitey! Black Power's Gon' Get Your Momma!* New York: Dial Press, 1968.

Lester, Julius, *Revolutionary Notes.* New York: Grove Press, 1970.

Lester, Julius, *The Long Journey Home.* New York: Dial Press, 1972.

Lipsky, Michael, *Protest in City Politics: Rent Strikes, Housing, and the Power of the Poor.* Chicago: Rand McNally Co., 1970.

Lomax, Louis, *The Negro Revolt.* New York: Harper & Row, 1962.

Mack, R., *Race, Class, and Power.* New York: American Book Co., 1968.

Malcolm X, *The Speeches of Malcom X at Harvard.* New York: William Morrow Co., 1968.

Malcolm X, and Haley, Alex, *The Autobiography of Malcolm X.* New York: Grove Press, 1966.

Marden, Charles F., and Meyer, Gladys, *Minorities in American Society.* New York: American Book Co., 1968.

Marx, Gary T., *Protest and Prejudice.* New York: Harper & Row, 1969.

Matthiessen, Peter, *Sal Si Puedes: Cesar Chavez and the New American Revolution.* New York: Random House, 1969.

McClellan, Grand S., *Civil Rights.* New York: H. W. Wilson Co., 1964.

McCord, John H., ed., *With All Deliberate Speed: Civil Rights Theory and Reality.* Urbana, Ill.: Univ. of Illinois Press, 1969.

McKissick, Floyd, *Three-Fifths of a Man.* New York: Macmillan Co., 1969.

McWilliams, Carey, *North from Mexico.* Westport, Conn.: Greenwood Press, 1967.

Meier, August, and Rudwick, Elliott, eds., *The Making of Black America.* New York: Atheneum, 1969.

Mills, Nicolaus, ed., *The Great School Bus Controversy.* New York: Teachers College Press, 1973

Muse, Benjamin, *The American Negro Revolution.* New York: Citadel Press, 1970.

Nabokov, Peter, *Tijerina and the Courthouse Raid.* Albuquerque: Univ. of New Mexico Press, 1969.

Newton, Huey P., and Blake, Herman, *Revolutionary Suicide.* New York: Harcourt Brace Jovanovich, 1973.

Oppenheimer, Martin, *The Urban Guerrilla.* Chicago: Quadrangle Books, 1969.

Osofsky, Gilbert, *Harlem: The Making of a Ghetto.* New York: Harper & Row, 1966.

Robinson, Armstead L., et al., eds., *Black Studies in the University.* New York: Bantam, 1969.

Rose, Peter I., *They and We: Racial and Ethnic Relations in the United States.* New York: Random House, 1964.

Samora, Julian, ed., *La Raza: Forgotten Americans.* Notre Dame, Ind.: Univ. of Notre Dame Press, 1966.

Schuchter, Arnold, *White Power; Black Freedom*. Boston: Beacon Press, 1968.

Scott, Benjamin, *The Coming of the Black Man*. Boston: Beacon Press, 1969.

Scott, Robert L., and Brockriede, Wayne, *The Rhetoric of Black Power*. New York: Harper & Row, 1969.

Seale, Bobby, *Seize the Time*. New York: Random House, 1970.

Silberman, Charles E., *Crisis in Black and White*. New York: Random House, 1964.

Skolnick, Jerome H., et al., eds., *The Politics of Protest*. New York: Simon & Schuster, 1969.

Steiner, Gilbert Y., *Social Insecurity: The Politics of Welfare*. Chicago: Rand McNally Co., 1970.

Steiner, Stanley, *The New Indians*. New York: Dell Publishing Co., 1969.

Storing, Herbert J., ed., *What Country Have I? Political Writings by Black Americans*. New York: St. Martin's Press, 1970.

Sugarman, Tracy, *Stranger at the Gates: A Summer in Mississippi*. New York: Hill & Wang, 1967.

Szwed, John F., *Black America*. New York: Basic Books, 1970.

Tovar, Ribes Federico, *A Chronological History of Puerto Rico*. New York: Vectorum Publications, 1973.

Vivian, C. T., *Black Power and the American Myth*. Philadelphia: Fortress Press, 1970.

Wagstaff, Thomas, ed., *Black Power: The Radical Response to White America*. Beverly Hills, Calif.: Glencoe Press, 1969.

Watters, Pat, *The South and the Nation*. New York: Pantheon, 1969.

Watters, Pat, and Cleghorn, Resse, *Climbing Jacob's Ladder: The Arrival of Negroes in Southern Politics*. New York: Harcourt, Brace & World, 1970.

Weinstein, Allen, and Gatell, Frank O., eds., *The Segregation Era, 1863–1954: A Modern Reader*. New York: Oxford Univ. Press, 1970.

Wenk, Michael, Tomasi, S.M., and Baroni, Geno, eds., *Pieces of a Dream: the Ethnic Worker's Crisis with America*. New York: Center for Migration Studies, 1972.

Wilkins, Roy, and Clark, Ramsay, *Search and Destroy: A Report by the Commission of Inquiry into the Black Panthers and the Police*. New York: Harper & Row, 1973.

Woodward, C. Vann, *The Strange Career of Jim Crow*. New York: Oxford Univ. Press, 1966.

Wright, Nathan, *Black Power and Urban Unrest*. New York: Hawthorn Books, 1967.

Young, Whitney M., Jr., *Beyond Racism*. New York: McGraw-Hill, 1969.

Index

Note: Numbers in italic type indicate pages on which a main entry appears in the "Individuals and Organizations" section.